Games of Empire

Electronic Mediations

Katherine Hayles, Mark Poster, and Samuel Weber, Series Editors

Games of Empire

Global Capitalism and Video Games

Nick Dyer-Witheford and Greig de Peuter

Electronic Mediations 29

University of Minnesota Press   Minneapolis / London

Chapter 4 was previously published as "Armed Vision and the Banalization of War: *Full Spectrum Warrior*," in *Fluid Screens, Expanded Cinema,* ed. Janine Marchessault and Susan Lord (Toronto: University of Toronto Press, 2007).

Published by the University of Minnesota Press
111 Third Avenue South, Suite 290
Minneapolis, MN 55401-2520
http://www.upress.umn.edu

Library of Congress Cataloging-in-Publication Data

Dyer-Witheford
    Games of empire : global capitalism and video games / Nick Dyer-Witheford and Greig de Peuter.
        p. cm. — (Electronic mediations ; 29)
    Includes bibliographical references and index.
    ISBN 978-0-8166-6610-2 (hc : alk. paper) — ISBN 978-0-8166-6611-9 (pbk. : alk. paper)
    1. Video games—Social aspects.   2. Video games—Economic aspects.   3. Capitalism—
Social aspects.   4. Imperialism—Social aspects.   I. de Peuter, Greig.   II. Title.
    GV1469.34.S52D94 2009
    794.8—dc22

                                                                                    2009029170

Contents

Acknowledgments

Nick Dyer-Witheford thanks his colleagues in the Faculty of Information and Media Studies at the University of Western Ontario for the creation of the exceptional academic program that has incubated *Games of Empire,* especially Tom Carmichael and Catherine Ross, for their leadership as present and past deans of the faculty; Gloria Leckie, for her mentorship in the black art of associate deanship; James Compton and Bernd Frohmann for years of academic comradeship; and Tim Blackmore, Jacquelyn Burkell, Jonathan Burston, Grant Campbell, Norma Coates, Ed Comor, Carole Farber, Amanda Grzyb, Alison Hearn, Keir Keightley, Sandy Smeltzer, Daniel Robinson, Daniela Sneppova, David Spencer, Sasha Torres, and Sam Trosow for collegial inquiries, suggestions, and conversations. An indispensable part in the composition of this book has been played by graduate students, as research assistants or participants in the "Games of Empire" seminar that was a laboratory for many parts of the project. Sarah Coleman was an early and extraordinary guide to online virtual worlds; Derek Noon, an ongoing example of gaming integrity and intelligence, whose insights inform the text at many points; Jeff Preston, a source for invaluable recommendations for Ferrari laptops. The research of Trent Cruz and Jen Martin underpins our analysis of virtual gaming in China; Stephen Swain supplied mind-bending facts about sports games; Henry Svec developed an outstanding analysis of *Guitar Hero* as a game of multitude that has found independent publication; Michael Schmalz endured the Marxist analysis of the industry in which he is a leading entrepreneur with enormous grace and good humor; Owen Livermore pointed out ominous connections between games and German expressionism; and Brian Brown rapidly made the connections between video games and the wider ranges of Web 2.0 aesthetics and politics. This book is a political project: salutations are therefore given to the student and faculty members of the Counter-Stryker collective, whose opposition to the University of Western Ontario's involvement in the production of Stryker light-armored fighting vehicles for the U.S. Army in Iraq was, during somber times, an inspiring instance of struggle in and against Empire. Beyond all these acknowledgments, Nick thanks his wife, Anne, not just for abiding the rigors of this book's composition but for a life lived in common.

Greig de Peuter thanks Mark Coté, Richard Day, David Firman, and Sharla Sava, for many memorable, and evidently inspiring, reading groups in Vancouver; Yuezhi Zhao, his doctoral supervisor in the School of Communication at Simon Fraser University, for being so consistently supportive throughout the preparation of this book; Adrian Blackwell, Christine Shaw, and Marcelo Vieta, for excellent conversations about theory and politics in the context of the Toronto School of Creativity and Inquiry project; Enda Brophy, for ongoing discussions about autonomist thought, from which he has learned a great deal; Roberta Buiani, Tanner Mirrlees, Todd Parsons, and Scott Uzelman, for a rewarding reading group in which some of the currents of theory driving this book were explored and challenged; students in political economy classes in the communication studies department at Wilfrid Laurier University, for reading parts of this book in early form and for their feedback on it; Albert Banerjee, for his sustained encouragement; and his parents, for being so tremendously supportive of his seemingly ludic pursuits. Most of all, Greig is immensely thankful to Sheila, for a contribution beyond measure; and, though he arrived late in this game, our son, Kieran, whose utopian joy is evinced each time he effortlessly diverts from work to play.

Nick and Greig together thank Stephen Kline, for his collaboration on our previous coauthored book, *Digital Play;* the many Canadian game developers who took the time to speak with us about their work and their industry; the Social Sciences and Humanities Research Council of Canada, for financial support for portions of the research that informs this book; Timothy Lenoir and Zach Pogue, for inviting us to present our work in their games lab at Duke University and for invigorating discussions; Catherine McKercher and Vincent Mosco, for facilitating the publication of our research in other venues; Siobhan McMenemy, for tremendously helpful comments on an early draft of this manuscript; Sebastian Budgen, Michael Hardt, Peter Ives, John K. Sampson, and Stevphen Shukaitis, for support for this project at various phases in its life course; Mark Poster and the other Electronic Mediations series editors for their enthusiastic reception of our initial proposal; Alberto Toscano and the anonymous reviewers for the University of Minnesota Press for their instructive remarks on the manuscript; and, finally, Douglas Armato, our editor, and editorial assistant Danielle Kasprzak, not only for welcoming this book into such a good home but also for their generosity throughout the publication process.

Introduction
Games in the Age of Empire

Ludocapitalism, Militainment, and Digital Dissent

A million avatars inhabit this archipelago. At any given moment thousands are navigating pixilated islands, flying over open waters, wandering among rococo architecture, imbibing at house parties, bending their gender, chatting with friends, attending rock concerts, enjoying erotic encounters, and much else besides.[1] You are among them. Curiosity excited by the massive publicity surrounding *Second Life*, the virtual world created by Linden Labs of San Francisco, you signed up, hoping in this new society to escape the getting-and-spending spin cycle of your everyday existence. Yet soon you discover your getaway was hardly clean.

"Basic play" in *Second Life* is free. But Linden Labs charges a monthly fee for the ownership of land. And sale and rent of virtual buildings are the major source of wealth generation in this online domain. You can also make vehicles—from cars to spaceships—furniture, works of art, and machines; design landscapes, fauna, and flora; and craft the skin and gestures of your digital character. These creations are legally yours: in a breakthrough in game-world economics, Linden recognized players' intellectual property rights to user-generated content. Such property can be sold to other denizens of *Second Life* for the "Linden dollars" that are its official currency. But these transactions link to a more mundane market. At time of writing, one U.S. dollar bought 250 Linden dollars at *Second Life*'s official LindeX currency exchange. Speculating on the chances of transforming virtual goods into actual profits, many entrepreneurs have flocked to

Second Life, and some real fortunes have been made. Yet the income distribution in *Second Life* is strangely familiar; while about 20 percent of its residents constitute a Linden-dollar-wealthy minority, the rest languish in virtual poverty.

Virtual poverty is, of course, not the same as actual poverty. Playing *Second Life* requires a computer and a broadband connection, which in itself limits access to the upper percentiles of global wealth. The majority of *Second Life*'s population are in their twenties, evenly divided by gender, living in Europe, the United States, or Japan (the most active players, however, are in the Cayman Islands, a notorious haven for shady financial capital, suggesting Linden dollars have become a means of money laundering) (Au 2007a, 2007b). Over 60 percent hold a college degree, most make at least $45,000 per year, and 40 percent earn $90,000 annually (Au 2007a). This is a demographic that attracts corporate marketers and fills the streets of *Second Life* cities with familiar logos. Apple, Adidas, Nike, Nissan, Volkswagen, Toyota, American Apparel, CBS, Dell, Sun Microsystems, and many other actual companies have an in-world presence, installing not just billboards but in-game stores where you can purchase virtual equivalents of offline products, supposedly stimulating actual sales, and certainly keeping property fees flowing into Linden Labs' coffers, building the company's current $20 million capitalization. Maybe you were *told* to join *Second Life:* employers are embracing it as a "fun" platform for training workers and conducting meetings; IBM owns several "private islands" that it uses for workgroups (Whyte 2007). However you came to enter this new dimension, your personalized avatar is powered not just by mouse clicks but by computer servers that, according to one estimate, annually use about 1,752 kilowatts of electricity per *Second Life* resident, as much as is consumed by an average actual Brazilian, and generating about as much CO_2 as does a 2,300-mile journey in an SUV (Carr 2006).

Inhabitants of *Second Life* are, in other words, class-divided, property-owning, commodity-exchanging, currency-trading, networking, energy-consuming subjects of a comprehensively capitalist order. Welcome to your second life—much like the first.

This is not enough for you. You want a virtual life that is more adventurous, more challenging. You want to be all that you can. Frustrated by your failed escape attempt, you sign up for another networked game: *America's Army.* Now you are in the Afghan mountains. It is the middle of the night. Your squad has been assigned to assault a terrorist training camp and secure a computer terminal storing valuable intelligence information. As a rifleman with the 2nd Battalion, 22nd Infantry Regiment, it is your job to penetrate the enemy compound, eliminating any resistance along the way. You turn on your night-vision goggles. The all-clear signal comes through on the radio. You charge the compound. When you're almost at the entrance, tracers start to fly over your head. A grenade explodes to your left, taking out one of your buddies. Ducking behind a large rock, you spot muzzle flash coming from a window on the second floor. You raise your M16-A2 assault rifle and fire a three-round burst. A terrorist falls out of the window like a rag doll. Invigorated by your first kill, you get up and rush forward again. As you pass through a door, there is another eruption of gunfire. Suddenly you're hit. Those tedious rounds of "Basic Training" you had to grind through before getting to actual combat clearly weren't thorough enough.

Downloaded over seven million times (Verklin and Kanner 2007, 90) since its release on the Fourth of July, 2002, *America's Army* is an online first-person shooter intended to put into playable form the military service performed by some of the nearly three million active soldiers and reservists employed by the United States. Money is no matter in *America's Army*; it is free to play online, courtesy of a publicly funded, multi-million-dollar investment by the U.S. Department of Defense. A more recent addition to the *America's Army* Web site is "Real Heroes," which includes a list of the accomplishments of soldiers from Iraq and Afghanistan who have earned awards for valor, and gamers can read profiles or watch video interviews of soldiers talking about their childhood and military experiences.

As you log in and out from your skirmish via the home page of *America's Army,* you have the opportunity to link directly to the Web site goarmy.com. Twenty-eight percent of all visitors to *America's Army*'s Web page click through (Au 2002a). It is a major recruitment site for the U.S. Army, one that reportedly has a higher success rate in attracting enlistments than any other method. The battle you experienced as a cathartic bloodbath, a bit of fun, is for the world's undisputed armed superpower a serious public-relations device targeted at a generation of game players and intended to solve the crisis of a military struggling to meet its intake targets for the fatal front lines of the war on terror.

Second Life and *America's Army* are both highly successful games. Recently, however, there have been some troubles in these virtual domains—small disturbances to the commercial economy of the one, to the recruitment lures of the other. The corporate influx to *Second Life* invited by Linden Labs provoked dissent from players who saw it as a violation of the libertarian ethic that they believed informed "their" virtual world. On the day that IBM's CEO appeared in-game, the Elf King, monarch of the influential Elf Clan, abdicated in protest. Acts of anticorporate satire, spoof, and sabotage have been rife: a CopyBot program ran amok with intellectual property, cloning copyrighted items in a cornucopian frenzy, and a guerrilla Liberation Army vaporized a Reebok store with nuclear weapons.

And while it sometimes seemed that Linden Labs could use a bit of help from *America's Army,* the Pentagon's game was itself disrupted. In March 2006, on the third anniversary of the Iraq invasion, the artist and professor Joseph Delappe of the University of Nevada logged in under the user name "dead-in-Iraq" and began using the chat channel to transmit the name, age, service branch, and date of death of real soldiers killed in the occupation (Clarren 2006). Meanwhile, back in *Second Life,* though elfin protest hadn't warded off Big Blue, things were getting virtually grittier. On September 25, 2007, IBM's "corporate campus" in *Second Life* was the site of a digital protest organized by an international labor union supporting striking Italian IBM workers—prompting one journalist in *Second Life* to ask, "Avatar-based workers unite?" (Au 2007c). These were not just fanciful exuberances but turbulences at the edge of virtual worlds embedded in wartime capitalism.

Which brings us to the argument of this book. The "militainment" of *America's Army* and the "ludocapitalism" of *Second Life* display the interaction of virtual games and actual power in the context of Empire, an apparatus whose two pillars are the military and the market (Burston 2003; Dibbell 2006). Consider that the virtualities of *Second Life* feed back into the actualities of capital via the medium of the Linden dollar, and that the virtualities of *America's Army* cycle into the actualities of combat via the Web link to the U.S. Army home page. Add, moreover, that the two games are connected: the high-energy consumption and consumer goods of *Second Life* are what *America's Army* recruits soldiers to fight and die for. The two games reassert, rehearse, and reinforce Empire's twin vital subjectivities of worker-consumer and soldier-citizen: *Second Life* recapitulates patterns of online shopping, social networking, and digital labor crucial to global capitalism; *America's Army* is but one among an arsenal of simulators that the militarized states of capital—preeminently the United States—depend on to protect their power and use to promote, prepare, and preemptively practice deadly operations in computerized battlespace (Blackmore 2005). Yet the examples of digital dissent in *Second Life* and *America's Army* show that not all gamers accept the dominion of what James Der Derian (2001) terms "MIME-NET"— the military-industrial-media-entertainment network. Minor gestures that they are, these protests nevertheless suggest a route from game virtualities to another sort of actuality, that of the myriad activisms of twenty-first-century radicals seeking to construct an alternative to Empire.

Our hypothesis, then, is that *video games are a paradigmatic media of Empire*—planetary, militarized hypercapitalism—*and* of some of the forces presently challenging it. But investigation of this claim requires setting down some intellectual foundations.

Play Factory

Some forty years have passed since digital games were invented in the nocturnal hacking of Pentagon programmers who whiled away tedious hours tending giant military computers by transforming the electronic screens of nuclear war preparation into whimsical playgrounds. Within a few years, Atari, the first commercial games company, had converted this bold experiment in computer liberation into an entertainment commodity. Over the following decades, a string of legendary game firms—Nintendo, Sega, Sony—perfected and popularized the hardware and software of this commodity: by 2000, the sale of over one million newly released PlayStation 2s in the console's first week on the market confirmed that gaming had become a staple in the media diet of young people. Today digital play is a vast industrial enterprise. News in 2007 that the first day of sales for Microsoft's *Halo 3* reached $170 million heralded the most commercially successful media entertainment launch in history (BBC 2007a), or that about twelve million people around the planet disport themselves as orcs, elves, trolls, and paladins in the massively multiplayer *World of Warcraft* (Caoili 2008), or that a merger between two giant game companies, Blizzard and Activision, commanded a market value of some $18.9 billion are just a few of a stream of factoids announcing the market triumph of virtual play (*Economist* 2007a, 2007b). Although networked virtual worlds such as *Second Life* and *America's Army* are rapidly expanding and are often predicted to succeed television as mass entertainment (Castronova 2005a, 2007), they are only a corner of a much bigger field of digital gaming. By far the most populous and lucrative part is that contested for by competing video game consoles, the distant and infinitely more powerful "seventh-generation" descendants of Atari's primordial TV-connectable gaming device—Microsoft's Xbox 360, Sony's PlayStation 3, Nintendo's Wii. A smaller but still vital sector is devoted to games played on personal computers. Indeed, mobile gaming on devices from the handheld consoles that started with Nintendo's Game Boy, now succeeded by its DS and Sony's PlayStation Portable (PSP), to play-capable cell phones, is now giving programmed-play culture a 24/7 availability. Taken together, this combination of digital game machines and gaming practices—an ensemble that we shorthand as "virtual games"—amounts to a techno-cultural-commercial nexus of formidable depth and scope.

The common boast about virtual games is that they are now "bigger then Hollywood." This disguises a more complicated reality. In North America, sales of games rival the cinema box office, though globally they lag behind them (Lowenstein 2005; BBC 2007b). But games lack the ancillary revenue streams of film, from advertising to DVD and cable television release. So cinema remains a larger commercial enterprise, although this may change as "advergaming" experiments intensify. On the other hand, games do seem set to overtake the music industry in revenues (Andersen 2007).

More significant than either of these comparisons, however, is that games are increasingly integrated *with* film, music, and other media. In a world of fiercely bargained cultural properties, titles and themes are traded between cinema, comics, and video games; *Spider-Man* becomes a game, *World of Warcraft* a film, and *The Simpsons* travels from television to both video game and film. For a music industry facing flagging CD sales, licensing tracks to digital games is now a vital revenue source and has become a way for bands to extend their exposure. The runaway success of *Guitar Hero* exemplifies the way virtual games are not just contending with older media but, as important, melding and morphing with them in a convergent entertainment complex.

A decade ago, it might have been countered that, profitable as gaming is, its influence remains limited to a subculture of adolescent and preadolescent males. But these demographics are changing: the Entertainment Software Association claims that in 2008 some 60 percent of North Americans play virtual games (ESA 2008a). The altered composition of digital play is especially clear in regard to age: people who grew up with games persist with them as adults, so that the average gamer's age now hovers around thirty. Gender is more problematic. In North America, industry surveys, which have in the past made hyperbolic claims of near-gender-equity gaming, now admit that some 60 percent of players are male, 40 percent female (ESA 2008a). The testosterone profile of games, though waning sharply since the early 1990s, is far from abolished. But the success of apparently female-friendly devices such as the Nintendo Wii points to further shifts. Moreover, in Asia, where digital gaming's future expansion will probably be fastest, gendered patterns of play are significantly different from those in North America, with more women participating in a culture of primarily online games than in the West (Krotoski 2004; Maragos 2005a). So even though women play fewer virtual games than men, and often play in different ways (see Kerr 2006), it does seem that game culture is becoming more gender universal.

Planetary game revenues are forecasted to soar in 2009 to $57 billion (Androvich 2008c). Such figures are often held to qualify virtual games as a "global media industry" (*Economist* 2007b). Most of the sales of this supposedly global media are in North America, Europe, and Japan, with the United States still the largest single market. Game culture is thus heavily concentrated in the developed, rich zones of advanced capitalism. Rapid expansion of digital games into Asia is, however, giving it a new territorial dimension. Moving from South Korea—one of the most intensive gaming cultures in the world—into China, a game industry focused on online play in collective cybercafé settings is opening up vast new player populations. Nonetheless, for the majority of the world's inhabitants, a mint copy of *Halo 3*, let alone the Xbox 360 on which it plays with its $400 price tag, remains a luxury for all but elites. This does not, however, mean that games are completely out of mass reach. Both large-scale pirating of game software (which the officials of the global media industry energetically try to stamp out) and the market in old consoles and game devices give games a circulation outside the planet's affluent regions, into Latin America, the Middle East, and southern Asia: we have seen sports games played in wooden booths on the streets of Cairo's Old City, black-market game bazaars in the center of Delhi (where an "original" current hit—that is, an initial copy—goes for five dollars, with a copy of a copy selling for even less), and Game Boy handhelds in the slums of Mexico City.

There is another aspect to the internationalization of digital games: it is not just consumption but production that is going global. As much as any other industry, the video game business works with transcontinental value chains. The U.S. and Japanese console manufacturers—Microsoft, Sony, and Nintendo—have their new machines assembled offshore, in Latin America, eastern Europe, and now, especially, southern China (in factories that provide video games as part of recreational facilities intended to contain workers in their dormitory-style compounds). North American, European, and Japanese game publishers are increasingly driving back production costs by outsourcing sections of software development to studios in Bangalore, Bucharest, or Ho Chi Minh City (see Gallaugher and Stoller 2004; Johns 2006). And ultimately the components of game machines come from sources such as the mines of the Congo and end up in the electronic waste dumps of Nigeria and India. In both consumption and production, play and work, the game industry is omnipresent around the planet, though its pleasures and its pains are unevenly distributed.

This fractured economic order is far from stable. In 2008–9 a compounding series of crises shook the market system, from subprime crisis to stock market plunge to credit crunch to full-bore recession. Amid the ongoing convulsions, however, global capitalism has one consolation left for its increasingly desperate subjects: you may have lost your job (or will never be able to retire from it), you can't afford to go out, but you can always stay home (if you still have one) and play a video game. As Lehman Brothers, Bear Sterns, and Merrill Lynch fell and General Motors, Ford, and Chrysler reeled round the edges of their graves, North American sales of game hardware and software hit all-time highs in 2008. Forecasters claimed that virtual play was recession proof; a maturing audience of stay-at-home gamers would cocoon around the Wii, Xbox 360, or PS3 or migrate to *World of Warcraft* or *Second Life* to enjoy a diversion from economic disaster. Such estimates of game-business resilience may prove optimistic: by 2009 job losses and studio closures were announced by game-industry icons such as Sony and Electronic Arts.

To these quantitative measures of the digital play industry's importance should be added another, qualitative one. To a greater degree than perhaps any previous media other than the book, virtual games are a direct offshoot of their society's main technology of production. From their origins in nuclear-age simulations, games have sprung from the machine system central to postwar capital's power and profit—the

computer. Born out of the same military research matrix that generated the personal computer and the Internet, virtual games continue
to be a testing ground for some of the most futuristic experiments in
digital technology: online play worlds incubate artificial intelligences,
consoles are linked into grid computing systems, and games are the
media of choice for neurobiological experiments in emotional stimu-
lation and telekinetic digital devices driven by brain activity alone.
More mundanely, games once suspect as delinquent time wasters are
increasingly perceived by corporate managers and state administrators
as formal and informal means of training populations in the practices
of digital work and governability (see Beck and Wade 2004). A media
that once seemed all fun is increasingly revealing itself as a school for
labor, an instrument of rulership, and a laboratory for the fantasies of
advanced techno-capital; all the more reason, then, to subject virtual
games to political critique through a theoretical optic whose key concept is Empire.

Empire Theory

"Empire" is a term with a long and bloody genealogy (see Pieterse
2004 and Colás 2007 for overviews). To connect it to virtual games
is not to import some distant, gloomy concern to the carefree world
of play. Games themselves nominate "empire" as a theme in a strategy
genre that runs from the text-based *Hamurabi,* an important game in
the freeware culture of the early 1970s, to Microsoft's *Age of Empires*
franchise to the even more frankly named *Empire,* the latest iteration
of Creative Assembly's *Total War.*[2] If one were to throw into the mix
a few games about business dynasties *(Casino Empire, Restaurant
Empire, Circus Empire),* an entire study of games about empire could
be written. This, however, is not our purpose. Instead we set out to locate virtual games within a larger analysis of, and controversy about,
actual global Empire.

Our point of departure is the recent and controversial definition
offered by Michael Hardt and Antonio Negri (2000) in their book
Empire. They claim we are witnessing the emergence of a new planetary regime in which economic, administrative, military, and communicative components combine to create a system of power "with no
outside" (Hardt and Negri 2000, xii). Earlier examples of imperialism,
such as ancient Rome, sixteenth-century Spain, or nineteenth-century
Britain, were in their time rooted in specific nations that dominated the

world map. What distinguishes Hardt and Negri's Empire from these earlier empires is that it is not directed by any single state. Rather, it is a system of rule crystallized by what Karl Marx (1858) called the "world market." Empire is governance by global capitalism. This domination works, Hardt and Negri say, through "network power" (2000, 167). Its decentered, multilayered institutional agencies include nation-states but extend to include multinational corporations, like Microsoft and Sony, world economic bodies, like the World Trade Organization and the International Monetary Fund, international organizations like the United Nations, and even nongovernmental organizations, like the Red Cross. What results from the interaction of these nodes is an imperium more comprehensive than any preceding one.

But this is not just an analysis of international relations. Hardt and Negri offer something more ambitious, a comprehensive account of conditions of work, forms of subjectivity, and types of struggle in contemporary capital. Empire is global in terms not only of its geographic reach but also of its social scope. Capital now taps its subjects' energies at multiple points: not just as workers (as labor power) but also as consumers (the "mind share" targeted by marketers), as learners (university degrees as vocational preparation), and even as a source of raw materials (the bio-value extracted for genetic engineering). Empire is thus a regime of "biopower"—a concept borrowed from the philosopher Michel Foucault (1990, 135–45)—exploiting social life in its entirety.

Within this system, Hardt and Negri (2000, 289–94) ascribe an especially important place to what they and others term "immaterial labor" (Dowling, Nunes, and Trott 2007; Lazzarato 1996; Virno and Hardt 1996). Immaterial labor is work involving information and communication, "the labor that produces the informational, cultural, or affective element of the commodity" (Virno and Hardt 1996, 262). The importance of immaterial labor to Empire, what makes it in Hardt and Negri's view the key activity in contemporary capitalism, can be grasped by thinking of how central media, marketing, communication, and surveillance are, not just in creating new commodities—such as video games—but also in managing the workplaces that produce them and in appealing to the consumers who buy them. It is through the fiber-optic cables and wireless connections of digital networks run by immaterial labor that the tendrils of business stretch around the planet, the equivalents for today's Empire of the Roman roads that tied together Caesar's dominion.

Yet if this picture of a world swallowed by capital is all there was to Empire, it would be just another account of corporate domination of a familiar sort. What made people take notice was that it spoke about opposition to capitalism—even of alternatives to it. That touched a contemporary nerve. The book came out at the high-water mark of the struggles against corporate globalization that were racing around the planet from the jungles of Chiapas to the streets of Seattle. Hardt and Negri declared this wave of activism signaled a new revolutionary power—"the multitude" (2000, 393–414). Precisely because capital is increasingly everywhere and has subsumed increasingly everything, rebellion against it upsurges at many points, from work to school to leisure, and from many agencies, including workers and unions but also indigenous communities struggling over land rights, students opposing the corporate campus, antipoverty groups fighting for a living wage, migrants contesting the oppression of borders, environmentalists demanding ecological conservation, open-source advocates promoting knowledge sharing, and many others. The multitude is thus made up of many protagonists pushing for a more democratic deployment of global resources. Transnational connections, cultural hybridities, and new technologies are seen by Hardt and Negri as containing immense potential for the multitude. Crucially, they spoke not of antiglobalization but of a movement for *another* globalization, an "exodus" from capital (210). Compared with the characteristic gloom of the Left, their book was a breath of hope.

Empire attracted wide attention not only from academics but also from activists and journalists (Eakin 2001). This was extraordinary, since the book was written at a high level of abstraction and openly declared a radical, anticapitalist position. Its success was in part due to timeliness: the reek of tear gas from the streets of Genoa, Seoul, and Washington seemed to rise off the page. But *Empire* also had intellectual and political credentials. Behind it lay Negri's history as a militant in the Italian *autonomia* movement (for overviews, see Cleaver 1977; Dyer-Witheford 1999; Wright 2002), a role that earned him imprisonment and exile; both authors' engagement with the work of the philosophers Gilles Deleuze, Félix Guattari, and Michel Foucault; and a series of debates within a Parisian Left locked in battle against neoliberal governments. *Empire* therefore encapsulated a wider experimental fusion of Marxist militancy and poststructuralist theory. It circulated novel concepts—biopower, immaterial labor, multitude, exodus—among students of globalization and its discontents and, in the process, catalyzed considerable excitement. It even seems to have at least partially inspired a computer game: a group of Serbian digital artist-developers produced *Civilization IV: Age of Empire*, displaying the highly multileveled power apparatus of global capital that Hardt and Negri described.[3]

Empire also drew fierce criticism, with some of the most incisive response coming from the Left (see Balakrishnan 2003; Boron 2005; Passavant and Dean 2004). There was intense debate between theorists of Empire and analysts of "imperialism." For many Marxists, the concept of a decentered transnational Empire seriously underestimated the continuing importance of the nation-state for capitalist power (Wood 2003). In particular, it fatally downplayed the importance of U.S. hegemony as a force driving globalization and, along with this, the continued subordination of the global South to Northern capital (Arrighi 2003; Seth 2003). There were also other objections to Hardt and Negri's work, and not only from more traditional left perspectives. Their concept of "immaterial labor" was widely criticized for emphasizing the importance of information work at the expense of older—but still alive-and-well—forms of drudgery and exploitation: what about all those factories in China, those mines in Africa? (Dunn 2004; Dyer-Witheford 2001; Moore 2001). And the idea of "the multitude," which Hardt and Negri seemed to propose as a replacement for the working class, was charged with being nebulous and romantic, resting on a rosy confidence in a revolt that would spontaneously self-organize from wildly disparate sources (Laclau 2004; Rustin 2004).

Criticisms gained force from the dramatic turn of global politics in 2001. Only a year after the publication of *Empire*, the attacks on the World Trade Center and the Pentagon, and the subsequent so-called war on terror, appeared to end the very project of corporate globalization of which *Empire* was in many ways an interpretation. The supernationalism of the Bush regime, the Iraq war, and the associated rift between the United States and its European allies made the idea of a unified international capitalist regime dubious. The daily swap of blood for oil around Baghdad reminded everyone that capital didn't just run on code, and that some vital resources weren't so immaterial after all. And the chill of post-9/11 wartime politics—think Patriot Act—subdued the Seattle-era oppositional optimism to which Hardt and Negri gave voice. The times suddenly seemed more conducive to analyses such as David Harvey's (2005a) account of a "new imperialism"—essentially a continuation of old imperialisms based on resource grabs by nationally, and particularly U.S.-based, corporations (see also Chomsky 2003; Lens 2003).

More or less holding the line, Hardt and Negri's 2004 follow-up to *Empire*, *Multitude: War and Democracy in the Age of Empire*, emphasized the role of military force in maintaining capitalist order, cited global mobilizations against the Iraq war as an example of the multitude in action, and argued that the protracted fiasco of the occupation demonstrated that "go-it-alone" U.S. unilateralism was, in fact, unsustainable. Other writers have attempted a synthesis between the conflicting accounts of Empire and imperialism and have introduced new elements to the analysis. *Afflicted Powers* by the collective Retort (2005, 5, 4) describes a pugnacious "American empire" driven by oil capital and the military-industrial complex, opposed from one side by reactionary jihadis and from another by the "multitudinous" progressive forces theorized by Hardt and Negri. Retort stresses the importance of media spectacle and its various "emotion machines" in these struggles (Anderson, cited in Retort 2005, 21).

We too take an intermediate position. In our view, Hardt and Negri were right to suggest that post–Cold War planetary capital is a new social formation whose analysis demands the reworking of many categories of critical political thought. They also, however, overstated several of their points and missed some important features of an emergent scene. So we work with a revised and modulated version of Empire. By Empire, *we* mean the global capitalist ascendancy of the early twenty-first century, a system administered and policed by a consortium of competitively collaborative neoliberal states, among whom the United States still clings, by virtue of its military might, to an increasingly dubious preeminence. This is a regime of biopower based on corporate exploitation of myriad types of labor, paid and unpaid, for the continuous enrichment of a planetary plutocracy. Among these many toils, immaterial labor in information and communication systems, such as the media, is not necessarily most important. But it clearly occupies a strategic position because of its role in intellectually and affectively shaping subjectivities throughout other parts of the system. This Empire is an order of extraordinary scope and depth. Yet it also is precarious. It confronts a set of interlocking crises—ecological (global warming), energy (peak oil), epidemiological (HIV/AIDS and other pandemics). Its governance is threatened by tensions between a declining United States and a rising China that could either result in some supercapitalist accommodation, consolidating Empire, or split the world into warring Eastern and Western empires. Its massive in-equalities catalyze resistances from below. Some, such as al-Qaeda, are disastrously regressive. Others, like the global justice movement—whose complex diversity Hardt and Negri's multitude gets closer to than any other category their critics can offer—contain the seeds of a better alternative. Empire is flush with power and wealth, yet close to chaos. This is the context in which we place virtual games.

Ludic Scholars

The growing body of academic game studies presents both insights for and obstacles to the perspective that orients this book. Schematically, scholars can be said to have responded to this young medium with one of three broad stances: condemnatory, celebratory, or critical, positions whose popularity and influence have approximately followed a chronological sequence.

The first, and longest, condemnatory phase, from 1972 (the year of the foundation of Atari) to just before 2000, was one of malign neglect. Relatively little was written by academics about virtual games. Much of what was bore the characteristic mark of generational "moral panic" about new media. Authors were unfamiliar with video games, and the culture surrounding them, and displayed an a priori distaste; the focus was on the "problem" of video game play, preeminently the alleged role of violent games in causing real-life crimes (Dominick 1984). Psychological studies were often based on simplistic models of "media effects," supported by laboratory research isolated from real-world contexts and variables (see Gunter 2004).

Other perspectives were rare. There were no major studies of video games by critical political economists comparable to those of news-papers, television, radio, or cinema. Cultural analysis of video game content was almost equally scarce, at least until Nintendo made its mark on North American children. Marsha Kinder's *Playing with Power* (1991) provided a nuanced analysis of videogaming in the wider networks of commodified children's toys and media. More typical of this phase, in both its hostility and its knowledge base, was Eugene Provenzo's *Video Kids: Making Sense of Nintendo* (1991), a searing indictment of video games' misogynistic violence. Such bluntly condemnatory perspectives—which persist to this day—surged after the Columbine school shootings in 1999, whose teenage perpetrators were, journalists rarely failed to mention, avid *Doom* players, a connection that was cemented by texts bearing titles like *Stop Training Our Kids to Kill* (Grossman and DeGaetano 1999).

Studies of this period raise issues of continuing importance: we too will engage with the game violence debate. But the narrowness of the psychological theories on which they are based is of limited relevance to the broad-level analysis of societal power we wish to contribute, and their denunciatory mode is at odds with a perspective that sees an appreciation of the pleasures and the possibilities—in short, the ambivalence—of virtual games as crucial to the analysis of this medium.

Eventually scholars, many of whom had by now grown up with consoles, got game. Around the turn of the new millennium, a second phase of game commentary emerged, whose trademark stance was *celebratory*. This shift was started mainly by an increasingly sophisticated body of work published outside academia by game reviewers, game journalists, and amateur game historians (Herman 1997; Herz 1997; Kent 2001; Poole 2000). Contrasting sharply with earlier perspectives, these commentators presented video games as media at least potentially as rich as literature or film; took games' aesthetic and narrative qualities seriously; found complexity, conviviality, and cooperation—rather than isolation—in game culture; and were skeptical about its stigmatization by moral authorities.

Academics also contributed to this more affirmative evaluation. A leading figure was Henry Jenkins, a professor in MIT's Comparative Media Studies Program, who has written prolifically about the aesthetic merits and cultural importance of games (Jenkins with Fuller 1995; Jenkins 2005), supported the "girl games" movement (Cassell and Jenkins 1998), defended video games from the charge of being "murder simulators" at U.S. Senate hearings (Jenkins 1999), and enthusiastically situated DIY game-making activities such as "mods" (player-made modifications to commercial games) and "machinima" (game-generated cinema) in the wider context of participatory fan cultures (Jenkins 2006a). While not entirely uncritical of video game culture, Jenkins's assessment of the medium is generally optimistic, an outlook that has encouraged game companies to support his influential program with donations to the Convergence Culture Consortium, demonstrating that, as academics become more sophisticated about games, the industry has become increasingly savvy about academic alliances (see Young 2007).

Upbeat reevaluations of the medium helped lay the foundation for the emergence of game studies as a recognized academic field, complete with its own journals *(Games and Culture),* conferences (DiGRA), anthologies (Raessens and Goldstein 2005), citations from the canonical texts of play theory (Caillois 1958; Huizinga 1944), and in-house disputes, such as the polemics between "narratologists"—who view games as stories or as texts to be analyzed in the same way as books, films, and television—and "ludologists," who want to discuss games as sports, structured by rules, goals, and strategies (see Aarseth 2001; Wardrip-Fruin and Harrigan 2004).

Much of this literature is concerned with delineating the specific properties of games as media, describing their genres and conventions, and forming a lexicon with which to describe them. When the literature does look to games in their larger context, the assessment is often positive, asserting the creative empowerment of game players compared to the audiences of the broadcast media. Rob Cover captures this sentiment when he writes, "Interactivity achieves a new stage in the democratization of user participation with the electronic game" (2004, 173). If in the earlier, condemnatory phase the gamer was a bad subject, delinquent, or victim, in this second, more enthusiastic period, she is the empowered denizen of the postmodern mediascape, happily prepared by play for rewarding digital careers. The title of Steven Johnson's best-selling book conveys the inversion: *Everything Bad Is Good for You: How Today's Popular Culture Is Actually Making Us Smarter* (2003).

Such eager, sophisticated game studies, which ride a wider wave of academic enthusiasm for popular culture, are a corrective to the not-so-well-informed condemnations of the previous phase. But in giving this media some overdue respect, they often bend the stick the other way, ignoring the political and economic contexts of virtual games, skipping lightly over the conditions of paid and unpaid labor in game production, reinscribing platitudes about the information-age jobs that gamers are training themselves for, and failing to raise awkward questions about the global order for which gamers are now the new model of empowered participants.

Intertwined with the emergence of academic game studies is, however, a third position, the one that we see this book as working within. It tempers both knee-jerk condemnation of, and celebratory euphoria about, virtual games with a critical political analysis of the medium. Again, the impetus comes not from purely academic voices but also from media artists, independent game designers, and media literacy advocates who are developing hacks, alternative minigames, and curricula that trouble, probe, or depart from the norms of official game culture (Bogost 2007; Ochalla 2007; Schleiner 2002, 2004).

These theorists write critically about games not to dismiss them but often in the hope that they might be otherwise. They situate digital play within formations of societal power and thus depart, to varying degrees, from the formalism of much of game theory. This research does not deny the singular attributes of digital play—but neither does it assume they simply transcend "old-media" problems of ideology and political control. And unlike earlier generations of media-effects perspectives that emphasized individual psychologies, the new research addresses social structures, corporate contexts, and institutional forces. Finally, in contrast to the boosters who have discovered the training merits of gaming, it does not assume that socialization for the prevailing social order is benign; instead it looks at games, and the discourses surrounding them, as vectors of contending interests and agendas, and as inculcating skills that can serve—but also potentially subvert—established norms.

Among the currents here are those addressing gender, race, militarism, and corporate power. Probably the most sustained is the criticism of virtual games as a masculine domain from academic feminists, women working in the industry, and female gamers, hackers, and digital artists (Alloway and Gilbert 1998; Flanagan 2002; Laurel 2001). Initially these critiques of "toys for the boys" focused on the gender inequities of game company employment and the traces this left in virtual worlds where women were invisible other than as "virgins and vixens" (Buchanan 2000). More recent takes acknowledge the ambiguities of increasingly common Lara Croft–type action sheroes (Deuber-Mankowsky 2005; Richards and Zaremba 2004). How recent changes in the gender composition of game culture—slow but significant in game play, near imperceptible in game production—will affect feminist critique remains to be seen. Meanwhile, although critical race-theory work on games has taken longer to emerge, depictions of ethnicity in games like *Grand Theft Auto: San Andreas* have stimulated analysis of a new media whose screens and studios are overwhelmingly white (Chan 2005; Everett 2005; Leonard 2003, 2004, 2005, 2006; Marriott 1999; Ow 2000).

Two recent waves of social activism have added new elements to this critical game politics. The first was the wave of counterglobalization protests that culminated in the protests of Seattle and Genoa, the second the international mobilizations against the Iraq war. Both generated a politically spirited alternative game culture and an accompanying analytic literature. The sort of digital dissent from both corporate and military power that we have already mentioned is discussed in Anne-Marie Schleiner's texts on her own game hacks (2002), Alexander Galloway's search for a "countergaming" tradition (2006a, 107–26), and Ian Bogost's work on the design of "persuasive games" for political issues (2007). Looking at the situation from the other side of the hill, the study of military links to games, though predating 9/11 (Lenoir 2000), has been accelerated by the war on terror (Der Derian 2001; Halter 2006a; Herbst 2005; Stockwell and Muir 2003).

In all of this, gaming's relation to the combined military and capitalist power of what we term Empire has not been ignored. Important grounds for such an analysis were prepared some time ago in an extraordinary essay by Julian Stallabrass (1993), "Just Gaming," later included in his book *Gargantua: Manufactured Mass Culture* (Stallabrass 1996). Writing from the perspective of the Frankfurt school, Stallabrass discussed computer games' fascination with war and the incessant reproduction within their worlds of market structures, concluding, "In their structure and content, computer games are a capitalist and deeply conservative form of culture" (1996, 107). The essay is suffused with a sardonic contempt that veers close to a condemnatory antigame rant. Yet Stallabrass zeroed in on issues such as "virtual trading," which would a few years later attract a great deal of attention. Although Stallabrass flattened out elements of conflict and contradiction within virtual play, we find his account an important backdrop to our own attempt to understand the interaction of games and capitalism.[4]

More recently, McKenzie Wark's *Gamer Theory* (2007) has visited this terrain, though arriving at different conclusions. He argues that video games provide an "atopian" refuge from a real-life "gamespace" dominated by a "military-industrial complex" whose arbitrary power plays rule our lives. Virtual play is, he proposes, a revelatory antidote to the false promises of neoliberal capitalism: "The digital game plays up everything that gamespace merely pretends to be: *a fair fight, a level playing field, unfettered competition*" (Wark 2007, para. 21). This is a persuasive account of the compensatory pleasures of gaming in a cynical age—though the point we want to press is how far the forces of armored neoliberalism have already broken into this ludic refuge via networked games like *America's Army* and *Second Life*, compelling critical gamer theory to explore responses more radical than atopian immigration.

We aim to build on the existing body of critical game analysis to construct something that is so far lacking: an account that explores virtual games within a *system* of global ownership, privatized property, coercive class relations, military operations, and radical struggle. We began this task in an earlier collaborative book that examined the video game industry as an aspect of an emerging postindustrial, post-Fordist capitalism (Kline, Dyer-Witheford, and de Peuter 2003). Now we offer a more directly political perspective on what we call "games of Empire."

Games of Empire

Virtual games are exemplary media of Empire. They crystallize in a paradigmatic way its constitution and its conflicts. Just as the eighteenth-century novel was a textual apparatus generating the bourgeois personality required by mercantile colonialism (but also capable of criticizing it), and just as twentieth-century cinema and television were integral to industrial consumerism (yet screened some of its darkest depictions), so virtual games are media constitutive of twenty-first-century global hypercapitalism and, perhaps, also of lines of exodus from it.

Why are virtual games *the* media of Empire, integral to and expressive of it as no other? They originated in the U.S. military-industrial complex, the nuclear-armed core of capital's global domination, to which they remain umbilically connected. They were created by the hard-to-control hacker knowledge of a new type of intellectual worker, immaterial labor, vital to a fresh phase of capitalist expansion. In that phase, game machines have served as ubiquitous everyday incubators for the most advanced forces of production and communication, tutoring entire generations in digital technologies and networked communication. The game industry has pioneered methods of accumulation based on intellectual property rights, cognitive exploitation, cultural hybridization, transcontinentally subcontracted dirty work, and world-marketed commodities. Game making blurs the lines between work and play, production and consumption, voluntary activity and precarious exploitation, in a way that typifies the boundless exercise of biopower. At the same time, games themselves are an expensive consumer commodity that the global poor can access only illicitly, demonstrating the massive inequalities of this regime. Virtual games simulate identities as citizen-soldiers, free-agent workers, cyborg adventurers, and corporate criminals: virtual play trains flexible personalities for flexible jobs, shapes subjects for militarized markets, and makes becoming a neoliberal subject fun. And games exemplify Empire because they are also exemplary of the multitude, in that game culture includes subversive and alternative experiments searching for a way out.

At the start of *Empire,* Hardt and Negri say that they see their book as "a toolbox of concepts" (2000, xvi). We have already mentioned some of these—biopower, immaterial labor, multitude, exodus. But there is an array of other ideas associated with their line of thought, elaborated by authors with similar perspectives but distinct voices: cognitive capitalism, machinic subjectivity, futuristic accumulation, cynical power, lines of flight, general intellect (Lazzarato 2004; Vercellone 2007; Virno 2004). These are intellectual tools we use in our inquiry into games of Empire. A useful concept, write Gilles Deleuze and Félix Guattari, "makes us aware of new variations and unknown resonances" (1994, 28). Opening new pathways of thought, concepts "pack a potential in a way a crowbar in a willing hand envelops an energy of prying" (Massumi 2002a, xv). It is in this prying, pragmatic way that we pick up concepts from autonomist Marxism and poststructuralist radicalism (and from critics of both) and put them to work on virtual play, setting up encounters between theoretical concepts and game activity so that each might shed light on, and critique, the other.

The rest of the book is structured in three parts. Part I, "Game Engine: Labor, Capital, Machine," looks at the main ingredients of the corporate game complex. We begin in chapter 1 with a bottom-up history of digital play, focusing on immaterial labor. It shows how video games, hacked into existence forty years ago by a Pentagon-mobilized technical workforce as part of vibrant freeware culture, were captured by entrepreneurs, commodified, and transformed into a colossal corporate complex. The continuing dynamism of the game industry has depended on trapping the innovations of game player-producers within commercial structures. Today this process culminates in a situation where virtual games are being sent "back to work," where they are used as a means of training new generations of immaterial labor across all sectors of capital.

Arguing that the game industry is at the front of new forms of cognitive capitalism hinging on property rights over intellectual and affective creation, chapter 2 undertakes a case study of this sector's publishing giant, Electronic Arts (EA). EA's game development studios, rinse-and-repeat game franchises, high-intensity marketing, fanatical corporate culture, and U.S.-based but transnationally distributed production webs provide a state-of-the-art example of how to make billions from digital play. But the unexpected outbreak of a scandal about the overwork of EA employees shows how trouble can flare up even in the smoothest-run fun factory.

Chapter 3 moves to the game machines that, connected to gamer bodies, power the corporate game complex, focusing on Microsoft's game console, the Xbox, in its most recent iteration, the Xbox 360, but also glancing at its rivals, Sony's PlayStation 3 and the Nintendo Wii. Game consoles, we argue, are not just hardware but techno-social assemblages that configure *machinic subjectivities*. They operate as corporate machines, eliciting ongoing expenditures on software; as time machines, commanding hours of attention; as biomachines, initiating intimate relations between players, artificial intelligence, and networked collectivities—but they also sometimes operate as nomadic war machines, appropriated by hackers and pirates challenging proprietary controls and raiding corporate revenue streams, within the larger biopolitical machine of Empire.

Part II, "Gameplay: Virtual/Actual," looks at the relationship between games and reality, body and avatar, screen and street, first life and second life. It examines how game virtualities arise from and cycle back into the social actualities of markets, battlefields, sweatshops, and law courts. Any particular interaction between game and gamer remains singular and unpredictable. But there are also regular pathways, sometimes institutional, sometimes clandestine, along which the traffic passes. We trace pathways through which virtual play materializes, with digital virtualities and corporeal actualities combining in the reality of Empire. Our examples—of subjectivities shaped for war, for work, and for only those rebellions that can profitably be recuperated—do not pretend to cover all of virtual game culture. Just a lot of it.

We examine the deep linkage of games and war in chapter 4, where we present an in-depth study of *Full Spectrum Warrior*, a military-civilian coproduction that doubled as a U.S. Army trainer for urban warfare and a "fun" variation on conventional shooter games. In its sanitized normalization of the carnage in Baghdad or the Balkans, *Full Spectrum Warrior* amply demonstrates the role of virtual games in the banalization of war, the habitual identification of civilians with "our troops," and the acceptance of an armed vision that perceives the world through the preordained categories of the war on terror. But our example shows what can go wrong with the best virtual plans as dissidents at home question the boondoggles of high-tech military contracting, and enemies abroad start to adopt the same techniques of virtual training and indoctrination.

Chapter 5 examines the massively multiplayer online game *World of Warcraft*. Our key concepts here are *biopower* and *futuristic accumulation*. We look at the interaction between two regimes of capitalist biopower—Vivendi/Blizzard's *Dungeons and Dragons*–style virtual world, and the marketization of China. The two are linked through the practice of "gold farming"—the selling of virtual goods for actual money—which now sustains a Chinese digital-sweatshop industry of thousands of workers. Many of these are migrants from rural communities being destroyed pell-mell by the entrance of, among others, the very electronics companies who produce the computers and consoles on which virtual games are played. The link between primitive accumulation in the Pearl River and futuristic accumulation in corporate game worlds is symptomatic of both the complementarity and the potential conflicts between the Western and Eastern halves of Empire.

A complex spiral of virtual/actual interactions is presented by the infamous *Grand Theft Auto (GTA)*, which we discuss in chapter 6. At once the most celebrated and reviled of video games, *GTA*, developed by Rockstar Games and published by Take-Two Interactive, stands at the center of the protracted controversy about violence (and some sex) in virtual worlds. But its more important contribution is, we think, not as a "murder simulator" but as an "urban simulator"—virtually re-creating the great metropolitan centers that are key sites of Empire. Our discussion here pursues the way in which *GTA* constitutes the politics of city space in ways that are not just generically urban but characteristically imperial. Its digital sandbox arises, we argue, from a specific moment in global capital's creation of world cities and, in turn, reproduces imperial territorializations of class and race. We examine three turns in this spiral of virtual and actual city building in Rockstar's famous franchise. In *Vice City,* we look at how *GTA*'s Miami is constructed as a virtual space exemplary of a "neoliberal urbanism" driven by a free-market logic whose imperatives are, literally, the rules of the game. In *GTA: San Andreas* we examine how the game's urban configurations recapitulate and reinforce the racialization of space in American cities. When we turn to Liberty City—the virtual New York of *GTA IV*—we shift focus to observe how not only the play but also the production of *GTA* contributes to the imperial cityscape, showing how Take-Two's own role in the media industry's remaking of its headquarters global city "slips and segues" into the world of criminal capitalism it depicts. Finally we consider the complex, contradictory blend of insight into, and complicity with, urban corruption that *GTA* represents, and argue that the category of cynical ideology explains why the "punch line" that Rockstar's virtual cities deliver is, ultimately, that of Empire's brutalism.

Having examined virtual games' integration in Empire, we invert our perspective in Part III, "New Game," to look at aspects of alternative gaming culture that challenge or subvert the dominant order. We have referred to the interplay of the virtual and the actual in Empire—meaning by the virtual the digital world fabricated by the computer or game console, and by the actual the corporeal, embodied world off-screen. But there is another meaning of "the virtual" relevant to our discussion. In recent philosophical discussions of ontology—the nature of being—"virtual" denotes *potentiality:* the manifold directions in which a given arrangement of forces, in any concrete situation, *might* develop (see Deleuze and Parnet 2002; Lévy 1998; Massumi 2002b; Shields 2003). The technological and ontological virtual, digitization and potential, are distinct; they should never be conflated. But there is an oblique relation. Computers create compelling, dynamic digital depictions of potential universes. Their simulations extrapolate from what is to what might be, fancifully or plausibly. In a sense, the slogan of every gamer is "another world is (temporarily) possible." There is nothing necessarily dissident about this. Many—probably most—digital virtualities amplify and reinforce imperial actualities, as we have discussed. And flight to imaginary worlds can be a dead-end escape. But aspects of gameplay can and occasionally do link to radical social potentials. It is in this light we apply to digital games Hardt and Negri's assertion that "the new social virtuality" is the substance of the multitude's "productive and liberatory capacities" (2000, 357).

So here we ask: Can there be "games of multitude"? Chapter 7 therefore looks at how digital-play culture implants capacities and follows trajectories that exceed and disturb its own commodified circumference. These lines of flight include gamers' abilities to sometimes play against the grain of even ideologically loaded games; dissonant development from a handful of mainstream game studios; the tactical games produced by counterglobalization and antiwar activists; the ambivalent social planning potential of "serious games";

experiments at radical self-organization in online virtual worlds; and the emergence of software commons challenging information capital's intellectual property regimes. Modest as these virtual initiatives are, they nonetheless open toward a remaking of ludic practices along lines connecting to an array of struggles against Empire.

Our conclusion, chapter 8, contrasts two contradictory aspects of virtual games. The very real wonders of the increasingly complex game "metaverse" display this medium's potential for virtually conceiving and exploring alternative worlds and social possibilities—a capacity of evident interest to radicals seeking an exodus from Empire. At the same time, however, virtual games are deeply embedded within global capital, a point we underline by reflecting on the working conditions in the African coltan mines and Asian e-waste sites that lie at the beginning and end of the console-production value chain. Assessment of the emancipatory possibilities of digital play, we conclude, must take into account these opposed, but simultaneously existing, sides of the game.

"A Sky Steeped Blood Red"

Games have always served empire: from Cicero's claim that gladiatorial sports cultivated the martial virtues that Rome required to the Duke of Wellington's apocryphal assertion that the Battle of Waterloo was won on the playing fields of Eton or the Prussian general staff's Kriegspiel rehearsals of their World War I Schlieffen Plan. But games have also been turned against empire, in ways ranging from the bloodbath of Spartacus's revolt to the gentler revenges of West Indian cricketers defeating their colonial British rulers (James 1966).

Today's academic writings on virtual games often prefer to start not with such charged and conflictual aspects of play but with the work of the conservative medieval historian Johan Huizinga and his concept of the "magic circle," enunciated in his great *Homo Ludens* (1944, 10). Huizinga's famous account of play as a quasi-sacred "autotelic" activity, conducted purely for its own sake, in a space and time ritually segregated from everyday life, is a favorite in recent game studies, where it tends to underwrite a formalist approach to digital play, with the video game controller, display screen, and introductory cut scene marking the liminal boundaries of an enchanted space set apart from the turmoil of global markets, preemptive militarism, and street protest.

Yet Huizinga himself, writing in the shadows both of the recently concluded World War I and of the approaching European fascism that would eventually take his life, was well aware of what Ian Bogost describes as "a gap in the magic circle," such that "instead of standing outside the world in utter isolation, games provide a two way street through which players carry subjectivity in and out of the game space" (Bogost 2006a, 135). This recognition of the inescapable relation between "magic circle" and "material power" is subtly present in *Homo Ludens*. But it is paramount in Huizinga's less-remarked-on study of decaying feudal power, *The Autumn of the Middle Ages*. There he shows how games such as jousts and tournaments cultivated the skills of chivalric elite, whose supremacy his account, despite its romanticism, unmistakably reveals as based in military barbarism and armed expropriation (Huizinga 1921, 90–97). The medieval magic circle of play, with all its visual pageantry and elaborate rules, is firmly set in the context of declining empires convulsively gripped by plague, war, and peasant revolt, with the game theoretician's eye "trained on the depth of an evening sky, a sky steeped blood red, desolate with threatening leaden clouds, full of the false glow of copper" (xix). It is in a similar light that we examine virtual games in today's age of Empire.

I
Game Engine:
Labor, Capital, Machine

1. Immaterial Labor:
A Workers' History of Videogaming

Working-Class Hero

Mario, hero of the most famous video game series in the world, is a worker—an overall-clad, cloth-capped industrial artisan who liberates Princess Toadstool by overcoming a series of bosses. He is, it is often observed, the quintessential "little guy." As such, Mario invites identification from every child pitted against the big world of adults (Kinder 1991), but his adventures also invoke the plight of every wage slave striving to beat a capricious, powerful, and frustrating system. Mario's "working-class hero" (moviebob 2007) status is also, however, significant in a more complex, contrapuntal way. Part of the charm of Mario games is the whimsical contrast between the weighty, industrial materiality of our hero's ostensible trade, plumbing (underlined by the prominence of pipes as a mode of transportation), and the weightless, leaping, running, bouncing, acrobatic, explorative exuberance he can, with sufficient player skill, be made to display as he hurtles from platform to platform. Mario was originally "Jumpman." The contrast, we suggest, crystallizes a moment of cultural transition between two epochs. One is the era of mass industrial work, often known as Fordism, when to be an everyman was to face a life committed in one way or another to a world of manufacturing production, factories, heavy machineries, and assembly lines. The other is the postindustrial, post-Fordist life of jobs mediated by computers, networks, and virtuality.

This shift occurred in North America, Europe, and Japan over the very period of Mario's climb to fame, from *Donkey Kong* in 1981 to

Super Mario Galaxy in 2008, and, more broadly, spans the rise of videogaming as a whole, from the 1960s to the present. As kids' play, an activity that young people "got" as they mastered the game console while parents were left bemused and clumsy, Mario games were a symptom of this tectonic shift. Their chaotic, colorful celebrations of virtual joie de vivre were a playful promise to generations of new, upcoming post-Fordist workers—a promise of escape from the hard, soulless Fordist labor their parents or grandparents suffered into a world of digital freedom and possibility. That this virtual promise has, in actuality, largely been betrayed is something we have plenty to say about later: it is, indeed, the point of our analysis. What we want to highlight here is the link between virtual games and a new kind of work—immaterial labor.

Immaterial labor is, according to the theorists who devised the term, work that creates "immaterial products" such as "knowledge, information, communication, a relationship or an emotional response" (Hardt and Negri 2004, 108; Lazzarato 1996, 2004; Virno 2004). It is not primarily about making a material object, like the work that makes a car roll off an assembly line or extracts coal from a mine. Rather, immaterial labor involves the less-tangible symbolic and social dimensions of commodities. There are various subcategories of immaterial labor: high-technology work manipulating the codes on which computers and networks run; affective work, generating emotion of, say, ease or excitement; and work involving social coordination and communication in a wide range of neomanagerial tasks. Immaterial labor is less about the production of things and more about the production of subjectivity, or better, about the way the production of subjectivity and things are in contemporary capitalism deeply intertwined. Immaterial labor is, Hardt and Negri (2000) say, the leading or "hegemonic" form of work in the global capitalism of Empire. This ascendancy is not quantitative—they recognize that not everyone works with computers or in a creative industry—but qualitative: immaterial labor is the activity that advanced capital depends on in its most dynamic and strategic sectors.

Though theorists of immaterial labor sometimes overstate their case, we agree that a new constellation of technological, affective, and communicational work is a feature of twenty-first-century capital. The video game offers a telling site for its critical exploration. One only has to think of how the development of a *Mario* game involves the advanced technological skills necessary in making hardware and programming software, the affective skills of many kinds of artists, from animators to musicians to concept designers, and the coordination of all these activities in collaborative studio teams to see how closely such work corresponds to the definition of immaterial labor. The ultimate product of this labor is, no doubt, material—once a game cartridge, today a disc—but its success or failure as a commodity depends on the creation of a relationship: the willingness of a player to identify, perhaps for hours, perhaps over the span of an entire lifetime, with a diminutive, running, jumping, red-capped plumber. Making and playing digital games involve combining technical, communicational, and affective creativity to generate new, virtualized forms of subjectivity. This is not the only sort of work involved in making games—later we will encounter some all-too-material labor far from the game studio, in electronics factories, e-waste dumps, and coltan mines—but it is a crucial element in their creation.

So in this chapter we present a short history of the video game from the perspective of immaterial labor. What distinguishes the concept of immaterial labor from theories about postindustrialism, knowledge work, or a creative class is its link to ideas of autonomy and struggle. It comes from a line of thought that emphasizes not the right and power of corporations to control life in the name of profit but the way workers' desires exceed, challenge, and escape that control (see Dyer-Witheford 1999). Capital's attempts to constrain this autonomy within the limits of profit lead to recurrent cycles of struggle. It is actually often these struggles that drive capital forward to new horizons as it attempts to crush, or co-opt and capture, resistances, deploying new technologies, trying new organizational forms, and seeking new global locations in a frantic flight into the future that, however, only creates conditions for fresh conflicts.

Immaterial labor emerges from one such cycle of struggle—that of the labor, student, and social movements of the 1960s and 1970s. This worldwide turbulence was marked by an eruption of new subjectivities, desires, refusals, and capacities: students who wouldn't submit to teachers, soldiers who wouldn't fight in Vietnam, factory workers who wouldn't watch their lives pass by on assembly lines, women who walked out on household drudgery. It was also a period of experiment with new techno-cultural forms—music, drugs, and strange digital machines. These interweaving resistances destabilized power. They drove corporations to restructure their technologies, replacing assembly lines with robots and networks; to switch managerial techniques, encouraging (limited) "participation" rather than dumbed-down routine; to leave old industrial heartlands in search of exploitable sites offshore; and to recuperate many of the themes of radical counterculture into new commodities, corporate stylings, and political creeds. This restructuring is variously described as a shift from industrial to information capital, from Fordism to post-Fordism—or from the centrality of material labor (in the factory) to a focus on immaterial labor (in the network).

In ways often insufficiently acknowledged, virtual play was an invention of, and ingredient in, the radical counterculture of the sixties and seventies. It was only subsequently, and after dramatic failures, assimilated into a business model that grew vast for-profit game empires. Even in the commodity form, however, games have continued to depend for their vitality on a constant infusion of energies from a do-it-yourself player-producer culture that embodies the autonomous capacities of the new echelons of immaterial labor. The protagonists of our snapshot video game history are therefore not so much companies or technologies or individual artists but creative assemblies of immaterial labor: the hacker clubs of the 1960s that liberated games from the Pentagon; the long-haired labor force of gaming's 1970s golden age, who drove the suits mad; the delinquent *manga* artists that animated Japan's revival of a burned-out American industry in the 1980s; the outsider female players and developers who challenged the old boys' game networks in the 1990s; the do-it-yourself culture of micro-innovators, modders, massively multiplayer online (MMO) game populations, and machinima artists who by 2000 were a major force driving game culture—and game company profits. We conclude by reviewing how, approaching 2010, games are increasingly being applied to training myriad other kinds of immaterial labor. What we want to suggest is how, in virtual play as in other aspects of life, "Empire is a mere apparatus of capture that lives off the vitality of the multitude" (Hardt and Negri 2000, 62).

Midnight Phenomenon

In 1972 the maverick futurist Stewart Brand wrote in *Rolling Stone* of an "irrepressible midnight phenomenon" at Stanford's Artificial Intelligence laboratory (Brand 1972). Among "the freaks who design computer science," at "any nighttime moment" hundreds were "locked in life-or-death space combat . . . joyously slaying their friend and wasting their employers' valuable computer time." They were playing a computer game—one of the very first, with an oscilloscope screen on which players could navigate rudimentary spaceship-blips and fire virtual space torpedoes at one another. *Spacewar* was "part of no one's grand scheme" and "served no grand theory." It was, Brand observed, "heresy, uninvited and unwelcome," yet also a "flawless crystal ball of things to come" in computer use: "interactive in real time," graphic, encouraging user programming, "a communication device," promising "richness and rigor of spontaneous creation and human interaction," and "delightful." *Spacewar* announced "computer power to the people" (Brand 1972).

This radical innovation emerged from an unlikely context. All contenders for the title "inventor of the video game"—William Higginbotham, who made a simple tennis game on an analog computer in 1958, Steve Russell, who created *Spacewar* in 1961, and Ralph Baer, who in 1966 devised the first TV-connected game console—were employees of the U.S. military-industrial complex. These workers were among the first mass draft of immaterial labor, the highly educated techno-scientific personnel recruited to prepare, directly or indirectly, for nuclear war with the Soviet Union. Their workplaces were academic research centers at Stanford University, the Massachusetts Institute of Technology (MIT), and other universities, to which the Department of Defense streamed military funds through channels such as the Advanced Research Projects Agency (ARPA); the nuclear National Laboratories of Lawrence Livermore, Los Alamos, and Brookhaven; and the massive defense-contracting system, in which the giants of U.S. corporate power, including information and telecommunications companies such as IBM, General Electric, Bell Telephone, Sperry Rand, Raytheon, and RCA, prepared for doomsday (Edwards 1997; Halter 2006a; Lenoir 2000). In this military-academic-industrial complex, computing science, born in the code breaking, ballistics calculations, and atomic programs of World War II, grew up in "a closed world, within which every event was interpreted as part of a technological struggle between the superpowers" (Edwards 1997, 44).

Computer simulations were integral to this closed world, a crucial means to calculate the options of nuclear strategy, to think the unthinkable. "Red versus Blue" war games were by the late 1960s starting to be computerized on the massive mainframes of the day, playing out the mega-death scenarios of nuclear exchange, not to mention the many subsidiary hot conflicts of the Cold War (Allen 1987; Edwards

1997; Halter 2006a). But simulations could also be a diversion from working on mass death if they were cut loose from serious application, enjoyed for their technical "sweetness" and oddity without instrumental purpose, transformed into play. Such escapes were possible because the military allowed its immaterial workers a lot of latitude. Computer scientists and engineers were the only people who understood the new digital machines. Transgressing standard procedures, fooling around with computers, was at least tolerated because that was the way to discover new uses and options (Kline, Dyer-Witheford, and de Peuter 2003). Such transgressions included making games.

All the first virtual games were unofficial, semiclandestine, or off-the-cuff projects. Higginbotham, an engineer who had worked on the first atomic bomb before becoming head of Brookhaven (he would go on to become prominent in Science for Peace), concocted *Tennis for Two* for an annual visitors' day display, where it featured alongside a duck-and-cover exhibit, "Methods of Protection against Nuclear Radiation" (Poole 2000, 29)—and was then promptly consigned to the archives and forgotten. Ralph Baer created his console by hijacking the resources of the five-hundred-person department he directed as chief engineer for Sanders Associates, a large military electronics firm, loyally filing patents in his employer's name but telling his managers nothing, working on the project in complete secrecy until it was completed. Russell's *Spacewar* was made on a PDP-1 minicomputer produced by Digital Equipment Corporation, a company specializing in military cybernetics, in an MIT department saturated with funding for air-defense systems.

Higginbotham's game preceded Russell's; Baer's invention had greater commercial significance. But it is *Spacewar* that is regarded as the ur–video game. This is surely because it was such an integral expression of the culture of computer-science "freaks"—a culture often at odds with the military institutions that funded it. At MIT, access to the PDP-1 was heavily monitored. Getting access was the mission of the Tech Model Railroad Club (TMRC), which brought together students for what they began to call "hacking." No political-activist collective, TMRC members nonetheless "believed in a cooperative society and . . . a utopian world in which people shared information, sometimes without regard for property rights" (Kent 2001, 17). Circulated via the Internet's precursor, the military ARPANET, *Spacewar* proliferated across campuses and wired labs, where people within and outside Russell's circle added features and graphics, making it an early instance of participatory design, freeware, and open-source development.

This digital experimentation tied in to a counterculture of psychedelic drugs and of political dissent. As campus protests against the Vietnam War rose toward a bloody crescendo with the Kent State shootings, disaffection was at near-revolutionary levels. Military computer laboratories were assisting electronic battlefield projects like Operation Igloo White, the remote-control B-52 bombing of the Ho Chi Minh trail, but the students in those labs were resisting the war. When Brand (1972) observed *Spacewar* at Stanford, he noted the "anti-Establishmentarianism" of the students who played it in a setting plastered with "posters and announcements against the Vietnam War and Richard Nixon." *Spacewar* was just one instance of a "counter-computer" movement in "moonlight mode" whose other manifestations included programmed letters supporting strikes against the war, computerized coordination of demonstrations, and projects for "investigative work on corporations, assisting free health clinics, community computer education," aiming, as Brand put it, "to plant dynamite in the very heart of the Combine."

There were thus *two* red scares at work in the origin of virtual games: the external threat of the Kremlin, inspiring the Pentagon to an escalating trajectory of digital research, and the internal subversion of counterculture where hacking met the New Left. John Markoff (2005) has traced this interweaving of hacking with political radicalism through forums such as Ted Nelson's 1974 *Computer Lib* (its cover sported a power-to-the-people clenched fist on a black background and the imperative "You Can and Must Understand Computers NOW") and organizations such as the San Francisco People's Computing Company (PCC), founded by programmers involved in the Berkeley Free Speech and War Resisters League, whose philosophy was "You make the software available for free, and anyone could do anything they wanted with it" (Markoff 2005, 262). PCC founders wrote one of the first DIY game design manuals and held "game nights" where the many successors of *Spacewar*—*Hurkle, Snork, Mugwump*, digital versions of *Star Trek*, and, most famously, *Hunt the Wumpus*—were devised, played, and swapped for free in the same space that political organizing proceeded apace (Markoff 2005, 268).

Watching the Stanford computing science students, Brand (1972) thought "something basic is going on." Retrospectively, many social theorists have agreed, selecting the year he observed *Spacewar*—1972—as a convenient point at which to date the transformation from industrial to postindustrial era, from Fordism to post-Fordism (Harvey 1989). Hardt and Negri pick that very year to locate the military, monetary, and economic crises that marked "the shift of hegemony of economic production from the factory to more social and immaterial sectors" (2004, 39). In this process, military power was, they suggest, essential, "adopt[ing] and extend[ing] the technologies and forms of large scale industry and add[ing] to them the new innovations of social and immaterial production . . . primarily through communications and information technologies" (40).

These innovations proved, however, impossible to control. In the hands of the immaterial laborers who made them, the communications and information technologies created for the military-security state were subverted into playful expressions of digital delight. The irony, however, was that in liberating computers, and games, from the Pentagon, "deterritorializing" them from the realm of nuclear death, hackers inadvertently set the stage for their "reterritorialization" by capital in pure commodity form (Deleuze and Guattari 1987).

You Are About to Be Captured

It was 1979, the golden age of video games, the epoch of classic arcade hits and the first deliriously addictive console games. One programmer was already disenchanted. He had worked exhausting hours transforming a text-based adventure game into virtual form, creating a digital labyrinth filled with fearsome foes and magic loot, a task his supervisor had said was impossible. He had done it anyway. Now the game was completed. But success would bring little recognition or reward. His employer, the most famous and profitable company in the newly booming video game business, had recently been bought by a huge media conglomerate. It refused to give designers royalties for games or even name credits on the game boxes, a clear move to reduce the bargaining power of a workforce whose strange technical powers its managers could barely comprehend. The programmer reflected and made one finishing touch. In the depths of a gray catacomb, he coded a single-pixel dot, the same color as the game's background. If a player detected and picked up the dot, it would allow access to a secret room. No one would find the room for quite a while, far too late to recall the thousands of game cartridges that had already been sold. On a wall of the secret room, running down the middle in flashing letters, the programmer wrote "Created by Warren Robinett." Then he quit.

Robinett's addition to Atari's *Adventure* is legendary in game culture as the first "Easter egg," a secret feature designed into a game awaiting player discovery (Connelly 2003; Gouskos with Gerstmann 2008). Such surprises soon became a staple feature in game design. That they originated in an act of protest not only demonstrates how capital gets some of its best ideas from the resistance it provokes but, more broadly, shows the problems that attended the conversion of hacker games into a for-profit industry driven by a new type of wage labor.[1]

A decade after *Spacewar,* video games had become a six-billion-dollar business, rivaling the music industry of its day, amassing profits from a stream of quarters. The counterculture that had confronted the military-industrial complex was morphing into a cyberculture whose "Californian ideology" of digital utopianism mixed with free-market fever fit smoothly into an America about to elect Ronald Reagan president (Barbrook and Cameron 1996). This process had many moments, from Bill Gates's appropriation of homebrew hacker culture as the basis of his Microsoft millions to the conversion of utopian "virtual communities" such as Stewart Brand's WELL (Whole Earth 'Lectronic Link) into a global business network (Turner 2006, 7). For games, the process ran through an enterprise named Atari, which in the Japanese game of Go means "you are about to be captured."

Atari arose on the border of two worlds that defined the future of virtual games—computing science and the entertainment industry. Its founder, Nolan Bushnell, was an engineering undergraduate at the University of Utah who frequented the laboratories of its military funded graphics-interface computer program (Lenoir 2000). But as a holiday worker in the fairgrounds of Salt Lake City, he was familiar with the midway ball toss, coin-op electronic amusements, and a business model that profited from expensive machines by a relentless drip of coins. Little surprise that when Bushnell discovered *Spacewar,* he "saw commercial opportunity" (cited in DeMaria and Wilson 2002, 16). He spent his California evenings in 1971 re-creating a version of the game to run on a stand-alone arcade machine, using components stolen from the engineering companies where he and his friends worked (Kent 2001). *Computer Space* sold few units. But Bushnell was further inspired when he saw a demonstration of the Magnavox Odyssey, the first commercial version of Baer's console idea, and sampled a simple ball-and-paddle game harking back to *Tennis for Two.*

Bushnell's next appropriative tour de force was the release of *Pong*, the first epic arcade success. In one of the intellectual property disputes that would characterize the game industry, Magnavox sued, but by the time the suit was settled out of court in 1976, Bushnell was the world's premier video game capitalist (Festinger 2005).

The company he founded, Atari, put joysticks in the grip of tens of millions of young North Americans, first luring them to the arcades, then entering their homes with its famous "2600" TV-connected console. Within a decade it was the "fastest-growing company in U.S. history" (Kent 2001, 52). Traditional American businesses, like the automobile industry, were flagging in the economic crisis of the 1970s. Capital was seeking new strategies that "put a premium on 'smart' and innovative entrepreneurialism" (Harvey 1989, 157). Atari was a technological innovator at the heart of a burgeoning Silicon Valley computer culture. The future founders of Apple computing, Steve Jobs and Steve Wozniak, made games at Atari before departing to make their fortunes in personal computing. The young, highly educated Californians Bushnell employed were a mutation in the workforce, a new stratum of techno-scientific creativity.

The student movement had rejected the prospect of monotonous jobs in industrial plants and offices. Atari paradoxically made this "refusal of work" its key to commercial success. With a "work smart, not hard" philosophy, an Aquarian constitution ("a corporation is just people, banding together"), a legendary lack of bureaucracy, small development teams who "bid" on games they wanted to design (and were rewarded by result), and parties awash in drugs and alcohol, Atari promised "play-as-work." The fusion of counterculture and corporate capitalism soon, however, revealed its contradictions. From the start, Bushnell had difficulties balancing the play-as-work formula. Atari made both hardware and software: there were tensions between the freewheeling "immaterial" ethos of game programmers and the routinized tedium of minimum-wage workers assembling arcade machines and consoles: after the assembly workers failed in a unionization attempt, "the theft was incredible," Bushnell remembered (Kent 2001, 52).

In 1978, seeking an infusion of cash to manufacture Atari's new in-home console system, Bushnell sold the company to the giant media corporation Warner Communications for twenty-eight million dollars. Soon after the sale, Atari's founder, manifestly unable to discipline his anarchic workforce, became one of the first victims of the takeover: he was dismissed as manager and replaced by a Warner-installed executive with a background in textile manufacture. What followed was a clash between traditional management and immaterial labor, a civil war between "suits" and "ponytails" (Cohen 1984). The new regime tightened security and subjected Atari to industrial cost-benefit practices. This aggravated programmers who were used to high levels of autonomy. Minor rebellions—from satiric self-made movies to T-shirts poking fun at Warner—erupted; as we have already seen, Robinett took discontent over wages and recognition into the game itself.

Resistances galvanized the next step in the expansion of the video game business. A number of Atari employees defected to start their own game companies. One, Activision, made cartridge games to play on its former employer's hardware. Since Atari was selling hardware at cost and making profit only on the software, it was threatened by this strategy and sued Activision every six months or so. Nonetheless the company was an enormous success and added a whole new arm to the structure of the video game industry, the "third-party" game-development sector separate from console manufacture (Kent 2001, 227). Atari's problems were, however, much larger than Activision. Hundreds of rival companies had entered the market. The same free-booting genius that had served Bushnell so well was glutting the market: in 1982 there were fifty companies making games for Atari's 2600 (DeMaria and Wilson 2002). Bootlegged software—an ineradicable legacy of hacker culture—was rampant, quality control nonexistent, and the mounting involvement by Hollywood studios and giant toy companies resulted in a series of embarrassing failures, the most notorious being the bathetic *ET* video game based on the film by Steven Spielberg.

In 1983 the mix of incompetent management, employee discontent, overproduction, and rampant piracy exploded. When Atari failed to reach projected profits, its stock fell—and the company abruptly plunged toward bankruptcy. It carried with it the entire industry it had previously drawn upward on its ascent. Toy stores and amusement arcades that a year before had been enraptured with games now as suddenly declared them terminally passé. As trailer loads of surplus game cartridges were bulldozed into landfills like so much radioactive waste, the North American game industry annihilated itself in one of the most complete sectoral disasters of recent business industry, a demonstration of the volatility of emergent digital industry that foreshadowed on a smaller scale the larger dot-com boom and bust that would come years later. Atari and its imitators had captured the playful genius of immaterial labor but failed to find the organizational and disciplinary forms to contain it: that discovery would have to come from somewhere else.

Media of a New Humankind

A second Pearl Harbor; a foreign invasion; a yellow peril! New machines playing games featuring entrancing entities in bizarre stories were infiltrating American homes, hearts, and minds. Digital play was being saved by *Asian* immaterial labor. The outlines of the Japanese video game coup that in the 1980s aroused protectionist panic among U.S. capitalists (though certainly not among U.S. children) can be summarized quickly. In 1985 Nintendo, a Japanese company with a foothold in the U.S. arcades, defied the conventional wisdom that digital play was dead, and released its Nintendo Entertainment System console in New York. The machine's superior graphics and *Mario* platform games won instant success. For a few years, Nintendo enjoyed a near monopoly of virtual play, until it was challenged by another Japan-based enterprise, Sega. The Sega-Nintendo "game wars," fought with rival mascots (Sonic versus Mario), waves of ever-higher-powered consoles, and lavish marketing, restored videogaming as a major entertainment business. This attracted the attention of a third Japanese company, one of a whole new magnitude, the multinational electronics and media giant Sony. The launch of Sony's PlayStation console in 1994 initiated a brief period of triangular warfare. Sega plummeted to disaster, Nintendo was demoted to a niche in children's games, and Sony emerged as the world-dominant console maker for the remainder of the twentieth century.

What was remarkable about this revival of virtual play was that it came not only from outside the United States but from a country that had experienced America's power in its most annihilatory form. Video games were rescued not by the military-industrial complex from whence they had sprung but by the victims of its atomic bomb. Nintendo, Sega, and Sony all made or remade themselves under conditions of Japan's post-Hiroshima "disrupture, defeat, and despair" (Allison 2006, 11) and amid the forced internationalization of U.S. occupation. Originally a maker of traditional Japanese playing cards, Nintendo adapted to the new conditions by printing Disney characters on its cards before moving into electronic games. Sega (an abbreviation of Service Games) changed hands between American and Japanese owners as it supplied arcade amusements for GIs. The founders of Sony, returning from war work as weapons researchers to rebuild their bombed Tokyo factory, turned to repairing radios damaged by American bombs or Japanese censors, then to manufacturing electric rice cookers, and finally, while U.S. companies researched military applications of transistors, to making consumer electronics.

The irony of U.S.-Japanese postwar relations was that the defeated culture excelled in adopting the victors' techno-cultural innovations. In the 1970s, as industrial reconstruction flagged, Japan took the idea of a "postindustrial society" as a policy guide, sponsoring "fifth-generation" artificial-intelligence research, producing the world's largest national population of robots, making itself an upstart global cyborg laboratory. In this context, video games spread rapidly. Namco and Taito licensed console production from Atari. Then domestic game developers emerged. In late 1970s, Tokyo "bowling alleys, pachinko parlors, and even small vegetable stores" replaced their inventory with rows of coin-op machines playing Taito's *Space Invaders:* production of 100 yen coins was temporarily quadrupled to meet demand (Kohler 2004, 21).

Japan's game artistry transformed the new media. U.S. games, made primarily by computer scientists and engineers, had created lively, diagrammatic worlds of stick-figure shooters, mazes, sports, and puzzles. But from the moment of *Pac-Man,* the first game with an identifiable *character,* Japanese developers added something else: graphics and narrative. These images and stories came from a distinct tradition: *manga*— broadly, Japanese comics. *Manga* art is characterized by iconic figures, clear genre conventions, and strong story lines filled with "small real world details" and "emotionally expressive" graphic effects (McCloud 2006, 216). While *manga* content ranges from the innocently childish to the demonically violent and sexually sublime, its worlds are usually chimerical, full of fantastic organic/machine, animal/human, natural/supernatural hybrids. It was perfect for games.

Japanese *manga,* like American hacking, was a suspect subculture. Though originally a children's medium, it attained prominence among Japanese youth born during postwar reconstruction, the *shin jinrui* or "new humankind" separated from authority and tradition by the trauma of Hiroshima (Yoshimi 2000, 210). This was a generation that in the 1960s and 1970s was a hotbed of student radicalism, Marxism, anti–Vietnam War protest, and anti-nuclear-testing activism. *Manga* was "'border art,' a new type of democratic medium accessible by cultural amateurs" (Kinsella 2000, 5). Enabled by cheap, portable offset printing and photocopying, urban migrant workers and radical students made *manga* a "shadow cultural economy" that incited the same sort of "condescension and loathing" among the Japanese establishment as "far-left political parties and factions . . . in the USA" (Kinsella 1998).

Video games absorbed *manga* talent. "Where American game designers were culled from a group of computer hobbyists," Chris Kohler observes, "Japan searched for computer tinkerers but also *manga* fans" (2004). *Manga*'s iconic conventions suited low screen resolution: "small, cute characters had fewer pixels per inch" (Herz 1997, 162). Even so, for years, consoles could not do justice to *manga* graphics. But box art and advertisement could. *Manga* influenced game designers such as Toru Itiwani *(Pac-Man)*, Tomohiro Nishikado *(Space Invaders)*, Akira Toriyama *(Dragon Quest)*, and, most famously, Shigeru Miyamoto, the designer of the *Mario* and *Zelda* series that made him the world's most famous game auteur and a Nintendo corporate powerhouse. Miyamoto was at college when his "eyes opened to *manga*" (Kohler 2004, 26); he took courses in industrial design and went to work for Nintendo only because he feared failure as a professional *manga* artist (Kohler 2004, 281). Miyamoto's work derives mainly from children's *manga* traditions rather than the darker adult strains. But even his games display not only *manga*'s fantastical inventiveness but also the populist sensibility of the *Mario* games that pit "a manual laborer who works very hard" against difficult "bosses" (Kohler 2004, 56).

Japanese media corporations, aided by a nationalist promotional apparatus, eventually "made a market of the new intellectual interests and aesthetic tastes of postwar Japanese youth" (Kinsella 1998). From the mid-1980s, *manga* was changed from an anti- to a pro-establishment medium (after this commercial absorption, amateur *manga* once again became a target of suspicion and censorship in the panics about "antisocial" *manga otaku,* or "*manga* nerds," that swept Japan in the 1990s). Companies such as Nintendo were part of this recuperation and normalization of *manga* dissidence, which was smoothed out within the highly disciplined machinery of Japanese game studios. When Ken Kutaragi, designer of the PlayStation, first came to work at Sony, he looked at the red flags of the "spring labor offensive," symbol of the labor militancy with which *manga* had once been associated, with incomprehension and distaste (Asakura 2000).

The Japanese video game companies, however, showed much greater sophistication than their American counterparts in managing immaterial labor. They recognized the primacy of designer creativity by perfecting the razor-and-blades model that gave consoles away at or below cost to make money on games; they recognized the affective appeal of *manga*-based mascots like Mario and Sonic and made them central to ambitious marketing and promotional efforts; and they celebrated their most talented artists—the status Nintendo bestowed on Miyamoto, for example, contrasts with Warner's crass attempt to deny Atari game makers name recognition. Nintendo also learned from Atari's catastrophe to exercise much greater attention to quality control, with detailed vetting of games by committees of designers, and it waged a relentless war on the piracy that had glutted North American markets, both through technological locks on its cartridges and with a notoriously aggressive legal department (Sheff 1999).

The stylistic vitality of *manga* thus continued to fuel the productions of Japanese studios. Though the popularity in North America of "Japanimation" only exploded in the 1990s with films like *Akira* and *Princess Mononoke,* "video games were the can opener" (Kohler 2004, 11). To see the abiding influence of *manga* on virtual play, and perhaps even a faint, residual trace of its dissident politics, one only has to think of the exquisitely wrought and massively successful *Final Fantasy* role-playing game series. Its world of fantastically good-looking ideal characters in romanticized neofeudal settings seems the extreme of spectacular gaming beloved of large-scale corporate game studios. The famous seventh game in the series, however, revolves around a conflict between a group of disaffected youth and a multi-national conglomerate, Shinra ("New Rome"), a weapons developer whose attempt to drain the planet's vital energy sources makes it both a world government and the cause of massive ecological destruction—a saga that strangely connects the postnuclear legacy of the dissident *shin jinrui* to today's anticorporate movements.

Gaming was the first media in which U.S. post–World War II hegemony over global culture was decentered toward a more complex, diffuse capitalist order. Anne Allison (2006), writing of the international *Pokémon* craze of the 1990s, specifically links the success of Japanese *manga*-inspired toys and games, with their "endless bodies, vistas, and powers that perpetually break . . . [and] reattach and recombine," to Hardt and Negri's account of Empire. She attributes *manga*'s "polymorphous mutability" to two factors—an atomic-bomb-bred sense of mutation, literal and metaphoric, and the pell-mell pace of Japanese postwar high-tech development. Both, she argues, fed an imaginary "of mixed up worlds, reconstituted bodies, and transformed identities" (Allison 2006, 11).[2] In the closing decades of the twentieth century, however, this imaginary "assumed the cutting edge in popular play aesthetics" because its popular culture spoke to the "millennial" condition of *global* techno-capital where "everything is at once fluid and boundless . . . a lived world of flux, fragmentation and mobility." This is the world of immaterial labor, of which Japanese video games were the first transnationalized expression.

Becoming Woman?

While virtual play culture was triumphantly encircling the planet, it was running into problems on the home front. In 1995 an Australian feminist group, VNS Matrix ("Venus Matrix") launched *All New Gen,* an online art piece and political polemic presented as a prototype computer game (Galloway, n.d.; Breeze, 1998). In a "transplanetary military industrial imperial data environment," the Renegade DNA Sluts do battle with the forces of Big Daddy Mainframe. Guided by Oracle Snatch, they must overcome Circuit Boy, a "dangerous techno-bimbo," and disarm him by removing his detachable penis and turning it into a cellular phone. This piece, a companion to VNS Matrix's "Cyberfeminist Manifesto for the 21st Century" (1991), was a contribution to a much-wider digital dissidence linking women in academia, the art scene, and new media—a revolt of *female* immaterial labor that in the 1990s took as one of its major targets the masculine dominance of virtual play.

In the same year *Spacewar* was invented, the birth control pill was released in North America. A decade later, as Bushnell debuted *Computer Space,* Betty Friedan and Gloria Steinem started the National Women's Political Caucus. Atari and *Ms.* magazine were both founded the following year. First-wave video games and second-wave feminism were contemporaries. From the start of virtual games, there were women game makers and girl players.[3] Yet despite this, the history of hackers, *manga* artists, and game developers is mainly a tale of men and boys. If, as Gilles Deleuze and Félix Guattari (1987) suggest, sexual subjectivities, rather than being naturally given, emerge in a process of "becoming" that combines not only bodies and social codes but also technologies, the game console has been very much part of the apparatus of "becoming man," and not of "becoming woman." No topic in the sociology of games has been more discussed than this gendered division of play; we will not attempt to review all its dimensions here, just to open some windows on it from the perspective of immaterial labor.

In the 1960s and 1970s, a generation of women walked out on unpaid toil—the bearing and raising of children, the cooking and cleaning, the caring for the young, sick, and old that were the hidden requirement of an industrial capitalism that put men in the factory and kept women in the home (Dalla Costa and James 1972; Federici 2006; Fortunati 1995). Leopoldina Fortunati (2007) relates the "machinization" of immaterial labor to this exodus. While domesticity involves material chores, much of it, she notes, is "reproductive immaterial labor"—"affection, consolation, psychological support, sex and communication," or, in short, "care labor" (140). With children, such work often involves media and toys: "fairy stories, read to send them off to sleep, or toys that serve to sustain games." In advanced capital, these supports increasingly become technological devices, by means of which "reproductive immaterial labor [is] machinized and industrialized" (140). This tendency, begun with radio and television, was, Fortunati suggests, accelerated by the feminist revolt of the 1970s. The refusal of women to do domestic work and the reluctance of men to take it over created conditions where "the grand offensive of the economic system" was to produce machines to "replace at least in part the immaterial domestic labor that was no longer carried out" (149). The video game console was part of this "grand offensive," the perfect latchkey-kid-care techno-device for a world of working women, double-income families, and single-parent households.

This machinization of unpaid domestic labor was accompanied by a new gender split *within* the world of waged work. While the decline of manufacturing jobs sent young men toward computer-related industries, capital's reply to women's domestic rebellion was to turn the activities they had performed for free into jobs in the service sector. Both service work and high-technology jobs can be defined as forms of immaterial labor; technology jobs, Hardt and Negri (2000, 2004) say, mobilize cognition and intellect, and service work often involves affect, caring, and serving—what feminist theorists have long defined as "emotional work" (Hochschild 1983). But the common categorization obscures real differences. Service jobs are usually worse paid, less prestigious, often more physically demanding—more material—than information work, and they are differently gendered. The old divide between male production work and female homework, apparently super-seded, was reconstituted inside immaterial labor. If Pac-Man went to program in Silicon Valley, Ms. Pac-Man was more likely to end up cleaning his office or working at the front desk (see Mathews 2003).

In the 1970s and 1980s, some women made careers in high tech-nology, and more in professional or managerial positions. But the mass of women in service jobs were subordinated within the new informa-tion order. They might work in digital networks, as teletypers or call-center operatives, but with a much less playful relation to computers than male programmers, system administrators, and technology devel-opers, "enveloped" in digitization, not "directing" it (Menzies 1996). There was also a huge residue of household tasks waiting at home, with millennia of gender socialization prompting women, not men, to a "second shift" of unwaged work (Hochschild 1990). Women had less free time at home for hacking at the Commodore 64 or mastering moves on the Sega Genesis. This was reflected in the socialization of girls, who, looking to their mothers and sisters for example, saw video games clearly on the list of "guy things."

While elsewhere male prerogatives were being challenged, virtual games thus congealed as a sphere of cultural "remasculinization" (Kim 2004). As late as the mid-1990s, 80 percent of players were boys and men (Cassell and Jenkins 1998). The military origins of simulations, the monasticism of hacker culture, the bad-boy arcade ambience, tes-tosterone niche marketing, developers' hiring of experienced (hence male) players, game capital's risk-averse adherence to proven shooting, sports, fighting, and racing formulae—all combined to form a self-replicating culture whose sexual politics were coded into every Game Boy handheld, every *Duke Nukem* double entendre, and every booth babe at industry conferences, where women appeared only as imper-iled princesses and imperiling vixens, a male head-start program, building and consolidating the gender stratification within immaterial labor (Haines 2004a, 2004b; Krotoski 2004).[4] Even when virtual play did acknowledge women, it was in a tellingly stereotypical way. In 1996 Mattel's *Barbie Fashion Designer* computer game, computer-printing dresses for its famous doll, sold a half million copies in two years. Girls perhaps now knew enough about new media to be targeted as a market, but Ken would clearly be the dot-com millionaire.

The cyberfeminism of the 1990s, of which VNS Matrix was one instigator, took fire from the increasing familiarity of young women with the Internet and was part of a wider "third-wave" feminism that built on previous movements but also reacted against their limitations (Fernandez and Wilding 2002, 17). In the world of virtual games, it took two directions. Girl Games (Cassell and Jenkins 1998) was a project of female entrepreneurialism to make commercially success-ful, nonsexist games for girls, predicated on the belief that there were identifiable "female-friendly" game features (a position that some-times drew criticism for reinforcing the idea of stable gender identi-ties). Grrl Gaming was a more kick-ass affair, appearing in the hyper-violent world of online shooting games through the amateur player production of female "skins" or avatar identities (by both male and female players) and the formation of female game clans such as PMS (Psycho Men Slayers) or Babes with an Attitude. It was aggressive, provocative, and campy, mixing virtual transvestism, separatism, and violence, sometimes with a dash of anticapitalist hacktivism and free software thrown in (Schleiner 2002).

Both movements altered the trajectory of the game industry, though not necessarily in the way either anticipated. Girl Games fizzled out after the collapse of its flagship company, Brenda Laurel's Purple Moon. But Jenkins (2003) argues that its "gender specific" goals were obliquely realized in the "gender equity" of one of the most popular games of all time, *The Sims,* whose domestic simulation of personal relationships, family formation, child raising, and household consump-tion appeared in 2000. *The Sims* was produced by a studio, Maxis Games, that boasted a majority of female employees, and the game attracted roughly equal numbers of female and male players. Grrl Gaming, on the other hand, may have engendered the Lara Croft char-acter (Schleiner 2004). Eidos Interactive's 1996 release of *Tomb Raider,* with its "a heroine for women to want to be and men to want to be with" (Deuber-Mankowsky 2005), certainly appeared just after player culture had put female warriors into cyberspace. She was followed by a bevy of combat-ready female protagonists—Samus Aran, Aya Brea, Joanna Dark, and many others. By the turn of the century, some sec-tors of the game industry seemed be celebrating the demise of virtual patriarchy with a festival of lethal heroines and unisex domesticity.

The game industry's recuperation of cyberfeminism also, how-ever, stripped out the most radical elements of its revolt. There was not much trace of the Renegade DNA Sluts' battle against Big Daddy Mainframe left. Rather, women were included *within* the transplanetary military industrial imperial data environment. The gender-neutral world of *The Sims* is driven by commodity consumption: sexual equality means universal shopping. The new mainstream game "sheroes" (Richards and Zaremba 2005) are corporate-military professionals, death-dealing, punishment-absorbing exemplars of what Camilla Griggers (1997) terms "becoming-women who kill"—avatars for an era of female national security advisers and an equal-combat-opportunity U.S. Army. The protests of Girl Games and Grrl Gaming had been captured in the virtualities of an imperial feminism compatible with militarized capitalism.

At the same time, the place of women and girls in video game culture remained strangely equivocal, at least in Europe and the United States. The Entertainment Software Association (ESA 2008b) has claimed since 2003 that roughly 40 percent of North American players are female, a doubling over the last decade. But other research suggests that men continue to be the primary owners of consoles and play more persistently than women, and that female gaming is concentrated around specific genres of games, such as "casual" games and online card and board games, often regarded by the industry as peripheral to its main action (Kerr 2006, 106–28). The employment of women by game companies continues, despite exceptions such as Maxis, to mark an abysmal extreme of the "underrepresentation" of women in technology industries (Cohoon and Asprey 2006).

This continuing gender bias seems to throw into question our claim that virtual games are exemplary media of Empire. How can they claim such representative status if, despite slow change, they remain a predominantly male domain? In our view, however, it is precisely this asymmetrical sexual composition that makes virtual play so perfectly fitted to global capital. The world market is a dynamo at drawing people into the circuit of production and consumption, but it neglects, to a catastrophic degree, social and ecological reproduction—care for households, community, and environment. The ongoing sexism of virtual play mirrors this imbalance. Reproductive work, material and immaterial, has historically been performed overwhelmingly by women, and this, even after successive waves of feminism, still largely continues to be the case. The virtual play industry addresses itself to an ideal male subject, a "digital boy" (Burrill 2008, 15) who can spend hours at game play and game production, and positions women, if not now as completely invisible other, still as a subsidiary participant, a "second sex," making the dinner, sustaining relationships, and gaming occasionally, "casually." It is precisely this non-universality, this prioritization of consumption and production over social and ecological reproduction, that makes virtual play so symptomatic of Empire.

Playbor Force

The way players created female avatars for online games before the game industry provided them, and the manner in which the industry subsequently and profitably adopted the innovation, highlight a process that has become increasingly prominent in virtual play: the mobilization of the players themselves as immaterial labor. As the console side of virtual play became a carefully guarded proprietary oligopoly, the open architecture and networked connections of the PC fostered a culture of enthusiasts who prototyped, modified, circulated, and repurposed games for free. This volunteer activity, generated from adolescent experimentation plus cheapening technology, was initially a highly autonomous, semi-illicit activity. But such "participatory culture" (Jenkins 2006a) was soon recognized by game capital as a source of ideas that could be harvested, and by the turn of the century it was reaping these fields with increasing thoroughness.

Theorists of immaterial labor suggest one of the characteristics of intellectual and affective creation is a blurring of the boundaries between work and leisure, creating a continuum of productivity, and of exploitability, that is "beyond measure" (Hardt and Negri 2000, 356). Tiziana Terranova (2000), building on such autonomist theory, has pointed to the prevalence of "free labor" in digitally based cultural industries that rely on fan excitement and user-generated content. Nowhere is this more pronounced than in virtual play. Julian Kücklich (2005) has termed this gamer do-it-yourself activity "playbor"—a neologism that perfectly captures the hybrid of work and enjoyment. We will examine four aspects of the emergence of a "playbor force," roughly in chronological order of their appearance: microdevelopment, modding, MMOs, and machinima.

Virtual play began in the free invention of hackers. As the digital game industry grew, it continued to benefit from voluntary prototypes. A striking example is *Tetris* (Sheff 1999, 292–349). The famous falling-block puzzle originated in the 1980s, in sight of the Kremlin, with Alexey Patjinov, an employee of the Moscow Academy of Science, who created it on an archaic Electronica 60 microcomputer entirely in his spare hours. Given its visuals and adapted for IBM machines by a sixteen-year-old hacker friend of Patjinov's, the brainteaser circulated

for free around the computing laboratories of a crumbling state socialism. In the closing years of the Cold War, *Tetris* became booty for
speculative capital. A Hungarian black marketer sold the "rights" to
Robert Maxwell's British media empire, triggering a chain of commercial claims that culminated in a bizarre three-way intellectual
property dispute between the Maxwells, Atari, and Nintendo. The
Japanese company won and made *Tetris* a flagship game for its immensely profitable handheld Game Boy. Patjinov, who initially got
nothing for the game, eventually immigrated to the United States as
a Nintendo employee, just as the whole Soviet Union underwent the
same privatization as his game, but he never matched the brilliance of
his initial creation.

Millions of young men, however, yearned to achieve the celebrity
Patjinov finally attained. Game making was a line of flight for digitally
adept youth seeking escape from the tedium of service or industrial
jobs. Well before the dot-com boom, games were generating a rush of
desperate ventures financed by whatever means were at hand—day job,
credit card, university grant. A handful became famous companies:
id Software, makers of the first-person shooters *Castle Wolfenstein,
Doom,* and *Quake;* Cyan, creators of the art-hit *Myst;* Origin, the
producer of *Ultima* role-playing games—these and others brought
their garage inventors fame and fortune, though many of these enterprises would eventually be bought up by big publishers. But these suc-
cesses rose out of an invisible, seething ferment of immaterial micro-
innovation in which most projects crashed and burned, perishing only
to provide an emergent industry with a critical mass of free creations
from which a handful of winners could be picked.

The companies that did succeed relied increasingly on networks of
immaterial work reaching far beyond the studio and the waged development team. One aspect of this was "modding." Players of PC
games modified games by altering the programmed code to change
characters' skins, adding weapons, creating fresh missions, even
building whole new games out of old engines. The resulting mod then
circulated for free, with or without the cooperation of developers.
Modding was only truly popularized in the 1990s, with its first famous success being the conversion by preadolescent boys of id Games'
Nazi-hunting shooter *Castle Wolfenstein* into a gnome-slaughtering
parody, *Castle Smurfenstein* (Kushner 2003). When id later released
its bloodcurdling *Doom,* it took account of fans' demonstrated capacity to alter its software and included editing tools for them to make

their own scenarios, or levels, which could be shared on the Internet. This generated near-inexhaustible interest in the game and also supplied id with a voluntary pool of production talent, which its recruiters soon learned to tap by checking the work of admired modders and phoning them with job offers.

Other companies followed suit. Modding history was made when a player-adapted game won more success than the original. Valve's *Half-Life* pitted the sole survivor of a laboratory disaster against hideous mutants and sinister security forces. A Canadian computer science student, Minh Le, son of immigrants fleeing the Vietnam War, adapted it to create *Counter-Strike*, a terrorist/antiterrorist game played online by networked teams. *Half-Life* was a smash hit, but *Counter-Strike* became the most popular online game in the world. Minh Le went to work for Valve, which bought the rights to his game. Within a decade, games such as the role-playing fantasy *Neverwinter Nights* were as much an editing tool kit as a stand-alone experience, and a game failing to release development tools to players was "more worthy of comment in a review than a game that does" (*Edge* 2003, 57). Game companies routinely bought back successful mods and hired the teams that created them, and some hosted modding competitions with lavish cash prizes (Todd 2003).

A larger-scale, more-complex mobilization of the playbor force occurred in MMOs such as *Ultima, EverQuest,* and *World of Warcraft* (Castronova 2005a; Taylor 2006a; Dibbell 2006). Prototypes of these games include text-based Internet MUDs (multiuser domains) and online *Dungeons and Dragons*–type games (such as Robinett's *Adventure*) with typed-in text commands. These were volunteer creations, played for free, experiments in self-organized virtual community. In the 1980s, some MUDs experimented with graphics interfaces requiring software both expensive to develop and easy to charge for, a change that laid the basis for profitable entrepreneurship. As a wider commercialization of the Internet gained momentum, MUDS became MMOs, in which tens of thousands of networked players interacted in persistent virtual worlds with elaborate avatars and exotic landscapes, at a price.

Meridian 59, the first commercial, 3-D massively multiplayer game, was published in 1996. Its more famous successor, *Ultima Online,* suffered persistent problems (Kline, Dyer-Witheford, and de Peuter 2003). In 1997 the game experienced a "peasant revolt" in which players used their avatars to protest the unrestrained killing of novice players, lagging servers, and catastrophic world crashes. Scores of serfs invaded the virtual castle of Lord British (a.k.a. Richard Garriott, the self-made game millionaire who was now only a corporate vassal to the game's publisher, Electronic Arts), drank their master's wine, ate his food, danced naked in the halls, and vandalized his chambers while loudly presenting their grievances. These were simultaneously pursued in a real-world class-action suit against Electronic Arts (Brown 1998). Three years later, another class-action suit was initiated by an *Ultima* player who claimed that in volunteering as an in-game community leader, answering questions and offering guidance to novices, she had unwittingly been performing a full-time, unpaid job (Brown 1998). Though all these challenges were unsuccessful, they highlighted the degree to which MMO management depended on the cooperation of its playboring populations.

Later MMOs, preeminently Sony's *EverQuest,* perfected a revenue model that turned the energy of these populations into a lucrative open-ended profit stream. Players not only purchased the initial software and paid monthly subscriptions, as well as expansions and add-ons, but also through their social interaction provided much of the game content. MMOs are thus a "co-creation" of player communities and corporate developers (Taylor 2006a, 155). This ambivalence has provoked considerable debate about who actually "rules" the worlds. While some suggest that publishers depend on player associations to sustain their games' interest and profitability (Jakobsson and Taylor 2003; Lastowka 2005; Taylor 2006a), others sees MMOs as a co-optative triumph for game capital, which appropriates the "immaterial, affective, collective production" of their virtual population (Humphreys 2004, 4). As we will see when we look closely at *World of Warcraft* in chapter 5, this activation of MMO playbor power is not without problems for publishers; but phenomena such as the large-scale illicit "gold farming" in such games are a logical, if antisocial, response to the harvesting of MMO activity by game capital.

A more recent manifestation of playbor ingenuity is machinima—cinema made from games. In the 1990s, players realized that the graphics and engines of *Quake* or *Unreal* could create quick, cheap films (Lowood 2005). A digital camera could be programmed to operate from the point of view of an in-game character, with voice and music dubbed in later. The most famous machinima creation is *Red vs. Blue,* made from Microsoft's science-fiction-combat console game *Halo,* featuring sardonic exchanges between bored soldiers waiting for battle and released on both the Web and DVDs for retail sale. In the United States, machinima creators filming from a game without permission could be prosecuted for EULA violations. Many game companies have, however, been willing to accommodate and profit from machinima. Microsoft distributes *Red vs. Blue,* clearly believing that, however irreverent, the spoof increases the cultural cachet of *Halo.* Id has allowed the *Quake II* engine to be converted to open-source software, providing machinima artists a valuable resource. After 2000 games such as *The Sims Online* and *The Movies* were being produced with machinima capacities as a featured attraction, and full-length machinima features tour film festivals, machinima music videos rotate on MTV, and machinima sections play on cable gaming channels (Kahney 2003).

Playbor continues the tradition of hacker culture from which games sprang, transforming it from esoteric art into a more general capacity for autoproduction, networked collaboration, and self-organization (Himanen 2001; Wark 2004). But while hacking was initially a subversive threat to corporate control of digital culture, the game industry has increasingly learned to suck up volunteer production as a source of innovation and profit. When we later examine Microsoft's Xbox console, released in 2001, we will see that a feature of this corporate giant's campaign to invade the video game market was the porting of do-it-yourself computer game practices into the console side of the business—encouraging networked play, machinima making, and homebrew game development in ways that outflanked its rival Sony. Commercial game production today culls the prototypes of micro-enterprises, buys back mods, assimilates machinima, and makes MMOs a source of endless subscription. This capture is not seamless; the capacities that make playbor so productive also make it troublesome. We argue in chapter 7 that piracy and other intellectual property border wars, disputes between MMO publishers and populations, and the emergence of an activist, anticorporate world of tactical gaming and politicized machinima all mean that the dance of capture and escape persists. But one side of this process is the conversion of virtual play into measureless immaterial labor, a tendency that now extends into new dimensions.

Back to Work: From *Spacewar* to Seriosity

At the start of their history, virtual games were a refusal of work: they signified leisure, hedonism, and irresponsibility against clock punching, discipline, and productivity. The first commercial appearances of virtual play were in dubious male refuges from toil—bars and arcades—and then, as the console entered the home, as machines for children and adolescents, devices on the border between innocence and delinquency, but in either case not at all serious business. Playing games on the job was seen by managers as the most corrosive habit of a computerized labor force. There were tales of weeklong dips in U.S. economic productivity immediately following the release of new versions of *Doom,* and *Tetris* came with a "boss key" on its menu that would draw a spreadsheet over the screen "to protect office workers who might be playing the game at their desks and need a quick rescue in case the boss walks by" (Bogost 2006a, 108).

As video game culture advanced into the new millennium, however, a strange reversal occurred. Games turned their coat, transforming from workplace saboteur to managerial snitch. Once again, the incubator was war. We have seen that virtual play was a spin-off from Pentagon planning. Though *Spacewar* liberated it from these grim purposes, games never fully shook off this genesis: in chapter 4, we will see how the U.S. military has followed the tracks of its runaway virtual slave, run it down, and reenlisted game culture into the business of training people for effective killing. In the 1970s, other sectors of the state, from city planners to air traffic controllers, were also exploring the possibilities of simulator training. And by the 1990s information-era capital had latched on to games as a means of preparing all kinds of immaterial labor for the digitized workplace.

One of the most enthusiastic adopters was the financial sector. In 1997 a junior trader working for German finance house posted an offering of 130,000 bond futures contracts online. Training in a game-like workplace simulator, he believed the virtual gambit was just an exercise. But the play was for real. He had "pressed the wrong button . . . a mistake easy to make, according to traders" (Associated Press 1998). His firm, contractually obliged to carry out the transaction, took a loss of some US$16 million. At around the same time, the stockbroker Ameritrade created *Darwin: Survival of the Fittest,* a game distributed free to customers to teach online trading—just in time for them to participate in the 2001 dot-com stock market crash. In 2004 the BBC reported that Geneva Trading, a Chicago-based house speculating on "anything from Brent crude to precious metals and pork bellies" and monitoring "small fluctuations in the market, easily missed on a bank of trading screens filled with fast moving numbers," *required* applicants to complete a video game exercise (Logan 2004).

The company president observed, "It is unlikely that we would hire someone who didn't show good proficiency at a Game Boy or online poker or similar video-type game" (cited in Logan 2004). By 2007, putting games to work had become an industry in itself, with the market for corporate e-learning estimated at US$10.6 billion (Michael and Chen 2006, 146). The Serious Games Initiative movement was exploring the applications of simulations to a wide variety of settings (Michael and Chen 2006). These included a wing of socially activist and politically critical games that we will discuss in chapter 8. The majority, however, were aimed at workplace training of differing kinds, sometimes integrating gamelike simulations with electronic hiring tools, psychometric personality tests, and cognitive skills measures. Corporations like video games for these purposes because they are cost-effective. Simple games are, by industry standards, cheap to make and cheaper to use: "Why pay for someone to fly to a central training campus when you can just plunk them down in front of a computer?" a *Business Week* journalist rhetorically inquires; even better, "employees often play the games at home on their own time" (Jana 2006).

Virtual training pushes all types of work toward immaterial labor. Since 2000 the fashion company L'Oréal has used an online, gamelike simulation in which players "invested in research and development, debated about how much to spend on marketing and looked for ways to cut production costs" to competitively select management candidates from twenty-eight countries: recently this was linked to a TV game show (Johne 2006). Canon, the digital reproduction multinational, has repairmen play games in which they must drag and drop parts into the right spot on a copier; a light flashes and a buzzer sounds if they get it wrong. More inventively, Cisco prepares its workers for on-call corporate crisis management by having them game fixing a network in a virtual Martian sandstorm. A California ice cream chain has a training game in which players practice scooping cones against the clock and perfect "portion control"; the company claims that more than eight thousand employees, about 30 percent of the total, voluntarily downloaded the game in the first week of its release. "'It's so much fun,' says one manager, 'I e-mailed it to everyone at work'" (Jana 2006). And games also engage the affective dimensions of immaterial labor. Cyberlore, now Minerva Software, is developing a training game to teach customer-service workers to be more empathetic. The basis of the simulation is Cyberlore's *Playboy Mansion* game, set in a lavish Hugh Hefner–esque pad, where gamers had to "persuade" models to pose topless; the new, workplace version simulates a store, complete with point-of-purchase display, and requires players use the art of persuasion to sell products (Jana 2006).

Business enthusiasm for virtual play extends, however, beyond training simulations and serious games. It is now *all* games—silly games, time-wasting games, fantastic orc-slaying and alien-blasting games—that are seen as beneficial for an immaterial labor force. Scientists studying the effects of game playing on sixty employees in a Dutch insurance firm concluded that "playing simple computer games at the office could improve productivity and job satisfaction" (BBC 2003a). In *Got Game: How the Gamer Generation Is Reshaping Business Forever*, the hipster management theorists John C. Beck and Wade Mitchell (2004) argue, on the basis of a few dozen interviews with Harvard MBAs, that the content of games, be it carjacking or dragon slaying, is merely the occasion for intensive skill acquisition in multitasking, flexible role play, risk evaluation, persistence in the face of setbacks, inventive problem solving, and rapid decision making—all, of course, precisely what corporate employers claim to want. Playing on the office computer was once an audacious escape from tedium: now a high score at *Space Giraffe* is de rigueur for the up-and-coming careerist. A corporate consultant claims that it is "increasingly common . . . to list things such as running *World of Warcraft* guilds in applications" and for employers to "recognize the organizational, managerial and inter-personal skills such experience bring[s]"; devices that tabulate gaming scores, such as the Xbox 360 Gamer Card, widgeted to a personal blog, "will give a future employer a great deal of information on how much time someone spends gaming, how skilled they are, how obsessive, how collaborative, how determined" (Robertson 2008).

Prospects for an even more complete absorption of games into work are offered by schemes such as Amazon.com's Mechanical Turk experiments. These aim to create an online, on-demand precarious workforce for quick or ephemeral jobs such as transcribing podcasts and labeling photos, to people around the world. The workers would process the tasks for a few pennies per minute or item and, it is suggested, will be able to perform them "in lieu of watching TV or fooling around on MySpace" (Hof 2007)—or, presumably, playing games. Incorporating labor process elements into a game, so that work is indistinguishable from play, has already been done. In the so-called *ESP Game,* a player, gaming with either a human or computer partner, strives to agree on words that match images within a set period of time—an activity harnessed to optimizing search engine performance indexing online pictorial content (Gwap 2008). Ventures such as the ominously named Stanford University spin-off Seriosity proudly declare their ambition to "steal sensibilities from games and virtual worlds and embed them into business" (Hof 2007). Observing that people in online role-playing games such as *Star Wars Galaxies* "spend countless hours carefully doing what looks like a job" not only battling Empire troops but also "building pharmaceutical manufacturing operations and serving as medics," the company is testing the possibility of "having players view real medical scans inside the game to find signs of cancer," which, its owner reassuringly asserts, "gamers could do as well as an actual pathologist" (Hof 2007). Virtual play, after what may in retrospect seem a brief early period of childhood innocence and teenage delinquency, is being sent back to work.

From its origins in the nocturnal digital experiments of the 1960s to the vast twenty-first-century entertainment complex, virtual play has required extraordinary digital skills and new capacities for cultural creativity—immaterial labor. This has not been easily or automatically converted into drive power for a commercial motor. It has often escaped, temporarily propelling other social machines, some politically radical, many seeking to escape the limits of commodified culture. Nonetheless, over its short history, the playful energies of immaterial labor have increasingly been subsumed by capital, and virtual games transformed from rebel innovation to vital relay in the planetary work machine.

It will be useful to recap a few key points about our use of the term "immaterial labor." As we said earlier, in our view some of the autonomist theorists who introduced the idea of immaterial labor overstate their case and overlook the material labor on which capitalist production continues to rely (see chapters 4 and 8). Nonetheless there are important differences between the labor that is performed in a game studio and that on, say, an assembly line. Immaterial labor is defined both by the cognitive and affective aspects of the commodity produced and by the production processes characteristically involved: for example, a high degree of communicative cooperation, use of networked technologies, and a blurring of the line between labor and leisure time. According to Hardt and Negri's hypothesis, these forms of immateriality are becoming hegemonic. What they mean is that features of immaterial labor are beginning to reshape more traditional forms of work as well as broader aspects of social life. Think of how, in recent years, the language of networks has come to permeate and reconfigure sociality. Unlike terms such as "knowledge worker," which carry a certain elitist tinge, immaterial labor is something in which a broad swath of people are engaged, in ways not limited to paid employment but extending to everyday life activities that are productive but nonetheless unpaid.

There is, however, more at stake in the concept of immaterial labor than just production processes under contemporary capitalism. It is bound up with political questions—of antagonism, of alternatives to capitalism—that are not immediately posed by mainstream terms such as "knowledge work," "creative class," or "digital labor" that attempt to describe similar terrain. Hardwired into the category of immaterial labor is the premise that resistance actively alters the course of capitalist development. When capital increases its reliance on this type of labor and commodity, it unwittingly creates tools for autonomy (as we saw with mods) and becomes more vulnerable to attack (as with piracy), albeit in ways that are hardly pure in their outcome. We will return to the implications for combating Empire throughout this book, but for now, the way this chapter has presented its history of games displays the conflict between autonomous invention power and capitalist co-optation intrinsic to immaterial labor.

This conflictual process has followed three main routes in the history of gaming. The first was the corporate recruitment of hacker invention and *manga* artistry to provide the basis of an internationalized video game workforce, producing virtual games as a commodity. The second was the deepening involvement of various forms of free, voluntary, immaterial playbor as a costless means of renewing industry profits. The third is businesses' adoption of digital play as a generalized form of work preparation for immaterial laboring, through simulations and training, but also generically as a benchmark of virtual skills. All these stages have been marked by gender asymmetries, with the women and girls whose work is still so heavily required for reproductive labor being absorbed into the new corporate game machine of play-production and play-consumption far more slowly and unevenly than men and boys. Despite this, the envelopment of virtual play by capital is increasingly comprehensive. From New York to Tokyo, Moscow, and Beijing, virtual play is becoming a medium in which Empire excites, mobilizes, trains, and exploits its new planetary workforce. We started our history with videogaming's working-class hero,

Mario. But it seems this is a game in which he can't beat the bosses. Do the Marios and Princess Toadstools of immaterial labor still have a chance for liberation? That is a question we return to later in the book. For the moment, we'll press on, deeper into the lair of their antagonists, into the palace of the Koopas, the abode of big virtual-game capitalism.

2. Cognitive Capitalism: Electronic Arts

"EA: The Human Story"

Game industry insiders recently made two surprising announcements. The first, by the industry's main employee organization, the International Game Developers Association, was of an initiative known as Employment Contract Quality of Life Certification. Certified game-development studios would, in writing at least, be obliged to meet specified humane workplace standards (Hyman 2008). The second, by John Riccitiello, CEO of one of the world's largest video game corporations, Electronic Arts (EA), was the frank admission that virtual games, including many recently developed by the company he heads, suffer increasingly from "creative failure" (cited in Androvich 2008a). Both announcements have connections to an unexpected workplace disruption that occurred a few years earlier, which challenged not only lingering dot-com-era myths about how liberating new-media work is but also the reputation of the gaming sector as a boundary-pushing branch of popular digital culture. A post to a blog sparked the disruption.

On November 10, 2004, a post titled "EA: The Human Story" threw into question the video game industry's work-as-play image. Signed by "EA Spouse," the entry was an open letter authored by the "significant other" of an employee of EA. EA Spouse (2004) described how her partner's initial enthusiasm for a job with a company listed as one of *Fortune*'s "100 Best Companies to Work For" had evaporated as seven-day, eighty-five-hour work weeks, uncompensated either by overtime pay or by time off, became routine. It told of a "put up or shut up and leave . . . human resources policy." This, EA Spouse further alleged, reflected this game studio for what it was: a "money farm," in which creativity was decomposing amid the rapid churn of commercially safe franchise games. Describing a company pressing its workers to "physical health limits," EA Spouse wrote of how "the love of my life is coming home late at night complaining of a headache that will not go away and a chronically upset stomach, and my happy supportive smile is running out." She concluded with a question for EA's then CEO, Larry Probst:

> You do realize what you're doing to your people, right? . . . That when you keep our husbands and wives and children in the office for ninety hours a week, sending them home exhausted and numb and frustrated with their lives, it's not just them you're hurting, but everyone around them, everyone who loves them? When you make your profit calculations and your cost analysis, you know that a great measure of that cost is being paid in raw human dignity, right?

Comments on the post poured in, and Web sites throughout the game development community linked to the letter, rapidly making it obvious that EA Spouse's narrative, far from being an isolated case, articulated a reservoir of discontent within the studios where video games are made.

Such moments of conflict make visible the power relations underlying capitalism, namely, the struggle between labor and capital. This chapter takes the discontent expressed by EA Spouse as a point of departure for a closer look at the employer she targeted, Electronic Arts—a corporate exemplar, we argue, of what some autonomist theorists have termed "cognitive capitalism."

Cognitive Capitalism

Cognitive capitalism refers to a system of production in which knowledge plays the integral role (see Lucarelli and Fumagalli 2008; Morini 2007; Vercellone 2007a). Carlo Vercellone, an exponent of the concept of cognitive capitalism, is careful to distinguish the term from "liberal theories of the knowledge-based economy" (2005, 2). Unlike those theories, the cognitive-capitalism concept emphasizes the continuation of capitalist imperatives, like that of "the driving role of profit and the wage relation." According to Vercellone (2007b), cognitive capitalism arose in response to the economic crisis of the 1970s and marks a new "configuration of capitalism" whose defining traits include the transformation of knowledge into a commodity and dependence on the kinds of immaterial work described in chapter 1. Against technological-determinist views, Vercellone adds that cognitive capitalism "cannot be reduced to the computer/IT revolution" (2005, 7). Instead it is about mutations occurring within human subjectivity itself: "It is labour and not capital which is 'cognitive'" (8). *Cognitive* capitalism therefore emphasizes the dependence of corporate enterprises on the thinking—the cognition—of its workers, and the distinctly cognitive dimension of "the forms of property [that is, intellectual property] on which the accumulation of capital depends" in the current era (2).

A video game studio executive we talked with in the course of a series of interviews with developers and managers unwittingly summed up the essence of cognitive capitalism for us. Speaking about the intelligent, imaginative, and enthusiastic young developers who composed his company's workforce, he explained, "[Our] machinery . . . is the mind of all these people who . . . come up with these great ideas. . . . Our collateral walks out the door every night." When the "mind" walked out the door, he added anxiously, "[You] just hope like heck that they . . . show up on Monday." But he quickly mentioned the great upside of this risky business: "Unlike machinery that stops working at 5:00, ours might be home, [but] they're thinking of new ideas, and their whole life experience is creating the potential for new ideas."[1] Cognitive capitalism is this situation where workers' minds become the "machine" of production, generating profit for owners who have purchased, with a wage, its thinking power. But the mental machinery this executive describes—because it is also a living subject—constantly poses a problem of control for those who employ it. This raises another point of the cognitive-capitalism perspective: it directs our attention to outbreaks of conflict, "new forms of antagonisms," taking shape within this economic regime (Vercellone 2007a, 32).

Of course, employers have always depended on their employees' intellect. Even the most rationalized assembly lines of industrial capitalism only ran (and continue to run) courtesy of workers' tacit knowledge. To speak of cognitive capitalism is specifically to suggest the recent rise to prominence of a set of industries for whom the mobilization, extraction, and commodification of advanced forms of collective knowledge are foundational: the computer hardware and software industries; the biotechnology, medical, and pharmaceutical sectors; the financial analysis sector, marketing, and data mining; and an array of media and entertainment enterprises, including video games. All these industries, in turn, presuppose a socially "diffuse intellectuality," generated by an increasingly vast educational apparatus (Vercellone 2007b).

Although each of the sectors of cognitive capital has its own unique characteristics, they share some basic features. First, they rely on, and often produce, software aimed at recording, managing, manipulating, simulating, and stimulating cognitive activity. Second, their primary mechanism for securing revenues is intellectual property rights, with patents, trademarks, copyrights, and other instruments anchoring a knowledge "rent economy" (Vercellone 2007b). Third, although individual businesses vary in scale, the sectors of cognitive capital often tend toward world-market scope, operating across extensive geographic territory with regard to both consumer markets and production facilities. Fourth—and in play in all of the foregoing—cognitive capital depends on the organization, disciplining, and exploitation of an immaterial workforce with formidable technical, intellectual, and affective skills, a workforce Franco Berardi (2007) refers to as a "cognitariat." Knowledge under cognitive capital not only is incorporated into fixed machinery but also is integrated into, and emanates from, the subjects of living labor. Fifth, and finally, as the EA Spouse episode confirms, cognitive capital is a terrain of conflict between workers and owners.

Corporations mediate all these features. Indeed, cognitive capital involves many of the largest corporations of our age, from General Electric to Electronic Arts. Thus to analyze video games as a form of cognitive capital, this chapter proceeds as a discussion of EA via the sequence of features we have just outlined—software, intellectual property, globalization, cognitariat, and conflict.

Software: Publisher Power

Started in 1982 in California by former Apple employee Trip Hawkins, EA helped create the interactive-entertainment sector it would soon have a controlling stake in. When EA was founded, Atari, the major games company of the day, was facing its own problem of disgruntled designers. Doubtless hoping to avoid similar conflicts, Hawkins made the promise of "treating creative talent like artists" (cited in DeMaria and Wilson 2002, 165), promoting its game designers much as a record label promotes its bands, packaging its games in album-cover format, giving designers photo credits in full-page magazine ads, and also offering profit-sharing schemes. This novel treatment, albeit short-lived, enabled EA to attract some of the brightest game creators and set it on a trajectory of commercial success that eventually led the company to be described, within just a couple of decades, as "the juggernaut of the industry" (Ross Sorkin and Schiesel 2008).

If you game, odds are you've bought an EA product. A NASDAQ-traded corporation, today EA has nearly nine thousand employees (Hoover's Company Records 2008); annual revenues projected to reach six billion dollars by 2010 (Wingfield 2008); licenses to behemoth brands like the NFL, FIFA, and Harry Potter; and production studios and consumer markets around the planet. EA publishes about seventy titles a year (Takahashi 2000), across almost all genres, and regularly dominates the list of top-selling games. EA executives have claimed that their plan is to build the "largest entertainment company in the world" (cited in Frauenheim 2004). Although its future promises to be as volatile as the industry it occupies, what is certain, however, is that EA is a bona fide member of the club of "huge transnational corporations" that "construct the fundamental fabric" of Empire (Hardt and Negri 2000, 31).

EA exercises its formidable corporate power at virtually all points within the broader structure of the games industry. Historically, the digital-play business has comprised two major wings: video games and computer games. Only three video game console manufacturers have traditionally proved viable, and these have always been the commercial giants of the industry; today these are, of course, Microsoft, Sony, and Nintendo. Computer gaming is a commercially subsidiary but more variegated part of the business, which includes stand-alone PC games as well as the growing area of online gaming, from casual games to the burgeoning field of MMOs. In addition to these two wings is the emerging mobile gaming segment. EA has a presence across all these branches and makes games for all the major platforms.

The games business is organized around four core activities. Development entails the design of a piece of game software; publishing involves the financing, manufacture, and promotion of a game; licensing enters the mix if a game integrates intellectual property owned by an external corporation; and distribution refers to the shipping of game hardware and software to retail stores. A single company can perform just one or a combination of these four activities. EA is, again, engaged in all these activities, from developing its own games to distributing its titles and those made by other studios.

Of all these activities, game development is the industry's creative wellspring and the lifeblood of the game commodity. Although Sony, Microsoft, and Nintendo all operate in-house studios, these console makers cannot make all the games they need. As a result, they license outside companies like EA, known as third-party developers, to produce games for their platform. Consequently the development side of the business has historically featured studios of diverse sizes: micro-enterprises, with fewer than ten employees, perhaps prototyping a console game or designing simple Web-based games; small studios employing upward of fifty people, typically with a game under contract but still scrambling to survive; midsize studios with perhaps a couple of hundred staff, capable of launching a couple of games annually; major studios, employing over two hundred developers, and working on a small handful of titles in parallel; and finally multinational studios employing over one thousand people and working on potentially more than ten games (Alliance NumériQC 2003). Along with its corporate rival, Activision, EA is one of the two largest multinational development studios in the industry.

The era of this multiscale corporate organization is, however, winding down, with current trends favoring the biggest studios. One explanation often given for this is that the latest generation of platforms has doubled, if not tripled, the average cost of developing a console game (BBC 2005). Each new platform throws those developing titles for it on a steep learning curve, requiring they learn how to program for the new machines and how to optimize on the expanded affordances of the latest consoles. This relates to something Vercellone (2007b) says about communication technologies in general: they "correctly function only thanks to a living knowledge that can mobilize them— because it is knowledge that controls data processing, information remains nothing but a sterile resource, like capital without labour." Producing console capital therefore "rests on the knowledge and versatility of a labour force able to maximize the capacity of training, innovation, and adaptation to a dynamics of continuous change." Cultivating knowledge of the new consoles consumes time and thus raises the labor costs of game development, costs that in turn are more easily absorbed by the multinational studios with deeper pockets and bigger staff (Nutt 2007). Longer hours of play afforded by the new machines' greater storage capacity and more sophisticated graphics enabled by faster processors also contribute to the growing size of development teams—illustrating the increasingly *social* character of the knowledge that cognitive capital must tap. Indeed, EA's Riccitiello estimates that developing a triple-A title now requires a two-hundred-member team—"a collective of people that is much greater . . . and paying those salaries is a much greater cost" (cited in Androvich 2008a). It is not surprising, then, that EA, via its University Relations division, actively pursues partnerships with various universities: mass higher education produced the "diffuse intellectuality" that cognitive capitalism's emergence required, and now the corporations of this expensive economic system are returning to those institutions to have their R&D and training costs subsidized.

The crucial arena for strategic control in the games industry is, however, publishing. Publishers control financing, marketing, and distribution and thus exert tremendous influence over what games are made. Many publishers—like EA—operate in-house studios, which can be gigantic, like EA's 1,600-strong EA Canada site outside Vancouver. Beyond in-house development, publishers contract various third-party developers to make games for their label. Publishers pay these independent developers' wage costs as an advance on royalties. In games, as in other cultural sectors, these "'independent' production companies . . . absorb high product risks and labor costs for the giants, which maintain their control over the critical areas of finance and distribution" (Mosco 1996, 109).

Many virtual games, especially for PCs, mobiles, and handhelds, continue to be made in small- and medium-sized development companies. In such enterprises relatively flat management structures are commonplace, and a degree of cooperative chaos is frequently held to be a prerequisite for creativity. Game developers often talk about space for creative freedom in relation to their studio's "flat" organizational structure, which seems to be most common in small to midsize studios. A small studio founder we talked to in Vancouver termed this model of cooperation "working anarchy." "We have very little hierarchy, very little formal structure, very little 'understood' ways of doing things. . . . In a situation where everyone more or less knows their role, it works out well: everyone just divides the work, you work on your bit, and everyone knows what to do. It just works out." Another programmer at a midsize studio described the communication within his development team:

> Everybody is crossing paths with everybody else. I have been very impressed that there aren't any barriers to communication. I can go

to talk to someone in our tools department or I can go to talk to someone on the art side. I'm not going to run into their "director" later, who'll say to me, "Why didn't you go through me?" We keep each other informed.

Thus in certain smaller game studios the "management" of collaboration is increasingly immanent to, rather than externally imposed on, game laborers. The legacy of Atari's "Aquarian" workplace is far from dead in game development, persisting both as a powerful nostalgic myth and sometimes as a reality (see de Peuter and Dyer-Witheford 2005).

Nonetheless it is the giants of cognitive capital who today shape the field of game development. The point is not just that the intensifying consolidation of ownership in the industry is reducing the enclaves of "working anarchy" in favor of the more rationalized production processes of the giant studios. It is that these studios increasingly determine when, where, and for how long the more anarchic enclaves will exist. It is customary for a would-be game entrepreneur to start his or her career working in a big studio—as a programmer, a designer, perhaps even as a game tester—before attempting to strike out on his (and occasionally her) own. This is why big international publishers provide the vital anchors for cities that become hubs of game development, with a proliferation of small enterprises spinning off from and surrounding them. In Vancouver, for example, it has been EA's huge studio, created by the takeover of a local company, Distinctive, in the early 1990s, that established the city as an international game development center over the next decade. Smaller studios—Radical Entertainment, Black Box, Barking Dog, Relic—were formed by defectors or deserters from this mega-enterprise.

At the other end of the process, however, it is common for start-ups that prosper to be bought by big publishers, sometimes by the same ones that spawned them. As Dimitri Williams notes: "Development teams used to be mainly independent operations, but have increasingly been purchased by publishers and distributors seeking to vertically integrate the development function in-house." While "the savvier publishers purchase the developers but leave them largely untouched operationally" to reap the benefits of molecular innovation, this semi-autonomy depends on the strategic priorities of the massive owner (Williams 2002, 46). To return to our Vancouver example, by 2005 nearly all the initial wave of smaller Canadian domestic studios spun off from EA showing any degree of success had been reabsorbed, either by EA itself or by other multinational publishers such as Vivendi, THQ, or Take-Two Interactive (Dyer-Witheford and Sharman 2005). The cycle then started up again as deserters from these reassimilated companies struck out on their own, following the dream of small-company autonomy and creative freedom (Smith 2006). It is, however, clearly the metabolic rhythms of the leviathans of game capital such as EA, their financial and organizational pulsations and cyclical sheddings and reabsorptions of immaterial labor, that determine the degree of latitude for the small game-making fry boiling in their wake.

Independent developers we spoke to said that they are typically disadvantaged in relation to publishers, to whom all but the largest or most famous developers must surrender creative control and intellectual property rights. Without a hit in their record, says one former studio manager, developers are "the David; the publisher is the Goliath." "Indentured servitude" is how another studio representative described the relationship. In reply to such accusations, publishers point out that they face the dilemma of a hit-driven business, where 10 percent of the games make 90 percent of the money. Publishers must balance a portfolio of games, the majority of which will sink without a trace. Little surprise, therefore, that publishers are notoriously risk averse—and why they believe that scale is required to help development firms spread costs and risk. EA, as we discuss in greater detail later, seems to have profitably mastered such risk management: in 2007 more than twenty of its titles sold over one million copies, and a handful sold more than five million (Richtel 2008a).

All these factors have over recent years contributed to a consolidation of ownership among a dozen or so multinational superpublishers (Wilson 2007). These include Sony, Nintendo, Konami, Namco, and Capcom from Japan; Vivendi and UbiSoft in Europe; and Activision, Atari, THQ, and Take-Two, among others, from the United States. The game-software empire that towers above the rest in terms of the rush to consolidation is EA. Over the past decade it has acquired dozens of studios: Black Box, BioWare, Criterion, Maxis, Pandemic, Westwood, and numerous others, and in 2008 it attempted but failed to buy out Take-Two. The company has, on account of its acquisitiveness, been the recipient of harsh criticism from industry insiders and gamers alike: "Electronic Arts has spent hundreds of millions of dollars acquiring acclaimed development studios . . . and then essentially running them into the ground because the corporate mothership did not allow those studios to maintain their creative independence"

(Schiesel 2008a). Now, ironically, even EA executives have come to share that opinion (Wingfield 2007). The question of how EA got to this size, and self-reflexivity, requires a look at another core feature of cognitive capitalism—intellectual property.

Intellectual Property: "Where's Madden?"

Accumulation of cognitive capital involves the conversion of "living knowledge" into "dead knowledge" (Vercellone 2005). A predominant form of dead knowledge under cognitive capitalism is that of intellectual property, and EA is, if anything, a corporate empire of intellectual property. This is an empire that expands through a highly calculated approach to intellectual property, the strategic cornerstones of which are direct purchase, licensing deals, and franchise management. Guiding all of these is a sentiment that EA's Riccitiello expresses well: "The developer today is right at the edge. In many ways, it is create a hit. Or else" (cited in Androvich 2008a).

The purchase part is straightforward. From the 1990s on, as noted earlier, EA began an accelerating round of acquisitions, buying or gaining a controlling share in smaller third-party studios. Usually these studios had developed at least one proven hit game: EA bought Origin, creator of the successful *Ultima* role-playing game line; Maxis, the developer of Will Wright's epic *Sims* series; and Mythic Entertainment, creator of the famous *Dark Age of Camelot* MMO; and it attempted to acquire Rockstar's *Grand Theft Auto* franchise. It is not just the purchase of game intellectual property that EA pursues, however. It also wants to buy access to innovation in the form of game-making technologies or game-related services. In 2008, for example, it bought ThreeSF (a company started by Napster's founder) for its beta version of a social-networking site for gamers (Jenkins 2008a), and it also swallowed Super Computer International in 2007 for its game client software (Alexander 2007). While living knowledge is the producer of these valuable resources, EA's executives perceive only dead knowledge, abstractly referring to recently acquired award-winning studios BioWare and Pandemic, for instance, as "an incredible pipeline of intellectual property" (Gibeau, cited in News Services 2007).

In addition to EA's direct acquisitions, the company's intellectual property pipeline is extended through licensing deals with other entertainment firms, a key site of the "high degree of interconnection between the video games industry and other cultural industries" (Johns

2006, 177). Through licensing arrangements, characters, story lines, and play concepts from other media are integrated into games. While EA is hardly alone in this, it is both a renowned pioneer and expert practitioner of a license-based approach to game development. To take just a couple of recent examples, EA purchased the rights to make games from blockbuster films like *The Godfather* and books like *The Lord of the Rings,* all of which have sold in the millions. Indeed, it has been suggested that as game sales continue to surpass box-office receipts, the major Hollywood studios are increasingly approaching game publishers to capitalize on their intellectual property (Jenkins 2008b). Licensing agreements extend beyond movies, however, with, for instance, EA entering deals with corporate mainstays of children's culture, like Disney and Hasbro.

Accessing others' intellectual property not only allows EA to reduce the expense of in-house idea generation but also enables the company to capitalize on characters, narratives, and themes that already have established recognition—a J. R. R. Tolkien book, a Hasbro board game, a Def Jam rapper, and so on—among its target audience. "We go after the [licenses] where there is a body of underlying fiction, so that people are already familiar with the characters and storylines," explained EA's former CEO Larry Probst (cited in Florian 2004). Emphasis on "familiarity" illustrates how cognitive capitalism makes shared cultural knowledge "directly productive" (Vercellone 2007b). The consumption of one form of entertainment during so-called free time creates the very conditions for the generation of further entertainment commodities, a dynamic related to the argument that cognitive capitalism "makes it necessary to redefine social productivity" itself (Morini 2007, 54). In all of this, EA, as cognitive capitalist, economizes on production costs by buying the rights to faces, images, and names that have already been cognitively worked up, and of which players are, we might say, precognizant.

For EA, licensing is hardly a one-off deal: "we look for properties where we know there will be multiple iterations" (Probst, cited in Florian 2004). When Probst made that remark, more than 70 percent of the publisher's annual releases were "based on established brands" (Pomerantz 2003). This strategy of studied unoriginality is explicit, with EA perfecting a method of risk aversion, preferring clones of proven hits to experimentation. EA, as one commentator summarized its corporate history, "became the world's biggest maker of video games by relying on a formula now widespread in the industry: pumping out sequels of familiar franchises that consumers bought almost on cue" (Ross Sorkin and Schiesel 2008). This investor-pleasing gambit takes us to the third pillar of EA's intellectual property empire, that of franchise management.

Nowhere is this more refined than in EA's most famous field—sports. Soon after it was founded, EA released a basketball game, *Dr. J and Larry Bird Go One on One*, "the first true licensed sports computer game" (DeMaria and Wilson 2002, 178). The impact this license-based approach to game development would have on EA's corporate strategy, and on gaming culture and commerce generally, is difficult to exaggerate. After *One on One* came EA's momentous 1986 deal with the National Football League (NFL) icon John Madden, which led to the launch of *John Madden Football*, a franchise whose success remains unbroken to this day. *Madden* is the birthplace of EA's extraordinarily profitable "wash, rinse, and repeat" model of game development (Florian 2004). Today the company unquestionably dominates all competitors in the sports genre.

In addition to the NFL, EA holds multiyear licensing deals with professional sport leagues including the National Hockey League (NHL), Fédération Internationale de Football Association (FIFA), Professional Golfers' Association (PGA), National Association for Stock Car Auto Racing (NASCAR), and Major League Baseball (MLB). These licenses grant EA the legal right to design games based on these real-life leagues, and the company releases upgrades annually, updating team rosters and player statistics. Data collected on everything from "annual salary to torso size" provide EA with a body of minute athletic differences that forms the rationale for re-releasing each of these sports games year after year (Delaney 2004a). In addition, by using the latest development technologies, "each year, the franchise title has some new 'hook,'" like the possibility of importing a personal picture into *Tiger Woods PGA Tour 08* to create a golfer-likeness of yourself (Pausch 2004, 9). Being able to reuse much of the underlying game code, as well as leveraging that code across different sport games, EA's sport games are capital-efficient, low-risk cash cows: updating a title like *Madden NFL* costs an estimated $8 million, while in 2003 alone that game was expected to earn nearly $250 million. As of 2008, the football franchise had sold more than 60 million units (Bulik 2007). Not surprisingly, these games are the publisher's cornerstones, the flagship brands of EA's most lucrative label, EA Sports.

Such games take what the media critic Sut Jhally (1989) dubbed the "sports/media complex" to the next level. Sports are, as Jhally analyzed, a capitalist business built on the commodification of the intense affective investment of millions of players and fans, culminating in a massive advertiser-driven media spectacle. EA's virtual games are multiply articulated to this complex: they *simulate* this complex, they *redouble* sport's commodification through the creation of a new layer of mediated capture, and they can even *alter* the way the games they simulate are watched and played.

Madden NFL is, again, a good example. "It's in the game" is the current slogan of EA Sports. At the outset, EA wanted its games to mimic NFL matches as realistically as possible. At the center of EA's sport games is the company's Vancouver-area motion-capture studio, "the highest-volume studio in the world," equipped with more than fifty cameras for which professional athletes rehearse their game (Zacharias 2008). In addition, EA "employs people whose sole job it is to watch thousands of hours of game films, noting players' habits, stadium conditions, and coaching strategies" (Ratliff 2003). In time, however, broadcast football began to mimic the camera angles of sport video games, some even using *Madden* for on-air play analysis. *Madden NFL* is now considered integral to building NFL's television audience, and some NFL players report using the game as a training tool (Ratliff 2003). The confusion between virtual and actual sport is intentionally heightened by EA's involvement of real NFL players in *Madden* video game events. For example, in "Madden Nation" (2005–7), a group of NFL players toured the United States in a bus while playing *Madden NFL,* a tournament road trip that finished with finals played on a big screen in Times Square for a $100,000 cash prize: the tours provided the content for an ESPN reality TV show. EA also runs a virtual simulation of the Super Bowl using the latest game in the *Madden NFL* series, which usually accurately predicts the winner.

Ultimately, however, the basis of this symbiotic loop between virtual and actual sports—or, it might be better to say, between successively mediatized sports moments, in the stadium, on broadcast television, and in digital play—is a commodity relationship. Mutually beneficial marketing is at the heart of EA Sports' licensing deals with professional sport associations. *Madden* feeds the NFL's coffers, second only to apparel in the league's licensing revenues (Delaney 2004a). Reciprocally, sports games, made in its in-house studios, generate about half of EA's revenue, and the generous profit margins on these titles have bankrolled the company's acquisition spree (Ratliff 2003).

Financial analysts and company insiders are, however, beginning to catch up with gamer-critics by acknowledging publicly, as one games journalist put it, that

> in recent years bellwethers like Electronic Arts have come to treat the process of game making as a virtual factory: X dollars invested in graphics technology combined with Y dollars in marketing resources should yield Z return on investment. . . . Electronic Arts, once known for its bold vision, has stagnated both creatively and financially, reduced to churning out an uninspiring litany of sports sequels and run-and-shoot knock-offs. (Schiesel 2008a)

EA may have mastered the deployment of intellectual property as a mechanism for optimally exploiting technical and cultural knowledge, but they have done so only to confront, in the stagnating markets for its sports games, a familiar capitalist challenge, that of the need to continually expand the market for its products. Around its accumulated knowledge of sport, EA is beginning to experiment with new revenue streams to counter this market saturation. Enabled by the fan thirst for knowledge of professional sport, EA Sports, now under the leadership of the former head of Microsoft's game division, Peter Moore, has plans to "turn" this label "into a general sports brand" (cited in Schiesel 2007), potentially expanding into areas like broadcast sports, sports camps, and a fan social-networking site. Speaking like a true cognitive capitalist, Moore says, "I think we have an opportunity to aggregate information and bring it to life with video technologies" (cited in Schiesel 2007). Another avenue EA is pursuing is "dynamic in-game advertising" (Jenkins 2008c). EA entered a deal with one of the leading firms in this emerging industry, Massive Incorporated, a Microsoft subsidiary. Telling of *Madden*'s influence within the wider circuits of commercial culture, when Massive's ad executives started pitching the concept of in-game adverting to clients, "the inevitable question" they received was "Where's Madden?" (Bulik 2007). *Madden*'s participation is said to have served as "validation" that other companies must take this new advertising medium "seriously" (Bulik 2007). EA's search to increase its returns also plays out, however, on a geographic basis, and so we turn next to the globalization of this intellectual property empire.

World Market: The Play of Differences

Early on, the video game business assumed a highly globalized profile, with three distinct regional hubs—North America, western Europe, and Japan. EA, although headquartered in Redwood City, California, has operated across all these zones and is developing an increasingly transnational presence in the making and selling of its games. In this respect, EA is among the "hardware and software manufacturers, and information and entertainment corporations . . . expanding their operations, scrambling to partition and control the new continents of productive networks" (Hardt and Negri 2000, 300). EA's world-market scope and its differential management of geographic territory are additional facets of this corporation that are characteristic of cognitive capitalism and are illustrated by the publisher's offshoring, outsourcing, and game-localization practices.

Most of EA's studios are concentrated in North America and Europe, where 95 percent of its games are currently sold (Hoover's Company Records 2008), and where it has most readily found a pool of skilled cognitive workers. Its major studios are, in the United States, in Los Angeles, Redwood Shores, and Tiburon, Florida; in Canada, in Vancouver, Montreal, and Edmonton; and, in Europe, in Madrid and Ingelheim, Germany. EA often expands within these territories by, again, buying out successful local development studios. Early on, for example, EA acquired Canada's Distinctive Software and made it the center for what would become its—and the world's—largest development studio, and it advanced its European presence through the purchase of England's Criterion Games and Germany's Phenomic. EA also often sets up new facilities to exploit regional incentives. To take just one example, in 2007 EA moved its *NASCAR* game-development site from Florida to Research Triangle Park (RTP) in Morrisville, North Carolina (Gaudiosi 2007). This was done not only for proximity both to the North Carolina offices of the game's NASCAR license partner and to local top-tier universities but also because RTP is consistently ranked as one of the "best business climates" in the United States (RTP 2008; for a critique of RTP, see Holmes 2007). By operating studios in multiple locations simultaneously, says one company executive, EA has the flexibility to "easily expand there or here, depending on the tax outcome"; the world that EA sees and cements is smooth but striated, ordered around different "tax jurisdictions" (Wong, cited in Hasselback 2000, 143).

The space of game production is increasingly transnational. The economic geographer Jennifer Johns found that game "software production networks are bounded within three major economic regions: Western Europe, North America, and Asia Pacific" (2006, 151). Concentrations of game-production activity are beginning to shift within, and explode beyond, these bounds—particularly in regard to Asia. Though Asia currently accounts for only 5 percent of EA's sales, the publisher is expanding its offshore presence there, positioning itself to take advantage of the region's fast-growing online market. EA is penetrating the region via joint ventures with development firms already active there. In 2007 it increased its investment stake in Neowiz, a successful South Korean publisher of online games, with whom EA partnered for a Korean version of *FIFA Online,* which had beaten all previous records for online games in Korea (Dobson 2007). Central to EA's expansion plan is, however, China: with eighty million people connected to the Internet, China is poised to be the world's most lucrative online games market (see chapter 5). EA is setting up its own offices in and around the country, with studios in Shanghai and Singapore employing more than two hundred developers (Kiat 2008).

A less-visible facet of the globalization of game production is outsourcing. Like other high-tech companies (see Ross 2006), EA is increasingly subcontracting elements of the game-development labor process to third-party developers outside the geographic core of game capital. In most cases, the tasks that are farmed out include "porting" existing games to additional platforms, rote programming, and made-to-order artwork. One estimate is that outsourcing can cut game production costs by between 20 and 40 percent (Graft 2007). EA works with various vendors in both India and China (Carless 2006a; Reuters 2008), and the only obstacle to further outsourcing is probably a lack of qualified cognitive workers. But EA is also moving further afield, including Vietnam. There it parcels out development work to Glass Egg Digital Media, a company based in Ho Chi Minh City. Glass Egg offers EA a massive savings on labor costs, with a local programmer making about $4,000 a year, whereas "comparable U.S. talent would earn $70,000–$100,000" (Gallaugher and Stoller 2004). This outsourcing trend displays the rise of "neo-Taylorist functions" within global cognitive capitalism, which Vercellone (2007a) associates with an increase in the number of "precarious jobs in the new cognitive division of labour." This is not, however, as we shall see a little later in the chapter, a straightforward hemispheric divide.

The globalization of game production is also achieved through localization, a term that generally refers to the translation of in-game text and audio into the language of a non-English-speaking market. EA localizes its titles with precision coordination: their first *Harry Potter* game launched "in 20 languages and 75 countries on the day the movie opened" (Takahashi 2003). EA also operates regional sales offices, from Austria to South Africa to India, to coordinate a global marketing strategy that hinges around locally catered selling tactics. Localization also has to do with where a game is developed. Sport is again a leading example. Mobilizing local cultural knowledge, EA's stock-car racing game is, as mentioned earlier, made in North Carolina, where NASCAR has offices, and its *NHL* hockey series is made in Canada. There can, however, be unexpected territorial combinations, as in the case of EA's annual *Rugby* and *Cricket* games, which have been developed for the EA Sports label in a small town on Canada's Atlantic coast at a studio run by British expats—and sell well in South Africa and India respectively. With the "wash, rinse, and repeat" cycle perfected by EA Sports stagnating, EA is therefore attempting to break out of the North American/European axis of hockey and football games, a bid to expand and thus survive: "We don't want to be American exporters of sports that nobody cares about," confesses an EA executive in an interview about the publisher's launch of new cricket and rugby titles in New Zealand (cited in Brown 2003).

EA therefore pursues transnationalization through the careful management of locational differences—differences of cultural tradition, of economic development, and also of ludic skill. In terms of cultural traditions, EA's use of regional sport cultures to build a world games market is an example of the cultural complexities of Empire. Rejecting a simplistic either/or binary, Hardt and Negri note that capitalist homogenization (e.g., mass culture) and differentiation (e.g., cultural diversity) processes are not mutually exclusive but rather coexist on the cultural landscape that is taking shape in the age of the world market. Although EA certainly is a U.S. company, its business strategy has to go beyond the imposition of U.S. thematics: it has to work across a field of difference while at the same time making the localized themes material for the "wash, rinse, and repeat" cycle. In this way, the approach of EA Sports is a classic exercise in "glocalization," with globalization working *through* localization, homogenizing *as* it differentiates.

Localization also entails adapting to differences of income and technological infrastructure across diverse markets. For instance, in various Asian markets where console ownership is low, EA is focusing on the more affordable platforms of mobile and online gaming (Herald News Service 2008). While EA has plans for its own newly opened studios in the Asia Pacific to develop games for the local market (Alexander 2008b), the case of *FIFA Online,* localized in partnership with Korea's Neowiz, is illustrative of another of EA's glocalization strategies. "Realizing that it was impossible to sell *FIFA Online* in a country where piracy is rampant, Electronic Arts started giving away the game," making it freely available for download in 2006 (Pfanner 2007). Piracy has here led EA to an online business model that has proved extremely lucrative (Pilieci 2008). Central to this model are microtransactions: EA uses the free game to get players hooked, and then, for less than a dollar, "the company offered for sale ways to gain an edge on opponents," from "extending the career of a star player" (Pfanner 2007) to "special virtual cleats and jerseys" (Pilieci 2008). EA reports earning more than US$1 million a month in this way (Pilieci 2008). Continuing this approach, in a major move, EA is releasing the latest title in its *Battlefield* online franchise, *Battlefield Heroes,* for free download. *Heroes* will also respond to another traditional barrier to game-industry growth: the prohibitive difficulty of play. Via a database running in the background, *Heroes* will use "a match-making system that allows casual players to log on and play with others at their own skill level" (Pilieci 2008). Addressing the issue of accessibility, this move is a part of EA's broader strategy to use casual games as an entry point for new players, who, the publisher hopes, will incrementally build up the inclination and the knowledge required for, say, EA Sports titles.

The global scope of EA's operations makes it exemplary of the role of cognitive capital in extending and consolidating Empire. In consumption, EA's approach resonates with Hardt and Negri's point that under Empire capitalism relates to "every difference [as] an opportunity" (2000, 152). EA's differential management extends to skill, as we have seen, with the infinite variability of knowledge equating with the polyvalent possibilities for commodification. So too with production. Hardt and Negri observe that "the world market both homogenizes and differentiates territories, rewriting the geography of the globe" (310). EA's soaring profits depend on capitalizing on a modulating network of transnational differences—variations in wage levels, exchange rates, and government incentives—so as to maximize its profits. Increasingly, this entails moving production sites from the high-wage centers to other places where it can get the same work done at lower rates—a point that brings us to EA's development workforce, which is nonetheless, for now, still primarily concentrated on the northern side of the "global hierarchy of production" (Hardt and Negri 2000, 288).

Cognitariat: Composition of the EA Workforce

In the United States, the digital games industry in 2007 directly employed some twenty-four thousand people (Siwek 2007, 5). Of these workers, EA's nearly eight thousand game developers constitute a significant proportion (Hoover's Company Records 2008). Using reports from those who have spent time in EA—particularly an account from the computer-science academic Randy Pausch (2004), who cofounded a graduate program at Carnegie Mellon University that EA recruits from—and several general reports about employment in the video game industry (Haines 2004a, 2004b; IGDA 2005), and supplementing them with our own interviews with Canadian game workers, many of whom had been employed at some time by EA, we can provide a picture of the composition of the cognitariat that makes EA games, and of the labor process in which they are involved.

Since the genesis of the industry, the game workforce has been youthful. It is now aging slightly, with an average age of thirty-one, but by far the largest proportion of game workers are under forty (IGDA 2005). EA is no exception. Pausch notes that "employees over 50 are rare, even in senior positions"; EA, he jokes, "feels a bit like *Logan's Run*" (2004, 8). Video game workers generally have formal university-level training: 64 percent hold university or college degrees, and a further 16 percent have graduate degrees (IGDA 2005, 20). While historically EA has favored hiring people with industry experience, it predicts that 75 percent of its new recruits—as many as 750 per year—will soon come from universities, where so much of the cognition power for capital is trained (Pausch 2004). "We're looking at universities as the next-generation of talent," says former EA human resources executive Rusty Rueff (cited in Delaney 2004b).

In addition to its deepening partnerships with universities,[2] internally EA uses a centralized software program called E-Recruiter to address its recruitment needs. By 2001 EA had produced a database that contained details on over thirty thousand potential recruits (Muoio 2001). One of the ways E-Recruiter works is that people visiting the employment section of EA's Web site are invited to submit personal contact and employment-background information and register to receive job postings. "My dream," said Rueff, "is that this database continues to grow to a point where the community gets so large that we can become very targeted and . . . extremely personal in our approach. We're going to get to a point where I'll ping someone who registered when he was 16 and say, 'You're 18 now. Where are you? What's new in your life? Can I tell you about some things that are going on at EA?'" (cited in Muoio 2001).

Most developers are male. One survey, which received some four thousand responses, predominantly from North America, found that women made up only 11.5 percent of respondents, that "male workers heavily dominate most of the core content creation roles," and that there is about a $9,000 compensation gap between women and men (IGDA 2005, 12–13; see also Haines 2004a, 2004b). At EA, as elsewhere in the game industry, women tend to work in administration, human resources, marketing, and art. In the late 1990s, as game development teams grew larger and production cycles accelerated, there was some hiring of women for producer positions, because, as one female producer told us, "those teams needed a lot more communication skills . . . because the problems weren't just about making video games." But despite these shifts, the verdict of most women insiders on the industry's gender balance, and, indeed, on their coworkers' sexism, was scathing: "It's a totally old boys' club industry," another female games worker said. EA is no exception: Pausch notes that when an announcement that the production team for a game such as *Lord of the Rings: Return of the King* is 22 percent female "receives cheers" on the studio floor, "it is both a triumph and a reminder that EA, like the entire video game industry, is currently a heavily male, testosterone-laden culture" (2004, 10).

Salaries vary widely depending on rank, department, experience, and location. In the industry as a whole, celebrity designers make as much as $400,000. Programmers average some $70,000, artists about $60,000, while quality-assurance (testing) wages are far lower, with contract game testers often scraping by on minimum wage (see IGDA 2005). Salaries are often supplemented by other payments; EA also gives stock options, a classic Silicon Valley strategy for binding employees to a company. "Golden shackles" is how one developer we spoke to describes this. Unlike the stock options of many smaller video game companies, EA's are, however, actually worth something. According to workplace lore, certain senior employees don't need to work for money and are called "volunteers," their cubicles bearing signs such as "DFWMIFV: member since 4/1992," as in "Don't Fuck With Me, I'm Fully Vested" (Pausch 2004, 7).

There are also powerful nonmonetary attractions to work in the game industry. No other industry has been as successful in generating an image of work as play. Recruits to EA come from the "playbor" force of enthusiastic gamers we described in chapter 1. "If there is anything that is clear at EA," Pausch observes, "it is that the rank and file employees are absolutely passionate about making video games. They have grown up playing games, and for many this is truly their dream job. . . . Most grown ups do not realize how emotionally strong the draw is to this career path" (2004, 9). This emotional draw can be anatomized into three components: creativity, cooperation, and cool. Creativity refers to the artistry to which EA appealed to at its origins. The hope of making something exciting, beautiful, or technically astounding pulls people to the industry. Cooperation arises from the collective nature of this creativity. Game studios are sites of an intensely complex division of labor. Participating in this and seeing it come together in "the rush of being involved in a big project" are widely cited by games workers, across role and rank, as among the most thrilling and rewarding aspects of their work. The third factor, cool, is a complex ambience made up in part by perks and promises—flexible hours, lax dress code, free food, fitness facilities, lavish parties, and funky interior design, the cultural cachet of a glamorous industry—and in part by less-tangible qualities of attitude. Many game workers we spoke to referred to the "rebelliousness" of the game development workplace, which they contrasted to the stiffness and rationality of the "corporate world." As we will see, this anarchic self-image, a hangover from Atari days, though perhaps still somewhat true of small game companies, hardly stands up to an encounter with a behemoth like EA—yet it remains a mythic element in the allure of game work.

Individual creativity, collective cooperation, and an aura of cool make an attractive package. For many game laborers, virtual production is, at least initially, funky, flexible, and fun. It is impossible to understand the power of cognitive capital without coming to terms with statements like the following from its cognitariat: "Generally, when you go to work, it's not, '*Ah,* I gotta go to work.' It's, 'I'm going to work, *cool!*'" Or "You come in, you see your friends, you get to make video games, and you get to play some. It's pretty cool. It's really not even so much like work here." The irony, however, is that the very attractions that make employment in video games "not so much like work" can also turn it into a digitized iron cage and convert a dream job to a nightmare.

EA's major North American studios are all attractive physical spaces—and well advertised as such. It is symptomatic of cognitive capital that, at the same time as it implants recruitment programs in North American universities, EA refers to its own production facilities as "campuses" and promises academic-style settings that seem a million miles from factory conditions. Work areas are based on the cubicle model, but with an open-concept design to encourage communication among team members. But there are also many amenities: "The Redwood Shores campus sports a high-quality gym, four-story atrium and a large 'campus green' where people play soccer or Frisbee at lunchtime" (Pausch 2004, 8). EA's studio on the outskirts of Vancouver employs nearly two thousand developers and features a gym, pool tables, basketball courts, subsidized gourmet food, and even field trips—one journalist summarizes it as "the EA Magic Factory" (Zacharias 2008).

Inside this factory is a labor process that is, as one interviewee explained, both "extremely hard and very collaborative." At EA over the decade from 1994 to 2004, team sizes for a typical game grew from 20 to 100, with some games involving over 250 people (Pausch 2004). Teams involve designers, artists, programmers, testers, and producers. Designers establish the basic game concept, characters, play mechanics, and art. Artists work on characters, levels, textures, animation, and special effects; although graphic arts are the most important, sound and music are a growing field. Programmers, known also as engineers, write the code and create the digital tools—the game engines—on which a game's functionality and artwork are based. Testers play a game to evaluate it for bugs and playability. Producers lead the project and manage the development team, trying to maintain a coherent vision of the game's design, facilitate communication among various subteams, and deal with personnel, motivational, and quality issues. Because of the growth in team size, game developers have begun breaking teams down into smaller units with specialized responsibilities for a particular aspect of the game—lighting, weapons, command and control. Some companies term these subteams "strike teams." EA calls them "pods" or "cells" (Svensson 2005).

A game's development evolves over a period of between six and twenty-four months, depending on its scope, genre, and platform, and typically involves four stages. In preproduction the conceptual infrastructure is outlined, its look mapped, schedules created, and resources assigned. At EA the preproduction team distills the "core essence of a game" into its "'X factor': a pithy statement to focus both development and marketing" (Pausch 2004, 10). In prototyping, programmers create engines to build the game and rendering tools to iterate animation or special effects, permitting the creator to design, review, edit, and so on. Artists work on two- and three-dimensional models, developing textures and animation for the virtual world, while software engineers code the game mechanics and the story. The third stage is production, with its substages of alpha, beta, and final. Game engines are now complete, and characters and animations are iterated into a working game. At alpha the game isn't fully stable, but all the art, code, and features are present. Testers are evaluating levels and returning them for correction to the development team. At beta the game should be full and stable, adapted to the platform it will play on, and be undergoing play testing and review. At final the product—if it's a console game—is shipped to the platform manufacturer, which will run its own tests before approving the game's release.

In discussing immaterial labor, Hardt and Negri have suggested that control of technical and cultural workers requires a situation where "discipline is not an external voice that dictates our practices . . . but rather something like an inner compulsion indistinguishable from our will" (2000, 329). Similarly, Lazzarato speaks of workplace situations where "the prescription and definition of tasks transform into a prescription of subjectivities" (1996, 135). The kind of subjectivities EA wants are spelled out in the corporation's "A.C.T.I.O.N. Values," called the "underlying cornerstone of EA's business philosophy," exhorting employees to "Be the Values, Make the Culture Real" (EA Academy 2005): *A* is for achievement, including "meritocracy"; *C,* for customer satisfaction, including "co-worker(s)"; *T,* for teamwork, including "communicate" and "Think EA World"; *I,* for integrity, including "openness," *O,* for ownership, including "responsibility"; and *N,* for now, including "Urgency—Do It Now!" Employees are told, on the one hand, that they are responsible for their own fate (i.e., "ownership"), yet on the other, they are part of a collective in which "we maintain our vision of being a one-class society." In practice, the A.C.T.I.O.N. Values translate into what even sympathetic observers like Pausch describe as a "ruthless meritocracy," where failure to perform to expectation will rapidly result first in warnings and then, if uncorrected, in dismissal, processes administered through the "famously brutal project reviews that senior management periodically conducts of each title in production" (2004, 7–8).

In an interview, Neil Young, head of EA's studio in Los Angeles, was asked about the company founder Trip Hawkins's "rock star" approach to game developers. Young responded, reasonably enough, "That becomes disruptive. When you have 3,800 employees in the studios, I mean . . . who gets to be the rock star?" "More like hundreds of craftsmen," the interviewer then suggested, hopefully. With what one imagines might be a slight pause, Young replied, "What we have are basically spokespeople" (Sheffield 2006). A number of factors constrain the creativity that EA employees will exercise. The first and most important is management's determination to control, in a highly predictable manner, the outcome of a complex, potentially chaotic production process. Pausch notes that an "early chore for the pre-production team" is quite explicitly to "remove innovation" so that later stages proceed in a highly productive, parallelized fashion, on the premise that "developers fall into trouble when they have to innovate" (2004, 9). Second is the role of licenses and risk-averse products in the company's strategy; because EA "tends to license rather than internally generate intellectual property for characters and stories," the scope for artistic exploration is limited. The net result is that despite all the talk of creativity and innovation, EA's production facilities tend much more to a neo-Fordist, re-Taylorized disciplining of the cognitariat. In this environment, "the largest sin," says Pausch, "is not delivering a title on time" (8). Conversely, the "key virtue" to management is predictability and "control of process." This is important because the video game business is extremely time sensitive; games have to be completed for the all-important Christmas season, to synchronize with a sport's season opening or movie release, or simply to clear the decks for the next in a relentless stream of projects. In this churn, "making an outstanding game, but delivering it late, is not as profitable as making an acceptable quality game on time."

Not surprisingly, then, one journalist reported, "work inside the company . . . resembles a fast-moving, round-the-clock auto assembly line" (Wingfield and Guth 2004). Here it becomes clear that one way EA employees show their submission to the A.C.T.I.O.N. Values— and avoid a negative verdict in those "famously brutal" performance reviews—is by working long hours. This returns us to EA's campus settings. Even the former president of EA Canada, Glenn Wong, look-ing out over his company's spectacular Vancouver-area facility, once admitted that it was "just candy": "Here it is, 3:30, a gorgeous after-noon, and my soccer field is empty. But I can tell you that at 3:30 this morning, there will be 75 people in this building working their butts off" (cited in Taylor 1999). Why? "The guts of it that makes it a cool place to be is that the people here want to win. Trying is nice, mak-ing mistakes is okay, but it's all about winning." Wong has on occa-sion been even franker, declaring, "If a 60-hour work week is your maximum, then this isn't the place to be" (cited in Lazarus 1999). "It's not unusual for these guys to work 21 hours, sleep on the couch and get up and start working again" (cited in Littlemore 1998). Pausch is therefore quite correct when he warned his students, "EA employees must be willing to work very hard" (2004, 12). But he might have amended that remark, adding that EA's norm of "performance" de-pended on the routinization of unpaid hours as an expected part of work—fulfilling, in other words, the classic definition of *exploitation*.

Conflict: Crunch Time

This brings us back to our point of departure—the scandalous net-worked outburst of EA Spouse, and the issue whose disclosure so deeply embarrassed not only EA but the whole video game industry: the length of the working day. In the industry as a whole, hours of work vary widely, depending on the company, the stage a team is at in the development process, a worker's role on a project, and the worker's slot in the hierarchy. But as one interviewee told us, digital play is an industry where the "circadian rhythm is regularly broken." "Crunch time" is the industry term for an ostensibly unusual period of crisis in the production schedule, when hours intensify, often up to sixty-five to eighty hours a week, sometimes more: one-hundred-hour weeks are not unheard of (IGDA 2004a). The root of crunch time lies in the time sensitivity we have already mentioned, such as working to meet dead-lines for sales seasons and licensed media events. For smaller studios, the need to meet the development milestones set by publishers or to make the design changes they demand provides additional pressure; and for all companies, the complexity of game production, the likeli-hood of unanticipated bugs, and the difficulty of synchronizing the cycles of large teams do indeed provide plenty of opportunity for sud-den emergency.

But although the term suggests a state of exceptional crisis, abundant testimony shows that crunch time often becomes normalized over long stretches of the production cycle: it becomes "built into the equation" (Hyman 2005; see also IGDA 2004a, 19). But EA Spouse (2004), speaking of the "crunch" in which her partner suffered, wrote: "Every step of the way, the project remained on schedule. Crunching neither accelerated this nor slowed it down; its effect on the actual product was not measurable. The extended hours were deliberate and planned; the management knew what it was doing as it did it." In the discussions catalyzed by EA Spouse, an excuse given for this is that the "garage invention" model at the roots of the game industry is not well fitted to meet large-scale production; the "working anarchy" of small studios, while perhaps favoring creativity, does not scale. In this logic, the overwork issue is a problem of industry "maturity," a failure to develop sufficient managerial skills and organizational competence to keep pace with success, and, by implication, a problem that could be dealt with by a process of education. There is some validity to this explanation. But it has one obvious weakness. If recurrent crunch time results from insufficient managerial experience, one would expect the worst offenders to be new, small companies. And there is no shortage of horror stories from such places. But EA Spouse's complaint deals with a well-established studio: EA has been making games since the early 1980s. Many of these games are among the most formulaic—and hence planable—products in the business. If any company could be expected to overcome the managerial problems of preventing overwork, it would be EA. Normalized crunch time therefore points to an elementary economic fact: it is a good deal—a steal, in fact—for game companies.

In the United States, the Fair Labor Standards Act exempts companies from paying overtime to computer professionals engaged in a strictly defined set of tasks and making over a certain amount per hour: this is often interpreted as a blanket excuse to withhold all such payments. However, each state has its own regulations; the employer must follow the law or rule that provides the greatest protection to the employee. Labor law in California, where EA and other major publishers have studios, stipulates that companies do not have to pay overtime to software programmers if they make more than US$41 an hour and engage in advanced creative or intellectual work. In Canada, British Columbia, Alberta, and Ontario also have overtime exclusions for high-tech workers, and in British Columbia, EA and other game companies lobbied vigorously to secure this deregulation.

EA Spouse's blog post coincided with other revelations about working conditions in the game industry. These included lawsuits by disgruntled employees at major studios and reports on working conditions from the professional associations of workers in the industry. Together these disclosures about the video game business threw into sharp relief three aspects of cognitive capitalism we have highlighted here: first, and most obviously, the working conditions of the cognitariat, but also, arising from this, questions of ownership and intellectual property, and of globalization, transnational capital mobility, and world-market networks.

If we look first at the immediate flash point of labor-capital relations, EA Spouse's blog came as several groups of game development workers were launching class-action suits against their employers. One, *Kirschenbaum v. Electronic Arts,* filed in California, alleged that EA had improperly classified some of its employees so as to avoid paying them overtime (Feldman 2004). The claimant's lawyers argued that their client's job as an image production employee was not covered by California's overtime exemption because the job did not involve original, creative work (Takahashi 2004). In 2005 the case was settled out of court, costing EA $15.6 million. The settlement, which specifies that future entry-level EA employees will not receive stock options but will be eligible for overtime pay, has been hailed as marking a revolution in Silicon Valley culture. Meanwhile a second suit along similar lines was initiated by Leander Hasty, an engineer, revealed to be the husband of EA Spouse, a.k.a. Erin Hoffman—and eventually settled out of court for $14.9 million. A third suit by Tam Su was initiated in Florida. In 2004 a similar case, although involving the falsification of time records, was brought against Vivendi Universal Games (Smith 2004). In 2005 another class-action suit for unpaid overtime was brought against Sony Computer Entertainment. In 2006 a similar case was launched against EA's rival publisher Activision (Sinclair 2006).

At the same time, the International Game Developers Association (IGDA 2004a, 2004b, 2005) issued its reports on "quality of life" in the industry. Its conclusions were stark. While a majority of workers found their jobs stimulating, the industry was characterized by a culture of "forced workaholism" (IGDA 2004a, 6). While acknowledging that some game companies had responsible and humane management strategies, the report's aggregate portrait was of "horrible working conditions" (IGDA 2004b, 1). More than half of respondents said that "management sees crunch as a normal part of doing business"

(IGDA 2004a, 19). For just under half of respondents, overtime was uncompensated—and when it was, it was usually in the form not of direct payment but of time off at project completion, royalties, or profit sharing; only 4 percent of companies paid overtime in cash. The report highlighted stress and health issues. Asked how they felt after extended periods of crunch time, the responses of workers interviewed by the IGDA ranged from "exhausted" to "flipped out" (2004a, 71). There were many accounts of the damage done to social and domestic relationships. IGDA (2004a) discovered an exceptionally high rate of turnover in the industry, with a growing number of game developers leaving the sector altogether: more than 50 percent plan to leave the industry within ten years, 35 percent within five years.

Why do game workers put up with these long hours? Demand for skilled programmers and designers is high. Companies anxious about losing talent would seem to have an incentive to treat workers well. But while experienced game workers are in short supply, new entrants are plentiful and well aware of their disposability. Though excessive hours are widespread, they are disproportionately endured by the youthful contingent, whose stamina helps set a studio norm of overwork. One studio owner we spoke to, who had also worked for other developers, was straightforward: "Companies tend to get these young guys that come out of film school, game programming school, or art school and get them to work their asses off. The mechanism for doing that is the game industry's corporate culture: 'You don't have to leave because we give you all the Pepsi and all the potato chips you'd ever want.'" And while smaller studios can offer chips and a couch to sleep on, the attractions proffered by larger ones, such as EA, are more extravagant.

These various reports and the discussions surrounding them also raised the gendered nature of the video game workplace, with the "long-hours culture" seen as both a cause and effect of the industry's institutionalized sexism (Haines 2004a, 13). As a masculine dungeon, the game studio is a place of creative camaraderie, technological intensity, and cerebral whimsy, but it is also often obsessively hard driving, punishingly disassociated from rhythms of domesticity, sleep, and nourishment. The hours of work are a barrier to women, who often carry the responsibility for familial care—a barrier felt either as outright exclusion or as a "glass ceiling" halting promotion. Conversely, the female contribution to game development work is usually in the classic invisible role of reproductive labor, covering the deficit of household tasks and emotional labor of which their exhausted partners are incapable. This, of course, was precisely the position from which EA Spouse wrote: disgruntled workers refer to studios such as EA as a "divorce factory" (cited in Takahashi 2004).

As the disclosures multiplied, debate among game workers about remedies for the labor crisis raged. Two different approaches emerged. One, a conciliatory line, advocated an educational strategy to enlighten management on "best practices" to minimize the situations that provide the official pretext for crunch time (Della Roca, cited in Hyman 2005; Howie 2005). The other, more militant approach insisted that the large publishers would not "benevolently change today's abysmal work conditions without pressure," and argued for unionization (McPherson, cited in Hyman 2005). Some drew parallels with the tumult in Hollywood in the 1920s and 1930s that resulted in the formation of the Screen Actors Guild and Writers Guild of America, and others looked to labor initiatives in other high-tech industries, such as WashTech (Washington Alliance of Technology Workers), a local of the Communication Workers of America organizing Microsoft workers and temporary tech employees (see Brophy 2006).[3]

Game companies, too, responded to the dissent. There was a flood of promises to improve working conditions. UbiSoft's Montreal studio appointed a "VP of continuous improvement" to address quality-of-life and workflow issues and created a sixty-person *bureau de project* dedicated to "planning and streamlining production," with one aim being to reduce crunch time (Chung 2005). At the same time, some corporations asserted that long hours arise "more from a certain bravado or peer pressure than from management" (cited in Hyman 2005). In EA's response, the desire to prevent unionization was unambiguous. While claiming that EA is "in the forefront" of addressing "work-life balance," and also promising some reforms, one of the publisher's HR executives warns against "people who want to step in and take a piece of the pie or get in the middle of things without contributing to the growth of the business" (cited in Hyman 2005). Many workers and labor-law specialists were skeptical about the flurry of corporate good intentions; the lawyer representing the Kirschenbaum case said that "most employers rely on their employees being hesitant to bring lawsuits and just hope it will blow over" (Graves, cited in Chung 2005).

The crisis also highlighted other aspects of the industry, including its growing concentration of ownership, the consolidation of control in the hands of large publishers, and the consequences of risk-averse dependence on clones and franchises. One element in the lawsuits against EA was the deskilled, routinized, and rationalized nature of work on games such as those in its sports franchise: under California labor law, as already mentioned, only creative workers are exempt from overtime payment, and the plaintiffs' case against EA was that their work was not at all creative. Many game development workers, however, tolerate bad or monotonous working conditions because they see a period of corporate drudgery as a step to starting their own companies. In this respect, the EA Spouse disclosures coincided with, and fueled, a wave of interest in the prospects for indie game studios, expressed in initiatives such as Manifesto Games. These projects express the aspiration of game developers to increase their control over the quality and content of their work, constructing small companies committed to realizing the creative potential of games. However, the notoriously high rate of business failures in the video game industry and the costs of development discussed earlier mean that a worker considering starting or joining such ventures must calculate the likely possibility that his new job may vanish within a year or so—or, if successful, be bought up by EA or some other giant publisher. This was a point raised by EA Spouse, who cites the "collapse of dozens of small game studios, no longer able to acquire contracts in the face of rapid and massive consolidation of game publishing companies," as a reason why EA could get away with its alleged "If they don't like it, they can work someplace else" policy.

The EA Spouse crisis also overlaps with the issues of globalization and outsourcing addressed in the preceding section. In the wake of lawsuits, EA had decided to "move hundreds of employees to Florida and Canada after being forced to reclassify which positions are eligible for overtime in California" (Feldman 2005). Human resources manager Rusty Rueff cited EA's success in finding thirty people on short notice for the relocated project as an example of the success of the E-Recruiter database we described earlier (Muoio 2001). And more far-reaching relocation was on the minds of both workers and managers. EA's appointment to its board of Vivek Paul, vice chairman at Wipro, one of the leading companies performing software outsourcing work in India, was seen as a sign that EA was looking toward centers on the subcontinent to find a cheaper labor force (Takahashi 2005). Not surprisingly, EA's capital flight is a source of consternation for employees. "You can never take the full fear out of it," said one executive, referring to the effect of EA's overseas initiatives on its work source: "We're trying to make it an opportunity to develop skills around managing offshore projects and managing a distributed development environment" (cited in Overby 2003). One of EA's newer job classifications is, in fact, director of sourcing. The consequences of this on games workers are hardly lost. One game development worker told us:

> In my opinion, it's always been just a matter of time before, say, you get a place like Prague that has the same set of circumstances with a highly skilled workforce—and their discrepancy between the currencies is even greater. The other one that kind of scares everybody is Bombay—this big high-tech scene in India. It's the same thing: you've got a lot of talented people and they can undercut us. . . . You know, it's only a matter of time.

How justified these fears are is hard to say: but games workers can learn from their predecessors in auto factories and shipyards that the mere prospect of relocation is often enough to quash dissent. The huge fixed investment represented by EA and other big publishers in places like Vancouver, Montreal, and California will probably ensure that in the near to mid-future, much of the high-concept game development remains at these locations, even if formulaic components are increasingly outsourced. In the longer term, the cognitariat of game development will have to wage its fight for survivable working hours across a global battlefield.

M.U.L.E. Kicks Back

One of EA's earliest games was *M.U.L.E.* It was set on a fictitious planet where players accumulated surplus value by purchasing robotic wage slaves who were then put to work extracting resources. When they stored up enough profit, player-capitalists could buy still more labor and land, creating a virtuous circle of ever-expanding profit accumulation. Released in 1983, *M.U.L.E.* stood for "multiple use labor elements." It was, in essence, a simulation game of the relationship between labor and capital. The game sold only about fifty thousand copies, but it is no mere footnote to game history: Will Wright was inspired by it and even dedicated one of his games to *M.U.L.E.*'s designer (Gorenfeld 2003). In turn, as we have seen, the profits generated by Wright's spectacularly successful *Sims* franchise bulked up EA's coffers, furthering the company's power to act as a major force in the concentration of ownership in the game development and publishing sector. *M.U.L.E.* may be a forgotten classic to most gamers, but to EA business managers, this game's story line endures. With the EA Spouse scandal, however, the "mules" kicked back.

Not all video game companies are like EA. While some smaller companies have working conditions that are no better, and perhaps worse, there are others with much better practices. Not all large publishers organize their studios like EA, and indeed, not all of EA is like EA—in the sense that, while the majority of its workers churn out sports games and other franchises, the corporation also finances projects, such as those of Wright and the Maxis group, that maintain a higher degree of creative autonomy. But EA's licensed-property game factories are a massive presence in the game business; the corporation's vertical control of production, publishing, licensing, and distribution gives it a pervasive presence; and it exemplifies tendencies—toward concentration of ownership, repetitious licensed franchises, world-market business strategies, maximizing the advantages of "glocalization," and the highly disciplined and exploitative control of its cognitariat workforce—increasingly prominent in cognitive capitalism generally.

The video game industry's work-as-play ethos and its bad-faith rebel image have been one small element in an overarching mythology that presents digitization as dissolving the contradictions and conflicts of capitalism. The shattering of this ethos is a step toward a more realistic assessment. One could see the story of EA Spouse as just a disclosure of the problems arising from a specific industry, with an unusual history, an extreme gender bias, and a unique corporate culture. But the conditions of the video game industry are also suggestive of broader tendencies in cognitive capitalism. Indeed, one of the strengths of the IGDA (2004a, 10) quality-of-life white paper is that it opens its examination of long studio hours by observing that while the problems it documents may be "particularly strident in the game industry, we do not hold a monopoly on them by any stretch of the imagination," and it substantiates this observation with a section headed "Everyone Works Too Much," which places these issues in the context of a broader and well-documented North American crisis of workplace stress (Menzies 2005; Schor 1993). From this perspective, anyone inclined to read this chapter only as an account of the workplace troubles into which an echelon of young male game workers with a dubious cultural obsession have fallen might reflect on how similar their own problems of long hours, boundaryless toil, and workplace burnout are to those suffered by an apparently very different group of workers—students and academics. The implications of this chapter's story of overwork with respect to strategies of organized labor are also suggestive. The conclusions drawn by EA Spouse are similar to some made more than a century ago—namely, that if one wishes for a life in which human energy can "blossom forth," then "the shortening of the working-day is its basic prerequisite" (Marx 1867, 959). To strategize in this direction would be to take seriously, with EA Spouse, one of EA's corporate mottoes: "Challenge Everything!"

A final twist in the saga of this cognitive capitalist: As noted at the start of this chapter, in 2007, EA's CEO, John Riccitiello, criticized the "rinse and repeat" production model and expressed concern that the games business was "at risk of being a little less interesting than Facebook and iPods and the next cool cellphone" (cited in Wingfield 2007). It was widely reported in the games press that while EA can "pay the bills" with license-based franchises such as *Madden* and *FIFA* and film tie-ins like *Harry Potter,* the company recently "stepped up" its commitment to creating original content (*Economist* 2007c). The "trigger" for this policy change was, according to the *Economist* (2007c), the EA Spouse crisis and the subsequent class-action suit: "In the discussions that followed to resolve the problem, EA learnt that its developers most enjoyed working on original titles"—and expanding this sort of work might, as one studio head mildly put it, "improve morale" (cited in *Economist* 2007c). And on the gamer side, "feedback . . . showed that they preferred such titles to film tie-ins."

The sincerity of this self-criticism was soon tested. At a major games industry summit in early 2008, Riccitiello spoke about sectorwide "creative failure" (cited in Androvich 2008a). At the same conference one year later, Riccitiello could not ignore the topic of the full-blown market failure that had transpired over the past year. His perspective seemed counterintuitive: "I actually think the economic crisis is a blessing for the game industry" (cited in Irwin 2009). Riccitiello praised the financial implosion for the Darwinian flush it promised to deliver: "A lot of the riff raff is going to go broke. We're not going to have to compete with junk." Annihilating competitors was not the sole reason that the EA chief saw the market meltdown as serendipitous: it also amplified the legitimacy, speed, and scope of a corporate restructuring effort that was already under way at EA. The company's restructuring plans were not unconnected, however, from stock market dynamics. Financial analysts were increasingly displeased with EA's profit margins, which had narrowed from 27 percent in 2004 to 8 percent in

2008 (Richtel 2008b). Close to the lowest point in the 2008 market plunge, EA's share price had shed more than half its value in the previous year (Thorsen 2008). The discipline of the market reinforced a familiar trim-the-fat game plan. Downsizing its cognitariat was integral to the vision of a "stronger and leaner" EA (Riccitiello, cited in Kohler 2009). In the fall of 2008, the publisher announced it would slash 6 percent of its workforce; by December, as economic conditions worsened, the figure was hiked to 10 percent; by February it crept to 11 percent, or about 1,100 employees (Alexander 2008a; Irwin 2009). Twelve studios would shut. It was only partly true, however, when hatchet-wielding EA executives described the cuts as a "global reduction" (cited in Alexander 2008a). Continental drift is more precise: EA pledged to eliminate positions in "higher cost" locations while simultaneously increasing the proportion of its workforce in "relatively low-cost regions," such as India and eastern Europe, by 5 percent to a total of about 20 percent (Richtel 2008b).

The downturn affected other aspects of cognitive capital accumulation at EA as well. As retail sales slumped, the publisher announced it would "narrow its product portfolio to focus on hit games" (cited in Alexander 2008a). As *Edge* reported, Riccitiello now emphasized that "sequels can be just as innovative as new intellectual property" (Irwin 2009). If EA did not soon unload underwhelming PC games, said one commentator, the publisher would witness its "cash horde being eaten faster than the tape of an eight-track cartridge" (Phillips 2009). At the same time, EA would need to adapt to a consumer who in a time of recession may be unable or uncomfortable to part with the "luxury good" of a $50 console game. The turn in market conditions redoubled a change in how EA conceived of its business model. Like other industry players, EA devoted more attention to audiences and platforms "previously thought of as minority or emergent" (cited in Alexander 2009): casual gamers, and their preferred console, the Wii; mobile gaming, including developing applications for the iPhone; pay-to-play online games; microtransactions in virtual goods; and other price-conscious tactics for tapping a growing pool of gamers in an increasingly ubiquitous arcade. It is uncertain how EA's response to crisis and change within and outside its industry will turn out. What is certain, however, is that EA will continue to struggle to manage its ludic cognitariat, a collective subject that, with thanks to EA Spouse, is now more aware of its disruptive potential.

3. Machinic Subjects:
The Xbox and Its Rivals

There Was the Machine

One November evening in 2001, on the roof of a toy store in New York's Times Square, the richest man in the world unveiled his new machine. The event had been delayed by the terrorist attacks of September 11, but now the trauma had waned sufficiently to allow the revelation: "He pulled a black shroud off a table, and there was the machine, a shiny chrome-finished device in the shape of a letter X, with a big green jewel at its center" (Takahashi 2002, 1). With this gesture, Bill Gates launched Microsoft's first video game console, the Xbox. He promised to "amaze people with the power that's in this box" (cited in Schiesel 2003). Machine power was a feature designed into the console's very appearance. The green light in the middle of the chrome X on the demonstration model was, according to Microsoft's promotional teams, symbolically exuding "nuclear energy" and glowed when the machine turned on, as if it were "thinking" (Takahashi 2002, 159). Focus groups had shown that "people always associated green with technology": "It is wizard-like and magical. Think of witches stirring a pot of something secret, or the blood of aliens in movies" (126, 159). Microsoft marketers invented a "brand mythology" for the machine with a story about Antarctic explorers discovering "glowing green pods" marked with an "acid-green X" that transport them through a wormhole to an energy source on the other side of the universe: "This X is peeling open and revealing the access to this energy" (156–60). In this chapter, we peel open the Xbox, its successor, the Xbox 360, and its rivals, the PS3 and the

Wii, to discern the energies that flow into and out of an omnipresent machine of Empire: the video game console. First, however, we ask, "What is a machine?"

What Is a Machine?

Our answer comes from the work of Gilles Deleuze and Félix Guattari (1983, 1987; Guattari 1995, 1996), theorists whose works influenced Hardt and Negri's concept of Empire. Machines are usually thought of as artifacts like cars, lawnmowers, and vacuum cleaners—tools, though complicated ones, with moving parts and power sources, large (hydroelectric dams) or small (nanobots), but basically instruments with which humans transform nature. Deleuze and Guattari call such tools "technical machines" (1987, 406–11). Technical machines develop in particular families and genealogies of related devices. Broad "phyla" demarcate, say, weapons from kitchen utensils, but there are finer distinctions: the sword lineage is different from that of spears, bows, or guns, and within it are offshoots such as sabers or rapiers, each with its own particular properties and techniques of production.

Technical machines are, however, themselves components of larger "social machines" (398). A social machine is a functionally connected assemblage of human subjects and technical machines, people and tools. So, for example, the curved saber is part of an assemblage that includes the armored warrior, the trained horse, the stirrups stabilizing the striking rider—a whole military apparatus or "war machine" (391–404). Seeing social formations as machines is not unique to Deleuze and Guattari; theorists such as Lewis Mumford (1970, 263) suggested that hierarchical power complexes, from pyramid-building Egyptian pharaohs to Pentagon command-and-control systems be understood as "imperial megamachines." Everyday expressions convey the same intuition: working in a corporation or a university, we may feel like a "cog in a machine" or, like our computer systems, need some "down time."

Indeed, the most radical aspect of Deleuze and Guattari's machine theory is that humans themselves are "desiring machines" (1983, 1). Subjectivities are not natural or given but assembled from biological, societal, and technical components in an incessant process of "becoming" that produces new alignments of bodies, cognition, and feeling. Take, for example, the male warrior, the "man of war," a figure that has dominated Western culture for centuries. This subjectivity, Deleuze and Guattari argue, was generated as an assemblage of specifically sexed bodies, skill with carefully crafted weapons (swords, lances, bows, armor), relationship with animals (think of the importance of horses to war, as mounts or totemic symbols), and social projects of colonization and conquest (1987, 353). Over the centuries, this military identity changes as its elements alter—with, for example, guided weapons and computers superseding swords or muskets. Subjects are fabricated, machined, made up from elements that include, among others, technical machines.

When Hardt and Negri say that Empire "appears in the form of a very high-tech machine" (2000, 39), they are using the term "machine" in the expanded sense proposed by Deleuze and Guattari to suggest how global capital assembles itself from interlinked social, technical, and subjective components. Console play displays the fusion of these elements. Guided by Deleuze and Guattari's machine studies, we open up the Xbox and its console rivals as state-of-the-art *technical machines* made of chips and circuits; as components of giant *corporate machines;* as *time machine* for profitably using up software and other virtual commodities; as generators of *machinic subjects,* mobilizing the passions and practices of hard-core gamers; as contenders in the competitive *machine wars* of video game capital, but also at the same time of the transgressive, subversive *war machines* of nomadic gamer hacking and piracy; and last, through all these preceding machine moments, as part of the *global biopolitical machine* of Empire.

Technical Machine: Console Lineage

Let us start with the Xbox as a technical machine: in its first version, a 733 MHz Pentium III processor, with graphics and audio hardware, a small hard drive, a CD/DVD player, a processor for connecting to the Internet, and display capabilities for conventional and high-definition television, all packaged in a black box.

This device can be situated in the broad phylum of digital machines that includes all computers. A console is a computer with hardware and software dedicated to running games. Its key components are those of a computer: a central processing unit (CPU), random-access memory (RAM) for temporary storage of operations (in this case, games being played), and the software kernel or operating system that integrates the various pieces of hardware. Crucial for consoles and all digital machines are semiconductors—the silicon flecks inscribed with miniature transistors that convey electrical current through patterned flows, digitized in binary on/off code, enacting billions of logical operations every second. It is Moore's Law—the tendency for the improvements in semiconductor manufacturing to double the processing power on chips available at a given price every eighteen months—that makes it possible today to fit into a small box computing power that forty years ago required a room to house.

Both the game console and the personal computer arose at approximately the same time—the early 1970s—from this miniaturizing tendency within the phylum of digital machines. They are, however, forking lineages. The console, a unipurpose machine, was simpler, smaller, and less expensive than the PC. Consoles had a controller with buttons and toggles, not a keyboard. They lacked a hard drive, depending on a disposable storage medium, the game cartridge, for the major part of their machine memory. Most important, a console's video and audio outputs connected to a television, rather than a monitor, replacing the assemblage "worker-computer-monitor" with "player-console-television."

As the console lineage separated from the computer, it displayed a "Cambrian explosion" of mutations. If the Atari's 2600 can in retrospect be seen as pioneering the main evolutionary line, there were other contenders that are now of largely paleontological interest: Magnavox's Odyssey, Coleco's ColecoVision, Mattel's IntelliVision, consoles attached to electronic guns, with paddles to bat digital balls, with celluloid filters to color black-and-white screens, all just a few of numerous dead-end experiments (although, as the recent runaway success of *Guitar Hero*'s console-attached plastic guitar shows, one never knows what may suddenly leap back to life). Only after the 1984 video game crash did the console's basic form stabilize, through its Japanese branch. The corporate wars of Nintendo and Sega, dramatic as they were, nevertheless gave the console lineage a predictable path. They culled the proliferation of machines in favor of a small circle of branded leaders. By strictly controlling the compatibility of cartridges and consoles, as Nintendo did with "lock-and-key" devices, console makers could limit access to their proprietary platforms, restricting their use to games that they made themselves, or games produced by licensed third parties. The failure of new companies to break into the market with machines such as the Jaguar and 3DO appeared to confirm that only a handful of console makers would succeed.

Consoles now followed a regular cycle of innovation, driven by

Moore's Law and the spur of competition. A new generation of consoles appeared every four to five years, with better chips and improved performance, marching from the NES, the Genesis, the Nintendo 64, the Saturn, and the Dreamcast, from 8- to 16- to 32- to 64- to 128-bit power. The precise timing of each new console launch was a nail-biting business in which any wrong estimate of technical readiness or customer willingness to discard old machines could be fatal: it was just such a miscalculation with the Saturn that sent Sega to disaster. But the overall progression was inexorable. The console was thus consolidated as a dynamic but highly specialized lineage of digital machines. It generated its own sublineages, most notably the hugely successful handheld Game Boy invented by Nintendo, which spawned successors and rivals running from Nintendo's own Game Boy Advanced, and later its DS, to Sony's PlayStation Portable (PSP). The main line, however, remained the TV-connected game-playing machine.

Though consoles and PCs became common household technologies over the same period, they were distinct. Consoles were fun, and mostly for children and adolescents; computers were serious, and mostly for grown-ups, even if this demographic slowly changed as the "Nintendo generation" carried gaming habits into adulthood. One could game on a PC, and the balance between computer and console gaming varied regionally around the world. But the technical specifications of consoles and computers altered the gaming experience available on each. Without Internet connection, consoles lacked the multiplayer dimensions of computer play, though they were never purely solitary machines—sitting together using multiple controllers was a formative sibling and friendship experience.[1] For some time, the large price differential between consoles and computers produced significant class and ethnic distinctions in their distribution. In the early 1990s, for example, the huge majority of African American gamers played on consoles; these divides diminished only as the price of PCs slowly fell. Most importantly, the machines suited different kinds of games: the console controller was geared to action and sports, the computer keyboard favored the complex menus of strategy and role playing. Overall, the console was the major vehicle of digital play.

This process reached its consummation in the PlayStation (PS), created by Sony in 1994. Sony had entered into consoles obliquely; the PS was intended as a CD add-on to Nintendo machines. When this alliance failed, the PS was, under the hands of Sony's engineering genius Ken Kutaragi, morphed into an independent machine. Sony brought to consoles its major capital investments in full custom chip design, component manufacturing, and assembly plants. The result was a superbly efficient machine. So adept did Sony become at improving and compacting its chips that the PS shrunk over time: an early model seems clumsy beside the slimness of later offerings. The PS replaced specialized game cartridges with a CD drive. Its successor, the PS2, was the first console whose graphics outperformed contemporary computers. Because the PS sold well, developers loved to design games for it, and the PS2 broke precedent by having backward compatibility. All of this gave it a brilliant game library, devoted players, and vast installed base. After a brief period of three-way warfare between Sony, Nintendo, and Sega in the mid-1990s, Sega was eliminated, confirming the belief that the console market would support no more than two contenders, and Nintendo was subordinated as a maker of "kiddie" games to the global power of Sony and its PS2. At the height of its success, the PS2 provided 40 percent of Sony's revenues: with 100 million sold globally by 2006 (Kerr 2006, 67), the PS2 was the most successful console ever made. In this context, the first Xbox appeared.

Corporate Machine: Trojan Horses

Capitalism, Deleuze and Guattari say, is a planetary "production machine" (1983, 226), assembled from flows of labor, finance, and technology. This "world-wide capitalist machine" (231), they say, operates through processes of "deterritorialization" and "reterritorialization" (259). The quest for profit generates new technical machines, conjures up fresh products and practices, breaks down old habits, and throws all bounded domains—"territories"—of life, geographic, social, and subjective, into upheaval. Yet capital simultaneously "reterritorializes" this flux, enclosing innovations as property, drawing around them new legal boundaries, and policing access so that new technical machines and cultural creations appear as commodities produced and sold for profit.

There is no better example of this deterritorialization and reterritorialization than Microsoft. This capitalist behemoth emerged from the homebrew hacker culture that deterritorialized computers and liberated digital knowledges from the Pentagon. It was, however, founded on an act of reterritorialization. Bill Gates's 1976 "Open Letter to Hobbyists," threatening against unpaid use of his Altair Basic code, was a milestone in proprietary enclosure of software and a death knell to the hacker ethic of "information wants to be free." Gates's company then leveraged its initial development of operating systems to win control over, or territorialize, successive software levels, from DOS and Windows to office programs and text processing to Internet browsers. Its "embrace and extend" strategy for copying rival innovations and then crushing the originators (amended by critics to "embrace, extend, and extinguish") was applied against rivals from IBM to Apple to Netscape. In the 1990s, antitrust prosecution by the U.S. Department of Justice condemned Microsoft as a "predatory monopoly," but it escaped with minor penalties, rolling on as an apparently unstoppable corporate machine (see Auletta 2002).

It was amid these legal struggles, just after Gates's trial appearances, that Microsoft turned its eye to video games. So far it had largely stood aloof from virtual play, creating a few PC games (including *Age of Empires*) and producing authoring tools for developers, but without any presence in the most important games arena—consoles. A corporate culture of unimaginative but overpowering products, ruthless takeovers, and interminable court cases was, in the eyes of players and developers alike, the antithesis of play. What drove Microsoft to change this image was a threat from a competitor of comparable corporate bulk and girth—Sony. Microsoft had been invited to make the operating system for the PS but had refused. Soon this decision seemed a mistake. Not only had the Japanese company tapped a huge flow of games income, but, more serious for Microsoft, the PS2 soon revealed hidden dimensions. Playing not only games but also music and films, the globally successful console began to appear as a domestic beachhead from which Sony might define software standards for other entertainment and home-computing purposes. Microsoft had already tried to make inroads on home entertainment by integrating television and Internet in a "Web/TV" initiative. This had been beaten back by cable and communications companies unwilling to yield a crucial digital gateway. Now consoles were spoken of as a "Trojan horse" through which a host of digital media could surreptitiously be implanted in the home.

This was a possibility Microsoft could not yield to Sony: in the contest of mechanical mounts, the Xbox would be its steed. The tournament was dangerous. For twenty-five years, no more than two companies at a time had won enough players to sustain a console platform: Microsoft, Sony, and Nintendo made three. Sony enjoyed an established position, formidable expertise, an in-house infrastructure of specialized chip foundries and assembly plants, and a more diverse library of games than Microsoft could offer. Microsoft lacked console-making experience and chip production capacity and had an inauspicious reputation. On its side, however, it had size and wealth, with sixty thousand employees in over one hundred countries around the planet, and revenue flows of $40 billion a year, computer-programming knowledge that could be transferred to the new project, a massive "war chest" opened to finance it, and an array of intracorporate alliances.

Microsoft resorted to a production model common in information technology: a "flagship" company determines the design, but components are manufactured and assembled by networks of suppliers (Luthje 2004, 1). A Microsoft development team conceived and prototyped the Xbox, championed it through boardroom politics, and provided its operating system (a simplified version of Windows). But the vital microchips, a variety of other components, and the actual mass manufacture of the console were all contracted out. Microsoft's role was to coordinate the multiple interdependent cycles of its suppliers, shaving costs to the bone and getting the product to market in time. The process was hazardous. For the original Xbox, Intel and Nvidia made the CPU and GPU chips.[2] The integration of their production cycles with Microsoft's was nerve-racking. Semiconductor manufacturing is so precise that problems occur at any stage. Nvidia graphics chips ran flawlessly alone but, with millions of Xbox orders pending, failed catastrophically when integrated with other components, persistently freezing a test animation of a swimming dolphin until "near midnight," debuggers discovered an incorrectly typed specification, leaving engineers who "still have bad dreams about that dolphin" (Takahashi 2002, 313). Similar last-minute saves characterized the entire process.

But the machine ground on. The final stage in production was the actual assembly of the console—the "box build," performed by Flextronics, the largest electronics contract manufacturers (ECM) in the world, with 95,000 employees distributed in a global production network (Luthje 2004, 4–5). Unlike earlier assembly operations that relied for profit only on the cheap "nimble fingers" of sweatshop workers, ECMs today are often highly automated, minimize material and transportation costs by making and warehousing components on-site, and at the same time continue to benefit from low wages in Latin America, eastern Europe, and Asia. The Xbox was assembled at three Flextronics plants, in Guadalajara, Mexico; in Western Hungary, at

Zalaegerszeg and Sárvár; and at Doumen, in South China. Production was several times switched from one plant to another, with Xbox runs in Mexico reduced in favor of those in Hungary, which then suffered the same fate relative to the Chinese facility.

Console assembly is not immaterial labor. It is industrial and bluntly material: extruding plastics and sheet metal for box enclosure, connecting cables, installing circuit boards, attaching shells, and checking production flow. In a "new economy Taylorism," standardized work practices are devoted to "fast and flexible response" to changing customer requirements and rigorous quality control (Luthje 2004, 129). A "modern company paternalism" aims at preventing workforce unionization and stabilizing turnover, with dormitory-style residences and on-site amusements (including video games) (Luthje 2004, 12). Average wages in Flextronics' China plants were between $60 and $100 a month, including overtime, which, many reports suggest, is in such assembly plants often mandatory in practice even if not in law. The pace of work at the Xbox factories was fast; as the Guadalajara plant ramped up production for the launch, two tractor-trailer rigs of consoles left, and one semi full of supplies came in, every two hours.

The trucks plowing across international free-trade routes carried a formidable machine. The Xbox's processors made it, Microsoft frequently pointed out, the most powerful console yet to appear. It was the first console with a hard drive, starting games more quickly than others. The built-in Internet connection implied a new orientation toward networked play. But despite these features, Microsoft knew every Xbox rolling out of Mexico would *lose* the corporation money. Each contained $323 worth of parts and materials. It sold at retail for $299 (a price that eventually fell by more than one-third to compete with Sony's cuts to PS costs). If the Xbox was intended as a cash machine, it appeared to be one that disgorged money from Microsoft's vaults at a speed not matched by deposits. What could explain this apparent inversion of corporate common sense?

Time Machine: Surplus Value

Here we invoke Deleuze and Guattari's concept of "machinic surplus value" (1987, 458). Observing the importance of media in the capitalist machine, they suggest that while Marx wrote about workers being exploited at the point of production, the same idea could now be applied to audiences. Television advertising, for example, captures

people's time and attention even when they are not officially working, a process Deleuze and Guattari describe as "machinic subjection"
or even "machinic enslavement," in which people become "intrinsic
component pieces" in "recurrent and reversible human-machine systems based on internal, mutual communication" (458–59).[3] We want
to suggest how the Xbox and game consoles generally function, in a
way related to but different from television, as devices for the extraction of machinic surplus value.

We have already seen that the business model directing console
gaming is one of "razor and blades"; the money is in the software, the
blades, for which the hardware is the razor. The console is sold at or
below cost to establish a platform for the sale of games. It is a machine
for using up the ephemeral experience encoded in the game software,
which must be played enough that the gamer finishes or gives up and
then buys another game. For Microsoft to recoup its apparently sui-
cidal strategy of giving away Xboxes for less than they cost to make,
each Xbox owner had to buy about ten games, a least three of which
were made by Microsoft itself. If each game took thirty hours to complete or abandon, then gamers would have to spend about three hundred hours, controller in hand, to "repay" Microsoft for their Xbox.
Thereafter, however, each game purchase would bring profits—
potentially large ones. If the Xbox dislodged the PS2 as the vital node
in the player-console assemblage, it would claim the lion's share of
video game revenues that in 2001 for North America alone amounted
to $4.6 billion (Chairmansteve 2005).

There were, however, other dimensions to the console-based extraction of machinic surplus value. As the Xbox project developed,
Microsoft's version of the Trojan horse focused on making the console a point of entry to networked activity. By 2000, online computer games had demonstrated their commercial promise, both in
competitive match play and in MMOs such as Sony's *EverQuest* and
Microsoft's own, less-successful *Asheron's Call*. The prospects of
lucrative subscriptions, online advertising, and hard-to-manage but
potentially profitable virtual trading were apparent. Now mounting
processing power and widening broadband availability could make
the console a wormhole siphoning online time into commodity form.
This was the aim of Microsoft's gaming network, Xbox Live, which
debuted in November 2002. For about six dollars a month, gamers,
identified by a "gametag" that gave each an online identity, could play
one another and, using headsets, talk in real time. By 2004 there were

more than two million subscribers, and they had played—and paid—for 1.4 *billion* hours of play (Takahashi 2006, 21).

Microsoft strategists started to think that in the contest with Sony, Xbox Live might be their ace in the hole—the "differentiator" that would give them an edge over their powerful rival (Takahashi 2006, 11). The service was steadily elaborated. In 2004, Xbox Live Arcade enabled the download of games distributed online at prices from about $5 to $15. In 2005, with the launch of the Xbox 360, Microsoft revamped Xbox Live completely, introducing "Silver" and "Gold" levels of subscription, enhanced matchmaking and feedback systems, voice chat and videoconferencing, multiplayer games, tournaments, and special events. To the gametag was added a "gamer card" displaying a player's interests, skill level, competitiveness, and gaming accomplishments, measured by scores and achievements. Developers would be required to build a certain number of "achievements" into Xbox games. Player success in completing these would be aggregated into a "reputation" (marks 0 to 5), a sort of competitive exchange rate.

Improving this score required playing more games, which, along with all sorts of accessories, could be purchased online at "the Marketplace," where real money (via credit card) translates into points to buy additional content, demos, videos, music, and more through a microtransaction system. Microsoft said this would expand to an eBay-like model where gamers sold their own, user-created content to one another. A corporate spokesperson outlined the future:

> "Kirsten," a gamer's graphic-designer girlfriend, makes his character in a . . . game a "cool" T-shirt. He goes on Xbox Live, and his friends see him wearing it in his gamer profile—an online ID card of sorts that will feature photos of the gamer—and they all want one. Then the group all wears them online, and then thousands of people want one of Kirsten's shirts for their . . . character. . . . Now Kirsten opens a store online. She's making a dime, or whatever, per shirt, and now she's got a reputation online. She's got her "gamertag." She's got a gamer card. She's got a reputation. (Allard, cited in Thorsen 2005b)

And, presumably, Microsoft too will have an enhanced reputation, not to mention another subscriber, possible commissions on sales—and profitable advertisement placements.

Another promised Xbox Live feature was online game tournaments that thousands could enter and millions watch in a "spectator mode":

"Football, soccer, *Halo,* you name it. . . . Anything that can culminate in peer-to-peer, head-to-head competition can be built into a tournament mode," a Microsoft vice president declared (Thorsen 2005b). "People will watch. People will pay to enter, particularly if there is serious prize money at the end of it," another company spokesman said. And advertisers would pay too: "Companies like a Pepsi or a Nike would be delighted to get our consumer, who they are having a great deal of difficulty getting to right now." Speculating further, he went on, "I think then, we, as an industry, get into the broadcast business because hundreds of thousands of people will log in and watch" (Thorsen 2005b).

How far these corporate dreams could be realized was uncertain. But Microsoft's ambition for the Xbox was clear: it would combine a "new media" economics (the "razor and blades" model of software consumption), the "old media" version (selling eyeballs to advertisers), and a dash of e-commerce. The console would be not only a game machine but at once a new television set and an online market; this, Microsoft hoped, was what the future of machinic surplus value looked like.

Machinic Subjects: The Hard Core

For all of this to work, however, people had to buy Xboxes, and this was a question not just of technical machines but of human "desiring machines." Microsoft aimed to mobilize a specific sort of desiring machine: "If you look at the starting launch," said a senior vice president, "most of the target audience is what you'd call the hard core, a little over six million of them in the U.S.; age brackets 16 to 26, mostly male" (Bach, cited in Pinckard 2001).

"The hard core" is a demographic stratum well recognized in game marketing: young men who play intensively, have disposable income, adopt new hardware platforms early, buy as many as twenty-five games a year, are literate about genres and conventions, read the game magazines, and form opinions, through word of mouth or online, about games and machines. The hard core is thus distinguished from "casual" gamers, although marketers increasingly recognize intermediate segments; "cool" or "lifestyle" gamers, who play quite often but without dedication, or the "family gamer" who plays with children and spouses (Bateman and Boom 2006). It is the hard core, however, that has traditionally been seen as key to console success: reaching that core involves hardware, software, and networks.

The Xbox, a brutally bulky black box with a lurid green light, brandished hard-core appeal. The most telling feature was the game controller. With its array of buttons, and left and right analog sticks, the game controller specializes the console for play. Being hard-core is to control the controls with a tacit, tactile knowledge that makes play easy, fast, and smooth: "No control mechanism is too complex for a hardcore gamer, provided they like the core game activity" (Bateman and Boon 2006). The most important point about the Xbox controller was simply that it was like previous controllers: players who were already virtuosos would "get it," and those who didn't would be as clumsy as ever—a point whose significance would not become fully apparent until five years later Nintendo's Wii challenged this assumption of familiarity. What *was* immediately obvious was the Xbox controller's size. It was an artifact for people with large hands, like North Americans, particularly North American men (Takahashi 2002, 160). In Japan especially, players complained vociferously. Microsoft eventually introduced the smaller Controller S, but the message had been sent: the Xbox was for big guys—hard-core subjects.

Software is as important as design in activating the hard core. Hard-core players identify with a specific subject position: *the man of action*. The majority of console games have come from two genres, action/adventure, followed by sports, with smaller sectors of racing, fighting, and shooter games. Historically, they have mainly involved male protagonists in combative or competitive situations, requiring speed and agility, the accumulation of equipment, and progressive training through a repeated "save-die-restart" sequence. Yet though the man of action has dominated in console play, there are distinctions within, and exceptions to, this theme. During Sony's long hegemony, the male action hero, while still a norm, also became a subject for innovative variation. Sheroes à la Lara Croft; "stealth" games, pioneered by the ironic and self-reflexive *Metal Gear Solid;* survival horror games with female protagonists, like *Crimson Butterfly,* or introverted innovations such as the "sanity-bar" of *Eternal Darkness;* the strangely melancholic and beautiful art-house adventures of *Ico* and *Shadow of the Colossus,* and even the whimsical Oedipal conflicts of the puzzle game *Katamari Damacy*—all elaborated out from hard-core action into increasingly diversified nuances of play.

Microsoft, however, took things back to basics. Referring specifically to the hard core, an Xbox spokesperson said, "You see the type of games they play: sports, action, racing, fighting. You can bet that our portfolio . . . is going to be mostly concentrated in sports, action, racing and fighting at launch" (cited in Pinkard 2003). The console was launched with an array of games emphasizing speed, crime, and combat in a stereotypical hard-core mix.[4] The supreme example, far outselling all others, was a game made by an independent developer acquired by Microsoft, Bungie, and exclusive to the Xbox: *Halo: Combat Evolved* and its successor *Halo 2*. Some games define the "affect" of specific consoles, investing them with a particular emotional tone: *Super Mario Bros.* made Nintendo's NES synonymous with magical, madcap adventure; *Mortal Kombat* (with full fatality moves) established Sega's Genesis as a "bad-boy" machine. *Halo* set its signature on the Xbox.

Easy to describe, *Halo* is difficult to play well. It is a game of military science fiction: with uncannily good timing (given its release date near 9/11), the plot features Earth under attack by the Covenant, an alien species of fanatical religious warriors. You are Master Chief, cyborg-soldier, awakened from cryo-storage on a crippled spacecraft to help a few remaining Space Marines survive on a planet occupied by legions of Covenant enemies, from dwarfish reptilian "grunts" to acrobatic "ninja" jackals to towering metallic "hunters." This is a game of kill or be killed. It demands speed of movement (never stand still), accuracy of aim (and remember to reload), tactics (the marines you protect can protect you), shrewd choice of weapon (plasma rifle or shotgun?), and navigation skills (avoid vertigo). The artificial intelligence is capable of variation and surprise. Though the terrain fills with fallen foes and friends, there are no real atrocities. Covenant are fierce, frightening, yet also comic: upon losing their leaders, grunts despair and flee with squeaks of "run away, run away" or, in a nice mirror-moment, are horror-struck when surrounded by humans ("they're everywhere!"). *Halo* is virtual cowboys and Indians, or Allies and Nazis, or any of the other us-against-them scenarios boys perennially enjoy in playgrounds, streets, gardens, and old bomb sites around the world. Inviting the gamer exclusively to the masculine, armored, machine-warrior position of Master Chief (with, in *Halo 2*, brief interludes in the shoes of his equally armored Covenant opponent), *Halo* is nothing if not hard-core.

What consoles signify is, however, not just a matter of machine design or game theme but also of the social contexts of plays. In determining who would play the Xbox, and how, Xbox Live was definitive. The first really successful network experience in the history of console play, it opened up collective experiences of teamwork and collaborative innovation. Multiplayer *Halo 2* games, with their many variants—Team Skirmish, Slayer, the Rumble Pit—and detailed tabulation of individual and team scores bred an intense online culture. Modding software, common among computer gamers, came to the console as *Halo* fans created new "bots," skins, weapons, sounds, graphics, vehicles, and terrain on a scale unparalleled since *Doom* and *Quake* (see Cawood 2005, 2006). *Halo* and Xbox Live culture even generated its own ironic self-critique, the most famous machinima creation ever, *Red vs. Blue,* spoofing the basic conventions of online play—two teams of different colors in an arid landscape with no reason for being there other than their opponent's presence—as an existential absurdity.

But this networked culture could be savagely exclusionary. In an analysis of online play, Natasha Christensen (2006) notes two views about gender in cyberspace: one holds that "without the constraints of the body, gender . . . becomes fluid," the other that "gender is reproduced mimetically in cyberspace" in ways that "may be more stereotypical and rigid than in real life." Xbox Live typified the latter option. It rapidly became (in)famous for an online taunt culture of aggressive sexist, racist, and homophobic insult, including ritualized in-game sexual humiliations such as "teabagging" fallen *Halo* opponents. On a Girl Gamer Web site, a player whose gametag identified her gender sardonically advised Xbox Live players how to behave toward women gamers:

> It is imperative that you call her every name that you can think of which is specifically derogatory to her gender throughout the entire game. She will pretend that she doesn't like it, but a little known fact about the Girl Gamer is that she actually enjoys being called bitch, slut, whore and dyke every 2 minutes. Also, try to be helpful by reminding her of her (and her entire genders') place. Statements such as "Girls can't play *Halo*" or "This is a man's game, bitch" work nicely. (Paradise 2005)

On Rampancy Net, a major Web site devoted to *Halo* and other Bungie games, the administrator, conceding the "essential complaint" was "fair," nonetheless defended his community by saying that "as for being called bitch, slut, whore and dyke . . . just about every male gamer who has played on XBL for more than five minutes has been called each of these many times" (Narcogen 2005). Other forums corroborated the picture. Many posts rebutted charges of sexism in terms that confirmed the accusations; some were from male gamers complaining about the many "asshats" ruining gameplay (Ruberg 2005). The persistent hostile othering of women and sexual and ethnic minorities was not uncontested, but it did establish a distinct hypermasculine—hard-core—ambience around the Xbox.

The Xbox configured who would play it, and how: the console's design, the games made for it, and the social networks that surrounded it all denominated it as a machine for game-literate young men, inviting and amplifying this "major" gaming subjectivity, ignoring or actively repelling possible "minority" participants (Deleuze and Guattari 1987, 469). And by affirming that a machine for youthful male players should be a big black box with a huge, complex controller, providing a virtual imaginary of racing cars and cyborg warriors, embedded in aggressive put-downs and trash talk, Microsoft circularly corroborated presuppositions about youth, masculinity, and digital play: it reproduced hard-core subjects.

War Machines: Nomad Gamers

Just because capitalism generates new machinic subjectivities does not, however, mean they are fully controlled. On the contrary, Deleuze and Guattari emphasize the potential for emergent human-technical configurations to make unexpected connections and take disruptive "lines of flight" (1987, 55). They call this uncontrolled element in machinic subjectivity "nomadism" (351–423). The term alludes to the warrior horsemen of the Asian steppes who harried so many ancient societies, fearsome fighters and skilled weapons makers, assembling new combinations of horse, sword, bow, and rider to wage war on empires. When Deleuze and Guattari speak of a "war machine," they are referring not to a giant military-industrial complex but, on the contrary, to mobile, subversive uses of technology (351). The hacker practices that lie at the base of gaming are a modern form of nomadism. One way in which the war machine of nomad gaming manifests is piracy.

Piracy has always been part of gaming culture. Historically it has been especially strong on the computer side, where the open architecture and Internet connectivity of the PC make it easy to copy and circulate games. But it also affects consoles. The great software glut that destroyed Atari was partly caused by pirated games. One reason for

Nintendo's success with the NES was its technical and legal measures against copying. When Sony adopted the disc format for the PS, it was thought to make such protection still easier. But hacker-players always found ways to bypass these measures. Console hacking today includes modifying consoles by adding special computer chips—"modchips"— to overwrite security codes and allow the play of illegally copied games or to bypass "regional lockouts" that, while intended to stop piracy, also prevent playing legitimate imports; "homebrew" gaming, in which people make their own games for console play; playing "abandonware," or games that have gone out of circulation, often using emulators that enable the use of old games on new machines; and the use of in-game cheats and modifications.

The original Xbox gave console piracy a fantastic boost. Sony had long been prosecuting players who installed mod chips. But Microsoft's console combined strong computing power and weak security in a way that made it a target for more ambitious adaptations. Hackers' long experience in penetrating Microsoft's computer security systems could be ported over to the adapted Windows operating system of the Xbox. Two years after the console's release, hackers had turned at least 150,000 Xboxes into PCs that would normally cost $800 or more (Schiesel 2003). With a new start-up chip and a bigger hard drive, the Xbox could become an inexpensive media hub for storing and playing a vast quantity of games, movies, and music. "It's like putting custom parts on your car," said the Washington dockworker who hosted XboxHacker.com, logging some eight thousand visitors a week (cited in Schiesel 2003). German computer science students replaced the Xbox's Windows operating system with Linux, a line of flight especially unappreciated by a corporation famously hostile to open-source programming.

Hacking also spread to Xbox Live. *Halo* cheaters perfected techniques such as "standby" (interrupting connections to freeze other players) and "bridging" (taking control of hosting through a local computer). Bungie used its Banhammer program to track gamers' habits for trends that suggest cheating, but "stemming cheaters in a game is a lot like stemming music piracy online; for every account shut down, there are more being created" (Rider 2006). Some gamers simply bypassed Xbox Live: it took hackers two days from its launch to create the first Xbox Internet "tunnel" allowing gamers to connect to one another independently of Microsoft's official network; the software was openly available on sites such as GameSpy.com, whose president helped to devise the hack: "We did it to show we're really cool technologists," he said (cited in Acohido 2003).

Microsoft took Xbox hackers to court: cases resulted in the conviction of several and the imprisonment of at least one. Andrew Huang, a doctoral student in electrical engineering at the Massachusetts Institute of Technology, author of *Hacking the Xbox: An Introduction to Reverse Engineering*, campaigned against tightening intellectual property regimes, supported by the libertarian Electronic Frontier Foundation. "This is about fair use of something I bought with my hard-earned money," Huang said. "If Microsoft can stop me from running whatever code I want on a given piece of hardware, it could then extend its software dominance into hardware and lock up the entire computer market" (cited in Acohido 2003).

In chapter 7 we will look more deeply into the politics of piracy; here we will just point out that console hacking is a complex phenomenon. Many copied games are circulated by the sort of pirate that game publishers like to represent as typical—black-market criminal organizations operating on an industrial scale, frequently out of the developing world (hence dubbed "Asian piracy"). But piracy also involves a not-for-profit "warez" scene and games shared among friends. It arises, moreover, from the very attributes of the hard-core subjectivity the Xbox fostered, imbued with masculine techno-expertise and an audacity that sees repurposing code as just another dimension of play. As a game journal observes:

> While piracy on a grand scale involves organized gangs and relatively complex infrastructures, much of the technical work is initially performed by talented coders who simply relish a challenge. Ironically, many hackers continue to see the process as a game, and the modding communities that have already built up around the new machines suggest that tampering with the contents of the box is now an established part of videogaming culture. (*Edge* 2007d)

In response, console makers embedded increasingly sophisticated digital rights management (DRM) systems deeper into machines, with encryption inscribed into the firmware, the software programming integrated with the console hardware. The growing emphasis on network gaming in consoles marked by the advent of the Xbox made it easier to provide patches and close security gaps but also allowed pirates to more swiftly document and disseminate new hacks, so that the battle between corporate empires and nomad gamers followed a path of spiraling escalation. Microsoft's response to the epidemic of console hacking that greeted the Xbox was to promise the next version of the console would be technically invulnerable. But it also started to think about how the technical skills of nomad gamers might be co-opted and bought off. To see how this process played out, we must, however, look at the intersection between the war machine of the console hackers and the machine wars of the giant console corporations.

Machine Wars: The Three Kingdoms

Deleuze and Guattari emphasize the extraordinary dynamic turbulence of capitalism's innovative flux, "creating machines and . . . constantly introducing breaks and cleavages through which it revolutionizes its technical mode of production" (1983, 233). These "machinic processes" (Deleuze and Guattari 1987, 435) can spring surprises on even the biggest and best of capitalists. Nothing better illustrates this than an unexpected twist in the contest for console domination between Microsoft and Sony.

By 2005, the release of the PlayStation 3 (PS3), Sony's long-anticipated riposte to the challenge thrown down by Microsoft three and a half years earlier, was eagerly anticipated. In an unexpected preemptive move, Gates uncloaked another machine—the Xbox 360. It was a bold gambit; consoles usually make money only in the final phase of their five-year cycle. Having lost Microsoft some $4 billion and just starting to turn a profit, the Xbox would be consigned to obsolescence (see Hesseldahl 2005; Takahashi 2006). Its successor was white, not black, smaller, sleeker, concave rather than convex, more elegant. But it reaffirmed the same combination of computing power, now boosted by special chips that split heavy workloads into different threads dedicated to graphics, sound, physics, and networked capacity; Xbox Live was also upgraded, and capacities to download television shows and movies were announced. Microsoft spokesmen paid lip service to the need to "expand beyond the core audience of young men" and "turn video games into . . . a community experience," but the games lineup for the new console showed an undiminished commitment to the hard core (cited in Hermida 2004). *Halo 3* was the big promise, but in the meantime, 360 players made do with *GhostRecon: Advanced Warfighter,* a futuristic war game played from the perspective of U.S. Special Forces in Mexico City in 2013, and *Gears of War,* a science-fiction shooter that offers the chance to try out weaponry such as a "chain-saw bayonet" on alien opponents.

Speculation about Sony's counter to the Xbox was rife. At the height of its reign, Sony had begun to experiment with new possibilities in the design of play machines and gamer subjectivities. EyeToy, a device similar to a Webcam, allowed PS2 and PSP players to interact with games using motion, color detection, and sound. *Guitar Hero,* first published for the PS2, was a play-along rock music simulator wildly successful with people usually far outside the orbit of games, as was Konami's *Dance, Dance Revolution,* also available on the PS2, where players synchronized dance steps to a chosen song. All invited "nontraditional" gamers. This, combined with Sony's record of success and Kutaragi's reputation, raised hopes that an extraordinary machine was in the works.

Yet when, after a series of baffling delays, the PS3 was finally released in late 2006, it was extraordinarily symmetrical to its Microsoft rival. In appearance it was like the first Xbox: big, black, shiny— "Darth Vader's tea kettle," one unkind blogger put it. If the PS3s sixty-gigabyte hard drive and new cell processors were more powerful than the 360, it was also, with a $600 price tag, more expensive. The Trojan horses were now in full collision: the PS3's most advertised feature was the Blu-ray Disc, a high-definition optical-disc format promising exceptional display of game, film, and video, backed by Sony, Sun Microsystems, Dell, HP, and Apple. The 360 sported Blu-ray's rival, the HD-DVD system supported by Microsoft, Toshiba, and Intel. A "standards war" over multimedia entertainment was under way. But the 360 and the PS3 were strikingly similar machines, technically awe inspiring, clearly aimed at the hard-core gamer, deeply unoriginal in their repertoire of virtual play. The PS3's flagship game was *Resistance: Fall of Man,* another futuristic shooter. Microsoft and Sony were fighting for the same machinic subjects.

The surprise came from another direction. Nintendo had been deemed an also-ran, confined to a minor juvenile market subordinate to the big game of hard-core play. Nintendo's neat but conventional GameCube, which appeared at the same time as the first Xbox, did nothing to change this impression. But when Nintendo's new console, the Wii, was released almost simultaneously with the PS3, it outflanked and dumbfounded both its giant opponents.

Far less technically powerful, and less expensive than the 360 and the PS3, the Wii's wireless remote directed onscreen action with full body movement. A swing of the arm produced a virtual tennis serve or saber cut. The grounds for its success had been prepared by an earlier Nintendo innovation, the DS, a handheld with a touch screen that allowed play without pressing buttons. It had proved enormously successful. Building on this lesson, the Wii even more dramatically broke with the tradition of controller virtuosity; its technical fresh start meant new players were not disadvantaged by a learning curve already mastered by console veterans. This broke the codes of gender and age that had dominated console design. A truly "disruptive technology," the Wii replaced the human-machine "hard-core/controller" assembly with a radically different one: "remote/casual gamer."

Anecdotes abounded of young men humiliated by grandmothers and infant sisters who "got" the Wii feel. These urban legends were amplified by Nintendo's viral marketers. Declaring that "Wii sounds like 'we,' which emphasizes that the console is for everyone," and mounting a television advertising campaign showing courteous Japanese salesmen demonstrating the console to urban bacchanalians, hillbillies, and grandparents, Nintendo positively reveled in its repudiation of the hard core. Wii designers pitched to a figure who, if no less mythologized than the young male gamer, was in many ways its antithesis: the mom. "We thought a low-cost console would make moms happy," said Sigieru Myamoto in an interview, "easy to use, quick to start up, not a huge energy drain, and quiet while it was running" (cited in Hall 2006). With the repetitiveness that signals a marketing mantra, another Wii designer, Ken'ichiro Ashida, chipped in: "We didn't want wires all over the place, which might anger moms because of the mess" (cited in Hall 2006). The console lineage was mutating; *Cooking Mama: Cook Off* was going up against Master Chief.

Miyamoto remarked that "power isn't everything for a console." "Too many powerful consoles can't coexist," he elaborated. "It's like having only ferocious dinosaurs. They might fight and hasten their own extinction" (cited in Hall 2006). It was hard not to like the nimble, equal-opportunity Wii. Nintendo was, however, like its competitors, a ruthless corporate machine. The innovative casual-gamer strategy was, in regard to content, a risk-averse ploy, recycling Nintendo's repertoire of family-friendly games—*Zelda, Metroid, Mario, Pokémon*— with a novel technological twist. And while the Wii enlarged the world of gamers, it entangled them just as much as Microsoft's Xbox Live in a web of commodification. Using the remote, one could navigate the Disc, Mii, Photo, Wii Shop, Forecast, and News channels. Some offered social networking—for example, exchanging Mii avatars with friends—but all had advertising potential; the first to be activated was the Wii Shop, where players used credit cards to buy Wii points, redeemable against merchandise. Before its release, the Wii was briefly called "Revolution," a name Nintendo then revoked in favor of something safer, nicer, and more infantile. Since the console was indeed an extraordinary innovation in console gaming, it in some ways lived up to its original moniker; but in another sense, the name change was an all-too-apt parable for a system that promised radical change but ends up resembling a familiar pastime—e-shopping.

The impact of the Wii on the Microsoft-Sony confrontation was nonetheless extraordinary. Because the 360 was released a year before the Wii, Microsoft was not as seriously affected as its rival. For Sony, however, the coincidence of the two launches was a catastrophe; PS3s languished in stores while Wiis rushed off the shelf. Sony marketers resorted to shock advertising—white women slapping black women, goat sacrifices—that smacked of desperation. Even apparently long-planned Sony initiatives, such as the PlayStation Network, modeled on Xbox Live but with a more family-oriented ambience, such as that Nintendo cultivated, came off as frantic catch-up. In 2007 Kutaragi resigned—the admission of corporate defeat that Microsoft executives had longed for, yet hardly the victory they anticipated, won by another's machine.

Meanwhile all console makers continued to be raided by digital nomads. Sony's handheld PSP console had been hacked to become a hotbed of homebrew game development (Rubens 2007). By late 2006, hackers were using PS3's Linux operating system to load games onto external hard drives and "rip" them from there (*Edge* 2007d). Very shortly after the release of the Wii, the Chinese market was flooded by ripped games, along with consoles modified to play them that commanded a better price than the official version. Yet all of this was no cause for Microsoft to celebrate: despite its claims for a watertight launch of the 360, the firmware was hacked in March 2006, with titles sold in China for as little as 30 yuan ($2), a favorite, appropriately enough, being *Hitman: Blood Money*.

The game companies replied by attempting to capture this restless hacker energy. As Deleuze and Guattari note, empires often try to enlist nomad console warriors as allies and mercenaries (1987, 424). Sony had once attempted to create user-generated content for the PS2 through its Net Yaroze system, but the plan never reached fruition. In 2005

Microsoft announced that an integral part of the 360 would be XNA, a set of tools and technologies that would, for a fee and a subscription, enable owners to develop their own games on the console—"YouTube for games," with Microsoft regulating content and intellectual property rights. Nintendo followed suit with a similar plan for the Wii. An apparent democratization of game development, these schemes were also a way of reducing the ever-rising costs of game development for the new platforms and of adding new revenue streams from subscriptions. As the great console corporations slugged out their machine battles, deploying technologies that at once expanded the scope of gaming and integrated gamers ever more deeply into commercial kingdoms, nomad hackers waged a flickering border war along the very frontiers of the commodity form, and game capital furiously tried to capture the very skills that subverted its dominion.

Eight years after the release of the first Xbox, no decisive winner had emerged in the console wars. Nintendo had done best: by 2009 cumulative worldwide sales of the Wii surpassed fifty million units, about as many as those of the PS3 and Xbox 360 combined. This was an especially delicious success because Nintendo's cheaper machines, unlike its rivals' consoles, were not actually losing it money. The Nintendo DS was also the leading handheld games device, with sales of some 100 million—twice as many as Sony's PSP (*Economist* 2009). The crucial issue in video game economics is, however, not just the amount of hardware purchased but also the quantity of software sold for each console. It remained uncertain whether the many new, casual Wii users would actually buy games in the quantities and at the prices that hard-core users of the Xbox and PS3 were inured to. The Xbox 360 and the PS3 were bleeding money (the PS3 initially sold at $300 less than it cost to produce), but Microsoft and Sony continued to battle toe to toe in what could for either of them be a ruinous contest. Microsoft led in North American sales, and its seventeen million Xbox Live subscribers dominated online console play (Thorsen 2009). Sony had been thrown even deeper into crisis by the economic recession, shedding thousands of employees and closing chip foundries. Nonetheless it still held its edge in the important Japanese video game market; Sony executives hoped the PS3 might prove to have a longer life cycle than the Xbox 360, giving the PS3 a long-term advantage. Both corporations were determined to regain the march that Nintendo had stolen on them with its remote controller. At the 2009 E3 video game industry jamboree, each unveiled new devices:

Sony demonstrated a prototype wand similar to the Wii remote, and Microsoft revealed its even more ambitious Project Natal, a camera-based motion sensor that potentially removed the need for a controller completely by responding to players' gestures and spoken commands. Without a clear victor in sight, and with all contenders racing to rearm themselves, videogaming seemed set for a prolonged period of inter-imperialist rivalry.

Imperial Consoles

As Hardt and Negri observe, "Machines and technologies are not neutral and independent entities. They are biopolitical tools deployed in specific regimes of production, which facilitate certain practices and prohibit others" (2000, 406). The Xbox, the PS3, and even the charming Wii are machines of Empire; their technological assemblages of circuitry and cell processors build the corporate territories of Microsoft, Sony, and Nintendo, which in turn are components in the worldwide capitalist machine. Earlier we referred to Deleuze and Guattari's concept of "machinic subjugation." This may seem absurd in regard to game consoles—which are, after all, fun, are they not? Even if playing video games does sometimes have a compulsive aspect, we don't intend a discourse about game addiction shot through with double standards and moral panics. But to say that consoles are enslaving is not to deny that they are pleasurable; it is to say that pleasure itself channels power.

Consoles are intimate machines, seamlessly inserted into our domestic or personal space or even carried close to our skin, responsive to our skills and prowess, becoming, with the Wii, remote body extensions. Eugénie Shinkle (2005, 27) suggests that intense game play invites and requires a corporeal-affective involvement arising from a virtuoso relation the console, akin to Glenn Gould's relation to the piano, a state "not about using an instrument but being an instrument" (the comparison is germane, given the predigital meaning of "console" as a musical keyboard). Shinkle argues that the experience of play cannot be comprehended in terms of the "manifest content (narrative, symbolic, emotional or otherwise)" of a game, but that it has dimension of affect—the "feel" or intensity of a game, which is synesthetic, involving auditory, kinetic, and tactile dimensions (25). To make this case, she emphasizes games low in manifest content but high in synesthetic input, such *Rez,* with its synchronization of "trance" techno music and shooting; but her point, we believe, obtains for all games.

Console play is thus a paradigm case of the cyborg (Haraway 1985) human-machine prosthesis that Hardt and Negri see as integral to an Empire where "the multitude not only uses machines to produce, but also becomes increasingly machinic itself, as the means of production are increasingly integrated into the minds and bodies of the multitude" (2000, 406). This symbiosis promises in the near future to attain an intensity that will make not just the Xbox's big-handed controller but even the Wii's deft remote seem clumsy and anachronistic. In 2005 the journal *New Scientist* reported that Sony had patented "a device for transmitting sensory data directly into the human brain" by sending "pulses of ultrasound at the head to modify firing patterns in targeted parts of the brain"; this would create "'sensory experiences' ranging from moving images to tastes and sounds" (Hogan and Fox 2005). By 2008 reports were circulating that IBM was on the brink of marketing a technology that would enable gamers to interact with the virtual world using their thoughts and emotions alone, via a "neuro-headset" that "picks up electrical activity from the brain and sends wireless signals to a computer" (Waters 2008).

This machine subjectivity will be a component part to a larger social machine. Today, holding the 360 controller or the Wii remote, we are already within an "imperial normativity . . . born of a new machine, a new economic-industrial-communicative machine—in short, a globalized biopolitical machine" (Hardt and Negri 2000, 40). To become an Xbox or PS3 or Wii player is to plug oneself into a network of techno-human relations, which even as it offers cognitive skills and affective thrills also inserts subjects into a commodity web involving not just the initial console purchase but that of the subsequent game software, the online subscriptions, the music and video services, and a whole branded identity built around gamer tags, achievement points, and the transfer of avatars, a grid of machinic coordinates engineered to the tolerances of corporate profit. When Microsoft designers referred, rather eerily, to the prototype 360 (then known by the science-fictional moniker "Xenon," after a colorless, invisible, pervasive gas) as "a living entertainment experience powered by human energy" (Thorsen 2005b), they unknowingly came very close to articulating the theory of "machine enslavement" in which people become "intrinsic component pieces" in "recurrent and reversible human-machine systems" (Deleuze and Guattari 1987, 458).

Deleuze (1992) wrote of a "society of control" that shapes its subjects, not primarily in distinct, formal, disciplinary institutions, such as schools, barracks, or asylums, but in a diffuse, infiltrative, molecular way, for example, via networks that permeate our everyday spaces and saturate apparently private time. This society of control is coextensive with Empire (Hardt and Negri 2000, 23). Alexander Galloway observes that that video games fit well this apparatus of what Deleuze termed "ultrarapid forms of free-floating control" (Galloway 2006, 87). This machinic subjugation is, however, unstable. Because cyborg identities are new, they disclose aspects unanticipated by power and dissonant with the social machine that generated them. To paraphrase Spinoza, "Who knows what a body at a game console can do?" Empire creates capacities excessive to its functional requirements. In its search for profit, capital is incessantly throwing itself into commotion, deterritorializing established domains, creating new states of flux. The history of console innovation, with generational cycles of machines, exemplifies this. For long periods, the process can run along well-worn, risk-free routes—witness Microsoft's and Sony's dedication to the hard-core gamer—but eventually something unexpected, such as the Wii's opening for nontraditional players, generates disturbances. Combining human subjectivities and progressively higher-power machines produces unpredictable effects, unforeseen permutations of desire and capacity that give cyborgs degrees of autonomy, latitudes of action. The battles over console hacking, homebrew, and piracy are a manifestation of this. Whether such gamer nomadism is doomed to be recaptured as a catalyst to further capitalist innovation or might join with other lines of flight in a counterassemblage of what Matteo Pasquinelli (2005) refers to as "radical machines against the techno-empire," we will examine later. For the moment, we will end with a quote from Guattari (1996b, 221) apt to the gamer-console assemblage: "Something of the machine seems to belong to the essence of human desire. The question is to know which machine, and what it is for."

II
Gameplay:
Virtual/Actual

4. Banal War:
Full Spectrum Warrior

The Sequence

A Humvee drives along a desert road. Ahead, a sandstorm brews. The convoy's helicopter escort overhead veers away, the beat of its rotors fading into the distance. Suddenly gunfire breaks out, mortar bursts straddling the vehicle's route: an insurgent ambush. A spreading, clammy dread sets in; the driver wipes the sweat from his brow, removes his goggles . . . and takes a break, a luxury only *Virtual Iraq* affords.

This simulation has a seriously niche audience: about 15 percent of U.S. soldiers returning from combat in Iraq suffer from post-traumatic stress disorder, with symptoms including "anxiety, nightmare, flashbacks, emotional numbness, extreme jumpiness and physical pain" (Gordon 2007). Bodily wounds such as concussions and crushed limbs are compounded by such psychological anguish. To assist soldiers in recovering from, and *returning* to, duty, the Pentagon has devised "virtual therapies." These are based on the theory that exposure to digital re-creations of traumatic experience allows patients to recover repressed memories, safely confront their fears, and gradually overcome them. "You don't want to send someone who is traumatized back to Iraq," says a military psychiatrist leading the research. "This allows us to bring someone back, but within the situation here" (cited in Gordon 2007).

The "situation here"—here in the apparent safety of simulation—is technologically extraordinary. Elsewhere in the military hospital apparatus, veterans may endure bureaucratic inefficiencies and substandard housing, but in the realm of the digital, no expense is spared.

This virtual healing machine provides the images and sounds of war, vibrates to emulate vehicle engines and detonating weapons, and even feeds in olfactory cues. "They can set off simulated explosions and gunfire . . . add fog, smoke and night-vision effects, along with the smells of body odor and Iraq spices" (Gordon 2007).

There's a good chance a go at *Virtual Iraq* might result in soldiers recalling more than their direct experience of war: it may also flash them back to their *preparation* for war—the very preparation that was presumably meant to preserve them from wounds and trauma. This is because the basis of *Virtual Iraq* is a digital combat simulator, *Full Spectrum Warrior (FSW),* used in the training of U.S. infantry in the early years of the twenty-first century. When traumatized troops reencounter this simulator in hospital, soldiers will find it has undergone some improvement since they first met it: the vibrating platform, the full-immersion goggles, the smells. In its original training application, *FSW* was quite simple—like your run-of-the-mill war-themed commercial video game. And, indeed, it *was:* in its second life, *FSW* was a commercial title, purchasable off the shelf of your local video game retailer. Originally released in 2004, with a sequel in 2006, *FSW* has sold hundreds of thousands of copies. The "sequence," as one of *Virtual Iraq*'s developers proudly puts it, was "from training to toy to treatment" (cited in Gordon 2007).

FSW is also, however, illustrative of another sequence important to this book's argument: the cyclical connection between the actual and virtual dimensions of Empire. Combat simulators are *the* classic example of this link: the intensely, arguably ultimately, corporeal activity of war is rendered into a digital world that rehearses subjects—soldiers—for battle, learning onscreen to make choices (flanking maneuver or frontal attack? use the RPG or call in air support? wait and see, or open fire now?) that then translate into life for some and death for others in the suburbs of Baghdad or the hills outside Kandahar. The psychic wounds the soldier-subjects suffer in these bloodily material encounters are then (ostensibly) healed by yet further simulations, such as *Virtual Iraq,* the better to resupply the actual slaughter. Add into this that combat waged by high-tech armies, of which the U.S. forces are the paragon, is today itself digitally mediated through computerized targeting, mapping, surveillance, and communication systems of contemporary battlespace, and we see how deeply compounded virtuality and actuality are in the reality of Empire. This link from actual to virtual war is not, moreover, contained to boot camp and battlefield: the connection from military simulation to commercial games—which, as we have seen, is primal and originary for digital play—provides a channel through which training for war spreads into a more widely militarized culture.

This chapter examines *Full Spectrum Warrior* as an example of the technological weapons of "armed vision" (Crandall 2004) essential to new complexes of military power. *FSW*'s double life as actual trainer and virtual toy, we argue, aptly demonstrates the "banalization of war" (Hardt and Negri 2000, 12)—the enveloping sociocultural-emotional process habituating populations to the perpetual conflict of the war on terror.

Banal War

"The world is at war again, but things are different this time," write Hardt and Negri (2004, 3). The world wars of the twentieth century and the cold war confrontation of competing nuclear power blocs seem, for the moment, distant. Sharpening tensions between the United States and either China or Iran could radically change that. But for now, such massive conflict between nations is not the order of business. Yet the world is at war. The 1990s saw a series of savage, but by historical standards minor, conflicts, waged by international coalitions of militarily powerful countries in the name of global order: NATO's interventions in the former Yugoslavia, and the first Persian Gulf War, sparked by Iraq's invasion of Kuwait and met by a U.S.-led, but United Nations–approved, coalition. Then came 9/11, followed by the U.S. invasion of Afghanistan and Iraq.

The aftermath—the war on terror—provides a fuller illustration of Hardt and Negri's thesis that, in Empire, war is waged not to resolve disputes between states but to maintain order within a global territory where "there seem to be minor and elusive enemies everywhere" (2000, 189). The Bush regime's declaration of the war on terror, ostensibly targeting al-Qaeda, though also providing the pretext for the removal of former ally Saddam Hussein and the occupation of Iraq, is a paradigmatic case: military mobilization undertaken not against an external enemy state but against a shadowy foe, who may take up temporary residence either in rogue states or domestic sleeper cells, and whose threat is sinisterly amorphous and borderless.

This new context of war has several important consequences. First, it is *interminable.* Unlike wars between two nation-states ended by formal surrender or negotiation, there is rarely a definitive moment of victory over today's foes, so that "one cannot win such a war, or, rather, it has to be won again every day"; war thus becomes "a permanent social relation," "a general phenomenon" (Hardt and Negri 2004, 14, 12, 3).

Second, because the enemy is diffuse and ubiquitous, so too the scope of military activities to defeat the opponent *lacks boundaries.* Security becomes the keyword: "Whereas 'defense' involves a protective barrier against external threats, 'security' justifies a constant martial activity equally in the homeland and abroad" (Hardt and Negri 2004, 21). Within the concept of "security," boundaries between civilian policing and war fighting blur: "The separation of tasks between the external and internal arms of power (between the army and the police, the CIA and the FBI) is increasingly vague and indeterminate" (Hardt and Negri 2000, 189).

This situation brings with it a third consequence. Endemic hostilities tend to generate a "state of exception"—that is, an "exceptional," but ongoing, suspension or erosion of civil rights, declared necessary for the preservation of democracy itself (Hardt and Negri 2004, 7–9). One can think here of the debates over the USA PATRIOT Act, but also of the suspensions of civil liberties in many countries justified in the name of the war on terror.

Fourth, this environment of nebulous, dispersed, and protracted conflict means that quasi-war conditions tend to become a way of life—"the new normal." War organizes not just military forces abroad but civilian life at home. "War has," in other words, "become a *regime of biopower,*" as "daily life and the normal functioning of power [have] been permeated with the threat and violence of warfare" (Hardt and Negri 2004, 13).

The socialization necessary for populations to endure and endorse such an ongoing condition of life brings us to the concept of "banalized" war. In this situation, war becomes part of the culture of everyday life, with "the enemy" depicted as "an absolute threat to the ethical order" and "reduced to an object of routine police repression" (Hardt and Negri 2000, 13). The long-standing interaction of video game culture and the military apparatus is a component in this process of the banalization of war.

MIME-NET and the Institute for Creative Technologies

Full Spectrum Warrior is a spectacular instance of what the collective Retort concludes is "the total obedience of the culture industry to the protocols of the War on Terror—its immediate ingestion and reproduction of the state's paranoias" (2005, 28). It is a by-product of the military-entertainment complex, or what James Der Derian (2001) calls MIME-NET: "the military-industrial-media-entertainment network." Digital play and military simulation have shared genealogies (Burston 2003; Lenoir 2000; Stockwell and Muir 2003). Early on, the dominant partner was the U.S. national security state, with Pentagon funding supporting the computer laboratories where some of the first virtual games were created in the 1960s and 1970s. By the 1990s, however, with military budgets declining after the end of the Cold War, commercial games had advanced so fast as to be *superior* to the Pentagon's in-house simulations. A newly frugal military began not only to adopt or adapt civilian games for training purposes but also to directly collaborate with private-sector studios to create customized war games.

The attacks of September 11, 2001, gave this rapprochement a massive boost. The military poured funds into codesigned simulations to anticipate the new challenges of the war on terror. Meanwhile developers of commercial games rushed to capitalize on market opportunities created by media coverage of terrorism and the invasion of Afghanistan and Iraq. Sales of war games rocketed, and developers able to cite collaboration with the military gave their products the cachet of "authenticity" that console warriors craved (see Nieborg 2006).

Some instances pushed the intersection of virtual and actual war to the extreme. In our introduction, we discussed the U.S. Army's online game, *America's Army,* launched in 2002 to recruit young Americans with no experiential connection to war, but plenty to video games. Another is *Kuma War,* an online gaming service, launched in 2004, marketing itself as "a series of playable recreations of real events in the War on Terror" (Kuma War 2006). Kuma invites subscribers to "re-live" recent war events in the form of "playable missions" carrying titles like "Freedom's Heroes: The Road to Baghdad," "Baghdad Checkpoint Attack," and "Operation Red Dawn," the latter giving you the chance to help capture "the Butcher of Baghdad" himself. While *Kuma War* is a commercial operation, overlaps between the military and the game industry have grown ubiquitous: the Department of

Defense Game Development Community (2005), a network aiming to connect "the entire community developing games within the U.S. military," currently lists some forty games "custom-made" for military purposes, and about twenty-five "off-the-shelf" products considered useful.

Even with this formidable competition, the Institute for Creative Technologies (ICT) stands out. The ICT epitomizes the intersection of military planning, computer simulation, film studios, and video game developers in what Der Derian terms "a new configuration of virtual power" (2001, xi). Based at the University of Southern California, the ICT was created in 1999 by the army and funded to the tune of $45 million to tap into the entertainment industry's high-tech expertise. A senior official describes its goal as being "to produce a revolution in how the military trains and rehearses for upcoming missions" by "develop[ing] the art and technology for synthetic experiences" to a pitch "so compelling that participants will react as if they are real," thus providing a "quantum leap in helping the Army prepare for the world, soldier, organization, weaponry, and mission of the future" (Macedonia 2002). The ICT hired talent from game companies and film studios to collaborate in this mission: artists who designed special effects for *The Matrix,* screenwriters for films such as *Training Day,* a designer from the *Alien* movies, and so on. The deal was clear: the military got sophisticated training aids for its soldiers, entertainment companies got insider military knowledge, and the university got external funding.

The ICT's résumé is extensive: simulations with "branching story lines" to train U.S. officers in negotiating with Afghan warlords; anticipatory visualizations of future war, such as the award-winning film *Nowhere to Hide,* "a sweeping vision of the Army's Future Force in action"; FlatWorld, which "allows users to experience virtual worlds—say a Baghdad street corner under enemy fire—without wearing clunky goggles"; and the Sensory Environments Evaluation program, an "immersive virtual-reality tunnel that can re-create unpleasant environments"—such as abandoned bunkers filled with bats—"with astonishing verisimilitude" (Kushner 2004). The aim, according to one ICT spokesperson, is "to create veterans who've never seen combat" (cited in Kushner 2004). Not the least of the ICT progeny are a series of gamelike training simulations, including *Full Spectrum Warrior.* To understand these developments requires a short excursion into military doctrine.

Full-Spectrum Dominance

Full-spectrum dominance is a concept whose centrality to Pentagon thinking was announced in *Joint Vision 2020,* a planning document released in 2000 by the Joint Chiefs of Staff. Its opening pages declare the U.S. military aim over the next two decades to be the achievement of "full spectrum dominance: persuasive in peace; decisive in war; preeminent in any form of conflict." It goes on:

> The label full spectrum dominance implies that U.S. forces are able to conduct prompt, sustained, and synchronized operations with combinations of forces tailored to specific situations and with access to and freedom to operate in all domains—space, sea, land, air, and information. Additionally, given the global nature of our interests and obligations, full spectrum dominance requires that the U.S. "maintain its overseas presence forces and the ability to rapidly project power worldwide." (Joint Chiefs of Staff 2000, 6)

So the term "full spectrum" designates military force that can flexibly modulate its activities across different types and theaters of operations, scaling its responses up and down as goals and circumstances require, shifting seamlessly from, say, tactical nuclear options to guerrilla urban warfare, with planetary reach (see Mahajan 2003).

The possibility of full-spectrum dominance is opened by what U.S. war planners know as the Revolution in Military Affairs (RMA), a transformation in military practices occasioned by the shift from industrial to informational warfare. The possession of overwhelming strategic, operational, and tactical advantage is determined by superiority in high technology, especially in communications and computing, rather than numbers of troops or even equipment. RMA identifies a situation of "virtual war," fought out "onscreen," in which the enemy becomes visible, knowable, and destroyable through the mediation of digital technologies, from satellite-generated maps to heads-up display systems and computer-controlled and dispatched weaponry.

What causes the greatest disquiet to U.S. war planners, however, is the threat of low-tech opponents and "asymmetrical conflict." The NATO and Red Army forces that faced each other in the Cold War were "symmetrical" enemies, mirror images, each with missiles, tanks, artillery, air, and infantry, as well as tactical and operational doctrines, which, though distinct, fell broadly within the same plane of military logic. But the U.S. troops fighting in Iraq or Afghanistan face "asymmetrical" foes: insurgents massively outgunned in terms of high-technology firepower, far less well trained, but retaliating with practices, such as suicide bombing, assassinations of civilian collaborators, and other forms of terrorism, that seem to imperial eyes alien, uncivilized, and inhuman. *Joint Vision 2020* identifies such "asymmetric approaches" as "perhaps the most serious danger the United States faces in the immediate future" (Joint Chiefs of Staff 2000, 5).

Associated with asymmetric conflict is yet another acronym: MOUT, or Military Operations on Urban Terrain. Pentagon strategists, as Mike Davis (2004) has noted, now consider the "Third World city" to be the "key battlespace of the future." The view that "the slum has become the weakest link in the American empire" is based not only on the disasters that befell U.S. occupations of Mogadishu and Beirut but also on Israeli experiences in Gaza and the West Bank. If "the future of warfare . . . lies in the streets, sewers, high-rise buildings, and sprawl of houses that form the broken cities of the world," then special training is required for the soldiers who will fight in such conditions. MOUT tactics are applied on a daily basis in cities such as Baghdad, Fallujah, and Nadjaf, and preparation for such fighting involves incessant war games, both physical and virtual (see Dawson 2007; Graham 2007).

The ICT's simulations are part of these rehearsals, most of them digitally modeling asymmetric combat: their title *Full Spectrum Command* aims to train company-level leaders, in charge of about 120 members, and *Full Spectrum Leader* works at the level of a 30-member platoon. Dealing with small-scale squad-level operations, *Full Spectrum Warrior* is intended by the army to help soldiers understand what their leaders are asking them to do: "By taking the 'boss's job,' soldiers might deepen their appreciation for the correct execution of dismounted battle drills in the urban context" (Korris 2004).

What really distinguishes *FSW*, however, is that it is a military-civilian codevelopment with *two* versions: the military version teaches soldiers how to make (or at least follow) smart decisions in the nightmare of urban combat; the civilian version, released in 2004, makes this an entertainment experience. Under the auspices of the ICT, the video game company Pandemic Studios developed both versions, with Sony Picture Imageworks doing special effects. The giant game publisher THQ later prepared the game for commercial sale. Civilian and military versions alike are playable on Microsoft's Xbox, and the commercial version was later ported to other systems. From the army's point of view, "leveraging Xbox" saved on special simulation devices and capitalized on young recruits' familiarity with game consoles, creating a "potential efficiency" in "training for training" (Korris 2004). The army invested $5 million. Pandemic and Sony did the development, promising $2.6 million worth of in-kind work. In return, they got the rights to the commercial game. It is with this "entertainment" version of *FSW* that we begin.

Mission to Zekistan

Load *Full Spectrum Warrior;* skip the manual; jump directly to the first mission. Here is the dusty, deserted, sinister Middle Eastern town, with its labyrinth of winding streets. Here "we" are, your point of view embedded in the midst of a U.S. infantry squad. Already, barely visible enemies have opened fire from ambush. In front of you, a truck burns; its driver lies wounded. Automatic weapons chatter; distant explosions reverberate. You are a soldier-subject in the war on terror: kill or be killed, and obey orders. This is all you really need to know.

After a few mission failures, you may return to the tutorials or the manual. There you find the backstory. Zekistan is an imaginary Central Asian country with a "three thousand year" history "punctuated by violence and bloodshed" (FSWIM 2004). After guerrilla struggle against Soviet invasion came a civil war in which "Mhujadeen fighters," led by the charismatic "Mohammed Jabour Al-Afad," emerge supreme. Al-Afad's regime converts the country to "fundamentalist worship" and persecutes the "ethnic Zekis, the nomadic mountain people that had originally settled the region," practicing "genocide" and "forced sterilization." Thousands of "ex-Taliban and Iraqi loyalists" set up "terrorist-training facilities and death camps." Following a "devastating wave of terrorist attacks" across "Europe and South East Asia," U.S. intelligence tracks the source to Zekistan. After "repeated warnings and failed diplomatic resolutions in the UN," NATO votes to invade. Massive air strikes prepare the ground for infantry and armor to begin the land war—which is where you, the virtual warrior suddenly inserted beside a burning truck on a dirty street, come in.

This is a complex geopolitical story. But it is basically irrelevant. All the parts are familiar from innumerable CNN reports, news photos, and movies; the political premises, the allotted roles, and the desired outcome are all predictable. Writing about the first Gulf War, Brian

Massumi observed how the legitimation of state violence operates primarily in "an affective register, through the mass media" (1998, 44). This "affective circulation" depends on a series of conversions, elisions, and blurs. On the one hand, the enemy combines attributes of military opponent, despot, terrorist, thug, and genocide perpetrator—omni-purpose evil. On the other, there is an implied identification between U.S. soldiers and media audiences, and foreign populations supposedly being philanthropically aided by "our" side. As Massumi puts it, "All you need do is feel—a oneness with the prospective dead hero, and, based on that, hostility for the hypothetical enemy" (45).

Such is the universe of *FSW*. "Zekistan" is Iraq, Afghanistan, Kosovo, Iran; "Al-Afad," bin Laden, Saddam Hussein, Mahmoud Ahmadinejad; the "Zekistan Liberation Front" are composite tyrannical, ethnic-cleansing, weapons-caching terrorist malefactors. You, the player, are "our" troops, at once defending the homeland and liberating oppressed inhabitants of invaded countries. One of the U.S. soldiers, whose position the player adopts, displays on his helmet the letters NYPD. Is this a cue that U.S. soldiers in Central Asia are, indeed, planetary police? In a moment of scripted dialogue, after a ferocious firefight has left bodies strewn all across the streets, one of our infantrymen reflects, "I think just by being here we help."

First-Person Thinker

The virtual experience of *Full Spectrum Warrior* is that of commanding two four-person teams of U.S. infantry: Alpha and Bravo. The player's point of view is normally from behind the shoulder of the sergeant commanding a team. Orders—"Bravo, pay attention! Move!"—are executed by the fire team as a group. The player's in-game subject position is complex. One can switch from leader of Alpha to that of Bravo and back again. And if it is necessary to get a specific line of site on an enemy position, one can "see" from the position of any member of the team. So it could be said that the player's implied position is that of a "ninth" officer, invisible and invulnerable, commanding both fire teams. Ultimately the player of *FSW* has a trans-individual position, the consciousness of a collective military entity.

The player must complete a series of increasingly challenging missions. Alpha and Bravo clear streets, evacuate wounded, relieve surrounded comrades, discover mass graves, eliminate antitank weapons halting U.S. armor, call in air strikes on enemy vehicles, fight their way through a palace, a university, and an oil refinery, rescue captured aircrews, and eventually unearth Al-Afad himself.

The necessary skills are rapidly learned through the in-game MOUT Training Course. There are two types of commands: fire and movement. Fire commands select weaponry, targets, and the intensity of fire: "point fire" takes out specific targets, "suppression fire" unleashes a maximum volume of bullets, compelling foes to keep their heads down or die. Movement commands direct the team to its next location, with the cursor showing exactly where each member will end up; teams can "rush," moving with maximum speed, or "bound," advancing cautiously, keeping weapons trained where enemies may appear.

The player, as squad leader, doesn't directly fire weapons but rather orders others to do so. The art of the game is the balance of fire and movement; the rapid detection of enemies; the location of covered positions with commanding fields of fire; and the interplay of support between the two squads, maneuvering one so that it can cover the other's assault—all while managing ammunition supplies and navigating through a city. The process is remarkably cerebral: in contrast to conventional "first-person shooter" games, *FSW* has been called "a first-person thinker" (Macedonia, cited in Adair 2005).

Alpha, Bravo, and the Tangos

But *Full Spectrum Warrior* has its affective dimensions. It goes to some lengths to personalize the members of Alpha and Bravo, whose backgrounds are described in detail in the game manual and, in the Xbox version, in introductory scenes. Of Sergeant Santiago Garcia Mendez, we learn that he is a "first generation American," born to Cuban immigrants who instilled "his strong work ethic and drive to better himself and his community," and that he is a "fiercely protective and loving father, a trait which comes through in dealing with his squad" (FSWIM 2004). Corporal Andre Ellis Devreux—"Crawdaddy"—is an African American who had "a typical suburban middle class upbringing, complete with little league, summer camp and a trip to Orlando, Florida when he was ten. That was the summer before he lost his mother to cancer." "Nova" Picoli "grew up in a crowded household with four older sisters" and joined the army to escape debt. Private "Gidget" Ota is "the middle child of single working mother in Honolulu." In a bow to Middle Eastern amity, the squad includes both the Arab American private Asher Shehadi Ali ("although he finds aspects of his parent's culture fascinating and takes pride in his heritage, he is also a proud American" and considers himself "no different from any other Southern California guy") and the "Caucasian," clearly Jewish private "Philly" Alexander Isaac Silverman, who is Alpha team's "resident smart ass."

One of the game's main tropes is thus that of the "band of brothers," familiar from war movies. In their mix of ethnicities and classes, Alpha and Bravo are an equal-opportunity paradigm. Of their eight members, three are Caucasian, two black, one Arab, and one Polynesian. There are four high-school diploma holders, one graduate from university (pre-law), two from college, and one from police academy. Though painfully programmatic in its inclusiveness, this is actually a semiplausible representation of a combat squad in the actual contemporary army, which is "in essence a working class military," enlisted from people who are "upwardly mobile," but from families "without the resources to send them to college" (Halbfinger and Holmes 2003). With "minorities overrepresented and the wealthy and underclass essentially absent," its composition resembles that of "a two year commuter or trade school outside Birmingham or Biloxi." Alpha and Bravo are somewhat better educated, and more ethnically diverse, than the statistical norm, but not unbelievable.

This militarized multiculturalism is explicitly thematized in the game. In a cut scene at the end of one mission, one of the white soldiers raps. "You are not, nor ever have been, black," says one of his African American team members. "Blackness is a state of mind, brother," the white soldier retorts. Sergeant Mendez then intervenes with a proper assertion of uniformed race blindness: "There's only one color in this army: green." "Philly" Silverman pipes up, "With respect sir, I think that's brown"—presumably referring to the actual color of camouflage battle gear. "Yo, shit brown," quips another black trooper. In the imperial army, race and class antagonisms are subsumed not only in the common uniform but also in the shared, shitty grittiness of soldierly life.

The "buddy" ethos is sustained throughout the gameplay. When a squad member is hit, his team members cry, "They got Philly!" (or Mendes, or whoever). Soldiers comment on the heat, "I wish I had a pop, nice and cold"; the pathos of war, "It doesn't have to be this way"; and inactivity, "Nothin' wrong with chillin' for a while, I suppose." They become agitated if exposed to fire without cover: "I thought standing out in the open was pretty much what they told us *not* to do!" Remarks range from the salacious, "You should see my wife in the morning, just after she gets out of the shower"; to the properly domestic, "Should be a letter waiting for you from your family"; the derogatory, "This place sure is fucked up in all kinds of ways"; and the virtually reflexive, "When we get back to base, I'm going to whip your ass on the Xbox."

The enemy is, of course, different. Apart from the Osama bin Laden surrogate, Mohammed Jabour Al-Afad, the opponents are nameless and mostly faceless. At the beginning there is a fast-cut scene displaying masked figures opening a crate of rocket launchers as the U.S. troops roll into town. Other than this, the Zekistan Liberation Army always appear from the perspective of its U.S. opponents as rather rudimentary figures, usually in the middle to far distance, at the end of streets, behind sandbags, or on rooftops spraying fire down the street. Scarves often hide their faces. When they are spotted, Alpha and Bravo identify them as "Zekes," "Motherfuckers," or, most often, "Tangos," from "T" for "target." They appear with small icons above their heads indicating whether they are "under cover," "engaged" (that is, pinned down by incoming fire), or dead—marked with skull and crossbones. They thus do seem like targets on a firing range. When they die—and, of course, they must die, nearly all of them, for the player to succeed— they crumple into inert heaps. As Alpha and Bravo pass by, they occasionally give the dead an epithet: "Should have done something else today, Zeke."

Armed Vision

Full Spectrum Warrior suggests aspects of contemporary warfare beyond simply the firepower and discipline of U.S. light infantry, aspects specific to new media of visualization and virtualization. In an incisive analysis of "armed vision," the artist and media theorist Jordan Crandall (2004) posits that in the history of visual technologies such as photography, cinema, and video, one can distinguish two major perspectives: "horizontal" and "vertical." The horizontal orientation is set at "ground level" and is concerned with "the advance or retreat of sightlines and perspectives along the terrestrial expanse of the earth." The "vertical," or "aerial," orientation is concerned with "looking downward rather than sideways." The vertical dimension is in origin an optic of surveillance and command: "Mapping changes and discovering patterns, the objective was to understand what moves (troops? construction materials?), how it moves, and how that movement can be intercepted or exploited." It adds to our visual experience "an orientation that is somehow ultimately not 'for us'" but rather is "the perspective of a militarized, machinic surround," an eye involved in "positioning, tracking, identifying, predicting, targeting, and intercepting/containing."

Each loading of *FSW* opens with a vertical perspective, a view as if from a surveillance satellite: first the earth from space, then a continental view of the Persian Gulf and Central Asia, then a city image, finally zooming to an overhead view of the streets where combat is occurring. These aerial views are granular, with static interference; it is the optic of military command scoping out the battlefield from an "eye in the sky." Soon you are down at street level with Alpha and Bravo, in the composite collective eye of the squad, making your way through Zekistan. Here you progress horizontally, street by street, building by building, corner by corner.

The urban landscape is lavish. Papers blow across the streets, burned-out cars litter the intersections, smoke from conflagrations billows thickly upward, crows and cats rise and run as your squad passes. The squalor of debris, the beauty of tilework in Islamic palaces, the colors of flaming sunsets glimpsed at the end of streets—all are created in gorgeous detail. But be entranced at your peril. Simply finding a designated objective can be a challenge. And since Alpha and Bravo are often outnumbered and always moving in the open—awaiting enemies, vulnerable to ambush—it is only by getting some advance warning that you'll find what you need: in other words, by invoking vertical vision.

At any moment, the player can press a button to obtain a view via his Global Positioning System (GPS) receiver. Here you see a city map with a view of several blocks surrounding your current position. The two teams are marked; your field of view shows as a green cone; medical aid points and objectives are displayed; and enemies appear as red icons. Additionally, you can request helicopter reconnaissance. This invocation of vertical armed vision is especially strongly marked, because the helicopter pilot, although only present as a radio voice, is the one persistent female presence in the game (the only other women are medics and aid workers who appear fleetingly): "Louise." So the move from the horizontal orientation of the grunt infantry on the ground to the vertical, aerial dimension breaks the game's gender code.

If a flight is available, the pilot confirms her approach via radio.

The helicopter can be heard and, in some of the game's most striking visual moments, seen, circling in the sky through gaps in the city skyline. As it passes overhead, Louise marks enemies on the GPS and informs the player whether their presence is heavy or light: "Tangos galore," "Tangos like ants on soda," "Targets up." Such flights are, however, limited: use too many, and Louise may respond to your panic-stricken request with a cool "Sorry Charlie, that's a negative."

Sometimes fire can be summoned from the sky. A crucial role for Alpha and Bravo is not directly defeating the Tangos in firefights but spotting for devastating air or artillery strikes. Here the role of the infantry is thus, in Crandall's (2004) words, "to act as a direct human interface to a machine that cannot yet fully interface with all of the ambiguities of a material world"—a function performed in-game by placing a special green bomb icon on target. After a few moments the screen is rocked with spectacular explosions, providing a pyrotechnic gratification acknowledged by one virtual soldier's scripted comment: "Ahh never get tired o' that."

This interplay of vertical and horizontal is, of course, integral to the doctrine of full-spectrum dominance, which depends on the combination and cooperation of air force and army into a single, invincible striking power. The first Gulf War was christened the "Nintendo War" because it introduced television watchers to gamelike perspectives of gun-sight and bomb-nose cameras. *FSW* takes things further by offering both vertical and horizontal perspectives on war in a situation where the role of the human horizontal sight is to vector in the apocalyptic power released from the vertical heights. We experience, virtually, what Crandall terms "the integration of analyst, operator, database, and weapons network into a smart image . . . unlike anything we understand in civilian perspectives." *FSW* is one of what he calls the "new kinds of militarized formats" in visual media, fusing "technological innovation and the erotic charge of combat" in "renewed, compulsive militarization."

War Is Peace

That video games are too violent is a common claim. But *Full Spectrum Warrior* is perhaps not violent enough. The price of failure is remarkably low. If soldiers in Alpha and Bravo are lightly injured, blood spatters across the screen. If one is more seriously wounded, he falls, and if unaided, he will eventually die. He can, however, be carried by his squad back to a Casualty Evacuation point, where healing is almost immediate. The wounded man staggers to his feet to upbeat comments from the commander: "You've still got your looks"; "Wow, am I glad to see you again, Sarge!" "He's one tough son-of-a-bitch."

If two or more soldiers are seriously wounded, the mission ends abruptly. There is a sudden cut to cinematic animations of your team falling to enemy fire. Soldiers jerk back, crumple to the ground, or are lifted off their feet by the impact of bullets and hurled through the air; fountains of scarlet blood jet from the punctures stitched across their bodies. The animation and game physics involved in these moments are extraordinary. Bodies fall realistically in the precise situation where they were hit. When an infantryman seeking cover among a stack of crates is caught in a burst of machine-gun fire, not only is the chipping of containers by bullets striking them and ricocheting around visible, but the unfortunate soldier's cheek slams against the side of the crate as he is hit, his head snapping back convulsively before he slides to the ground.

All of this, however, only lasts an instant. Almost before you register that you have led Alpha and Bravo to death and disaster, a voice-over comes up with some good advice for next time, "Always use cover." Then the "Mission Over" screen appears—with the "Return to Last Save" option, which restarts the game at the most recent of the designated save points scattered through its course. This may mean having to repeat several minutes of maneuvers and re-kill a number of Zekes. Let this happen a few times, and whatever horror you may have felt at the deaths of your men turns to exasperation. It is essential to *FSW* that time can be reversed, and every mistake undone; the "save-die-restart" sequence makes Alpha and Bravo immortal. This is, of course, the big lie of war-as-video-game.

There are other subsidiary lies in *FSW*'s virtual war. That missions end if you have more than one serious casualty reflects the U.S. military's well-known concern for (and success in) minimizing politically volatile losses to its highly trained post-Fordist techno-soldiers. "The U.S. Army has zero tolerance for casualties!" the manual sternly declares (FSWIM 2004). But it also means you never witness the annihilation of large numbers of your own troops. And—need it be said?—this is war where no one lies for hours gut-shot and shrieking for his mother; has his testicles blown off; or wakes in the hospital finding he has lost a limb. It is war without mutilation or post-traumatic stress disorder. It is also war without moral dilemmas. And there are almost no civilians. The miracle of Zekistan is that its streets are deserted and houses empty, apart from the ubiquitous Tangos (who all die instantaneously when hit). Air and artillery strikes do not hit wedding parties. There is no collateral damage. War is peace.

HA2P1PY9TUR5TLE: Decline and Fall?

The package of *Full Spectrum Warrior* boldly declares, "Based on an actual training aid for the U.S. Army." Immediately after release it was discovered that entering a "cheat code,"—HA2P1PY9TUR5TLE— into the Xbox commercial game unlocked the Army version (this option was disabled when the game was ported to the PC and PS2, suggesting the disclosure was unwelcome to the military). As many reviews attest, a major attraction of *FSW* was that it gave gamers a glimpse, if not of real war, at least of real military virtuality.

The military version plays like the commercial game, but with significant differences. It spans two theaters of war, the Middle East and the Balkans. The personalization of, and banter between, soldiers is removed. So is much of the graphical polish, special lighting, blur effects, and visual detail. There are no cut scenes. The audio quality is markedly lower. The rich musical score that added excitement and exoticism is gone. Apart from faint wind and distant gunfire, all is quiet in the streets—with one exception: in the military version there are more civilians, and they speak to your soldiers more often. In the commercial game, this happens very occasionally and is entirely benign: in one cut scene, the Arab American private Shehadi gets directions from a friendly Zeke (after a lengthy dialogue in Arabic, the Sergeant asks, "What did he say?" "North," replies Shehadi). In the military version, there is some of this fraternization—"Come this way, America"—but also many expressions of hostility: "Filthy American pigs!" "This is our home, capitalist pigs," or, when the U.S. troops are facilitating elections, "Go home, don't vote." While the civilian game presents a war of liberation, the military version familiarizes U.S. soldiers with being unpopular.

Less spectacular than the civilian version, the military game is harder to survive. Cover is scanter; fewer onscreen icons give information about the vulnerability of friends and foes; there are more civilians, so identifying "hostiles" is harder. The enemy attacks more aggressively, from a greater variety of directions; the awkward behavior of weapons like grenades is more accurately represented. Instead of the GPS, the soldier gets a crude hand-drawn map of the missions, although the interplay between vertical and horizontal vision is preserved by the ability to lift the camera hundreds of feet into the air, seeing the entire map from bird's-eye view in real time. It is possible to modify the quantity and aggressiveness of opposing forces and civilians and also to change the capabilities of one's own troops, altering their accuracy and reaction times. Wounded soldiers cannot be carried to evacuation points: you gather their weapons and ammunition and move on. On balance, the military version is a sparer, but more complex and challenging, simulation than the civilian game.

But perhaps not complex and challenging enough. In 2005 scandal erupted around *FSW* when Taxpayers for Common Sense, an organization critical of the Bush regime's military spending, suggested that Sony, Pandemic, and THQ had obtained massive public subsidization for a commercial venture that fell far short of military training needs. News reports suggested that *FSW* should be reinterpreted as "Full Spectrum Welfare" and that the army had been "out-gamed" (Adair 2005). The source was a whistle-blowing graphic artist, Andrew Paquette, who claimed he was fired from the *FSW* development team after writing repeated memos warning that the game would not be realistic enough for the army. Most of the city buildings, Paquette pointed out, are just facades: those that have interiors can be entered only on one level. Hence what is usually considered the worst part of urban combat—floor-to-floor house clearing with enemies lurking in cellars or upper floors—simply doesn't exist in the game. "What they did," Paquette said, "was give the Fisher-Price version of a city" (cited in Adair 2005). Suing both Sony and Pandemic for wrongful dismissal, he said the companies "didn't pay attention to what the Army needed," and that their attitude was "We don't care about the Army, we're making money off this." Paquette lost his case. But his complaints were echoed from other sources. Taxpayers for Common Sense unearthed internal ICT e-mails warning, "we have a huge problem on our hands" because the army "was not satisfied" (Conroy 2005). Military training personnel corroborated this, saying that the game was "incredibly shallow" and had a "very limited set of situational challenges" (cited in Adair 2005).

ICT spokespeople responded by ceding ground, declaring *FSW* a useful experiment that would improve other training aids. "We have learned a lot," said one army official involved. "And that's the purpose of research—to learn those types of things, not to deliver a product"

(Macedonia, cited in Adair 2005). Set against the daily death toll in Iraq and Afghanistan, the scandal around the ICT expenditures seems trivial. But it provides an insight into the Achilles' heel of full-spectrum dominance: the Iraqi insurgents or the Taliban cannot beat the U.S. Army in the field, but they may spend it into the ground. The low-casualty (for the United States), high-technology strategy on which the Pentagon depends is monstrously expensive. Empire's vulnerability is not battlefield defeat but economic crisis caused by the collapsing over-hang of military budgets. The heist of five million dollars from the U.S. Army by Pandemic, Sony, THQ, and Microsoft is dwarfed by the war profiteering of corporations such as Halliburton, but it offers a micro-cosm of imperial decline and fall.

In the short term, *Full Spectrum Warrior* was nonetheless a suc-cess. The commercial game earned enthusiastic reviews and industry awards, sold about a million units, and grossed US$50 million. In 2006 Pandemic released a sequel, *Full Spectrum Warrior: Ten Hammers*. It continued the saga of the Zekistan expeditionary force, though with new weapons and troops. *Ten Hammers* was developed independently of the Pentagon; Pandemic was now using its well-subsidized military expertise for a purely commercial project.

Nor did the company escape political controversy. In 2005 Pan-demic had joined with the Canadian video game company BioWare to create a new "superdeveloper" studio, a $300 million deal financed by the venture capital firm Elevation Partners (Thorsen 2005a). One of the main investors was U2's front man and celebrity activist, Bono. Shortly after the formation of the new company, Pandemic an-nounced a new game, *Mercenaries 2: A World in Flames,* a game that follows soldiers of fortune as they topple a "power hungry tyrant" who "messes with Venezuela's oil supply" (*Mercenaries 2,* 2007). Responding to that obvious allusion to the troubled relationship of the United States with Venezuela's socialist leader Hugo Chávez, the Venezuelan Solidarity Network (2006) wrote a letter to Bono, point-ing out Pandemic's *FSW* connection to the Pentagon, criticizing the anti-Venezuelan propaganda of *Mercenaries,* and petitioning him to use his influence to cancel the game: "Our concern is that this game will only deepen an already antagonistic relationship between the U.S. and Venezuelan governments. Millions of Venezuelans fear an inva-sion from the U.S.; knowing that a company that works for the U.S. military has created a game in which their country is completely de-stroyed will increase those concerns." These concerns were echoed by a Venezuelan congressman, who said, "I think the U.S. government knows how to prepare campaigns of psychological terror so they can make things happen later" (cited in BBC 2006a). Pandemic, apparently feeling a little liberated from even putative military authenticity, shook off the objections, saying, "One of the key reasons Venezuela was chosen for the setting of *Mercenaries 2* is that it is a fascinating and colorful country, full of wonderful architecture, geography and culture" (cited in Buncombe 2006). Despite the furor over the funding of *FSW,* on November 20, 2004, the U.S. Army awarded ICT a new five-year, $100 million contract.

"Everyone's a General"

Full Spectrum Warrior also has a context beyond the institutional linkages we have described. Here we return to the notion of full-spectrum dominance and the role of the banalization of war within that. Implicit in this doctrine is an understanding of war as a project with not only military but also ideological and political dimensions. Maintaining an imperial populace's will to fight is as important as battlefield dominance. In a U.S. context, this is reflected in neo-conservative determination to cure the so-called Vietnam syndrome of peacenik disaffection to which the country's historic humiliation in Southeast Asia is ascribed. From this point of view, whatever the success or failure of simulators such as *FSW* in preparing soldiers for Baghdad, their role in habituating civilians to perpetual war may be as, or more, important.

To suggest games such as *FSW* prepare not only soldiers but also civilians for war is to enter a complex and frustrating debate about the links from virtual to actual. The success of military simulators in improving soldiers' battlefield performance—for example, learning to fire swiftly and accurately—has led video game critics such as David Grossman (1996) to claim that first-person shooters constitute informal "training to kill." Such assertions, widespread after the Columbine massacres, have been revived by the demagogic lawyer Jack Thompson (2005), who, while seeking publicity for victims of alleged video-game-induced shootings, denounced the ICT as a "tax payer rip-off" responsible for "training" terrorists.

We find these unilinear media-effects claims simplistic and unconvincing. Positions inscribed in games are never necessarily replicated by players. The effectiveness of simulators in military training arises from their specific insertion as one relay in the war machine of military institutions. In that context, virtual violence is part of an ensemble of practices aimed at disinhibiting, disciplining, and directing deadly aggression, ferociously etching direct lines from simulation to actuality. The idea that these conditions are replicated every time a shooter is played in a civilian living room is naive.

By the same token, however, when the same militaristic identities and assumptions are reiterated by numerous media channels and asserted by many institutions, the chances for their reproduction rise. In societies on a war footing, militarization, as we mentioned earlier, becomes part of everyday life, from downloading a free mission from the *Kuma War* Web site to CNN reporting the daily threat level based on Homeland Security's color-coded terror alert system (see Massumi 2006). The boundary between the barracks and the living room is thus imploding, and we enter the war on terror version of what Deleuze (1992) called "the society of control." Hatred toward an officially designated enemy, triumph in his death, or at least indifference toward its necessity, vigilance against his wiles, acceptance of casualties in the course of struggle, uncritical loyalty for "our side," and so on, all become values promulgated across a wide social bandwidth, on a full spectrum, from the president's podium to daily news reports. In the era of the war on terror, this is the situation in the heartlands of Empire.

What of the motivations for this current round of militarization of which *FSW* is a part? One response is suggested by the context surrounding *FSW*'s incubator, the Institute for Creative Technologies. The erosion of the boundaries between state and corporation represented by the ICT—as well as the opening up of its host university as a facility for producing intellectual property—is symptomatic of a process that is finding its purest and most vicious manifestation in the regions of the Middle East that are the setting of war games like *FSW*. That process, discussed in greater detail in the next chapter, is "primitive accumulation" (see Retort 2005, 10–12), capital's drive to satisfy its requirement of perpetual expansion by continually capturing new territories—be that education or a country—in which to implant its logic. Primitive accumulation's current delivery system is what Naomi Klein (2007) identifies as "the shock doctrine": the calculated method of seizing or fomenting crisis of various types as an opportunity to crack open zones formerly restricting capital's free play—an aim achieved now with the supplement of unprecedented military shock, or full-spectrum dominance. Shock fosters Empire. And Empire, we remember, is a regime unified by a single, capitalist economic system. In Iraq, the U.S. struggles, with extraordinary realism, to secure for itself the top slot in that Empire. In American living rooms, meanwhile, the armed vision of *Full Spectrum Warrior* and its ilk contributes to the culture shock necessary on the homeland to banalize the global violence of primitive accumulation: nothing more perfectly encapsulates the intersection of war, profit, and cultural shock than the attempt (eventually withdrawn) by Sony in 2003 to trademark that "brutally abstract" slogan "Shock and Awe" (Retort 2005, 16), Pentagon jargon for the strategy of overwhelming and disorienting force applied against Iraq, for use as a possible video game title (BBC 2003b).

In this setting, games such as *FSW* generate subjectivities that tend to war. They prompt not atrocities of gothic delinquency but displays of loyal support for "staying the course." Their virtualities are part of a wider polyphonic cultural chorus supporting militarization, a multimedia drumbeat for war. Dissonance is still possible: tens of millions marched in opposition to the invasion of Iraq, we cannot forget. But the battle song is loud. *FSW* contributes to the broader banalization of war by promoting uncritical identification with imperial troops; by rotely celebrating the virtue of their cause and the justice of their activities; by routinizing the extermination of the enemy; by diminishing the horrors of battle and exalting its spectacle; by forming subjects of, and for, armed surveillance; by investing pleasurable affect in military tactics and strategy; and by making players material partners in, and beneficiaries of, military techno-culture. Virtual involvement of civilian populations in actual imperial war makes military games a homefront component of full-spectrum dominance. "Don't bring out the General in you!" warned Deleuze and Guattari (1987, 24–25). As one of the developers of *Full Spectrum Warrior* said of this game, however: "The bumper sticker version is, 'Everyone's a general'" (cited in Silberman 2004).

The Tangos Get Game

But if everyone's a general, so, presumably, are all your enemies. In 2000 Osama bin Laden and his followers, fleeing U.S. cruise missile attacks on al-Qaeda's base in Sudan, arrived in Afghanistan. Bin Laden's children were with their father in the desolate caves of Tora Bora. While holed up in this uncongenial setting, the teenagers endured a "strange, unstable mix of boredom and mortal danger." The boys—though not the girls—had the opportunity to attend school but "did little other than memorize the Quran all day." There was, however, one line of escape. Bin Laden—reportedly regarded by his children as "quite liberal"—let his younger son "play Nintendo because there was not much else to entertain him" (Bergen, cited in Wright 2006, 253–54).

The countries of the Middle East have large youth populations who are just as fascinated by video games as those elsewhere on the planet. What the Institute for Creative Technologies may not have foreseen is that the United States' insurgent foes would use the same simulatory techniques as the Pentagon to train recruits and inspire support. A number of games by Middle Eastern developers are intended to counter the situation of Islamic youth playing "against themselves" in products such as *Full Spectrum Warrior* or *Delta Force,* which depict Muslims mainly as terrorist foes. Games played from the position of a protagonist in the guerrilla movements, religious militias, and nationalist regimes in armed struggle *against* the United States or Israel are what the games journalist Ed Halter (2006b) terms "Islamogaming."

Several examples involve the Palestinian struggle. One of the earliest was *The Stone Throwers* (2001), a relatively simple game that positioned the player within the *intifada.* This was followed by *Under Ash,* a first-person shooter in which the protagonist, Ahmed, progresses from throwing rocks at Israeli soldiers to destroying Israeli military positions. *Under Ash* was criticized for being too hard. Nonetheless its first pressing of ten thousand copies sold out in a week. Its sequel, *Under Siege* (2005), takes as its point of departure the 1994 massacre of Islamic worshippers by the Jewish extremist Baruch Goldstein at the Ibrahimi Mosque in Hebron and the subsequent street battles between Palestinians and Israeli troops. Both *Under Ash* and *Under Siege* are made by the Damascus-based Afkar Media, a subsidiary of the Syrian publishing company Dar El Fikr. Commentators have remarked on the similarity of these games to *Full Spectrum Warrior* (see Frasca 2005; Ghattas 2002; Oliver 2004a), but the games' author, Radwan Kasmiya, rejects the comparison, saying that players will be able to "tell the difference between a history game based on lives of real people trying to survive ethnic cleansing and a political propaganda that is trying to inject morals in future marines to justify their assaults on nations far away from their homeland" (cited in Oliver 2004b). Also in this genre is *Special Force,* a first-person shooter published in 2003 by Hezbollah, which invites the player to take the part of an armed member of the Islamic resistance to the Israeli invasions of Lebanon.

The virtual war over the Middle East recently escalated. In 2006, in the midst of international crisis over Iran's alleged nuclear weapons program, Kuma Reality Games—whose news-based simulations we mentioned earlier—released a playable mission called "Assault on Iran," in which U.S. Special Forces destroy Iran's Natanz uranium-enrichment facility. In 2007 it was reported that the Iranian group Islamic Student Societies planned to develop its own game in which a Iranian Special Forces hero, one Commander Bahman, must rescue one of his country's top atomic scientists, who has been kidnapped by U.S. forces, and battle with those forces fiercely in the course of events (Halter 2006b). Claiming enthusiasm for the ludic "dialogue," and certainly keen for the potential profits from the well-publicized game battle, Kuma (2006) promptly announced its forthcoming "response to the Iranian gaming counter-attack," *Assault on Iran Part 3: Pay-Back in Iraq.* At the time of writing, both games remain "vaporware," so simulatory war proceeds at a fully phantasmagoric level.

So-called Islamogaming takes its place alongside the growing mastery of the virtual by Middle Eastern movements varying in political inflection but sharing in an antagonism to the United States, Israel, and the West. Examples range from the Palestinian "digital intifada" to the cybernetworks of al-Qaeda and the online videos of the Iraqi insurgency. This highlights one of the limitations of Hardt and Negri's perspective on the contemporary situation. The two-sided collision between Empire and multitude that they describe is enormously complicated by the fact that since 2001 the major opponent to capitalist modernity to emerge is fundamentalist jihad aiming to restore a medieval caliphate. To take account of this, the binary opposition of Empire and multitude must be rethought as a triangular fight whose third point is theocracy. On this, Retort is correct to take the antiwar movement to task for failing to adequately confront the rise of "revolutionary Islam" (2005, 132–69). We anticipate that the coming years will see more games rendering this third protagonist, theocracy, playable.[1]

Hardt and Negri's analysis of Empire retains its cogency on a central point: a global capitalism with "no outside" is unable to control the technologies that uphold its supremacy. The fears aroused by "weapons of mass destruction" and nuclear proliferation in Iran and elsewhere register a dawning awareness of this situation. The seizure of the digital by militant jihadis demonstrates the same dynamic. The powers that created *Full Spectrum Warrior* to train soldiers to fight shadowy, nameless, faceless opponents—"the Tangos"—in the dusty streets of strange cities confront a dreadful reality: the Tangos have got game.

Meanwhile, undiscouraged, the Pentagon intensifies yet further its links with virtual games: in 2007 it announced the formation of the Training and Doctrine Command's (TRADOC) Project Office for Gaming, or TPO Gaming, a branch of the National Simulation Center at Fort Leavenworth. Perhaps with an eye to avoiding future debacles such as the one with Pandemic, one of TPO's first projects was to create an army game kit enabling military personnel to build and customize their own training scenarios "without needing a contractor to do it for them." Says TPO's commanding officer: "We will empower that soldier to build his own scenario rapidly so he can train for his specified task" (Peck 2007).

Instances of the gamelike virtualization of war continue to proliferate. The best directors of remote-controlled armed aerial drones such as the Predator and Reaper now crucial to the U.S. war in Central Asia are apparently not air force pilots but hard-core videogamers, who, installed in trailers in Virginia or Nevada, controller in hand and monitoring multiple screens virtually, deliver actual attacks on villages in Afghanistan and Pakistan, occasionally logging off for meals and family time (see Singer 2009). For an even more futuristic example of how virtual games spawn in and out of imperial battlespace, we can, however, take the Defense Advanced Research Project's plans for a Deep Green supercomputer that will generate automatic combat plans for military field commanders. Deep Green—a khaki variation on the name of IBM's famous chess-playing computer Deep Blue—has several interlocking components: "Sketch to Plan" reads a commander's doodles, listens to his words, and then "accurately induces" a plan, "fill[ing] in missing details." "Sketch to Decide" allows a commander to "see the future" by producing a "comic strip" of possible options; "Blitzkrieg" quickly models alternatives; and "Crystal Ball" figures out which scenarios are most likely and which plans are optimal (DARPA 2007). Skeptics say Deep Green will never work; but even as a multi-million-dollar boondoggle, it will generate innumerable spin-offs for the game industry. If it succeeds, future wars in Iran, Nigeria, Venezuela, or Kazakhstan will be truly plug-and-play, separated only by a few orders of computing power from a commercial war game such as the recent Tom Clancy–scripted *EndWar,* in which players give voice commands to air and infantry units deployed in global combat theaters.

To do justice to the likely destination of such projects takes comic book writers such as Anthony Lappe and Dan Goldman (2007), who in their brilliant graphic novel about militarized regimes, *Shooting War,* envisage an Iraq war ongoing in 2011, where U.S. forces include the "Tenth Infantry Division Remote Battlefield Operations," running miniature tanks controlled by a roomful of cubicled adolescents on "PS4s." One has only to imagine the encounter between such forces and jihadis trained on their own game-derived simulators to see the war on terror for what it is—a death match between Empire and theocracy in which most of the planet's population loses.

5. Biopower Play:
World of Warcraft

We recently made two journeys.

The first was on the back of a flying gryphon. Taking off from the city of Ironforge, it took a course over the snowy trees and mountains of Dun Morogh, past the lava and fires of the Burning Steppes, into the green forests and orchards that surround the city of Stormwind, and on to the port of Booty Bay. Leaving behind labyrinthine conurbations of palaces, shops, and courtyards, we swooped out over undulating countryside where open heath gave way to gradually thickening woods, dotted with the occasional intriguing settlements. Moving into Stranglethorn Vale, with its tropical forest and turquoise water bordered by sandy shores, we continued our flight to the harbor, anticipating the hospitality of a travelers' inn as we watched unfold below us the expanding vistas of exploration and adventure that draw so many to the lands of Azeroth.

Our second journey was by bus, from Macao to Guangzhou. The modern highway traverses the Pearl River Delta, crossing numerous bridges over estuarine waterways. These once supported the mulberry tree orchards that made the area a world-historic center of silk manufacture. Today the orchards are gone; air pollution killed the silkworms. Rows of high-rise blocks march back from the road, housing for workers employed in the booming electronics assembly factories for which Guangdong province is now a global center. Even as a red sun sank into a twilight thickened with industrial effluents, these dormitories were unlit, a reminder of power shortages that regularly brown out urban areas. From the beggars outside the customs crossing at the start of our journey to its end near the partially razed animal market suspected as the source of a global SARS epidemic, the ecological and social stresses of headlong industrialization were everywhere apparent.

In this chapter, we trace the connection between these two journeys, the virtual one in Blizzard's massively multiplayer online game *World of Warcraft,* the actual one in the People's Republic of China.[1] The concept that links them is *biopower.*

Biopower and Accumulation

The concept of biopower is used by Michel Foucault to describe regimes that administer and discipline "life itself" (1990, 143). Such regimes, he says, emerged some three hundred years ago with the rise of the modern state. Previously, feudal sovereigns had based their power on coercive force, spectacular torture, and the threat of death. But beginning in the eighteenth century, an increasingly rationalized government apparatus emphasized its powers to organize and sustain social existence—"to *foster* life or *disallow* it" (138).

Foucault identifies two types of biopower. The first, a micro-biopower, involves an "anatomo-politics" of optimizing, extorting, and disciplining bodies, for example, by drill in barracks, labor in factories, or constraint in prisons (139). The second, a macro-biopower, is "situated and exercised at the level of life, the species, the race and the large-scale phenomena of population" (137). It focuses on "propagation, births and mortality, the level of health, life expectancy and longevity, with all the conditions that can cause these to vary" (139). The establishment of clinics and hospitals, the eugenic management of heredity, and official codifications of race and sexuality are all instances of a power "bent on generating forces, making them grow, and ordering them," one that "endeavors to administer, optimize, and multiply it [life], subjecting it to precise controls and comprehensive regulation" (136, 137).

Foucault broke sharply with classical Marxism's focus on the factory, but he emphasized that "bio-power was without question an indispensable element in the development of capitalism" (140–41). The era in which the rationalized administration of populations began was precisely that of capital's founding moment. As Foucault observes, "The exercise of biopower makes possible the adjustment of the accumulation of men to that of capital, the joining of the growth of human groups to the expansion of productive forces and the differential allocation of profit" (141).

His account of biopower can be synthesized with Marx's narrative of capitalism's founding moment of "primitive accumulation" (see Read 2003). It was at the origin of the modern era that the Enlightenment states of Europe laid the basis of the world market. The colonial conquests that created the transatlantic slave trade, transporting entire peoples from one continent to another, were an exercise in biopower. So too was the massive displacement of rural populations through the state-facilitated enclosure of the peasant common lands by early agribusinesses. So too was the disciplining of these displaced and vagrant populations as they were forced into new urban centers to become the wage-labor force for the first capitalist industries (see Linebaugh and Rediker 2000).

Twenty-first-century Empire is an apparatus that takes biopower to new extremes in the service of a now-global capitalism. Under neoliberal regimes, the "old" processes of primitive accumulation continue, but now on a planetary scale. The enclosure of rural collective lands by agribusinesses in Latin America, Africa, and Asia is an ongoing process, resulting in recurrent land wars between peasant communities and corporate developers with powerful state allies, and vast migrations of the dispossessed to the slums and shantytowns of new industrial metropolises (Midnight Notes 1992; Retort 2005).[2] But alongside such time-honored exercises of biopower also appear a whole range of fresh variants deploying the most advanced technologies to enclose new areas of previously common life. The commercial development of life sciences—biotechnologies, pharmaceuticals, and nanotechnologies—profitably reconstituting the basic corporeal and psychic aspects of human existence, facilitated by the state through university research and intellectual property laws, is just one example (see Rabinow and Rose 2003).[3]

Synthetic Worlds

Another instance of these "new enclosures" (Midnight Notes 1992) is the commercial appropriation of virtual worlds. Ever since Raymond Williams (1976, 70–73) pointed out the shared root of "commons" and "communications," enclosure has provided a potent concept for understanding expanding corporate power in media and on the Internet (Bettig 1997; Lessig 2004). As academic-hacker traditions of free and nonproprietary Internet use succumbed to dot-coms and e-commerce, many analysts spoke of an enclosure of the electronic frontier (Boyle 1996; Lindenschmidt 2004). We have described this seizing of emergent digital territory as not primitive accumulation but "futuristic accumulation" (Dyer-Witheford 2002).

Among the most striking sites of futuristic accumulation are MMOs. As we saw in chapter 1, MMOs were a transformation of an earlier culture of mainly noncommercial, text-based online play worlds. In the 1990s, free MUDs and MOOs were transmogrified into graphically lavish, technologically sophisticated, commercially profitable games such as *Ultima Online, EverQuest, Asheron's Call,* and *Dark Age of Camelot* (see Torill 2006). Today, as many as seventeen million regular participants from around the planet inhabit such "synthetic worlds" (Woodcock 2008; Castronova 2005a). With revenues from these games already estimated at around $2 billion and expected to triple by 2012 (O'Dea 2009; Thorsen 2007), market pundits prophesy they will be among the fastest-growing forms of twenty-first-century mass entertainment, a burgeoning site of what Julian Dibbell terms "ludocapitalism" (2006, 299).

There is a conceptual match between biopower and MMOs. In these virtual domains, corporations really do rule the world: game publishers are at once the creators, owners, and governors of such digital realms. Managing an MMO is an exercise in administering "life itself"—or at least a "second life." It requires recruiting player populations, regulating the spawn cycles of NPCs, terraforming digital landscapes, and shaping the "anatomo-politics" of bizarre creatures while keeping all under panoptic surveillance and disallowing, by account suspension, the life of insubordinate subjects. Such management is in fact a parallel exercise in virtual and actual biopower, proceeding simultaneously at two levels—that of the in-game digital world, with its enchanted territories, heroic characters, and fearsome monsters, and the real-life apparatus of shard servers, system administrators, and fee-paying subscribers. This doubled sovereignty, superimposing the supervision of digital and corporeal life, exemplifies the enlarged scope of twenty-first-century biopower.

There is, however, an additional aspect of biopower that is important in the context of MMOs. Foucault (or at least most of his interpreters) emphasized the top-down exercise of biopower by sovereign authority. But autonomist theorists such as Maurizio Lazzarato (2002) and Hardt and Negri (2000, 22–42; 2004, 93–97), in their characteristic search for resistance and alternative, say that biopower always rises from the bottom up.[4] Regimes of biopower, they say, can ultimately only mobilize and constrain the life activity of collective subjects. In this view, biopower is a *capacity* that rulers must try to control and direct. Hence there is the possibility of friction between biopower wielded from above and "biopolitical production" rising from below. There is a tension between the "constituted" power wielded by sovereign authority and the "constituent" self-organization of the subjects on whom sovereigns ultimately depend (Hardt and Negri 2004, 94; Negri 1999, 2–4).[5]

This ambiguity is evident in MMOs. While an MMO's initial programming—code manufactured and owned by a corporate publisher—sets the constituted parameters for virtual existence, it is the constitutive bottom-up behavior of player populations, the interaction of thousands of avatars, that gives this form content, animates its parameters, and sometimes pushes against its preset limits. Corporate publishers must stimulate player activity from below, for this is precisely what gives the game life, makes it interesting, and bestows the "persistence" or longevity vital to commercial success (Jakobsson and Taylor 2003). But publishers must also ensure that players' biopolitical production of game life does not transgress the limits of profit maximization, disciplining and interdicting all sorts of demands, desires, and infractions. These conflicts have been described in a variety of MMOs in a scholarly literature debating questions such as "whose game is it anyway?" (Taylor 2003) or "who rules the planes of power?" (Lastowka 2005). Here we want not only to analyze their manifestation in the most eminent of such games, *World of Warcraft,* but also to demonstrate how, in an intersection of primitive and futuristic accumulation, virtual biopolitics intertwine with the most titanic terrestrial transformation of contemporary capitalism.

Azeroth: The Art of Government

By the beginning of the new century, the commercial MMO was a well-established genre, with some forty such games in operation—85 percent of them *Dungeons and Dragons*–style role-playing games—and many more in development (Woodcock 2005). The center of gravity of the MMO industry had already shifted to Asia, where South Korean games were recruiting players in the millions. In North America, however, the leader of the pack was *EverQuest,* which with over 400,000 subscribers had made the transformation of suburbanites into mages, paladins, and night elves a popular cultural phenomenon. But in 2005 it was abruptly overtaken by a new contender, *World of Warcraft,* which within two months of its release had enlisted more players than *EverQuest* had accumulated in five years (*Edge* 2005).

World of Warcraft (WoW) is owned by Blizzard Entertainment, a company with a successful record in Internet gaming and fantasy games, and a subsidiary of the French media conglomerate Vivendi Universal until its sale in 2008 to U.S. video game giant Activision. *WoW* featured better, brighter graphic environments than *EverQuest,* with cartoonish animations that translated sword-and-sorcery arcana into a Disney-esque vernacular; it was a simpler and more combative game, but it remained firmly within the familiar conventions of MMOs. Its fantastic land of Azeroth hence provides a good example of how such virtual worlds can be seen as a site of biopower.

Biopower is about the control of populations, and nothing more clearly reveals MMOs as case studies in biopower than the prodigious population-measuring exercises they incite. For *WoW,* the most complete records are those amassed by Blizzard, which only selectively releases this proprietary information. The official census is, however, supplemented by several unofficial counts by game players, scholars, economists, and psychologists (see PlayOn 2007; Warcraft Realms 2007; Yee 2007). From these sources it is possible to compile a fairly detailed statistical portrait of *WoW*'s inhabitants. They show that Azeroth contains about 7.6 million characters created by players, as well as numerous nonplayer characters (NPCs), of which more than 4,000 different types are listed in Blizzard's database.[6]

Foucault said that "factors of segregation and social hierarchization" were crucial to the sovereign exercise of biopower (1990, 140); they "allow power to . . . subdivide the species it controls, into the subspecies known, precisely, as races" (2003, 255). In Azeroth, the player can choose from eleven different races (humans, night elves, dwarves, gnomes, draeni, orcs, tauren, forsaken, undead, trolls, and blood elves) and nine different character classes (druid, hunter, mage, paladin, priest, rogue, shaman, warlock, and warrior). To select an avatar to live as in Azeroth is to engage in a graphically vivid anatomo-politics of the body. While Blizzard firmly dictates the range of choices that players have over their appearance (a control that causes some discontent), various body parts—hair, skin color, eyes, sex, and facial features—can be changed by menu choices, although only during the initial character creation. The permutation of race and class determines what attributes—agility, intellect, spirit, stamina, and strength—

an avatar possesses, as well as where it starts its existence, what modes of transport it uses, what spells it commands, what weapons and armor it can use, and so on. Choices about a character's race and class do shape "the optimization of its capabilities, the extortion of its forces . . . its usefulness and its docility, its integration into systems of efficient and economic controls" (Foucault 1990, 139).

Indeed, the selection of race determines one's place in an overarching division between Azeroth's two factions, Alliance and Horde. Since these groupings cannot communicate with each other, dominate different territories, and are in a state of permanent hostilities, the choice fundamentally shapes the game experience (at one time, certain classes were barred to each of the two main factions, but Blizzard recently relaxed these regulations, a decision exemplifying the sovereign exercise of biopower). This conflict might seem to sabotage the idea of Azeroth as a kingdom subject to the biopower of a single sovereign authority. But in fact war is intrinsic to Foucault's theory of biopower, which, he says, depends on the "maintenance of war as a primal and basic state of affairs" (2003, 266); sovereign control of populations is facilitated by a "general process of war" (266), and in particular by the sustained hostilities between racial groups, "a war between races," which functions as a regulative instrument of power (239, 267). Azeroth's perpetual antagonism between Alliance and Horde corresponds to Foucault's suggestion that sovereign biopower depends on war: "It divides the entire social body, and it does so on a permanent basis; it puts all of us on one side or the other" (268).

Biopower, says Foucault, involves the governance of subjects,

> in their relations, their links, their imbrication with those things that are wealth, resources, means of subsistence, the territory with its specific qualities, climate, irrigation, fertility and so on . . . [and] in their relations to things that might be accidents and misfortunes such as famine, epidemics, death and so on. (2000, 208–9)

And Azeroth, comprising the two continents of Kalimdor and the Eastern Kingdoms, as well as the Outland, an off-world floating land formed from the shattered remains of the planet of Draenor, is indeed full of "wealth, resources, means of subsistence," a territory where the traveler will stumble on the food, equipment, and magical artifacts necessary for survival, as well as raw materials such as cloth, minerals, metals, and hides, which can be worked up through "tradeskilling" practices into all kinds of equipment and precious artifacts. It is also, however, a territory full of sources of "accidents and misfortunes," mostly in the form of "mobs" (mobile objects) ranging from rats and lizards to dragons and even more titanic monsters, which if killed will drop loot but also threaten "death and so on." There are also other hazards; for example, in 2005 a virtual epidemic was unleashed when "corrupted blood" from Hakkar, God of Blood, splashed on a raiding party in the newly created Zul'Gurub dungeon and was carried by a character's pet animal to a nearby city, creating a viral plague that reportedly killed numerous avatars (Ward 2005a). While opinion differs as to whether this event was accidental or planned by Blizzard, it illustrates the problems and the possibilities confronting a wielder of virtual biopower.

Characters ascend the ranks of Azeroth's society by going out into the wilds and slaying creatures, completing preset quests and tradeskilling. Increases in "experience" are registered through the MMO convention of "leveling up." Each character starts at level one; the highest level, denoting maximum fulfillment of pregiven race and class capacities, was for a long time sixty; the arbitrary addition of another ten levels, after the Burning Crusade expansion pack is, again, a classic instance of virtual biopower in action. The position of any member of the population of Azeroth (and, indeed, of most other MMOs) can approximately be charted on an imaginary three-dimensional grid, with two horizontal axes, marking the race and class combinations that make up a checkerboard of starting subject positions, and one vertical axis, recording ascent through the levels. There is, however, no final "winning" of the game, which can be played indefinitely, particularly as new quests, creatures, and continents are added.

This game structure appears rigid, linear, and mechanical—and, as we will see, the "grind" of leveling up is not only a favored topic for player grumbling but also an incentive to large-scale transgressions against WoW's official biopower regime. What complicates the game is, however, that as in most MMOs, access to certain elements of game content is only possible through cooperation with other characters, usually of different races and classes, whether in short-lived "pick-up groups" assembled on the fly, or larger and longer-lasting "Guilds."[7] The vertical and horizontal lines of the game grid are thus cut across by a transversal path of player cooperation and self-organization. It is this cooperative requirement that gives MMOs the social complexity that engrosses so many players, and hence the persistence necessary for their publishers' commercial success (see Jakobsson and Taylor 2003).

For MMO publishers, generating and managing player associations are part of the "art of government" that Foucault (2002, 209) saw as key to biopower. WoW is the corporate property of Blizzard; the end-user license agreement (EULA), the click-through contract to which every player must assent, is unequivocal on its near-universal prerogatives. In everyday gameplay, however, things are vaguer. Blizzard's governmental arm inside Azeroth is the Game Masters (GMs), who can be "petitioned" to fix technical bugs or discipline social misbehavior. It is, however, a well-known feature of MMOs that what Edward Castronova terms the "Customer Service State" is often remote and inefficient (2005a, 210). As Foucault suggests, ruling large populations over expanded territories requires an "ensemble" of "institutions, procedures, analysis and reflections" (2002, 209). Straightforward, top-down monarchic sovereignty has to be parlayed into a variety of institutions, multiplying and ramifying administrative power through a diffuse complex of governmentality.

Much of the practical governance of MMOs is provided by guilds. In WoW, guilds vary in size, from less than 10 to over 150. Some emphasize social activity, others player-versus-player battles, and others large-scale raids on monsters that can involve forty-member teams, last from two to eight hours, and be coordinated through VoIP systems and user interface mods that track the performance of team members (see Taylor 2006b, 329). Most WoW Guilds are short-lived, but some last years, developing elaborate social protocols, entrance requirements, probationary periods, and complex divisions of labor (Williams et al. 2006, 345). Guild-mates know each other, group together, and assist novices by teaching tactics, orienting them geographically, and bestowing gifts; they maintain codes of behavior, train players, and even administer rough justice. Famous guild exploits—or infamous ones, such as the attack by the guild Serenity Now on a rival group, CROM, as it gathered for an in-game funeral commemorating the real-life death of one of their members—go down in the history of WoW, building a body of lore and tradition that informs innumerable fan sites and boards and deepens the ambience of the game.

Good MMO governmentality requires that *constituted* publisher power manage *constitutive* player power. Guilds act as channels of communication between the corporate sovereigns and their subjects, airing grievances, providing sounding boards for opinion about game changes. Guilds or other collectivities sometimes vigorously contest publisher decisions about disciplining players, changing (or failing to change) rules, or other game policies. Though publishers may override such protests, they sometimes back down. For example, when a Blizzard Game Master threatened to ban a *WoW* player who publicized her Oz guild as gay, lesbian, bisexual, and transgender "friendly" for a breach of "terms of service" about sexual references, the decision was met by mass protests. Other gay-friendly guilds, Stonewall Champions and the Spreading Taint, organized in game protest. Blizzard apologized and sent its administrators to sensitivity training (Ward 2006).

Running an MMO thus requires careful governance. And to what end is this elaborate apparatus of biopower, with its administration of vast territories, management of complex populations, and elaborate negotiations devoted? Why, for "the adjustment of the accumulation of men to that of capital, the joining of the growth of human groups to the expansion of productive forces and the differential allocation of profit" (Foucault 1990, 141). For *WoW* is all about profit. Blizzard has played an important part in turning the fortunes of its parent company around from near bankruptcy in the late 1990s. In 2006 Vivendi declared the dramatic 25 percent increase in its profits was "primarily driven" by the success of *WoW* (Thorson 2006). Three years later, Vivendi chief executive Jean-Bernard Levy ascribed his company's relatively strong performance even in the midst of the financial meltdown to the fact that 70 percent of its revenues are generated by "phone, Internet, pay-TV and online video games subscriptions," which help shield the company from economic crisis (Reuters 2009). "We expect video games to continue to show a nice growth," Levy said, adding, "We started the year with 12 million subscribers for *World of Warcraft,* which is a good base" (cited in Reuters 2009). It is therefore no surprise that Blizzard's most energetic exercise of biopower in *WoW* is directed at preserving this profitability and that the fiercest struggles about control of the virtual world hinge on issues of accumulation. To understand the scope of these struggles, we need to step outside Azeroth's boundaries and look at a more terrestrial exercise of biopower.

China: The Planet Wobbles

WoW is not a highly original game, but it is a groundbreaking one—the first MMO to operate on a truly global scale. It achieved this status by bringing together the previously largely separate worlds of Western and Asian online play. Other MMOs—*Final Fantasy, Ragnarok*

Online, Lineage II—had taken steps in this direction. But *WoW* was the first to bridge the gulf on a mass scale. When by 2007 it claimed some eight million players, over 50 percent of the entire planetary MMO population, it was estimated that about two million were in North America, one and a half million in Europe—and nearly all the rest in China (Woodcock 2006). Two years later, after the release of the *Wrath of the Lich King* expansion, the number of subscribers had grown to 11.5 million, but the ratio of players' international distribution did not seem to have changed significantly (Caoili 2009).

The conditions of this triumph were set by the largest biopower experiment on earth; the shift from the revolutionary state socialism of Mao Tse-tung to the authoritarian state capitalism of Deng Xiaoping. The absorption of China into the apparatus of Empire, a process benchmarked by its entry into the World Trade Organization in 2000, had been under way since the 1980s. While Silicon Valley entrepreneurs were tinkering with virtual worlds, new leaders in Beijing were launching a massive project to introduce the planet's most populous nation to the world market. Directed by what Yuezhi Zhao calls "a power bloc of bureaucratic capitalists of a reformed Party state, transnational corporate capital, and an emerging urban middle class, whose members are the favored customers of both domestic and transnational capital" (cited in Schiller 2007, 188–89), this reimposition of capitalism on a collectivist economy has been described as a vast contemporary instance of primitive accumulation (Holmstrom and Smith 2000; Webber and Zhu 2005).

The astounding scale of this project is documented in the film *Manufactured Landscapes* (2007), featuring the photographs of Edward Burtynsky, whose images of China's city-block-sized factories, decapitated mountains, moonscapes of waste, and ancient neighborhoods overwhelmed by proliferating skyscrapers convey the gargantuan transformation more vividly than any analytic account. Nonetheless some of its elements can quickly be enumerated: the dismantling of communal agriculture, triggering huge migrations from rural areas to cities; the establishment, often on abandoned agricultural land, of new industries, such as the electronics assembly nexus in the Pearl River; megaprojects such as the Three Gorges hydroelectric dam, whose construction displaced between one and two million people and whose reservoir is so large that, as it is filled, the earth momentarily wobbles on its axis (*Manufactured Landscapes* 2007); and the formation of a whole new set of cultural norms, habits, and proclivities among a freshly minted urban consuming class. This is indeed an exercise of power "at the level of population as a whole," complete with panoptic surveillance and a disciplinary security apparatus to repress the many unrests it engenders.

In the field of media, this transformation displays the untidy intersection of five major vectors (see Schiller 2008; Zhao 2008). First, dating from the moment of post-Maoist opening to global capitalism in the late 1970s, is China's positioning of itself as the electronic "workshop for the world" through the labor-intensive production of televisions, computers, game consoles, and other communication devices in the booming southern coastal manufacturing areas of the Pearl River; this has involved both foreign direct investment by companies such as Apple, IBM, Dell, Hewlett-Packard, and Motorola and the emergence of Chinese manufacturers, often partnered with these foreign multinationals, but also competing with them. Second is the emergence of China as itself a major zone of media consumption, a process fast becoming apparent by 2000 and that by 2008 made it the largest market in the world, in terms of population, for cell phones, and the second biggest for Internet access and personal computers. Third is the eagerness by foreign media, from News Corporation to Google, to take advantage of this vast new opportunity for subscriptions and advertising audiences, an effort whipped into a frenzy by the approach of the 2008 Olympics. Fourth, and most recent, is the determined drive by Chinese companies, including Internet service providers Baidu and Tencent, telecommunications corporations such as China Netcom, and cell phone enterprises like China Mobile, to themselves claim a share of these media profits; acting with state support and mobilizing a nationalist or even anti-imperialist rhetoric against foreign ownership, they are, however, often actually involved in strategic partnerships with foreign enterprises. Fifth, ongoing throughout all the previous moments, is the attempt of the "party state" to maintain its political hegemony and control of media content as it propels the country into the capitalist world market (Zhao 2008). Internet gaming in China is implicated in every aspect of this tumultuous and contradictory mediascape.

Many of these factors influence the virtuality of WoW, but the obvious place to start unraveling their effect is through the growth of Internet use and online games in China. Over a relatively brief period, China has become probably the largest and certainly the fastest-growing nation of Internet users. Over 180 million Chinese use the

Internet, most from the new urban middle class (*Economist* 2009a). Of these, over one in four—some fifty-five million—play online (Ye 2009). Widespread piracy makes MMOs—which cannot easily be copied because content is player generated—almost the only commercially viable form of digital play in China, accounting for some 80 percent of a market worth between one and two billion dollars and projected to expand rapidly in the next few years (Jenkins 2007; Ye 2009). The majority of players are young, from nineteen to twenty-five, and many are high school and college students (Xinhua News Agency 2006). Conditions of play differ from those in North America. Most gamers do not own a computer and play from Internet cafés—something of a misnomer, since we can say from personal observation that while some Chinese Internet cafés are on a scale familiar to North Americans, others, often located in the seedier areas of cities to ensure low rent, are cavernous halls with hundreds of computers.

Chan (2006) situates China's MMO explosion within a wider "East Asian online games boom" that started in South Korea. In a classic case of crisis-driven innovation, Korean MMOs broke through into mass popularity during their country's IMF-induced economic meltdown in the late 1990s, when thousands of unemployed men whiled away hours playing games in cybercafés or "PC bangs." Publishers were vigorously supported by a government that viewed games and broadband Internet as components of a high-technology development strategy. Companies such as NCSoft, whose *Lineage* is still one of the most popular MMOs in the world, pioneered "Asian" themed games based on martial arts, traditional folktales, and military and imperial history.

It was South Korean entrepreneurs who carried Internet play into China at the start of the new century, with MMOs such as the *Legend of Mir 2*, whose invocation of a fantastic and romanticized Asian past was, Chan (2006) suggests, consonant with the repudiation of Maoist revolutionary culture by the Chinese state and urban middle class. The success of Korea's MMO makers then led the Chinese government to emulate their state-supported business model. In 2004 it invested US$242 million in the Chinese National Online Game Development Project to seed domestic development (Chan 2006; Feldman 2004a). While Chan says that South Korean publishers retain a "stranglehold" on the Chinese MMO market, other analysts suggest their share is dropping sharply in the face of state-supported domestic companies (Maragos 2005b). In 2006 there were about ninety online development companies in China, with a handful of leading enterprises such as Shanda, Zhengtu Network, NetEase, The9, Optisp, Kingsoft, SINA, and Sohu poised to be placed among the world's leading game companies.

While the Chinese state supports domestic developers, it is also suspicious about the social effects of MMOs. All aspects of Internet use are subject to the panoptic surveillance of "the Great Firewall of China." But online gaming has become a site of moral panics about addiction and corruption even more intensely than in the West (see Funk 2007). Following highly publicized cases of the deaths and suicides of MMO gamers after long bouts of playing, and of murders arising from disputes about online goods, the government, in an exemplary piece of regulatory biopower, initiated "fatigue" rules by which online players in cybercafés would experience diminishing returns after three hours and be cut off after five.[8] These regulations were, however, so widely circumvented that they now seem to be applied only to minors (Koo 2007a).

State agencies also attempt to proactively counteract suspect ideological influences in MMOs. The Chinese Communist Party's official newspaper, *People's Daily,* launched a casual games site. The China Communist Youth League partnered with the MMO publisher PowerNet Technology to develop *Anti-Japan War Online,* featuring the liberation struggles of 1937–45, to give young players "patriotic feeling when fighting invaders to safeguard their motherland" (D. Jenkins 2005). In 2005 one of China's largest online game companies announced it would develop *The Chinese Hero Registry,* featuring People's Liberation Army soldiers performing good deeds ranging from the darning of socks to assisting the elderly (Ni 2005).[9]

Most Western publishers were marginalized in China's MMO fever. Sony Online Entertainment tried to adapt *EverQuest II* by contracting a Taiwanese developer to design an optional set of "Orientalized" character types, but failed miserably to win a following. Blizzard, however, was already connected to the Asian scene. Its *Star Craft* science-fiction strategy game had become a cultural phenomenon in South Korea as the main attraction in televised multiplayer player tournaments whose competitors become pop-culture celebrities. Pirating of *Star Craft* and other Blizzard games gave the company widespread name recognition. But Blizzard did not attempt to directly operate *WoW* in China. It licensed the game to The9, a Shanghai company whose name affirms digital games as the "ninth art" following eight traditional Chinese arts such as painting, sculpture, and literature. The9 launched *WoW* in 2005, and despite a host of technical problems, it was a runaway success: by 2007 it accounted for 99 percent of The9's revenues (Koo 2007b). Its success was further accelerated by a TV promotion with Coca-Cola, which bent, and arguably broke, Chinese media regulation against advertising online games by attaching coupons for *WoW* cybercafé play to Coke cans and publicizing the giveaway in spots featuring Chinese pop stars and Olympic athletes (Koo 2006).

Millions of Chinese players have made *WoW* the unrivaled sovereign of MMO games. These gamers are not as profitable to Blizzard as their Western counterparts. Most do not subscribe in the Western sense of the word or buy the initial software package but rather purchase prepaid game cards for Internet café play at a rate calculated at 0.45 yuan (US$0.06) an hour. It is estimated that through its licensing deal with The9, Blizzard in 2006 received some $32 million from the Chinese *WoW* players, about one-seventh of the revenues that an equivalent number of American players would generate (Cole 2006). The mass entry of Chinese players into *WoW* epitomizes the paradoxes of Empire. That Western and Eastern players separated by thousands of miles share much the same virtual world demonstrates what Hardt and Negri (2000, 332) consider the "smooth space" of Empire, a cosmopolitan global order integrated through the world market. But Blizzard's differentiated marketing strategy, carefully adjusted to the disparity in incomes between Chinese and Western players, also demonstrates the stratified or "striated" nature of this global space, fractured by huge inequalities (Deleuze and Guattari 1987, 491–92). Azeroth, in fact, presents a classic site of what Trotsky (1962) called "uneven and combined development." Where the tensions arising from this are most apparent is in conflicts over "gold farming."

Gold: An Immense Accumulation

WoW shares with many other fantasy role-playing MMOs a paradoxical convention: the market economy. Insofar as Azeroth has an actual referent, it is presumably to the archaic societies on whose myths and legends it draws for its heroes, ogres, and dragons. In such premodern, precapitalist societies, resource allocations were organized around familial or feudal obligation, barter, and plunder. Markets and money, though not completely absent, occupied a minor role. Yet "neofeudal" MMOs tend to be dominated by market exchange (Stern 2002). Barter is possible and looting important, but virtual currencies—gold in *WoW*, platinum in *EverQuest*, adena in *Lineage*—are, by virtue of their convenient convertibility, at the core of economic activity, vital for acquiring goods, such as weapons, armor, or spells. The supremacy of this "play money" (Dibbell 2006) is, it should be emphasized, not something that affects only the venal or acquisitive player: it shapes the whole game ambience. For example, underequipped players cannot participate successfully in raids and other groupings or reciprocate favors or demonstrate generosity, so that even those who play mainly for the social aspects of the game are drawn into a web of market transactions. The wealth of Azeroth, its Nightstalker Daggers, Helms of Wrath, Earthstorm Diamonds, Ogremind Rings, Black War Steeds, and Moonglade Raimants, presents itself to the player as "an immense collection of commodities" (Marx 1867, 125).

In 2001 a U.S. economist, Edward Castronova, whose work we cited earlier, publicized what gamers had known for some time: currency—and armor, spells, property, even characters—in MMOs could be traded for *real-world* dollars. Dividing the value of *EverQuest* avatars' assets by the hours required to accumulate them, Castronova (2001) estimated that an average player "earned" $3.42 an hour, making the imaginary continent of Norrath the seventy-seventh-strongest national economy in the world, richer than Bulgaria. And this was not just a theoretical observation. Virtual trading—or RMT (real money trading)—seems to have begun with individual, ad hoc transactions on eBay and other online auctions. Soon, however, gamers playing for profit, known as "farmers," were systematically harvesting games for real cash resale.

A year after Castronova's essay, it was widely reported that a U.S. company, Black Snow Interactive, had hired and trained shifts of Mexican day laborers in Tijuana to farm *Ultima Online* and *Dark Age of Camelot*. Already in court over other shady Internet activities, Black Snow dissolved before the story could be verified or the legal implications tested (see Dibbell 2006, 10–32). But other transnationally organized, commercial game-farming enterprises soon followed. Operating out of Mexico, Hong Kong, and eastern Europe, though sometimes owned in the United States or western Europe, these companies used "low pay in poor countries to provide services for wealthy western players" (T. Thompson 2005). These services include the purchase of currency or of specific game items or, related to but distinct from RMT, "power leveling," by which a player pays a proxy to rapidly advance his or her avatar through the grind of gaining game experience.

The single most prominent company in this business is IGE. No hole-in-the-wall operation but an enterprise employing over four hundred people (sixty in its Hong Kong offices alone), IGE acts as an international RMT broker. Self-described as a maker of "secondary markets for the buying and selling of the virtual currencies and property used by players of multiplayer online games," IGE facilitates player selling of assets, conducts virtual auctions, and exchanges various game currencies, taking a commission on deals. IGE is central to a network of contractors that handle "delivery, supply, and sourcing" of virtual items and currency for a wide variety of MMOs, from *WoW* to *Final Fantasy, EverQuest 1* and *2,* and *Lineage* ("Eyewitness" 2005). A recent major study of global gold farming says that while the illicit nature of the practice makes its monetary value hard to estimate, it is probably worth about US$500 million a year, "though it could well be more than US$1bn," involves some 60,000 gold-farming firms worldwide, and employs between 400,000 and 500,000 people worldwide, though over 80 percent of them are in China (Heeks 2008, 10). This would make gold farming an industrial sector comparable in size to India's famous software outsourcing industry (BBC 2008b). Other estimates of the numbers involved are much higher (Ryan 2009).

While many MMO players admit to the occasional RMT, commercial farmers are widely disliked. Purchase of equipment and characters erodes the skill component of games and undermines community formation. The character you met last week may tomorrow belong to someone else; the level-seventy paladin on whom your raiding party is depending may be a rank novice who purchased his impressive standing. Moreover, farmers often occupy strategic sites in virtual worlds where they can, for example, kill the same respawning monster over and over again, repeatedly looting whatever treasures it drops. Such "camping" blocks other players, monopolizing the sources of loot, and is often maintained aggressively. In MMOs that include player versus player (PvP) options, farmers may "kill" those who intrude on their operations. Farming enterprises also increasingly use automated programs—"farmbots"—to scour game worlds, gathering gold or salable items without human monitoring, turning virtual communities into resource-extraction sites for acquisitive roving game golems.

The terms of use and EULAs for most MMOs make unauthorized sale of in-game properties illegal. But while many publishers attempt to repress farming, others tolerate or even encourage it. In 2005 Sony created a furor when it established its own Station Exchange to facilitate the sale of in-game items for cash on select servers in *EverQuest 2*, charging a listing fee and taking a cut on transactions. In its first year of operation, this generated $1.87 million in sales, with players paying as much as $2,000 for a character, and one seller earning over $37,000 from 351 auctions (Hefflinger 2007). The majority position among MMO publishers has, however, been to oppose virtual trading, especially large-scale commercial variants. Publishers have an interest in suppressing a practice that is widely unpopular and may cause players to abandon their game. By shortening the time that players take to grind through levels, RMT and power-leveling services may subtract from subscription revenues. Furthermore, the ill-defined legal status of virtual goods makes publishers reluctant to permit breaches of EULAs with uncertain future implications. Pressure from both publishers and players has led some game-related businesses to distance themselves from farming; game magazines have refused to advertise for IGE, and in 2007 eBay curtailed RMT auctions (Game Politics 2007).

Blizzard's terms of use for *WoW* expressly declare: "You may not exploit *World of Warcraft* for any commercial purpose," a point it then clarifies: "No one has the right to 'sell' Blizzard Entertainment's content, except Blizzard Entertainment!" "Accordingly," it continues, "you may not sell items for 'real' money or exchange items outside of *World of Warcraft*," a prohibition that includes performing power-leveling services to other users of *WoW* for real money. The warning concludes: "Blizzard is both able and willing to take action against players who violate these agreements by engaging in farming." To make good on this threat, Azeroth's owner has developed a regime of panoptic game surveillance, police enforcement, and "technologies of power"—a veritable "explosion of numerous and diverse techniques for achieving the subjugations of bodies and the control of populations" (Foucault 1990, 140).

In Azeroth, certain high-level goods, especially those found in dungeons, are coded as "bind on pick-up." This means that the item becomes instantly "soulbound" to the person who discovers it, and cannot be given, sold, or auctioned to other players, ensuring that gamers must work to get such treasures. The use of such "safeties" is, however, limited. A full set of measures to prevent farming would also kill the in-game economy that is an integral part of the *WoW* environment. Since farmers rely on the same systems to make money as players do—usually just in more extreme ways—eradicating farming could only be done by totally decommodifying the game.

At a more active level, Blizzard conducts regular disciplinary sweeps of *WoW*. Players are encouraged to report characters that they suspect are associated with, or played by, farmers. But *WoW* also automatically installs a spyware program, the Warden, on players' computers. The Warden searches for familiar signatures of cheating tools and looks at the contents of any windows open while *WoW* is running. In 2005 a software engineer, Greg Hoglund, disassembled the program and found it read hard-drive contents, e-mail, and Web-browsing patterns. When he publicized this information, the digital civil liberties organization Electronic Frontier Foundation characterized the Warden as a "massive invasion of privacy" (Ward 2005). Hoglund devised and distributed a countermeasure, "the Governor," which can be downloaded from the Internet to scour Blizzard's spyware from computers, but response to the Warden revelations from the *WoW* populace was muted.

Once Blizzard has detected infractions, it punishes them—mercilessly. On March 14, 2005, it closed over a thousand *WoW* accounts "of certain individuals who have been farming gold in order to sell it in exchange for real world currency" (Blizzard, cited in Jade 2005). It went on to delete over 89,000 player accounts between May and July 2006. Although Blizzard does not provide cumulative totals of accounts that have been banned for farming, it seems that well over 100,000 may have been deleted, a number greater than the entire population of many other MMOs. This is power to disallow virtual life—exerted on a large scale.

The battle extends beyond the game world. Blizzard fights farmbots (a subset of a wider policy prohibiting players from using third-party software for in-game advantages). When an avatar is reported or suspected of botting, a GM will contact it and ask a question to see if someone is actually playing the account. If there is no reply, the account will be banned. In response, farmers in many MMOs perfect communication systems to instantly alert them via cell phones or other devices when their bots are interrogated, so that they can reply on behalf of their automata (Dibbell 2006). Michael Donnelly, an American programmer, devised WoWGlider, code scripted to automatically perform quests and hunts in Azeroth, and sold access to it on the Internet for $25 per customer. In January 2006 he was visited at his home by a corporate officer and lawyer representing Vivendi and

Blizzard. Donnelly sued Vivendi and Blizzard for the alarm caused by the visit. In 2007 the corporations filed a countersuit seeking "monetary relief including damages sustained by Blizzard in an amount not yet determined" for

> loss of goodwill among WoW users, diversion of Blizzard resources to prevent access by WoW Glider users, loss of revenue from users leaving the WoW game as a result of the diminished game experience, loss of revenue from terminated WoW Glider users, and decreased subscription revenue from undetected WoW Glider users.

Maintaining sovereignty and sustaining the orderly accumulation of profit in Azeroth clearly require serious biopower.

Gold Farmers: Migrant Labor

It is around gold farming that China and Azeroth, Shanghai and Stormwind, Beijing and Booty Bay, are most dramatically superimposed. Among WoW players, the phrase "gold farmer" is often almost automatically rendered with an addition: "Chinese." While this is a racist epithet, stereotype and reality sometimes coincide; though gold farms and farmers are located all over the world, many, perhaps over 85 percent, operate out of China (Dibbell 2006; Lee 2005; Heeks 2008). In 2005 it was estimated there were about 100,000 people in China whose everyday work was farming MMOs; by 2009, some sources put the number as high as one million (Barboza 2005; Ryan 2009). China's gold farms developed alongside the South Korean origins of MMOs, from the Adena farming of the in-game currency of *Lineage* (see Steinkuehler 2004). *WoW*, however, presented an even stronger magnet for farmers, following the bipolar logic of a global Empire where "the greatest purchasing power resides in America while the lowest wages reside in China" (Steinkuehler 2006).

Several recent reports (Barboza 2005; Jin 2006; Paul 2005; Yee 2006) give a glimpse of an industry with its own management practices, labor process, and workplace problems.[10] China's gold farms are clustered in coastal Fujian and Zhejiang provinces, between Shanghai and Guangzhou, and also in the rust belt region of the northeast. Enterprises range in size from small shops to factory-like enterprises with hundreds of computers and employees. Companies purchase MMO accounts and, operating 24/7, rapidly advance avatars to their maximum levels so they can access the high-level, lucrative areas of the game. Employees work twelve-hour shifts, then hand off both the computer and the avatar they are playing to the next worker so that no time is wasted leveling more characters than necessary (Paul 2005). Some gold farms provide meals and dorms or perhaps just a sleeping pad beside the keyboard.

Players are assigned gold quotas to meet each shift; sometimes these are broken down and spread out over half or quarter shifts to ensure a steady pace of work. To meet their quotas, farmers complete quests with monetary rewards and kill creatures that drop currency or treasure. In most cases, goods such as weapons, armor, and clothing that are acquired are sold in-game, either to automated vendors or to other players, since currency—"gold"—is more easily negotiable. Within WoW, certain classes of characters, such as rogues and hunters, are better for farming than others because they can easily be "soloed," or played alone, without a group for support; rogues also have "stealth" ability to invisibly sneak past enemies and other players, avoiding interactions and battles that delay accumulation. Studies of the time various types of WoW characters are active show a high proportion of rogues and hunters being played around the clock, a sure sign they are operated by a gold farm, perhaps even running as bots.

Quotas are often difficult—some say virtually impossible—to meet, so employees fear losing their jobs and compete with each other. Relations between workers sharing a computer can be difficult, because shift changes raise issues as to whose quota loot from unfinished missions will be credited to (Paul 2005). Many farmers keep a clandestine cache of gold in case they run short of quota one day or perhaps to sell on the sly—"like stealing widgets from the factory to sell on the black market" (Paul 2005).

WoW is what is known as a "sharded" online game: its millions of players are divided up among a large number of servers, or shards, because no individual server could handle the full player base. Servers are organized by global region; North American players buy North American software intended to work with North American servers; Chinese players should only be able to access Chinese servers. To sell gold on the rich North American servers, it is therefore necessary for farms to have North American associates or to sell through brokers such as IGE (Paul 2005). But regional separation also brings certain advantages beyond the international wage differential on which gold farming hinges. In a handful of legal cases about the ownership of virtual goods, the Chinese judicial system has sided more strongly with players than have the American courts, supporting players' claims of personal rights against publishers' assertions of corporate owner-ship (see Steinkuehler 2006). There thus seems less legal threat to China-based companies buying and selling virtual goods than to their counterparts in North America.

Farming operations can be extremely lucrative; reports suggest some *WoW* gold sellers make tens of thousands of dollars a month. But most of the revenues from farming go to owners or RMT brokers (Huifeng 2005). Workers' wages seem to vary widely, with reports ranging from US$40 (300 yuan) to $200 (1,500 yuan) per month, though there are instances where farmers work only for accommodation (Huifeng 2005; Jin 2006). At the higher end of this scale, these wages are better than those of Chinese factory workers (Roberts 2006). Labor condi-tions are ambiguous. Some observers emphasize the long hours, lack of security, and repetitive nature of the work: "You try going back and forth clicking the same thing for 12 hours a day, six or seven days a week, then you will see if it's a game or not," says one gold farmer (cited in Huifeng 2005). Others say that workers take pride in game skill and prefer even a game "sweatshop" to the other available em-ployment (or unemployment) options.[11] Chan (2006) catches the ambi-guity when he writes of a workplace where "exploitation is entangled with empowerment and productivity is entangled with pleasure."

The gold-farming workforce seems to involve two main groups—college students and graduates, and rural immigrants to cities. The college students, familiar with computers, led the way in making money from MMOs: some now own or manage gold farms, which are increasingly employing a new workforce of rural migrants to cit-ies. These workers can be trained on-site in minimal farming skills and employed at extremely low wages. Barboza (2005) reports one operation in Chongquing owned by Luo Gang, "a 28-year-old college graduate who borrowed $25,000 from his father to start an Internet café" and now employs "23 workers making about $75 a month." Luo Gang says, "If they didn't work here . . . they'd probably be work-ing as waiters in hot pot restaurants, or go back to help their parents farm the land; or more likely, hang out on the streets with no jobs at all." Another owner, Wei Xiaoliang, the twenty-six-year-old proprie-tor of the Shenzhen Red Leaf technology company, which wholesales *WoW* gold to overseas brokers, says, "We prefer to hire young migrant workers rather than college students. The pay is not good for students, but it is quite attractive to the young migrants from the countryside" (cited in Huifeng 2005). He is "thinking of moving his company to Gansu or Shanxi provinces, where he could easily find scores of rural migrants to become 'farmers' at lower costs" (Huifeng 2005).

The migrant workers who are now recruited by gold farms are part of the largest mass migration in the whole of human history—that from China's countryside to its cities. This is the twenty-first-century version of the displacement of rural populations that was part of primitive accumulation in eighteenth-century England. By 2020, between three and five hundred million people will have shifted from countryside to city to provide the labor for Chinese capitalism (Xinhua News Agency 2003). As in the earlier case, the migration is not voluntary; if migrants are drawn to China's cities by the promise of factory wages, they are also driven by the destruction of the social guarantees that protected rural living standards ("breaking the iron rice bowl"). Many are victims of the compelled sale of farmlands to party-capitalist developers for middle-class housing, rural villas, and greenfield industrial sites. As many as seventy million farmers have lost their land in the past decade, a number expected to rise above one hundred million (Yardley 2004). Rural unrest that has to be repressed by military force is now a major internal security problem for the Chinese state; "authorities are confronted by continual outbreaks of disorder and dissent" (Schiller 2007, 198; see also BBC 2007c).

Here the intersection of Blizzard's digital biopower with the material biopower of Chinese capitalism snaps into sharp focus. When Blizzard polices the digital realm of Azeroth (a kingdom created from the commercial enclosure of cyberspace) for virtual gold farmers, the offenders it seeks are likely to be actual peasant farmers who have left or been thrown off their fields by Chinese capitalism's enclosures, abandoning an impoverished and ecologically devastated countryside for its cyber-connected cities. Some have probably been displaced by megaprojects such as the Three Gorges Dam, supplying the insatiable demand for electrical power, primarily for industry, but also for Internet servers, in China's eastern coastal cities. In an additional twist, the burgeoning growth of the Chinese electronics industry, both foreign and domestic owned, means that the computers used by WoW players all around the world are made by companies such as Dell, Compaq, HP, IBM, Acer, Wriston, and Lenova, whose factories (concentrated around Guangzhou) eat up China's agricultural land, dump their obsolescent products into the waste sites that riddle the landscape, and drive rural populations into the new urban centers. The lush lands of Azeroth arise on the ruins of the Pearl River delta; that Blizzard's parent company, Vivendi, was originally not a media conglomerate but a utilities enterprise that profited by outsourcing management of water supplies to China's new municipal complexes just gives a rococo flourish to this actual-virtual spiral (Vivendi 2002).

Gold farming's rural-to-urban migrants are also simultaneously a transnational migrant labor force. Nick Yee (2006b), an MMO demographer, recently suggested that farmers in Azeroth occupy a position similar to that of the Chinese laborers in nineteenth-century America who provided menial services in laundries and barbershops. By accumulating currency that can be purchased by wealthy players to speed progress through the game, or by leveling up avatars, they take on the grinding work of the *WoW* world. As immigrant laborers so often are, however, they are often repaid with rancorous hostility. When farmers are recognized (not only by patterns of play but also often by "the English test" of conversational skills), they are often subject to abuse and harassment from other players; asked how to evaluate how the "foreign players" he interacts with regard his activities, one farmer says, simply, "loathing." Noting that RMT and power leveling are at least as much problems of demand as supply, driven by North American players' desire to buy shortcuts to game success, Yee suggested this virulent distaste for farmers repeated a historically familiar pattern of Sinophobia and, more broadly, of Western racism against mobile, precarious foreign labor.

Yee's article provoked many replies to his well-known Daedalus Project Web site, most angrily repudiating the charge of racism by reasserting the illicit nature of farming and its deleterious effects on game play. A few recorded in-game conversations with gold farmers, in which, despite language barriers, they learned about the farmers' working conditions. One or two hoped Azeroth might become a place where North Americans gained a better understanding of disparities in life chances around the planet. But this was a minority response. By 2006 a host of postings and video clips on *WoW*-related Web sites suggested a wave of hatred against Chinese gold farmers (see "Catching the Gold Farmers" 2007; "Chinese Gold Farmers" 2006). Organized attacks by other players on gold farmers had already appeared in *Lineage* (Steinkuehler 2005). They are now common in Azeroth. One player wrote:

> After Timeless [a guild] was put together, we got a group of Timeless together in the form of Bowie, Sinnyin, Nobia, and Myself and we

went on the hunt. What were we hunting for? Chineese gold farmers of course! We would start our adventure in Azshara, going from
camp to camp repeatedly killing all of the gold farmers, Solbia,
Rotcherwind etc etc. After we had our fill with Azshara, we would
head on over to Felwood, going from satyr camp to Furbolg camp,
and anywhere in between and back picking up all the tubers / night-
dragons we could along the way. After pretty much clearing all of
Felwood, we would head up to Winterspring, and kill everyone we
saw at the lake, at the yetis, and hell, ganking anyone we could
INSIDE Everlook. That path we took was later dubbed the Ho Chi
Minh Trail. Another large part of the Chinese farmer farming was
in Tyr's Hand, With Me, Sinnyin, Nobia, and Wiggum, roof top
camping. Nobia dropping flares on the jump point to prevent nin-
jas, Sinnyin sniping people, and wiggums Mind Control disruption
with Thorium Grenades, wile I would jump down and assassinate
runners. (Marielo 2006)

Gold farmers, especially those in PvP environments, fight back. Some
commentators propose such interactions should be seen as a form of
additional game content. If so, it implants in *WoW* a low-intensity resource war with echoes of ethnic cleansing. Uncannily, the crusades of
Northern players against Chinese gold farmers reproduce the game's
basic trope of bipolar race conflict—Alliance versus Horde. The racialized features of the "evil" Horde have frequently been remarked
on (Castronova 2005b; Lastowka 2006). While these features allude
to a wide variety of peoples, from Jamaicans to North American First
Nations, the basic metaphor of the "horde" draws on the Western
fears of *Asiatic* hordes (see Allerfeldt 2003). If the virtual encounter
between American and Chinese players in *WoW* is a harbinger of actual relations between West and Eastern poles of Empire, it is hardly
an auspicious one.

Such developments bear heavily on the debate about Empire. As
David Harvey (2004) says, thinking not of Alliance and Horde but of
the United States and China, the world market, rather than deepening
the sort of unitary capitalist system described by Hardt and Negri,
"could dissolve into warring regional factions." The United States, as
Harvey explains, is multiply dependent on China, which provides U.S.-
based companies access to cheap labor, supplies affordable consumer
goods to the poorly paid U.S. working class, represents an emerging
market for U.S. goods, and funds much of the massive U.S. debt.

At the same time, the United States, with its declining manufacturing power and balance of trade and budgetary instability, is intensely anxious about the potential countervailing economic and geopolitical power of a "rising China." Speculation on conflict with China is rife in U.S. media—including video and computer play, where war games involving a triangular conflict between the United States, Islamic powers, and China have become a staple scenario in popular titles from *Command and Conquer: Generals* to *Battleground*. But *WoW* embodies the state of U.S.-China relations in a more complex mode, with the fraught relations between Chinese gold farmers and North American players encapsulating the current "bond . . . of reciprocal but tense dependency" (Harvey 2005a, 230) that links the two economies, while proceeding under the shadow of the Alliance-Horde trope that seems to foreshadow some massive racialized conflict between contending blocs of world capital.

Gold farming in *WoW* and, more broadly, real money trading throughout MMOs present a knot of political contradictions. MMO publishers manage an extraordinarily deep process of accumulation. Profits are not just a question of players' paying for software purchase and subscriptions. As players pay, they also in a sense work for the game owner—providing, through their ingenious interactions and collective construction, the content of the game world that sustains interest and attracts new players. As early as 2000, Tizania Terranova (2000), writing about the role of AOL chat room hosts and digital fan sites, identified the importance of "free labor" as a key element in commercial online culture. As Sal Humphreys (2004, 4) suggests, MMOs are an extension of this process, in which game capital benefits from the "immaterial, affective, collective production" of their population. This mobilization of free labor is risky, demanding high initial investment to lay the foundations of the virtual world. But as the success of Blizzard and other major MMO publishers shows, tapping into the collective creativity of millions of players can be highly profitable— one of the first successful commercial ventures in the "peer production" or "crowdsourcing" practices now so widely explored by the capitalists of Web 2.0.

Farming subverts this corporate control of player time. By turning MMOs into a revenue source for players, it challenges publishers' monopoly over the value-producing "playbor" (Kücklich 2005). In their study of the land enclosures of the eighteenth century, Peter Linebaugh and Marcus Rediker (2000) show that one response to the loss of the commons to business interests was an outbreak of poaching, highway robbery, and maritime piracy—a sort of diffuse criminal rebellion against primitive accumulation. Gold farming is a similar criminal revolt against the futuristic accumulation of digital capital, reappropriating the value-creating capacity that publishers privatize and fence around with intellectual property rights.

But such revolts are intensely ambiguous. Gold farming is not a revolutionary repudiation of ludocapitalism but itself a capitalist venture. Even in its transgression of EULAs and terms of use, it extends and deepens the commodification of the game and, in the eyes of many outraged gamers, destroys these worlds' playful qualities. The battle between publishers and farmers is a conflict between big, legal capital and small, illegal capital, a war of corporate business and criminal business. What further complicates the picture is that this war is fought across and within the global inequalities of the world market. The struggle is largely—though by no means exclusively—between the dominant North American and European sectors of game capital and emergent Chinese cyberbusiness. Gold-farming operations, moreover, like many black-market and criminal businesses, have their own deeply exploitative work disciplines: behind the hunter or rogue looting gold in Azeroth, there is a player who, while he or she reappropriates value from Blizzard, is her- or himself expropriated of that value by cyber-sweatshop operators and RMT brokers. This workforce, we have seen, is recruited from those dispossessed by the primitive accumulation proceeding around Guangzhou, Shanghai, and Beijing—a primitive accumulation that is itself, in a bizarre circularity, partly driven by China's new position as the global center of computer production and commercial Internet activity, including MMO play.

In 2009 The9 terminated its relationship with Blizzard, and the operation of WoW in China was assumed by another Chinese company, NetEase. The temporary closure of the servers during this transition was seen by many as marking the end of an era in Chinese MMO gaming, and a relative decline of the importance of WoW relative to domestically produced games such as The9's *Atlantica,* Shanda's *AION,* Kingsoft's *JX Online 3,* and Perfect World's *Zhu Xian Online* (Ye 2009). No one, however, expected any decline in virtual trading. The *Economist* (2009a) reported that at the start of 2009, "in the midst of a global capital shortage, the first company to list this year on New York's NASDAQ exchange not only needs no money; its source of profit is receiving cash for items that do not exist." Changyou, a spin-off from China's second-largest Internet portal, Sohu, was valued at about $820 million. Its business strategy was to provide free access to its games, "collecting revenue from the 10% or so of players who are prepared to pay for in-game extras such as weapons, medicine and shields." Although in 2009 the Chinese government imposed limits on virtual currency exchange, Chinese companies were embracing practices that gold farming had pioneered.

Alexander Galloway (2006b) has suggested that the mythopoeic universe of *WoW* can be seen as a nostalgic "utopia for the before," imagining life "*before* capitalism." This surely explains much of the promise of Blizzard's games and other "neomedieval" MMOs (Stern 2002). But it neglects the extreme betrayal of that promise in the actual unfolding of these digital universes. The controversy over gold farming displays the *dystopian* realities of social existence so saturated by commodification that it is impossible to escape even in play. *WoW*'s gold-farming crisis is a symptom of *hyper-subsumption*. "Subsumption" is a term used by Marx (1867) to describe the way capitalism gradually envelops the entire social environment, extending itself from the workplace into ever-expanding areas of culture, changing life habits, consumption practices, political practices, and interpersonal relations, creating what autonomists term "the social factory" (see Negri 1991; Vercellone 2007b) and making capitalism a fully Foucauldian regime of biopower. MMOs carry this process into virtual worlds. By recapitulating the accumulative structures of consumer capitalism within the archaic dream worlds of MMOs, game companies unleashed a profit-taking dynamic that exceeded their grasp. They let loose a viral, molecular microcommercialization that both destabilizes publisher control of game economies and threatens the communal ambience on which these games depend. Instead of the military-industrial complex, *WoW* gives us the Alliance-Horde gold-farming complex.

In a condition of extreme subsumption, even rebellion against capital and the struggle of poor against rich can often find expression only within the commodity form. They manifest in a distorted way as a battle between different forms of enterprises, corporate and criminal, and also between different types of exploited workers. The legitimate Western players whose "free labor" fills Blizzard's coffers revile the Chinese gold farmers for spoiling "their" game. What is precluded by these dynamics is any radical challenge to the commercial domination of virtual space. Such challenges, or at least some hint of them, can be found in a few other MMOs, as we will discuss later. But the degree to which gold farming and RMTs have become the central political issue in MMOs shows how powerfully games have been subsumed by capital. The emergence of virtual worlds entirely based on RMTs, such as *Second Life,* which we discussed in chapter 1, carries this process still further. Yet for the moment *WoW* remains a far more popular and globe-spanning game. And although the genres of MMOs are diversifying—it is now possible to join worlds of pirate adventure and intergalactic trade—the neomedieval role-playing fantasy remains dominant: if one wants to get away from things, where better than an imaginary of precapitalist folklore? How ironic, then, that these worlds become sites where primitive and futuristic accumulation now meet on a new frontier of profit. Indeed, while *WoW*'s universe appears to point back to a premodern world, its universe of altered humanoids and species hybrids, with its menu-driven character design, leveling up, and specialized bio-classes, seems also a parable for an emergent order of commodified posthuman self-modification, and the struggles between game companies and gold farmers over the circulation of beastlord avatars, shamanistic spells, and demonic weaponry a virtual rehearsal for a world where the choices for medical implants, longevity treatments, cosmetic improvements, sexual optimality, enhanced intellect, and means of mass destruction are contested only between legal or criminal markets. In the conclusion to his study of "synthetic worlds," Castronova (2005a, 274) expresses the conventional concern about MMOs—that such games will become so attractive that people will steadily abandon quotidian actuality to addictively sojourn in virtual fantasy. Perhaps so; but is this more disturbing than the converse possibility: that virtualities such as *WoW* will increasingly *coincide* with the actuality of Empire's biopolitical regime—a game of chimeras, populated by cyborgs, governed by capital?

6. Imperial City:
Grand Theft Auto

> We create an approximation, an abbreviation of a real city. . . . The game is about creating a reinterpretation of the U.S., a socially and visually distorted prism of the real thing. . . . Experience has taught everybody that it is better to make something that looks good, seems real, and carries a punchline.
>
> —*Dan Houser, cofounder, Rockstar Games (cited in Hill 2004)*

Metropolitan Punch Line

The city is a key site of Empire. If previous world-dominating imperial powers concentrated their authority and spoils in a single city-state, today the imperial order is articulated across an ensemble of "global cities"—New York, Paris, Tokyo, London—interacting with one another as nodes on a planetary network (Sassen 2001). The immaterial production that exemplifies Empire consolidates in, and fans out from, these strategic places. It is not surprising, then, that in recent writings Negri has come to stress the significance of the contemporary city as a terrain of conflicting possibilities. "The metropolis is above all a commons" (Negri 2005): "urban intensity" is "everyone's product . . . made of a great wealth of life styles, of collective means of communication and life reproduction," of "thousands of active singularities" (Negri 2002). If the political project of the multitude includes bringing into being alternative institutions, this must take place *somewhere:* "Nowadays, I believe that this place is the city" (Negri et al. 2007).

And yet the city is simultaneously what Negri calls a "biopolitical diagram": "the space in which the reproduction of organized life (social, political) in all its dimensions is controlled, captured, and exploited—this has to do with the circulation of money, police presence, the normalization of life forms, the exploitation of productivity, repression, the reining in of subjectivities" (Negri et al. 2007). The imperial city is, from this view, a vast territory of accumulation, whose sociospatial patterns reflect the "consolidation of global hierarchies" that accumulation both requires and generates (Negri 2002). Imperial cities are, then, places of "repression and blockage," with "the erection of walls to delimit zones the poor cannot access, the definition of spaces of ghettos where the desperate of the earth can accumulate." This is an arena where "zero tolerance has become the watchword," and where overt and subtle forms of "repressive zoning" sort the populace according to "skin color and race, or religious clothing, customs or class differences" (Negri 2002).

Negri's description draws on the insights of the radical urban analyst Mike Davis (1992, 1998, 2002), whose accounts of U.S. cities provide some of the most graphic portrayals of how modern capitalist urbanization combines gated communities, glittering towers of finance, and glamorous playgrounds of consumption *with* poverty, racialized segregation, gang activity, and militarized policing. We too take cues from Davis (1995), in particular his observation that the American metropolis compulsively "simulates or hallucinates itself." This simulation occurs, Davis says, in two ways. One is the "tourist bubbles" of the entertainment complex, epitomized in Disney versions of sanitized urbanity, re-created entirely as a consumer experience. The other simulation comes into being via "electronic culture and economy," with the city creating "its own virtual double through the complex architecture of its information and media networks." Davis is thinking of William Gibson's evocations of "three-dimensional computerized interfaces," with strangely beautiful, abstracted depictions of city territory that might "someday allow postmodern flâneurs to stroll through the luminous geometry of . . . urban cyberspace." Very soon after Davis wrote, "someday" had arrived: "cyberspatial flâneurs" (Simon 2006) were already drifting through the digital moonlit grid of great American conurbations. Not on a "stroll," however, but on a tire-screeching, music-pounding, car-thieving, drug-running, gun-slinging journey through one of the most sophisticated self-simulations of the imperial city—those in the video game franchise *Grand Theft Auto*.

From Moral Panic to the Ludodrome

Grand Theft Auto (GTA) offers an invitation to adopt the persona of an urban underworld denizen, jack whatever vehicle strikes your fancy, and begin completing a complex series of criminal assignments revolving largely around entrepreneurial thuggery, advancing to new missions as your villainous competencies, illicit social network, and financial wealth expand. When assassinating competitors, doing dirty jobs for corrupt cops and vicious mob bosses, and conducting business with a bazooka slung over your shoulder grows too cerebrally taxing (and it can), recharge with some freestyle urban exploration, maybe mugging a tourist in broad daylight, doing a drive-by in an inner-city neighborhood, or just cruising through the streetscape listening to talk-radio programs mocking the decadence of the virtual metropolis and the actual civilization you coinhabit.

Launched in the late 1990s, the *GTA* series is an offspring of the game industry's most determinedly deviant developer. Rockstar Games, with its parent company, Take-Two Interactive Software, has perfected a lucrative corporate strategy of making titles calculated to provoke moral panic: in the promotion of its highly publicized *Manhunt* game, for example, reviewers were sent "barbed-wire garrotes" (Kushner 2007a). While Rockstar is the producer of many titles, *GTA* is its flagship product, a title that carries the peculiar status of being probably the most celebrated *and* most vilified video game of all time. One reviewer says the franchise, which has sold over seventy million copies to date, has moved beyond "mere entertainment into something that can credibly . . . demand to be called art" (Manjoo 2008); savvy pop-culture defenders praise the series as "richly textured and thoroughly compelling . . . cultural satire disguised as fun" (Schiesel 2008b); and an appalled commentator advises that the morally repulsive inventors of this mature-rated game "should be stoned in the street" (cited in Au 2002b).

Controversy has focused on the game's violence. In the United States, Jack Thompson, (recently disbarred) lawyer and crusader against "murder simulators," had represented the prosecution in at least two (unsuccessful) multi-million-dollar civil cases against *GTA*'s developers, publishers, and retailers for inspiring "copycat crimes" (cited in Vitka and Chamberlain 2005). Less flamboyant, but more threatening to the game industry at large, is the array of political authorities that point to *GTA* as exemplary of the need for stringent regulation on the sale of violent video games. These range from Democratic senator Joseph Lieberman, who in 1998 singled out *GTA* in congressional hearings on the marketing of violent entertainment to children, calling it "graphic, gruesome, and grotesque" (cited in Hill 2002, 120), to California governor Arnold Schwarzenegger, who in 2005 signed a bill that would have retailers caught selling violent video games to minors fined—one of a spate of similar state-level initiatives, all of which have been annulled on First Amendment grounds.

Discussion about game violence generates frustratingly contradictory opinions. Recent research techniques such as the use of MRI scans to measure gamers' localized brain activity, increasingly sophisticated psychological studies that dispense with naive "blank-slate" assumptions about subjects, and meta-analyses synthesizing the results of previous studies do, however, permit some provisional conclusions (see Anderson 2004; Anderson and Bushman 2002; Sherry 2001). Playing violent games, research is suggesting, *does* make *some* people more aggressive—but only slightly so. Neither an uncontrollable incitement to homicide nor an utterly benign experience, playing violent games generates a marginal increase in aggressive affect, heavily moderated by the prior disposition of the subject toward anger (Giumetti and Markey 2007). In terms of *GTA* and the virtual-violence debate, players and game-industry organizations have not only festooned the controversial series with accolades and awards but also largely upheld its publishers' right to produce and sell games in which one can machine-gun a prostitute to death and finish off opponents with a chain-saw as a civil-liberties issue to be defended with self-righteous indignation. These defenses have often combined telling insights, pointing out that the incidence of violent crime in the United States has actually declined over the period when *GTA* swept the country, while remaining resolutely unwilling to consider *any* negative social-psychological effects of virtual murder as a staple of the modern media diet.[1]

What interests us about *GTA* here is not the game's inspiration to individual instances of criminal mayhem but the relation of its virtualities to the structural violence of Empire, that is, the systemic patterns of inequality and marginalization inherent to global capital, of which violence and crime are often only symptomatic. We will approach *GTA* not as a "murder simulator" but as an "urban simulator." There is general agreement that the great design achievement of the *GTA* franchise is its re-creation of major American metropolitan environments: its Liberty City is New York; its Vice City is Miami; its region of "San Andreas" contains versions of Los Angeles, Las Vegas, and San Francisco (see Bogost and Klainbaum 2006). *GTA* has been lauded as "one of the most sophisticated developments in commercial video gaming to render a highly traversable urban space" (Murray 2005, 91), and the latest addition to the series, *GTA IV* (2008), has been described as "a dark urban masterpiece" (Manjoo 2008).

On the basis of interviews with *GTA* gamers, Rowland Atkinson and Paul Willis (2007, 818) suggest that players of urban games become engaged in a subtle interplay between actual cityscapes and their media representations. Urban experience, they write, is "inflected by a range of interpretations, atmospheres, inherited viewpoints, dialogues and scenarios derived from . . . media." They found that *GTA* players, although of course aware of simulation, "slipped and segued viewpoints" in which the virtual and actual blur—an instance of how cities are "blended . . . with their portrayal." The result is that players inhabit what the authors term "the ludodrome," a "mediated space between immersion in urban simulation and a real world that is simultaneously generated, destabilized and blurred by . . . gameplay." Compared to the effects models typical of the game-violence debate, this analysis of the shuttle between virtual and actual is more subtle and comprehensive in that it addresses the relation of *GTA* to an entire urban environment. What is understated in Atkinson and Willis's discussion of the ludodrome is, however, the political nature of digitized cities—the way in which the virtual mapping of the metropolis in urban simulations such as *GTA* is informed by, and reinscribes, dominant relations of power.

This chapter investigates how *GTA* constitutes space in ways that are not just generically urban but characteristically imperial. This game franchise arises, we argue, from a specific moment in global capital's urbanization dynamic and, in turn, reinforces territorializations of class and race that typify Empire. We examine three rounds in this spiral of virtual and actual city making, using as our exhibits three titles in the *GTA* oeuvre. With *GTA: Vice City,* we look at how Miami is constructed as a virtual space exemplary of neoliberal urbanism, where market imperatives are literally the rules of the game. With *GTA: San Andreas,* we examine how the game's metropolitan configurations, particularly of Los Angeles, recapitulate the racialization of urban space. When we turn to *GTA IV,* set in a virtual double of New York, we observe how the production and profit of *GTA* shape the imperial cityscape, showing how Take-Two's participation in the

new media industry's remaking of its headquarters city "slips and segues" into the actual world of criminal capitalism the game depicts.
We conclude by considering the contradictory mix of insight into, and
complicity with, urban corruption that the *GTA* series represents, arguing that the punch line that Rockstar's virtual cities deliver is ultimately that of Empire's brutalism.

Vice City: Neoliberal Urbanism

It's 1986. You, Tommy Vercetti, are sitting in the back of a limou-
sine owned by property developer Avery Carrington, one of your first
business contacts in your new town. Carrington has hired you to help
him unlock a few opportunities on the city's hot property market. He
wants you to put some brass knuckles on the invisible hand and adjust
the going rate of real estate in a downtown neighborhood where he
wants to buy in. And, explains Carrington, "Nothing brings down real
estate prices quicker than a good old-fashioned gang war."[2] Your job
is to set it off by paying a surprise visit to a funeral for a Haitian gang
lord. Carrington, who is a white southerner, gets you, an Italian, to
"dress up like a Cuban"—the Haitians' rivals—head over to the funeral, chase down and kill a Haitian gangster, and bolt. "We'll just sit
back and watch the prices tumble," predicts Carrington, as the Cubans
and the Haitians go at each other. It earns you $2,500. Welcome to
Vice City.

Days earlier, you were freed from a fifteen-year prison sentence for
multiple murders. By background, you're Mafioso, and it will take
more than a stretch in maximum security to prompt a career change.
Your Family is awaiting your return, and even if you wanted a "real"
job, national unemployment is a lot higher than when you went inside: you don't see a viable alternative to recidivism. Your boss back
home in New York City, Sonny Forelli, has set up a job for you—a
cocaine deal—down south in Vice City. It promises to get you back
on your feet and to be the first step in establishing a drug cartel in
town for the Forelli Family. Trafficking has tended to be a no-fly zone
for other families, but Forelli reasons that moral virtue cannot allow
such profitable terrain to be occupied by competitors: "Vice City is
24-carat gold these days: the Colombians, the Mexicans, hell, even
those Cuban refugees are cutting themselves a piece of some nice action." At the moment, the bulk of your country's cocaine supply is
airlifted from the *fincas* of South America to the ports of Vice City.

But the transaction at the dock goes horribly wrong. Just when you and your men present the seller with the briefcases of cash for inspection, black-clad figures slink out from behind a stack of pallet boxes, shoot your colleagues and the seller dead, and steal both Forelli's money and the blow you were supposed to wholesale. By the skin of your floral print shirt, you dive through the rolled-down rear window of the getaway car and escape the ambush. Now you start to track your enemies to resolve this serious debt crisis with the Family. You begin your reconnaissance at a party on the yacht of Colonel Juan Garcia Cortez, a well-connected South American expat, who helped arrange your comeback coke deal. You are introduced to a motley crew of high-rolling venture capitalists and their political friends: Avery Carrington as well as a congressman, a film producer, "Mr. Coke" himself, and others. With these contacts, you will soon be woven tightly into Vice City's criminal tapestry. As your black book fills, as your hit-man skill is honed, and as your own private cast of cronies grows—"friends to help you create your own criminal empire" (Bogenn 2002, 5)—you'll ultimately forsake Forelli for a more independent entrepreneurial life of illicit profiteering, laundering your proceeds through a diverse portfolio of business properties, from a taxi fleet to a porn studio. Accumulate enough money, arms, and associates, and you will have a shot at territorial control over the criminal economy of Vice City, a virtual version of Miami during Ronald Reagan's presidency—a prime space and time of "neoliberal urbanism" (Brenner, Peck, and Theodore 2005).

Neoliberalism is a central concept in radical analysis of contemporary geopolitical power: Hardt and Negri (2000, 313) speak of the "neoliberal project of global capital"; Retort (2005, 14) of "military neoliberalism"; and David Harvey (2007, 2, 1) of "an emphatic turn towards neoliberalism" remaking "the world around us in a totally different image." The "neoliberal doctrine," Harvey explains, rests on a belief that "human well-being can best be advanced by liberating individual entrepreneurial freedoms and skills within an institutional framework characterized by strong private property rights, free markets, and free trade" (2007, 2). Often introduced by violent "shock" rather than electoral choice (Klein 2007), this doctrine consolidated politically in the 1980s through the governments of Margaret Thatcher and Reagan and institutions like the International Monetary Fund and the World Trade Organization. Familiar components of neoliberal policy include the privatization of state-owned industries, the reduction of social programs, the orientation of the state toward ensuring a "frictionless" business climate, the enhancement of trade and international capital mobility, the deregulation of industry, the lowering of corporate taxes, the assault on organized labor, and the elevation of entrepreneurialism to a higher ideal. Under neoliberalism, in other words, the imperatives of capitalism are almost completely unleashed—which ensures an extraordinarily volatile and, many argue, unsustainable socioeconomic order.

Critical geographers argue that the metropolis is an especially intense site of neoliberalism. What Neil Brenner and his coauthors (2005) call "neoliberal urbanism" is characterized by the evolution of the entrepreneurial city, with deindustrialization and budgetary cutbacks from national governments "forcing" cities to think more like businesses maximizing their competitiveness through revitalization initiatives, private-sector partnerships, and place-marketing strategies (see Harvey 2001). Cities are increasingly subsumed by the rule of capital, with business interests integrated into local policy and development, and the "creation of new spaces of elite/corporate consumption" (Brenner, Peck, and Theodore 2005). This is accompanied by deepening spatial segregation, marked by, on one side, "gated communities, urban enclaves and other 'purified' spaces of social reproduction" and, on the other, the marginalization of the urban poor. These "polarizing consequences" stoke fear of crime and a law-and-order agenda promoting "new strategies of social control, policing, and surveillance." "The overarching goal" of neoliberal urbanism "is to mobilize city space as an arena for both market-oriented economic growth and for elite consumption practices, while at the same time securing order and control among 'underclass' populations" (11). This dual goal reflects capitalism's "uneven geographical development," a contradictory dynamic that reveals itself within cities and across the planet as a whole in the accumulation of wealth in one area as poverty flourishes in another (see Harvey 2001, 2007).

One of the cities that exemplified these neoliberal dynamics and their wider geopolitical context in their early form is Miami, the urban actuality that *Vice City* references (see Beverley and Houston 1996; Portes and Stepick 1993). A longtime tourist hot spot, oceanfront Miami was undergoing an explosive growth phase in the 1980s that coincided with both rightward political shifts in the United States and neoliberal offensives in Latin America and the Caribbean. Miami was transformed by "land-rush economics," Latino and Haitian immigration, the globalization of the world economy, and the ascendance of financial capital (Beverley and Houston 1996, 32). The "Miami growth machine" (Nijman 1997, 165) generated social polarization, however, and visibly broke with the twentieth-century American narrative of "immigrant social mobility" (Beverley and Houston 1996, 24). With a primarily service-oriented economy, a low level of unionization, and a plentiful reserve army of migrant labor, Miami was described as an expanding "low-wage desert," albeit at the edge of glittering waters that promised escape (32). In the 1980s growth period, some immigrant groups, such as Haitians, lost badly, while others, such as (some) anti-Castro Cubans—"the most consistently right-wing ethnic voting bloc in the United States" (22)—and the henchpeople of exiled Latin American dictators preparing for return as the beneficiaries of U.S. counterrevolutionary wars, celebrated their winnings with an orgy of conspicuous consumption.

The drugs that brought Vercetti to Vice City had a big place in this urban growth machine. When he arrives at "Escobar International Airport," the game riffs on Pablo Escobar, then head of the Colombian Medellin Cartel, the world's largest cocaine smuggling operation, whose production chain linked Miami directly to a Latin American rural peasant class that ramped up coca production as they struggled to survive the consequences of neoliberal economic policies enforced by the institutions of Empire. On the U.S. side, the imported powder cocaine was culturally articulated to the 1980s as marijuana was to the 1960s. But whereas the sixties were about dropping out and slowing down, the eighties were about getting in and speeding up, and international trade in this expensive drug was driven from the demand side by the affluent Americans who benefited from Reaganomics. Despite all the Republican rhetoric of, and spending on, the "war on drugs," cocaine was early neoliberalism's ideal narcotic, not only because it provided an ideological cover for increasing class inequality but also because it boosted human energy for the accelerating pace of work and consumption.

Released in North America in 2002, at the very time when, after the punctuation of Clintonism, Republican right-wingers were once again in power with George W. Bush, Vice City's setting revisited a place and a time formative of neoliberalism. Although its portrait of Miami is mediated by numerous other representations (the television show Miami Vice, films such as Scarface), Vice City is a ludic homage to the moment of national and international victory for global capital in the closing decades of the twentieth century. One of the more telling examples of this is the game mission "Riot," where the action begins with the instruction "Let's crack some commie skulls." Your first task—throw some punches at (or just drive your car though) some striking workers, which instantaneously pits them against each other in distracting fisticuffs—alludes to the aggressive war against labor waged by Reagan in the 1980s. Not only does this signal the final phases of the Cold War, but the workers your action will lay off, and the land grab it is supposed to facilitate for a real-estate developer, also indicate the class inequalities being inscribed into the Miami of that era, a city with a level of unemployment and income inequality that exceeds the U.S. norm (Beverley and Houston 1996, 29). The streets of Vice City are fairly quiet, save for tourists and vagabonds, an echo of a Miami, where "in many parts of the city, unemployed and underemployed young adults, adults, and senior citizens idle away endless torrid days with few ameliorating amenities" (26). Given this historical connection, it is hardly surprising that *Vice City*'s lead, Tommy Vercetti, is neoliberal theory incarnate: if the most famous line of the eighties film *Wall Street* is Gordon Gekko's "greed is good," then the equivalent for *Vice City*'s eighties parody is Tommy Vercetti's statement "I work *for* money."

The terrain across which Vercetti operates is that of a city shaped by money—a Miami in which an idyllic semitropical environment is reworked by speculative capital, public disinvestment, growing spaces of consumption, and the unequal distribution of wealth. Sectioned off into multiple distinctly named territories, Vice City's cityspace spans the opulent Leaf Links, an island golf and country club for the city's affluent, with metal detectors at the entrance for their enhanced security, and, at the other extreme, Little Haiti, a run-down neighborhood where you'll find wooden shacks, including one inhabited by a Haitian gangsta matriarch, Auntie Poulet, and numerous dubious, and dangerous, businesses. But the aim of Vercetti's journey through this uneven socioeconomic landscape is to occupy it, activate it, and network it into a setting for optimal capital accumulation. Presenting players with missions carrying injunctions like "Kill the competition," and orbiting around "unlocking" accumulation opportunities, *Vice City* puts market imperatives and their rewards into playable form.

In a discussion of *Vice City*, McKenzie Wark argues that although the game's rules "call for a vast accumulation of cash, cars and cronies, of weapons and real estate," this content is irrelevant: "the story and the art are arbitrary, mere decoration," "just a means to discover an algorithm" (2007, para. 120). "Vast accumulation" is, however, precisely the point on which the game's narrative and the algorithm intermesh perfectly: the play logic *and* the plot line of *Vice City* are thoroughly neoliberal. Necessitated by Vercetti's personal debt situation, the motive to accumulate sets in early, with money acting as the reward for completed missions and a key to gaining advantages, like more safe spots, in the game. To truly advance through the game, Vercetti must own revenue-generating property, or "assets"; with enough petty-crime cash built up, he can acquire commercial operations like InterGlobal Studio and Malibu Club, which generate thousands of dollars per day and are, coincidently, in exactly the sectors that Empire expands: service work. Assets generate an ongoing stream of reward, wealth—a feature that, as one *GTA* player describes, "makes your money more useful" (GTA Place 2008). Possession unlocks new commercial possibilities for you in Vice City. This is a world where access to, mobility in, and knowledge of urban territory are complexly tied to accumulation's advance: how much city there is for you as player depends on how much money you have. But what makes *Vice City* properly neoliberal is that, as your financial tally rises, there is not a hint of labor, just the abstracted, increasing magnitude of accumulated capital.

There are other aspects to this embedding of free-enterprise axioms. Paul Barrett (2006), in a study of how neoliberalism suffuses *GTA*, calls attention to the respective roles of market and state in its ludic universe.[3] Within *GTA*, he says, "the state has absolutely no presence aside from a carceral role," and "other than the police, the military, the ATF and other similarly violent, disciplinary organizations . . . is completely vacant from the game." In the main action, there is, as Barrett says, nothing "remotely resembling a democratic, public state . . . no government representatives and no larger social institutions through which to pursue any sort of assistance" (104–5).[4] Vercetti is, in keeping with neoliberalism's preference, a self-reliant economic subject, and the city, the setting of dense commercial networks, formal and informal, is the optimum place to perform that self-reliance. In contrast to the diminished state presence, the market reigns supreme in Vice City: "not only does the player earn money for completing tasks, but there are a wide range of shops and malls in which the player can spend that money" (105). *GTA* is a ludic fulfillment of "the neoliberal dream in which the market becomes the apparatus around which all institutions are organized."

Vice City constructs a virtual town in which urban space is defined first and foremost as a venue of profit extraction, networking is the path to commercial success, and consumption is the dominant reward system. There is, simply, no countervailing logic. As Barrett observes, *GTA* "does an excellent job of representing a 'pure' neoliberal order, as any form of collective social responsibility is subordinate to the profit motive and market law" (105). So, paradoxically, *Vice City* may depict a deviant criminal subculture, but the game *works* through the habitual logic of the dominant order. Here we return to Tommy Vercetti's roots. The historian Eric Hobsbawm (1998), in a comment on North American audiences' fascination with *The Godfather*, on which *Vice City* liberally draws, says the Mafia's "business is business" mantra perfectly embodies the ideological logic of American capitalism: this slogan is a tagline not only of virtual Vice City but also of the neoliberal urbanism it celebrates. Yet the sociospatial polarizations that neoliberal urbanization exacerbates can be, as we shall see next, explosive.

San Andreas: Racialized Space

Every day I wonder just how I'll die / Only thing I know is how to survive. "The Ghetto" by rapper Too $hort is playing on the stereo while you drive to pick up your brother Sweet from a downtown Los Santos jail. The track's message hits home after the mayhem of recent weeks: your mother was sprayed in a drive-by shooting; your retaliation provoked a bloody gang war; the head of community policing blackmailed you into killing a whistle-blower on the force; you've been betrayed by your best friends from the hood, who, in cahoots with the gang who killed your mom, are now dealing crack, the drug devastating the city you grew up in; and you've been tossed in and out of jail so many times you've stopped counting. But you're building up a well-stocked bank account now, and you've got a nice house, too. "Don't forget where you came from, Mr. Uppity Ass Niger," demands Sweet, telling you that your old neighborhood has fallen under the control of your longtime rivals, the Ballas. Your standby shooter, the Kalashnikov, will be your one sure ally in the impending turf war. *There's only one rule in the real world / And that's to take care of you, only you and yours.* That you're still breathing is proof of that care, and your self-taught street smarts: marksmanship, regular exercise, business acumen, time management, staying clean, and, of course, carjacking. *Never be ashamed of what you are.* You are Carl Johnson, CJ, son of the black neighborhood of Grove Street in Los Santos, and protagonist in *GTA: San Andreas*.

One of the urban actualities *San Andreas* references is that of Los Angeles in the early 1990s. Then, some sixty black, Latino, and Asian gangs, including the Crips and Bloods, turned areas of the city into free-fire zones for crack dealers and street gangs to settle their scores, while a corrupt, militarized police force waged low-intensity urban warfare against people of color, and comprehensive surveillance systems, private security forces, and architectural fortifications of corporate zones and affluent neighborhoods spawned an "ecology of fear" (Davis 2002, 378). While inhabitants endured discrimination, economic misery, and daily fear, L.A.'s neighborhoods came to occupy an exceptional role in the social imaginary of Empire, not only via films such as *Colors* and *Boyz N the Hood* but, more lastingly, through the rap and hip-hop cultures that emerged from—and fed back into— these zones and spread outward into a massive commercial youth-culture complex.

Into this mix Rockstar inserted itself. *GTA* had always been about the violent interaction of identity, territory, and criminal commerce. Early games in the series introduced the Colombian Cartel, the Leone Family Mafia, the Jamaican Uptown Yardies, and the Japanese Yakuza, and *Vice City* added Cuban and Haitian gangs. But *San Andreas* was Rockstar's most provocative exploration of racialized subjects. CJ's African American identity was seen as a radical step in a game culture where every genre, apart from sports titles, had been overwhelmingly white (Leonard 2006, 84). Breaking this code, Rockstar constructed an alliance between two transgressive cultures—rap and games. As Rodrigo Bascuñán and Christian Pearce (2007, 189) note, with the success of *San Andreas*, urban crime games "featuring black or Latin American characters" became "part of the hip-hop experience." *San Andreas* would quickly be followed by clones, some featuring rappers themselves as protagonists, like *50 Cent: Bulletproof,* and others with rap soundtracks, like that by D12 for *Crime Life: Gang Wars*—all games where "big guns . . . dominate" and whose storylines more or less follow a formula of "former bad guy, faced with a dilemma, decides to do the right thing—while employing all his old tricks" (191). This template had been set by the saga of CJ, an urban gangster trying his best to get clean, who evidently has no other option but to end up brutalizing countless enemies and amassing extreme illicit wealth as means to the end of justice.

Opinion on the cultural politics of Rockstar's gambit split sharply. On one side, *San Andreas* was praised as a game showing it possible for a "black male protagonist to have mass appeal" (Murray 2005, 97). It was suggested that allowing white players to virtually occupy the shoes of the United States' most feared racialized other was educative. The game was, however, also criticized for reinforcing "hyperviolent and superpredator black male stereotypes" (Everett and Watkins 2008, 154). CJ is defined by his criminality, his violence, and his physique (mission success, for example, requires a fitness regime of gym workouts, a diet, and dates), making him another idealized black male who is "physical, typically sexualized, and rooted strictly in the body" (Barrett 2006, 98). Lives in *San Andreas* are, moreover, "marked as disposable and dangerous," with the black male "as both target and source of violence and terror" (98–99). Far from being an instructive ethical experience of marginalization, adopting the subject position of CJ was critiqued as "digital minstrelsy" (Everett and Watkins 2008, 148; Leonard 2004) or "racial 'slumming'" (Barrett 2006, 100) in which black identities and aesthetics could be tried on virtually without historical understanding or political solidarity. As Paul Gilroy writes in a discussion of the commercial opportunism that accompanies liberal multiculturalism, "the culture industry is prepared to make substantial investments in blackness provided that it yields a user-friendly, house-trained, and marketable 'reading'" (2000, 242). In *San Andreas,* as Tanner Higgin observes, everywhere people "perform roles according to popular myth. . . . Asians are suit-wearing triads, Italians are mobsters, and the people in the backwoods of San Andreas are skinny, slack jawed yokels"; so while the game is "certainly multifarious," it is also "homogenized," not only by each group's uniform "involvement in crime and violence" but by "staunch adherence to stereotype" (2006, 77–78).

This stereotyping extends beyond CJ to the urban space he inhabits. His hometown, Los Santos, is a place of ghettos where danger is ubiquitous. CJ's homecoming to Grove Street at the beginning of the game is synonymous with a return to violence: drive-by shootings are (if you're inclined) regular occurrences, baseheads wander the sidewalks, and gang wars are fought in public parks. The inhabitants, technically almost universally potentially dispensable, come across as helpless, doomed, or drawn to violence as if by nature. Critics therefore claim that *San Andreas*'s "ghettocentric" vision of black districts "defined by criminality, dysfunctionality and cultural chaos" confirms the discourses of a "new racism" (Leonard 2006, 64, 65). *GTA*'s urban grid of commercial opportunities is racialized territory: in the city that CJ moves through, the zones of safety and danger, the secure areas where friends can be found, loot stashed, and assets mustered, and those that must be bypassed, sped through, or entered only with serious force are coded by race. And although *GTA* presents a virtual multicultural metropolis that inscribes, to a much greater degree than almost any other video game, the multitudinous variegation of urban life, the layers of immigrant community, and the ethnic complexity of the contemporary United States, it is defined by violence and savage turf wars. It is a melting pot on the boil. By building segregation into its urban sandbox, *GTA* puts into play a dimension of actual imperial cityscapes, where spaces of wealth and poverty, privilege and dispossession, are inscribed along the lines of neoapartheids.

Discussing urban games in general and *GTA* specifically, Anna Everett and S. Craig Watkins term these virtualities "racialized pedagogical zones," "powerful learning environments" in which young gamers "understand, perform, and reproduce race and ethnicity" (2008, 142). The games' richly textured graphic and audio environments are "racially coded as black and brown spaces" not just "portraying" but inviting players to participate in a performance of race, mobilizing a whole set of assumptions about race. *GTA* configures its virtual urbanism around a "problematic" of race, setting a ludic agenda that, while it elicits a variety of responses, persistently addresses players in terms of ethnic identities. The array of stereotypes through which *GTA* communicates creates a virtual world in which racialized identities and ethnicized cartographies appear immutable, essentialized, and beyond transformation, hard-coded into the very streets of urban life.

How this racial problematic defines *San Andreas*'s vision of urban possibility is demonstrated in the last strand of game missions, called, simply, "Riots." You have by now, after hundreds of hours of running and gunning as CJ, assembled a set of allies that actually cut across the ethnic turfs that otherwise define this game world: your brother, Sweet; Cesar, your sister's Latino boyfriend; Catalina, the Chicana gangsta; and The Truth, a burned-out hippie. Your ragtag crew is at your mansion— acquired thanks to a side interest in the rap business—arrayed around the television. A newscaster reports live on a high-profile court case involving Frank Tenpenny, the crooked Los Santos Police Department cop who has been blackmailing you for years. But despite a litany of charges, from racketeering to narcotics, he has been exonerated due to the sudden death of a key witness (a mystery you may know how to solve). "That ain't no justice," Sweet shouts. "We all being used," you add. Suddenly noise surges from the street. Cesar glances outside: "The whole city's going up!" Disgust at the corruption and oppression is exploding into full-blown urban insurgence. You fly over to Grove Street to protect it from rioters. Sweet is sympathetic with the looters: "I guess it's better than staying home and watching the shopping channel." You take in the urban sensorium: helicopters are circling the city, sirens blaring, smoke billowing, voices screaming, bodies running. "Look around you, CJ," says Cesar, "the whole city is a war zone."

From your point of view, there's an unfinished task that will help get to the root of these problems—take out your former pal, Big Smoke, whose drug trade is destroying Grove Street. "Welcome to the Jungle" by Guns N' Roses plays on the car radio as you head toward Smoke's fortified crack palace. To break through, you jack a SWAT tank—brought to the streets by the state to restrain the looters—and plow in to perform some people's justice. Smoke is in the penthouse level on the couch, bong at his side, playing, of all things, a video game. After a battle in near darkness, he goes down, declaring that what drove him to cocaine imperium was the desire to leave a legacy before a certain young death in the hood. There's little time to reflect on this: where there's drug money, there's Tenpenny, so you're not surprised when he shows up to grab a suitcase of cash and make a run for it. "Half the city's looking for cops to kill, Carl. And I ain't about to get dragged out of a patrol car and get beat to death," says Tenpenny. After a harrowing street pursuit, you run him off a Los Santos road and watch him bleed to death on the pavement. Looking on, The Truth lauds you for achieving what he in his time failed to do: "Far out, man. You know, I mean, you beat the system!"

This cinematic finish references a real urban insurgency, the 1992 L.A. riots, three days of cross-racial uprising that followed the videotaped beating of Rodney King by white LAPD officers, resulting in forty-four dead, two thousand wounded, and one billion dollars worth of burning and looting (see Soja 2000, 373). How *GTA* rehearses, revises, and recuperates these events tells us a lot about its ludic logic. As Davis's studies of Los Angeles (1990, 1998, 2002) make clear, the social topography of the 1992 riots was primed by the long-standing racial prejudice of a white police force and political establishment—and neoliberalization. The tinderbox was prepared by the loss of Californian centers of working-class employment and public-sector jobs to global outsourcing and deindustrialization; by the Reagan-Bush cutbacks to welfare and social services; by affluent middle-class flight from L.A.'s center to the suburbs and then onward to various "edge cities"; and by new waves of transnational migrations, particularly from Central America, driven by counterrevolutionary wars south of the border. The riots were a manifestation of the grievances of intersecting class and race.

In the *GTA* version, the riots are not lit by white police violence: Tenpenny is African American. The game sidesteps the specific white racism of the Rodney King event for a universal cynicism: black cops can be corrupt, too. Even more telling is what defines CJ's alleged defeat of "the system." He overthrows a crack dealer from his own black community with a cross-ethnic and mixed-gender coalition of criminal capitalists. Far from suggesting that ending urban collapse requires repudiation of neoliberal policies, the game's one semiutopian moment is the product of a path of hybridized free enterprise. The game's conclusion obliquely references the extraordinary moment after the L.A. riots when the Crips and Bloods, in a truce, announced a reconstruction plan under the title "Give Us the Hammer and the Nails: We Will Rebuild the City," which demanded a massive influx of public funds for community facilities, parks, clinics, and affordable housing. Though the Blood-Crips proposal was ignored by authorities, the story of postriot L.A. discloses a series of social struggles by community and labor organizations, such as Justice for Janitors and the Los Angeles Alliance for a New Economy—slogan, "No Justice, No Growth"—to shape city development away from uncontrolled marketization in the direction of what Edward Soja (2000, 407–15) terms "democracy and spatial justice." These are the attempts to beat the system that have little to do with gangster glamour; and they are struggles that are, in terms of *GTA*'s virtual cartography, completely off the map. Because the game's array of fixed, essentialized, stereotypical racial identities obscures the social processes and histories that have positioned and defined various racialized groups within Empire, it cannot play out options that might really challenge this structure by challenging interlocking oppressions of race and class. *San Andreas*'s verdict on the segregated scene it plays out remains the fatalism of CJ, who, in the lead-up to the main action of the "Riots" strand, can only explain the pervasive oppression by saying, "It's just the way shit's stacked."

Liberty City: Criminal Capital

In the dark of night, Niko Bellic arrives at the ports of Liberty City. Dockworkers, upon catching Bellic's eastern European accent, taunt the migrant to "take over the world" someplace else. Bellic was pulled to this metropolis by a desire to flee a criminal past of human trafficking and to track down a former comrade who betrayed his army unit during the Bosnian War: "Life is complicated. I killed people, smuggled people, sold people. Perhaps here, things will be different." Bellic's hopes were excited by his cousin Roman, who claimed he himself realized the "American Dream" in this city, boasting in letters about a lavish lifestyle, a bulging bank account, and multiple girlfriends. But upon arrival Bellic learns that his cousin deceived him: Roman works at a modest taxi company, lives in a tenement apartment, and has accumulated nasty debts, behind which lie even nastier enemies. Released in 2008 to near-perfect reviews, *GTA IV* revolves around a story not of "extreme wealth and real estate," as in previous games in the series, but of "survival and existence" (Doree 2007).

Although *GTA: Vice City* and *GTA: San Andreas* are formidable achievements of urban simulation, there is no more striking similitude than that between the Liberty City of *GTA IV* and New York City. It is appropriate that the metropolis that Hardt and Negri (2000, 347) refer to as the epicenter of "money" in Empire is the setting of what, at an estimated $100 million, is probably the most expensive video game ever made (Androvich 2008b). With this choice of city, the *GTA* franchise adds a new dimension to the interaction of virtual and actual urbanism: now we examine not just how North American cities are represented within *GTA* but also how media corporations like Rockstar remake real urban space through their corporate wealth, which is itself often outside the law. New York and Liberty City are, we suggest, veritable twin cities: one real, the other simulated, the two nonetheless interacting criminal capitals.

Liberty City has been a setting for past *GTA* games. It appears as the major location in *GTA III*, the game establishing the franchise's credentials for three-dimensional city simulation, and is often referred to, or briefly visited in, other games in the series. While each iteration is a version of New York, it is in *GTA IV* that this simulation is the most comprehensive and detailed. Behind the digital mapping of this metropolis (done at Rockstar's Scottish studio) is a comprehensive research effort (coordinated from Rockstar's New York head office), which spanned time-lapse video recordings to monitor traffic patterns and rainfall, photographs of more than 100,000 locations, and regular site visits to investigate the ethnic "character" of different corners of the city (Bowditch 2008; Boyer 2008a). The simulated city is separated into districts with distinct populations and architectural styles, featuring many of the city's historic landmarks and urban destinations. Mirroring the uneven social geography of New York, the game features the bohemia of Brooklyn, the commercialism of Manhattan, the affluence of SoHo, and the shady areas of the Bronx. The high-definition graphics spotlight familiar sights like the advertising-saturated Times Square; bodies move hurriedly along the sidewalks, drunks are plentiful, and area-appropriate accents are audible. One commentator promises the sounds of this city are "as real as the ones we live and breathe in" (Doree 2007). The game even integrates use of today's means of urban communication: GPS for route navigation and a cell phone interface that allows Bellic to keep in touch with contacts and get instructions for his next crime job.

This urban backdrop is very familiar to those who crafted the *GTA IV* plot, wrote its script, and envisioned its environment, many of whom live in New York. Says Rockstar cofounder Dan Houser:

> We've been here for a number of years. . . . We could capture some aspects of the experience of living here—because you are actually wandering about and meeting some of the freaks that you meet on the streets here. And that's what it's all about—meeting the same kind of freaks you'd meet on the streets, the angry yuppies you'd met there. A big part of New York life is walking around the streets and meeting lunatics. That's something that we definitely tried to put into the game. (cited in *Game Informer* 2007)

Indeed, the story of Bellic resonates strangely with that of its creators, Rockstar, in an uncanny play of similarity and displacement, a story about both "extreme wealth and real estate" and "survival and existence."

Like Bellic, Dan Houser and his brother, Rockstar cofounder Sam Houser, are immigrants to New York. But they come from no mean streets. "Prep-school educated Brits" (Kushner 2007a), children of an entrepreneurial family, they emerged from their elite London private schools to work in the music and later the interactive media division of BMG in London within the German media conglomerate Bertelsmann. BMG had bought a Scottish game company whose *Race and Chase* car-boosting game was an ur-version of *GTA*. The BMG interactive division was bought in 1998 by Take-Two Interactive, a fledging New York video game publisher started by Ryan Brant, scion of a wealthy media family. Under Take-Two's corporate umbrella, the Housers went to New York to start a publisher, which they named Rockstar Games. Rockstar started out in a "cramped ground floor apartment in New York's Soho district nicknamed the Commune" (Kushner 2007a). The Housers found themselves "a second home" at the heart of a city being rapidly transformed by the dot-com boom—a boom for which the U.S. government doubtless happily granted visas to people like the Housers, and not the Bellics—to meet digital industry's demands.

Vincent Mosco has described the transformations worked on New York in this period by the "development of an integrated network of information and entertainment businesses" (1999, 107). In the 1970s, New York was on the brink of fiscal collapse, a saga ending in what David Harvey describes as "a coup by the financial institutions," which resulted in the substitution of "corporate welfare . . . for people welfare" and in an entrepreneurial turn in city governance (2007, 45, 47). Exacerbating urban inequalities in the eighties and nineties meant, says Harvey, that "redistribution through criminal violence became one of the few serious options for the poor, and the authorities responded by criminalizing whole communities of impoverished and marginalized populations" (48). In the 1990s Republican mayor Rudy Giuliani promised to "clean up the city," making it safe for business. All of this helped prepare the stage for the arrival to the city of new-media industries, which seemed to promise "a cyber version of the phoenix myth: in this case, the city reborn from the ashes of its industrial past" (Mosco 1999, 107). Two crucial points of digital implantation were the high-tech district known as Silicon Alley at the southern end of Manhattan and a Times Square complex of media conglomerates. In and between these points incubated an "agglomeration of . . . media industries connecting advertising, publishing, broadcasting, telecommunications, mass entertainment, contemporary art and fashion," invading a "collection of overlapping districts."

This influx set in motion a wave of gentrification as areas of the city were reconfigured for habitation by New York's dot-com owners and workers. The once-dubious reputation of urban neighborhoods was now marketed as an appealing edginess. Prices for New York "loft living" skyrocketed, often driving out the artists whose search for cheap studio space had unwittingly pioneered this new frontier of real estate development. It was within this scene of "dot-com urbanism" (Ross 2004) that the young entrepreneurs of Rockstar took root and flourished. The 1999 "Rockstar Loft" promotion parties organized by the Houser boys, events for which "gaining entrance was itself a game," demanding mysterious telephone calls and intriguing interrogations, were just one of a round of fashionable events for the urbanites of New York's new virtual class (Kushner 2007a). As revenues streamed in, Rockstar would eventually move into another loft space at 622 Broadway, where today Rockstar and Take-Two are located. The building they occupy was a classic victim of the gentrification process, with former tenants, like a long-standing dance studio, forced to move as rents skyrocketed to over $10,000 per month (Carr 2001).

As Mosco points out, much of the "new entrepreneurial spirit" of the Silicon Alley dot-coms was made possible by "government financial subsidies" that opened "prime rental space at well below market prices and helped to retrofit older buildings with technologies necessary to run an aspiring dot-com" (2003, 15). It also involved the proliferation of New York's Business Improvement Districts (BIDs)—in essence, corporate-controlled mini-municipal governments. BIDs acted to "police the streets, manage the parks, haul away trash, and remove the homeless," controlling public space "primarily to service upscale high-tech workers and their families" (Mosco 1999, 111). The shift was accompanied by a crackdown on the homeless and suspects of all kind. Licensing sidewalk artists, attacking street musicians, harassing news vendors, and silencing street protests, the NYPD and BIDs combined to make New York dot-com friendly by instituting a regime that combined "restrictions, privatizations, militant anti-welfare legislation, and overall support for giving big business relatively free rein to make use of public space for private purposes" (112). Rockstar, like other digital business, was the beneficiary of an urban class war that erased, marginalized, and moved on those very aspects of metropolitan life the developer would fictionalize and celebrate in its games.

In 2007 Dan Houser reportedly purchased a wired SoHo penthouse for six million dollars (Abelson 2008). Although Rockstar's story is, like Bellic's, one of New York immigrant entrepreneurialism, it has been worked out in a very different class ambience. *GTA IV,* says a Rockstar representative, captures the "gritty urban environment" of New York that "hasn't benefited from economic boom and it hasn't got Mayor Giuliani there" (cited in Doree 2007). But Rockstar could only capitalize on that grit because of the boom, the gentrification, and Mayor Giuliani's draconian law-and-order regime. The grittiness of Liberty City is, then, the digitized capture of class inequalities, which are shaped by radically different experiences of migration. Sam Houser, in reference to having recently become a U.S. citizen, has the privilege to be blasé: "I'm American. It's official" (cited in Boyer 2008a). The same luxury is not afforded the city's half million undocumented residents, without whom, the current mayor admits (Bloomberg 2006), New York would "collapse"—as would the plot of *GTA IV*. This is not a story of immigrant upward mobility. Bellic's life in America begins with debt, around which spins a ludic tale of informal economies and criminal capitalists, where the precarious exploit the very precarious. As with *San Andreas* and *Vice City,* you earn cash and status by completing missions for and against an increasingly complex social web of enemies, friends, and traitors. By the end of it, however, you may have some money in your account—but, as one reviewer says, "the name's ironic: There's no liberty in Liberty City" (Manjoo 2008).

This, however, is by no means the end to the strange relation of Bellic's Liberty City and Rockstar's New York. The money Bellic stands to make in Liberty City is chump change compared to the green that circulates every second in and out of New York City's NASDAQ, the stock exchange on which is listed Take-Two Interactive Software Inc., Rockstar's parent company. Never was this trading more frenzied than in the dot-com years during which *GTA*'s designers came to the United States. Then the stock market bubble burst in April 2001, not only laying to waste thousands of dot-coms but bringing in its wake a wave of prosecutions for cooked books. The video game business was one of the few sectors of information capital to escape widespread catastrophe; Rockstar seemed to share in this invulnerability as shares nearly tripled in value in the space of one year. But some of the suits behind *GTA* were about to follow the same path as the owners of Enron and WorldCom.

Take-Two has "for years operated under a cloud" (Richtel 2006). Various investigations relating to financial impropriety have been conducted into the firm since its inception in 1993. Trading of its stock was frozen for three weeks in 2002; in 2005 it settled a $7.5 million fine with the U.S. Securities Exchange Commission in a case where managers recorded a falsified volume of units sold in an attempt to raise the company's stated revenues; and it was served a criminal grand jury subpoena in 2006 that requested information on a range of corporate activities and concluded with a verdict of insider trading (Kushner 2007a, 2007b). The subpoena also led to the conviction in 2007 of the man at the top of Take-Two's family tree, its thirty-five-year-old founder Ryan Brant. Brant, along with other company executives and board members, held stock options. Although the date of each person's stock-option grant could vary, the suits who held these grants were poised for a windfall: consider, for instance, that the company's stock was trading at around ten dollars in 2002, and by 2004 it was shy of thirty (Kushner 2007b). Sweetening an already handsome prospective booty, Brant, who was both the company's board chairman and CEO at the time, illegally backdated the stock-option grants to a time when shares were trading lower. As a result, Brant and other top-level staff improperly "received millions of dollars in unrecorded compensation" ("Video Game CEO" 2007). Unlike Tommy Vercetti, however, Brant could not conceal his crime by racing over to Collar & Cuffs to grab a new pair of clothes. This episode climaxed with Brant being convicted of stock fraud, penalized over seven million dollars, and barred for life from holding "control management positions" in a public company. In a New York Supreme Court, he pled guilty and was sentenced to five years' probation. Asked about his feelings about Rockstar's controversial parent company, Dan Houser brushes it off: "It's what I associate with being in America: corporate drama" (Fritz 2008).

Rockstar is perfectly capable of producing its own drama, of course. Take-Two's woes were exacerbated by the "Hot Coffee" scandal. In 2005 a GTA fan released on the Internet a patch that disclosed hidden sex scenes in GTA: San Andreas. Although Rockstar initially claimed these scenes were created by hackers, it quickly became evident that the code was already latent in the game. The tide of moralistic condemnation, led by political figures such as Hillary Clinton, exceeded the furor over GTA violence. Even video game industry organizations, which had celebrated Rockstar as it produced scenarios of brutal beatings, recoiled at the spectacle of virtual sex. One can only feel sympathy for Rockstar in confronting this double standard. But the release of the game with the scenes—explanations range from carelessness to a (badly) calculated marketing ploy—were consistent with the company's style of in-your-face "bad-boy" business. The recall demanded by the Federal Trade Commission cost $25 million, further damaging

Take-Two's finances (Kushner 2007a). All of this reflected back on the frantic development of *GTA IV*. Although Rockstar made some half-hearted gestures at cleaning up its image, the reality was that its prospects hung on the irreverent *GTA* franchise: the illicit virtuality of Liberty City would have to save the actual New York company housing corporate criminals. But as *GTA IV* experienced delays in release, the situation at Take-Two spiraled; a shareholders' revolt turfed the board of directors, and a major takeover bid in 2008 was launched (but ultimately failed) by rival publishing empire, Electronic Arts. The fact that the Housers' contract with Take-Two will soon expire adds uncertainty to the publisher's future.

By 2008 the United States was in the grip of another financial crisis—one created by the avalanche of easy credit that the Federal Reserve Bank had released to stave off recession after the bursting of the Internet bubble. As *GTA IV* hit the stores, cities that had been reshaped by the gentrification and studio lofts of the dot-com boom were being worked over by another sort of capitalist urban design—one inflicted by the subprime mortgage crisis. People like Bellic were being thrown out on the street as mortgages were foreclosed in Cleveland, New Jersey, and Detroit. Focus was shifting from the creative accounting of information capitalists to the dodgy lending practices of banks and finance houses. Set against the collapse of Bear Stearns and the near implosion of the financial system, Rockstar's woes were minor convulsions in the capitalist firmaments. But Brant's conviction nonetheless adds video game capitalists to the bushel of so-called bad apples amid the corporate orchard: Enron, Halliburton, AOL, Arthur Andersen, and others. It is, however, a well-known feature of white-collar crime that the verified misdeeds of corporate capital receive dramatically less media attention than is dedicated to the hypothetical street crimes that may result from playing *GTA*.

In 2009, as capitalism's crisis deepened, Take-Two published a Rockstar title whose "addictive addition," said one reviewer, was the "thrill of turning a profit" (cited in Cowan 2009). This references the drug-dealing component of *Chinatown Wars*, a *GTA* game that was initially developed for the Nintendo DS, despite the younger demographic associated with this handheld. The Triad protagonist of *Chinatown Wars* can "earn his keep by selling drugs to progress further in the narrative. To be successful as a dealer, you'll have to buy low and sell high. Demand is always changing, creating situations where you'll have to sit on your supplies and wait for the right opportunity" (cited in Cowan 2009). Rather like the game's publisher. In 2008 the New York owner of "the most valuable franchise in the video game industry" successfully repelled a takeover attempt by Electronic Arts (Takahashi 2009). Some investors chided Take-Two for rejecting EA's offer. More recently, in a 2009 interview, Take-Two's CEO, Strauss Zelnick, suggested, however, that a sale should not be ruled out. "We're just trying to create value. If we could do that through a combination, we would pursue it. We're not religious about it. We're just trying to create value" (cited in Takahashi 2009).

Zelnick's mantra is expressed amid some concern about Take-Two's own *GTA* dependency: when a release like *GTA IV* generates a half billion dollars in sales weeks after its launch, it is inevitably followed by a relatively dry spell in revenues, leaving financial analysts wanting more stable value. A latest mechanism for satisfying major shareholders, and perhaps for attracting another industry bidder, is the delivery of small dosages of *GTA* content as downloadable episodes from Xbox Live, as with 2009's *The Lost and the Damned,* a Liberty City extension whose plot revolves around a biker gang. And so, once again, the virtual and the actual slip and segue. The latest games co-opt and depict the illicit street economies whose networks of informal labor are unlikely to contract in the context of the global slide into recession. At the same time, these titles impel and inculcate the same frenzied devotion to accumulation that fomented the crisis with which global capitalists are now struggling to cope.

It is tempting to speculate that the shady dealings of Take-Two in some way inform the publisher's fascination with ludic criminal underworlds. But clearly there are much-larger-level connections between capital and the crime portrayed in urban-themed games. The transnational crime rings of which Bellic is a fictional petty operative have flourished as a doppelgänger of transnational corporations. Global criminal organizations are a "McMafia" (Glenny 2008) to go with the "McWorld" (Barber 1995) of planetary capital. Here, taking the cue from *GTA IV*'s theme song, "Soviet Connection," we remember that Bellic hails from the former Soviet bloc, which has become lodged in the U.S. imagination as the home of corporate crime lords. While this image is well founded—the marketization of the post-Soviet economy has indeed unleashed a criminalized economy of unprecedented scale—it also distances the oligarchic and corrupt tendencies of American capital itself, which, by unleashing on the world economic policies of privatization, deregulation, and financialization, have opened the door to a veritable explosion of global criminality.

At the same time, there is a massive degree of difference between the street-level hoodlums like Bellic and the stock scams of capitalists like Brant. In one sense, games that dwell with fascinated attention on street crime deflect attention from white- to blue-collar misconduct: crime appears as gangsters, not suits; on mean streets, not in corridors of power; as drug deals, not stock options; in low-riders, not high-rises. Yet in another way, GTA's constitution of a metropolitan world entirely enveloped by, and subsumed within, crime also performs a normalization of corporate criminality. Its game world asserts that crime is the way the universe is—the way money changes hands, business is done, society organized; it is the nature of reality. Why be outraged when the financial rulers of the world disregard the pettiness of the law, since all of this just reveals their superior grasp of the rules of the game? The omnipresence of crime in Liberty City is thus one more cultural contribution to the generalized indifference that greets the news of corporate crimes in Empire, an indifference whose rational kernel is perhaps, as David Harvey observes, the popular assumption that criminal behavior is hardly "easily distinguishable from the normal practices of influence-peddling and making money in the marketplace" (2007, 166).

Corrupt Cities, Cynical Games

Hardt and Negri write:

> In Empire, corruption is everywhere. It is the cornerstone and keystone of domination. It resides in different forms in the supreme government of Empire and its vassal administration, the most refined and the most rotten administrative police forces, the lobbies of the ruling classes, the mafias of rising social groups, the churches and sects, the perpetrators and persecutors of scandal, the great financial conglomerates, and everyday economic transactions. Through corruption, imperial power extends a smokescreen across the world, and command over the multitude is exercised in this putrid cloud, in the absence of light and truth. (2000, 389)

If GTA depicts this corrupt state, why do we call it a game of Empire, not a game of multitude? Surely a game that exposes this condition is a blow against power? Surely all the more so, since its protagonists—its Vercettis, CJs, and Bellics—are drawn from the multiethnic, transnational, nomadic proletariat that Hardt and Negri see as a source of radical social transformation?

Rockstar's affinity for urban mayhem has always given it an ambivalent relation to radical activism. Around the year 2000 tens of thousands were involved in events such as the Battle of Seattle at the World Trade Organization ministerial meeting and the Quebec City demonstrations against the Free Trade Agreement of the Americas—events that turned the streets of North American cities into sites of struggle against Empire. In 2002 this metropolitan multitude was virtually replayed in the urban-riot video game *State of Emergency,* where one plays a "black bloc" activist intent on maximizing havoc. Some anticapitalist activists were excited by ludic recognition, others enraged by the co-optation; die-hard gamers were generally unimpressed by the quality of the capture. The game certainly accelerated its maker's delinquent image; a few years later we were talking with a senior executive for a major game company who, after delivering an impassioned diatribe against game censorship of hyperrealistic shooters, then declared that in depicting anarchist anticapitalists battling the police, Rockstar had "gone too far"!

Many politically left gamers like *GTA.* Admitting its rampant free-enterprise ethos and racial stereotyping, not to mention brutality, these players say that it is so "over the top" as to become by its very extremity a comedic exposé of U.S. politics. An aspect of the game that typically draws radical admiration is the in-game radio stations that players can tune into, stations whose advertisements and talk shows are a scathing parody of neoliberal sensibilities. Here is a sample commercial aired in *San Andreas,* advertising a character named Mike Andrews, author of a book called *Rags Are Riches:*

ANDREWS: Understand that it's okay to be poor. There needs to be poor people. We rich are the yin. You are the yang. We need you!

AUDIENCE MEMBER: Mr. Andrews, I've had a run of bad luck and I was wondering if the state could help me get back on my feet?

ANDREWS: This is the negative kind of self-obsessed greedy talk that doesn't help anyone. My program will teach you a new outlook on life. Instead of complaining about being poor, enjoy it. Watch TV. Don't vote. Who cares?

AUDIENCE MEMBER: But I'm homeless.

ANDREWS: You've got it all wrong. Society doesn't owe you anything. The government has better things to worry about, like
killing innocent people. You already have everything you need,
so enjoy your lives.

We too enjoy such mordant moments in our trips to San Andreas, or
watching an episode of *Republican Space Rangers* while hanging out
in our apartment in Liberty City. But there is nonetheless a manifestly
reactionary aspect to *GTA*'s vision of universal corruption. What is excluded from its virtuality is *any* alternative to the rottenness. In *GTA*
the populace of U.S. cities appears as a vicious multitude. The denizens of this video game are not the empowering multitude of Spinoza
but the multitude of the conservative theoretician Hobbes, locked in a
war of all against all, perpetually splintering into contentious and destructive factions, an auto-endangering multitude whose internecine
conflicts provide the legitimacy for the emergence of a massive disciplinary state Leviathan—except, of course, that in *GTA*, Leviathan,
too, is corrupt, with its drug-dealing CIA agents, grotesque media apparatus, and self-aggrandizing political dynasties. No one escapes a
whipping.

There is no shelter at all from corruption, violence, and "cruel seg-
mentation" (Hardt and Negri 2000, 340). The game presents a no-exit
situation. *GTA* contains occasional allusions to the fierce genealogy of
radical politics in North American communities of blacks, Latinos,
Asians, and other immigrant and minority communities—but only to
negate their potential. Though the narrative in *San Andreas,* for example, contains individualized moments of minority alliance against
repression, "these tantalizing possibilities are never fleshed out with
actual game-play" (Redmond 2006, 110). The game's "narrative dilemma" is, says Dennis Redmond, that the protagonist's "quest for
personal redemption cannot serve as a template of collective resistance
to neoliberalism." It is, in fact, vital to the ideological consistency of
the games' demonic satire that brutalization, racism, and greed be
ubiquitous. In *GTA IV* a prominent theme is that of the poor exploiting the very poor. There may be other options; *but you can't play
them*—and that is what makes *GTA* a game of Empire.

In an interview about *GTA IV,* Rockstar's Sam Houser remarked,
"We take our games very seriously, but we don't take ourselves very
seriously. Because I think that's a slippery slope for life. So we take the

piss out of ourselves, and we take the piss out of anything we can think of. It's sort of unilaterally offensive" (cited in Boyer 2008b). Indeed. We would say that the category most relevant to the *GTA* franchise is cynicism—an attitude that several commentators see as essential to the ethos of Empire. Slavoj Zizek speaks of "the cynical functioning of ideology: that in order to function ideology shouldn't take itself too seriously" (Zizek and Daly 2004, 35). "It is as if in late capitalism 'words don't count,' no longer oblige: they increasingly seem to lose their performative power; whatever one says is drowned in the general indifference; the emperor is naked and the media trumpet forth this fact, yet nobody seems really to mind—that is, people continue to act as if the emperor is not naked" (Zizek 1999, 18). In a context that bears directly on *GTA*, bell hooks (1995), reviewing Quentin Tarantino's *Pulp Fiction,* observes that the director "makes that shit [sexism, racism, oppression] look so ridiculous you think everybody's gonna get it and see how absurd it all is. Well, that's when we enter the danger zone. Folks be laughing at the absurdity and clinging to it nevertheless."

GTA is a cynical game that simultaneously satirizes, indulges, and normalizes individual hyperpossessiveness, racialized stereotypes, and neoliberal violence in a self-cancellation that allows these elements to remain intact, a structure that is, in a very precise way, conservative. This cynicism makes *GTA* undoubtedly complex, and certainly more ambivalent and interesting than, say, the unabashed affirmations of imperial power in *Full Spectrum Warrior.* The world city that most fully actualizes Rockstar's vision of ferociously violent, ethnically segregated gang war is American-occupied Baghdad. It is no wonder a marine records his urban experience in Iraq in the following terms: "I was thinking just one thing when we drove into that ambush . . . *Grand Theft Auto: Vice City.* I felt like I was living it when I seen the flames coming out of the windows, the blown-up car in the street, guys crawling around shooting at us. It was fucking cool" (cited in Wright 2005). At one level *GTA* exposes some basic operations of, and hypocrisies about, imperial economics, politics, and culture. Yet at the same time the rendering of these truths in the form of excess, mockery, equivocation, and ridicule functions to keep those same truths at safe distance—the distance necessary for their endless repetition in a world where all streets leading to an alternative have been blocked. Such distance is both cause and effect of cynicism, a defining feature of the "emotional situation" of politics today (Virno 2004, 84). Mike

Davis refers to "a supersaturation of corruption that fails any longer to outrage or even interest" (1992, 45). Endless corporate scandals, political sellouts, oil wars, and bank bailouts feed this condition. So too do virtual landscapes like San Andreas and Liberty City. In the case of *Grand Theft Auto,* we are inclined to side with Spinoza, the early theorist of multitude who opposed "satire" as that which "takes pleasure in the powerlessness and distress of men" (Deleuze 1988, 13). Cynicism, with the inevitability of the present that it implies, is among the best fortifications protecting the imperial city against its multitudinous potential.

III
New Game?

7. Games of Multitude

Street Games

Revolts within the gates, protests in the desert beyond, accusations of human-rights violations, and, embarrassingly for the private corporation running the compound, successful escape attempts—the Immigration Reception and Processing Centre holding nearly 1,500 refugee claimants in the desert at Woomera, Australia, was notorious. Detention is among the most draconian devices of imperial control. A government policy barring access by the press meant outsiders could only imagine living conditions within the center—until someone made these conditions a topic of virtual play. Built as a *Half-Life* mod, *Escape from Woomera* is an activist-made game that set out to recreate the camp's "architecture of intensity and fear" from the point of view of asylum-seeking inmates "ever-alert for what sources of danger lie around the corner" and trying to find a way out (Wilson 2005, 114). The game involved an alliance of digital designers, investigative journalists, and migrant rights activists (see Schott and Yeatman 2005, 84). The mere announcement of its construction stirred controversy about detention in Australia, especially since the game's early stages were financed by a government arts grant. *Escape from Woomera* didn't progress past prototype. But even as an unfinished demo, it contributed to the wider current of Australian antidetention activism that shut down the center in 2003.

Leap a year and a hemisphere. Late at night on August 28, 2004, as the U.S. Republican Party's National Convention met in New York City, a mobile troop of ludic activists took to the streets. Two female cyborgs, one with a laptop, another with a video projector, beamed visuals from *America's Army* onto downtown buildings as the game was hacked, in real-time, by coconspirators linking in from five different locations around the world. This was OUT, "a live action wireless gaming urban intervention." Playing on MOUT (Military Operations on Urban Terrain), the U.S. military doctrine we saw rehearsed in *Full Spectrum Warrior* (chapter 4), OUT's architects demanded, "The United States OUT of Iraq and the Middle East. Escalating worldwide Militarism and Violence, from whatever source, (right-wing oil hungry U.S. capitalists or wealthy Islamic fundamentalists), OUT of Civilian Life. The U.S. Army and Pentagon computer game developers OUT of the minds of prepubescent gamers." OUT was the brainchild of Opensorcery (2004), an initiative that for nearly a decade has troubled the militarist bent and gender norms of game culture through a variety of hacktivisms, its best known the *Velvet Strike* interventions in the multiplayer online shooter *Counter-Strike,* where it digitally scrawled peace signs and encouraged gamers to give each other virtual blow jobs instead of virtually blowing each other away. Now this crew of media activists dissolved amid the 800,000 protesters converging on the street during the Republican convention that nominated George W. Bush to run for his second term as president.

Jump another fifteen months and one continent, to Fortress Europe in autumn of 2005. The torched cars had barely cooled, tear gas hung in the streets, and the riot squads still stood ready for any rekindling of the four-week uprising by immigrant youths in the *banlieux* (suburbs) of Paris when a video account from the insurgents' point of view circulated around the Internet. Alternative-media messages are a familiar part of political crisis. But this one was different: *The French Democracy,* created by twenty-six-year-old Alex Chan under the pseudonym "Koulamata," was made using a commercial video game, *The Movies.* Published by Lionhead, *The Movies* invites players to manage their own Hollywood studio ("Build Your Own Movie Empire" is one of its marketing slogans) and includes machinima tools allowing player-producers to record computer-generated animated films in real time. Lionhead's promotion emphasized the creation of comedies, dramas, and other entertainment genres. But Chan made a thirteen-minute political documentary. It dramatized the police-pursuit death of two immigrant boys that had sparked the riots, and the racism, unemployment, white-fright indifference, and frustration of racialized communities reviled by politicians that were its wider context. Chan explained his intention: "to bring people to think about what really happened in my country by trying to show the starting point and some causes of these riots" (cited in Musgrove 2005). Posted to *The Movies Online* Web site, where Lionhead encouraged players to exhibit their productions so as to publicize its game, *The French Democracy,* made for a cost of some $60, was downloaded many times, for free, was uploaded to YouTube, drew widespread press attention, and was shown at film festivals, making it perhaps the single most effective communiqué from the *banlieux* to leap across the Atlantic and around the world.

Escape from Woomera, OUT, and *The French Democracy* show that players can and do fight back against games of Empire. They are examples of a different dynamic, that of games of multitude.

The Multitude and the Media

The multitude is the social force that is at once the motor and the antagonist, the engine and the enemy, of Empire (Hardt and Negri 2000, 2004). It can be defined in three different but connected ways.

First, the multitude refers to new forms of subjectivity (Hardt and Negri 2000, 195–97; Virno 2004, 75–93). It is based in emergent individual and collective human capacities, the fresh ways of producing, communicating, and cooperating that global capital requires to run its vast and complex Empire. The example central to our topic is the technological and cultural know-how energizing immaterial industries such as the video game business, though there are also other, and not unrelated, instances, such as the cosmopolitan literacies of the massive mobile migrant labor flows integral to the world economy. Capital needs and, up to a point, fosters these new ways of being human. Empire is, however, a thoroughly ambivalent system. To use an old metaphor from Marx and Engels (1848, 85–86), capital is like the sorcerer's apprentice, conjuring up forces it cannot fully control. Multitudinous subjectivity is not only technically astute and culturally creative but also potentially subversive because its skills, aptitudes, and desires exceed the uses to which Empire tries to confine them.

This takes us to a second manifestation of the multitude—new movements opposing global capital (see Notes from Nowhere 2003 for an overview). Hardt and Negri's main theme is the way Empire's subjects refuse to submit to its bottom-line logic. Despite all the apparent victories of the world market, time and again resistances to the total monetization of social relations and the primacy of profit erupt. Because corporate power has enveloped society so completely, there are myriad points around which insurgencies spring up: the environment, citizenship status, housing, employment, education, public space, art, and media. Grassroots mobilizations against corporate globalization from the jungles of Chiapas to the streets of Quebec City, international resistance to the invasion of Iraq, the struggles of nonstatus people, and the wave of ecological activism around global warming are all instances of a multitude contesting Empire.

Such movements open up a third dimension of the multitude—a capacity not only to resist Empire but also to develop, protect, and propose alternatives. Hardt and Negri (2000, 400) say the "political project" of the multitude is nothing less than constituting a world other than that of global capital. They have been—fairly—criticized for not providing a full account of this large task. But they do sketch some elements of a program: a "global citizenship"; the right to a social wage and a guaranteed income for all; and free access to, and control over, "knowledge, information, communication and affects" (396–407). Of particular importance to our discussion is the importance they give to wresting control of the means of communication away from capital. The "indymedia" of the counterglobalization movement, with their famous slogan "Don't hate the media, become the media," are a key expression of the multitude's "powerful desire for global democracy" (Hardt and Negri 2004, 305).

When all three dimensions of the multitude—subjective capacity, social movement, political project—coalesce, Hardt and Negri suggest they become a utopian arrow, pointing to a possible future life beyond Empire.

This optimistic account of the multitude is, however, tempered by other authors. Paolo Virno also explores the concept of multitude but emphasizes the way it can oscillate between subversion and submission. He stresses that contemporary capital is very good at adopting apparently iconoclastic practices and utopian ideas as management techniques and revenue sources. Information-age, post-Fordist enterprise, with its participatory workplaces and social networking, presents the face of what he terms "the communism of capital" (Virno 2004, 110)— a regime of profit that invokes team spirit, revolutionary change, and individual empowerment the better to harness people to work. Thus, Virno notes, while one "emotional tonality" (84) of the multitude is the radical energy that Hardt and Negri celebrate, its other side is a cynical opportunism and nihilistic resignation born of pragmatic adjustment to a world where capital seems to swallow everything. It is also ambiguity that Virno highlights in discussing the relation of the multitude to media. He begins with the category of the spectacle. From grumblings about Rome's "bread and circuses" to the Situationists' scathing account of the twentieth-century "society of the spectacle" (Debord 1967) to Retort's (2005) recent emphasis on the importance of spectacle to American global power, critics have long pointed to the role of extravagant media displays in exciting, intimidating, distracting, and ultimately pacifying the subjects of a social order. But today spectacle has, Virno suggests, a "double nature" (2004, 60). One part is the subjugation of culture to the commodity form; the other is intensifying "productive communication." In contemporary capitalism, the industries that create spectacle—the so-called cultural or creative industries—driven by their own profit-seeking dynamic, make and disseminate the tools of communication. To capture the attention of people, and even to involve and exploit new types of labor, they give people instruments for producing and reproducing media in a way that paradoxically diminishes capital's monopoly of spectacular power.

This analysis clearly applies to virtual games. Interactivity seems to break with the passivity traditionally associated with watching spectacular entertainment. The possibility for players to select even limited—though in new games, rapidly widening—options and to become involved in practices of modding, machinima making, and MMO participation appears to mark a quantum jump in engagement beyond that of, say, networked television audiences. We want, however, to insist on what Virno (2006) terms "the ambivalence of the multitude" and even to amplify his point. As we noted in the introduction, many scholars of game studies see interactivity as automatically empowering and democratizing. But although the capacity for "productive communication" Virno describes may overcome spectacle, it doesn't necessarily do so: on the contrary, it can be subordinated to, and even intensify, spectacular power. When a Canadian solider creates a *Half-Life 2* mod, *Insurgency,* allowing gamers to take *either* side in Iraq, it is not to challenge the logic of the war on terror but to enrich cultural militarization: "If you just want to get into the action and have some fun, grab your AK47 . . . and let loose as a Guerrilla or Paramilitary fighter." Similarly, when *Second Life*-ers sell their virtual construction skills to advertising agencies beaming brands to the virtual world, the outcome is deeper commodification. Here we recall Retort's point that contemporary spectacular life is a "self-administered reality" (2005, 187): subjects already deeply immersed in a commodified and militarized regime are provided the means to animate, elaborate, refine, and extend their own commodification and militarization, all the while having empowerment-through-interactivity trumpeted in their ears by acolytes of corporate power. People no longer just view wartime capital "accumulated to the degree that it becomes images" (Debord 1967, para. 34) but insert themselves into this image, labor at its accumulation, as its self-spectacularizing cocreators (see Wark 2007, para. 111). This is not a break with spectacle. It is an ever-deeper affective and intellectual investment in it.

An analysis of the multitude's relation to media after 2001 cannot, then, just applaud "indymedia." Rather, it has to recognize what Matteo Pasquinelli (2006) describes as conditions of "immaterial civil war" (see also Lovink and Schneider 2003). New media such as Web 2.0 applications, social software, the blogosphere, and, of course, recent generations of virtual games are both the terrain and the prize of a pitched battle, fought twenty-four hours a day across innumerable digital devices and platforms, between two sides of the multitude's collective subjectivity—creative dissidence and profitable compliance. On the one side are the prospects for what theorists such as Steve Best and Douglas Kellner (2004) and Henry Giroux (2006) term "interactive spectacle," in which the participatory capacities of digital machines are captured to reinforce imperial power; on the other, the possibilities that Steven Duncomb (2007) identifies when he discusses opportunities for "ethical spectacles" that turn media dream-worlds to radical ends.

Tracking this ambivalence is the project of this book. So far we have focused on how virtual games reinforce actual Empire. Yet our analysis also revealed conflict, from the unauthorized creativity of the first game makers (chapter 1) to the online denunciation of labor exploitation by EA Spouse (chapter 2), to Xbox hacking (chapter 3), to guerrilla war simulators (chapter 4), to MMO players' transgressions (chapter 5) and the controversies over the modding of *GTA* (chapter 6). Games and gamers get out of the control of their corporate military sponsors. Many of these lines of flight are recouped by game capital, and some are black holes of pointless or destructive energy, but all persuade us that it isn't quite "game over" yet. Game culture is full of glibly promoted "empowerment" and slickly marketed "participation" that provide game capital free labor and expanded revenues. Yet it is also and simultaneously shot through with instances of player self-organization, from warez collectives to tactical game makers, which intersect with movements against Empire. Despite everything, as Hardt and Negri say, "the spectacle of imperial order is not an iron-clad world, but actually opens up the real possibility of its overturning" (2000, 324). Games of Empire are thus also games of multitude.

So we turn now to what Alexander Galloway dubs "countergaming": the prospect of playing against—and beyond—games of Empire (2006a, 107–26). We survey six pathways of multitudinous activity that can be seen, sensed, or speculated on at the margins—and sometimes deep in the heart—of contemporary video game culture: *counterplay,* or acts of contestation within and against the ideologies of individual games of Empire; *dissonant development,* the emergence of critical content in a few mainstream games; *tactical games* designed by activists to disseminate radical social critique; *polity simulators,* associated with the educational and training projects of the "serious games" move-ment; the *self-organized worlds* of players producing game content independently of commercial studios, especially in MMOs; and fi-nally *software commons* challenging restrictions on, and monopoly control over, game-related intellectual property. Not all these often-intersecting paths are as explicitly militant as the "street games" with which we started this chapter; many are tentative, and some, skeptics may think, trivial. But though gamers' contribution to toppling the global power structures will, we suspect, be modest, it is not as irrele-vant as some might suppose.

Counterplay

Earth has been destroyed by war and ecological mismanagement. Humanity takes flight to another planet and divides into multiple factions: the Spartan Federation (fascist militarists), Gaia's Step-daughters (green pacifists), University of Planet (academic technocrats), Peacekeeping Forces (bureaucratic diplomats), Human Hive (state-socialists), Lord's Believers (Christian fundamentalists), and Morgan Industries (neoliberal capitalists). Each faction races to expand its colony, selecting political structures (police state, democratic, or theo-cratic), economic systems (free market, planned, or green), and cultural values (prioritizing wealth, power, or knowledge). Victory—planetary hegemony—might be achieved through conquest, diplomacy, economics, transcendence (collective consciousness), or cooperation (an alliance of factions). The permutation of these choices makes Sid Meier's 1999 *Alpha Centauri* among the more complex of civilization-building games. There's no doubt that it deeply embeds some premises of what Kacper Poblocki (2002), in an analysis of the game, terms "bio-cultural imperialism." *Alpha Centauri* is, after all, one of an inauspiciously named genre of "4x" games, as in eXplore, eXpand, eXploit, eXterminate.

But let's imagine a gamer, a unionized media worker—maybe a scriptwriter on strike against Hollywood's conglomerates—also involved in the antiwar movement and ecological activism, who regularly plays *Alpha Centauri*. Let's imagine she plays by forging a multitudinous alliance of Gaia's Stepdaughters, Human Hive, and University of Planet against the imperial powers of Morgan Industries, Spartan Federation, and Lord's Believers. This may not be an optimal gambit for winning, yet it could be both pleasurable for our gamer to try, and also virtually corroborative of her actual activism.

Games are machines of "subjectivation." When we play an in-game avatar, we temporarily simulate, adopt, or try out certain identities. Games, like other cultural machines, hail or "interpellate" us in particular "subject positions" (Althusser 1971). These subject positions may be utterly fantastic, quite realistic, or somewhere in between. But such in-game identities are never entirely separated from the options provided by the actual social formations in which the games are set, from which their virtualities derive and into which they flow back. Game virtualities remove us from, but also prepare us for, these actual subject positions. Mostly, as we have discussed at length, they simulate the normalized subjectivities of a global capitalist order—consumer, commander, commanded, cyborg, criminal—not to mention the rapid shedding and swapping between identities that is such an important aptitude of workers in "flexible accumulation" (Harvey 1989).

Contra enthusiasts for game "empowerment," interactivity does not mean virtual play is free from ideology; rather, it intensifies the sense of free will necessary for ideology to work really well. Players, of their own choice, rehearse socially stipulated subjectivities. The scope and substantiality of such choice vary from genre to genre, from games "on a rail" to sandbox games. Even in the most open game, it is only a range; one of our points in this book is that some games widely praised for their latitude—such as MMOs and sandbox games—are coded to constrain and channel toward imperial subject positions. Whereas the old broadcast media of industrial capital rather obviously (and often not very successfully) exhorted audiences to specific subject positions, interactive media manifest a more flexible order where users *of their own initiative* adopt the identities required by the system. In this sense, games are indeed exemplary media of an order that demands not just the obedience of assembly-line work but also the mandatory self-starting participation of immaterial laborers and global migrants. Empire wins only when played by multitude. But this mode of internalized media discipline, while potentially far more powerful than old-fashioned indoctrination, is also riskier. Shaping subjectivity is an ongoing process; people are exposed to various machines of socialization and contain multiple aspects, some of which may be surprisingly activated. Moreover, to be truly involving, a game often has to include some "bad" subject positions, renegade options, outlaw possibilities, even if the logic of play often tends to their being unattractive to play or unlikely to win.

In the case of our hypothetical *Alpha Centauri* player, the game machine is unusually aligned not with becoming a subject of Empire but with a wider process of becoming a multitudinous activist. This is an example of the process William Stephenson (1999) suggests when he asks: "What if the player elects . . . knowingly to be a Bad Subject? The power of the computer," he argues, "can be harnessed by the skeptical, dissident player." Here Stephenson is thinking particularly of empire-building games, like *Alpha Centauri* or *Civilization,* whose remote ancestors are the training exercises of old imperial elites, who had to know about the weaknesses of their own system and the strengths of their opponents to win global domination. The sweeping social, economic, and ecological choices of such games can be quite rich for politically dissident gaming, but it can occur in other genres, too. Declare your seventeenth-century *Europa Universalis III* territories republics, earning the enmity of all AI-controlled monarchies; queer your avatar's gender in *The Sims;* rejecting the attractions of superior weaponry and better "shock and awe," never play the fascists in *Combat Mission.*

Such game choices are what we call *counterplay against Empire.* That game players do not always accept the imperial option reflects a base-line capacity of "refusal." Not only do gamers sometimes "resist the dominant messages" encoded in games of Empire, but they can also "manage from within . . . to produce alternative expressions"

(Hardt and Negri 2004, 263). We don't exaggerate the subversion of dissident play or lower the bar on what counts as political engagement: it is easy to laugh at a ludic multitude thumbing through dissent rather than taking it to the street. But let's ditch double standards. Few political activists consider reading or watching films as always just time-wasting distractions. We extend the same courtesy to gaming. Just as in cinema, music, and literature ideologies are challenged, new subjectivities coalesce, and flashes of autonomy appear, so too sometimes with games. There is, however, no doubt that the scope of such expressions depends largely on the content programmed by their developers, to whom we now turn.

Dissonant Development

Given the origins of immaterial labor in the social movements of the 1960s and 1970s, and a gaming culture where a "rebel" stance is de rigueur to this day, it is not surprising that politically critical content *does* sometimes get into mainstream games. If we focus for a moment on shooters, the "evil corporation" is a standard game trope, from the Union Aerospace Corporation responsible for unleashing demonic forces in *Doom* to the Ultor against which you revolt in *Red Faction* or the Alliance conglomerate you struggle to topple in *Armored Core: Last Raven*.[1] Of course, this is such a commonplace in popular culture that it is almost a toothless cliché. In games as in other media, its subversive charge is usually canceled by story lines in which critique of capital comes down to a tale of bad-apple delinquency defeated by individual heroism. And this is a matter not just of plot but also of game dynamics: political reflection is eclipsed by high-intensity action, and analysis of Empire falls very fast to the imperative of getting that last sniper shot to complete your game.

In the late 1990s, however, at just about the same time as protests against global corporate power were gaining steam, this formula was elaborated in a number of "stealth" games, such as Hideo Kojima's famous *Metal Gear* franchise and Warren Specter's *Deus Ex* series. The play of these games emphasized guile and subterfuge as much as speed and violence, and their byzantinely complex plots revolved around the malign machinations of transnational elites and the role of high technologies, computer networks, and virtual realities in the maintenance of planetary power systems. Such games are clearly vulnerable to Fredric Jameson's critique of "conspiracy theory" fiction in general

Games of Multitude 195

as "a degraded attempt . . . to think the impossible totality of the contemporary world system" (1992, 38), exercises in misrecognition that emphasize mysterious cabals at the expense of systemic forces. But in the context of gaming's long domination by straightforward action narratives, the somber convolutions of these stealth games represented a sophisticated modulation in virtual play and a substantial injection of dissonant content.

Such dissident infiltration has intensified since 9/11. With books bearing subtitles like "America's Quest for Global Dominance" topping best-seller lists (Chomsky 2003) and Michael Moore's documentaries breaking big at the box office, so too have critical perspectives on the war on terror appeared among a handful of game developers. One example is *Bad Day L.A.*, whose protagonist is a Hollywood-executive-turned-homeless-man protecting Los Angeles' paranoid citizens from all manner of disaster, from meteor shower to "Mexican invasion." The game is openly promoted as a satirical "counter message," a "critique of America's fear culture." Its outspoken designer used the publicity around the game as an opportunity to criticize representations of certain ethnic identities in games (i.e., Middle Eastern) as "less than human because they are video game cannon fodder" (Totilo 2006).

Or take *BlackSite: Area 51*, a first-person shooter attuned to imperial blowback, war profiteering, and implosion of public trust. An infantry squad leader, you've been in Iraq on the hunt for weapons of mass destruction. Now you're back home in the United States in a dustbowl Nevada town, and something monstrous is emerging from the barren state-controlled lands on its outskirts. It's been manufactured by the U.S. government, which has been using the country's poor as raw material for the creation of designer militarized mutants, the Reborn. An ambitious solution to the recruitment problem—but the result was unpredictable: "The enemy you're mostly fighting is an insurgency on American soil," says *BlackSite*'s designer, "but we created the enemy that we're now sending our troops to fight, and somebody's profiting from that" (Smith, cited in *Edge* 2007a, 34). Again, the game's controversial wartime content is actively promoted by the developer: "We're getting a lot of people saying, 'I can't believe you're touching this subject matter.' And I'm like, 'I can't believe you're not'" (cited in Totilo 2007).

Perhaps even more strikingly critical, and rather subtler, is the highly acclaimed 2007 shooter *BioShock*, created by Irrational Games. It is set in an underwater city where a utopian experiment has gone horribly wrong, leaving behind monstrous residues. But *this* failed experiment in social and genetic engineering is the product not of socialist planning but of capitalist hubris. As the player proceeds through the ruins of The Rapture—so the city is called—s/he discovers from diaries and audio journals that it was founded in postwar America by the libertarian Andrew Ryan (a thinly disguised Ayn Rand), who believed in the power of the free market to create an Edenic future based in unconstrained techno-industry. The dream was slowly corrupted by war, black markets, and class conflict, leaving only a decaying submarine necropolis peopled by mutant "splicers," who had obeyed advertising exhortations to "evolve" via genetic modification, the victims of insane cosmetic surgeons obsessed with bodily perfection, and an ecological catastrophe of dying trees, rotting vegetation, and declining oxygen supplies. Despite a 1960s setting, The Rapture's combination of free markets and fundamentalist religion is irresistibly reminiscent of early-twenty-first-century U.S. neoliberalism, making *Bioshock*'s success a game-world sign of the fading luster of the post–Hurricane Katrina Bush regime.

That media giants find it profitable to produce games about the malignancies of capital is a symptom of the paradoxical relation of Empire and an antagonistic multitude.[2] When game magazines such as *Edge* (2007a, 31) discuss whether creations such as *BlackSite* and *Bioshock* can both reflect on "ideology, modern geopolitics and cultures of fear" *and* be "unashamed balls-to-the-wall first-person shooters," it is a sign of a shift in the political wind of game development. But the proposed answer—that success depends on imparting politics in small details "without impinging on the running and gunning"—shows the challenge such projects face in a commercial context where the domination of genre conventions means that dissident politics easily become no more than a novel twist to refresh tired formulae. In this context, it is interesting to note the boldness of one unusual mainstream game with the unequivocal title *Republic: Revolution*. Here the dynamics are not just "running and gunning" but the slow—even tedious—process of grassroots radical organizing to overthrow an unjust social order: ideological agitation, clandestine media, undermining the military, bankrolling the movement. . . . But note the setting: *Revolution* is plotted in Novistrana, a fictional post-Soviet country in eastern Europe, remnant of a former, fallen, hostile evil empire—and hence a safe site for virtual subversion. To find such frank ludic dissent against today's capitalist Empire, we have to step away from the center of its entertainment apparatus, to the equivalent of *samizdat* gaming.

Tactical Games

Drill a hole into every box passing your station on the assembly line. Go home. Wait. *Zip.* Sit at the front desk and answer the phone, e-mails, and intercom. Go home. Wait. *Zip.* Transport the boxes, one by one, from the truck to the conveyor; don't let the barking supervisor distract you. Get fired. Busk. Start over. Passage through this tedious sequence of random jobs, material and immaterial, performing rote tasks at ever-quickening pace, is facilitated by TuboFlexInc., a "staffing solutions" company whose breakthrough distance-defying tube technology permits nearly real-time transfer of employees, satisfying the requirement of the corporation of 2010 for labor to be supplied on an as-needed basis. This is *TuboFlex,* a small online game satirizing the hodgepodge experience of the perma-temp that arises from the corporate demand for maximum flexibility—a demand whose severity has spawned a trans-European activist movement that, linking together issues of labor and migration, is contesting the increasingly precarious conditions of social life under Empire.

Since 2000 a growing number of activist-made games—what the game theorist and indie designer Gonzalo Frasca terms "videogames of the oppressed" (2004, 90)—have circulated online. Most are preliminary experiments, but they represent the entrance of gaming into the toolbox of "tactical media" (Garcia and Lovink 1997). Made possible, like the culture of camcorder activism before it, by evolving technological know-how and lowering technology price points, tactical games mobilize the do-it-yourself digital practices that are so integral to gaming culture: the machinima making demonstrated in *The French Democracy;* the modding practices that enabled *Escape from Woomera;* the Flash authoring technologies behind *TuboFlex.* Tactical games connect such autonomous game-production capacities, and a small group of indie game studios trying to survive outside the orbit of the big publishers, with radical social criticism and global movements against Empire. We cited several such experiments at the beginning of this chapter. There are many more: Frasca's *September 12,* showing the inevitability of so-called collateral damage in the war on terror; the famous Flash game *Gulf War 2,* released six months before the invasion of Iraq, presciently foretelling the consequent chaotic descent of Middle Eastern politics; the *Civilization IV: Age of Empire* project we mentioned in the introduction.[3] Today, those who frequent sites, such as Kongregate and Klooningames, that host free online games can find titles such as *Raid Gaza,* which criticizes Israel's military strategy, *Trillion Dollar Bailout,* which savages CEOs saved by the state from the economic crisis they generated, and even *The Truth about Game Development,* which satirizes the exploitative practices of the game factory itself. But to examine the logic of tactical games, we'll look at more productions of *TuboFlex*'s makers, Molleindustria.

Molleindustria is a Milanese collective of media activists whose ludic critique of pedophilia in the Catholic Church led the Italian Parliament to shut down the group's Web site in 2007 until the game in question was removed. Operating out of a social center self-managed by and for activists, Molleindustria has developed a catalog of smart but simple online games addressing precarious labor, media concentration, queer politics, and street protest—themes that reflect the group's immersion in the social movements of contemporary Italy. Active since 2004, these self-described "videogame detractors" emerged from a milieu crosscut by two opposing tendencies (Molleindustria, n.d.): from one side, their country's communication system was overwhelmingly controlled by the prime minister, Silvio Berlusconi; and on the other side, the nascent counterglobalization movement demonstrated the activist potential of digital media. With the slogan "Radical games against the dictatorship of entertainment," Molleindustria has done much to add gaming to the repertoire of radical critique and to experiment with how the form of social criticism might be changed by the distinctive power of virtual play.

So, for example, Molleindustria's *McDonald's: The Video Game* turns upside down the "tycoon" game genre. Restaurant, headquarters, slaughterhouse, farmland—these four sites must be carefully managed in fluctuating market conditions. Real-time financial calculations determine the course of action. Begin on a farm, tending to matters of land, livestock, and crops. Purchase cattle and let them graze on the recently razed forest. Back at head office, command a public relations specialist to negotiate with the environmentalist threatening a campaign against the South American rain forest destruction. Get to the front line: hire another burger assembler to keep pace with the lengthening queue at the cashier, and award that slacking teller a star for model performance to ensure speedy service with a smile. Bustling business (and an isolated case of Mad Cow) has meanwhile emptied your slaughterhouse, so plump those calves with steroids and test out the new high-yielding genetically modified soy. All of this in a couple of minutes of virtual management multitasking. Motivated by research on the political economy of meat and marketing, this game puts into playable form the processes of the globalized fast-food production and consumption chain. Paolo Pedercini of Molleindustria calls it an experiment in "procedural critique" (cited in Dugan 2006). It makes its point through what behavior is allowed and rewarded, what action is required or excluded, by the game's programming (see Bogost 2006b). *McDonald's* doesn't give the gamer room for maneuver: accept the growth imperative (and the dodgy dealings it demands) or bankrupt your big business.

Molleindustria's countersimulations are intended to invite players to reflect on the nature of "the systems that produce those events" (cited in Dugan 2006). Its most recent productions include *The Free Culture Game*, "a playable theory" in which the player liberates digital resources from corporate capture and releases them into a media commons, and *Oligarchy*, which makes the player CEO of a petro-corporation: "explore and drill around the world, corrupt politicians, stop alternative energies and increase the oil addiction" (Molleindustria, n.d.). Such tactical games are frankly didactic. Their stripped-down, graphically rudimentary production sacrifices affect for instruction. The genre teeters between brilliant ludic alienation-effects and a digital-age version of socialist realism. But for Molleindustria and other tactical game makers, constructing a politicized game culture is about more than overlaying alternative imagery in established genre conventions; as Alexander Galloway observes, building "radical action" in game culture requires the creation of "alternative algorithms" (2006a, 125). Or as Pedercini says of Molleindustria: "We often claim that it is important for us not to produce games to entertain radical people, but (to make) radical games" (cited in Nitewalkz 2007). From the pamphlets printed by labor militants in the early twentieth century to the wikis maintained by network activists in the twenty-first, alternative media have cultivated oppositional intelligence: now games enter these ranks. But is the role of politicized games limited to that of agitprop? To answer this question, we must turn to some more ambitious, and more ambivalent, experiments.

Polity Simulators

Georgia Basin Futures Project is an "interactive social research" initiative by sustainable development scholars at Canada's University of
British Columbia (Robinson and Tansey 2006, 152). One of its components is inspired by Will Wright's *SimCity* and *SimEarth*. Simulating
the ecological and social makeup of Vancouver and its surrounding region, *GB-QUEST* invites players to set variables for regional economic
development and environmental policy, ranging from taxation and air
quality to land-use zoning, transportation, and unemployment. It then
generates a model of what the area might look like in 2040 based on the
user's registered preferences. *GB-QUEST* underscores the imbrication
of ecological, social, and economic factors and illuminates the complex
consequences of particular actions. The game's "backcasting" feature
allows users to reset their choices until they arrive at a configuration
that gets them closer to their desirable future. This platform not only
logs users' preferences regarding desirable future scenarios but could
also forward them to local government to give a sense of ludic public
opinion on ecological policy. The goals of the project are, the coordina-
tors explain, to allow users "to play iteratively with the model to explore
the trade-offs involved in alternate regional futures" and "to examine
whether tools such as *GB-QUEST* can be used to create an informed
constituency for social change" (Robinson and Tansey 2006, 153).

GB-QUEST is one of a range of games that we will call "polity
simulators." Involving players in issues of public policy formation, they
are a subset of what have recently become known in gaming circles
as "serious games." The Serious Games Initiative is a Washington-
based nonprofit organization promoting diverse social applications of
gaming. Broadly referring to games as a means of learning, "serious
games" has become a wildly inclusive label, spanning simulations on
topics from election campaigning to health care (Laff 2007). Much in
this category resembles the training games for Empire whose workplace applications we discussed in chapter 1 and whose military uses
have been a persistent theme in this book. But an offshoot movement,
Games for Change, is more ambiguous, encompassing social awareness
minigames aiming to educate players about a variety of international
political, ecological, and health crises (see Ochalla 2007). Often technically and graphically quite simple, usually playable for free online,
these games also feature links to associated materials about the social
issues addressed, and often include activist guides to "things to do."

This is an increasingly crowded game subfield. *Third World Farmer* addresses issues of global poverty and food supply by placing the player in the position of a struggling family of African agricultural producers; *Darfur Is Dying* simulates life and death in a Sudanese refugee camp; *Climate Challenge*, based on UN Intergovernmental Panel on Climate Change data, positions the player as EU President seeking a solution to global warming; *Food Force*, developed for the UN's World Food Program, takes on famine-relief missions; *Peacemaker*, a commercial game simulating Middle Eastern politics, makes the gamer either the Israeli or Palestinian leader seeking a two-state solution; *A Force More Powerful*, developed by the International Center on Nonviolent Conflict, trains players in civil disobedience strategy; and *Karma Tycoon*, a progressive twist on business simulators, makes the player a coordinator of not-for-profit organizations.

Most of these games emerge from and reflect the concerns of civil-society agencies such as nongovernmental organizations and their sympathizers in the game industry and academia. Outside the corporate-military axis, NGOs are nevertheless often part of the apparatus of Empire, appliers of sticking-plaster solutions to its endless wars and structural catastrophes (Hardt and Negri 2000, 35–36). Serious games reflect this. Most code neoliberal assumptions: *Food Force*, for example, engages players with issues of global famine but never really probes the structure of the world market. Other serious games are sponsored by flagrantly hypocritical corporate philanthropy: the sustainability game, *Planet Green Game*, is funded by Starbucks, emblem of global monoculture, and *Karma Tycoon* by JPMorgan Chase, a massive investment bank implicated in the Enron accounting scandal (responsible money management is touted as one of the game's pedagogical assets). *A Force More Powerful* is connected to the National Endowment for Democracy, whose projects for "revolutionary" free-market democratization of eastern Europe are supported by the U.S. Congress (Barker 2007).

But the compromised nature of many current serious games does not mean the genre lacks radical potential. Eroding the monopoly of the military-industrial complex over simulation tools, however modestly, to foster their use by ecologists, peacemakers, and urban planners, is a welcome development. While activist-made tactical games expose the catastrophic procedural logics of Empire, polity simulators can take a step toward envisaging alternative procedures. Critical discussions of deep alterations to Empire are, we believe, too often averse to the issue of planning. This is surely out of an understandable fear of the centrally planned command economies of the Soviet era. But like it or not, crises like global warming have put back on the table precisely what the unfettered market of the neoliberal era attempts to erase: massive social planning. The challenge is to explore forms of planning that escape the authoritarianism of state socialism and surpass conventional representative democracy. We think projects of counter-Empire require more attention to issues of participatory governmentality and longer-term planning—and even utopian envisioning—than many activists often allow, and that serious games with radical politics could contribute to this.

Of course, polity simulators face design challenges. Just as military simulators like *Full Spectrum Warrior* can proceed from spurious premises (no suicide bombers in occupied cities), making them worse than useless, so too civil-society games can embed dubious assumptions: "nonviolence always works," "individual recycling can save the planet," "philanthropic donations will solve poverty." But if, as Ian Bogost (2006a, 108–9) suggests, the pedagogical value of games lies in inducing a "simulation fever" in which players question the premises programming virtual (and actual) worlds, then games that allow players to edit or tweak such parameters—as in *GB-QUEST*—may be more politically educative that those that simply impose their own presuppositions on players. So while *GB-QUEST* was an academic experiment, it leaves us wondering whether such a platform could act as one tool among others for distributed, bottom-up, participatory planning around political, economic, and ecological issues affecting a locality. Asking this question, we are in good company: none other than the eminent *Sims* designer Will Wright, commenting on his next potential project, ponders, "If you could just get everybody to be a little bit more aware of the world around them, and how it works, and have that feed back into the course the world is taking, gaming could be an incredibly powerful mechanism for steering the system" (cited in Morgenstern 2007). We'll come back to this question of how virtual rehearsal might be linked to a system reboot. But first we'll take a look at another sort of virtual world building.

Self-Organized Worlds

Their world, it was announced, would be deleted; commerce decreed it no longer viable. Facing imminent erasure, three hundred residents assembled to discuss what could be done to maintain the society they had painstakingly labored to create—that was, in a real sense, collectively theirs. Apparently without recourse, they fled and settled in another land. But their former landlord had not destroyed the original territory, just left it dormant, his attention absorbed by more profitable pursuits. The evicted paid him a visit. Citing their competence, they negotiated a return, agreeing to expect little in the way of assistance; they would, as much as possible, self-organize and autocreate their society.

An actual story of a virtual event, this episode is the topic of a study by Celia Pearce (2006) investigating the "intergame immigration" of groups of players from the MMO *Uru* to other MMOs after the publisher pulled the plug on the game server. One proficient player guild—which had already established a rich diasporic culture within another persistent world—obtained from Cyan a transfer of control over the servers, enabling them to return to their "homeland." The result is that "players have quite literally taken it over and made it their own, carrying it forward to a new level" (Pearce 2006, 23). That a band of itinerant gamers could squat *Uru* in this way testifies to the advance of what Pearce dubs "autoludic culture" (23)—or what we will refer to as *self-organized* virtual play, yet one more extension of do-it-yourself game culture. Following Pearce, we'll focus on some of the multitudinous skirmishes with capital in the realm of MMOs, the digital domains substantially created by the collective efforts of their player populations.

We have already looked at the political conflicts in some corporately owned virtual worlds, with mixed conclusions. Gold farming in *World of Warcraft* (chapter 5) certainly showed how precarious publisher control of online populations can be, but also how transgressive player participation, driven by the basic market structuring of a world, can deepen microcommodification. In *Second Life* (introduction), we glanced at some instances of what Nancy Scola (2006) terms "avatar politics," such as the IBM workers' strike. There's no doubt that corporate-owned MMOs can become sites of audacious online activism: to add another *Second Life* example, the opening of a virtual office by the Front Nationale, a French neofascist anti-immigrant political party, was given a savagely carnivalesque greeting by demonstrators displaying antiracist placards in a protest that culminated with the explosion of a "pig grenade" that washed the zone in a sea of pink (Au 2007d). So we don't discount entirely the prospect of waging anti-imperial protest inside commercial virtual worlds.[4] But despite these outbreaks, the majority of avatar politics in mainstream MMOs seem tepid affairs, ranging from Save the Children selling virtual yaks for real money to U.S. Democratic Party politicians organizing "town halls" to support their election campaign. Virtual takeovers of "the party apparatus" (Scola 2006) sound all too much like politics as usual stepped up a notch, with virtual liberal democracy the natural complement to *Second Life*'s virtual market economy.

More exciting prospects, however, open up as players challenge the basic structures of corporate ownership over virtual worlds. One famous example occurred in Sony and LucasArts' *Star Wars: Galaxies*. Created in 2003, the game was originally a complex virtual world emphasizing strategic choice and a deep skill system, which encouraged elaborate avatar creation. In 2005, unsatisfied with the game's low profits, the publishers revamped it, making fundamental alterations to its architecture. The so-called New Game Enhancements, implemented like the video game equivalent of a structural adjustment program, converted *Galaxies* to a much simpler point-and-click combat system designed to generate frenetic firefights and attract younger players, and eliminated whole classes of characters. Many of the original players abandoned the game, forfeiting the days, weeks, and months of time invested in creating in-game identities. Not all the deserters went quietly. The Web sites they created commemorating their losses and declaring their grievances made *Star Wars: Galaxies* a notorious example of how *not* to cultivate digital community, especially since Sony's revised game was a conspicuous failure (see Varney 2007). The episode was especially poignant given the basic trope of the *Star Wars* mythos—rebels versus empire—a point underlined by the name of the main dissident Web site: imperialcrackdown.com.

Legendary as this episode has became in MMO culture, it is nevertheless a long way from shaking control of virtual worlds. Another group inched slightly closer to success. In 2006 Nevrax, the French developer of the MMO *Ryzom,* went bankrupt. Under the banner of the Free Ryzom Campaign, a coalition of former employees, committed players, and cyberlibertarians banded together to raise money to buy out the game. These campaigners promised to rerelease *Ryzom* as nonproprietary "free software," thereby enabling players to access, revise, and enhance the programming, while the hardware—the game servers—would be maintained by a nonprofit organization (BBC 2006b). Despite raising $200,000 in pledges, their bid was beat out by a commercial offer. Their effort was nonetheless considered a victory by many protagonists who point out that it drew game culture closer to the Free Software Movement, which views the development of a free MMO as "a high priority project" for their movement (Free Software Foundation 2006). The Free Ryzom Campaign has since morphed into the Virtual Citizenship Association (2007), which, declaring "virtual worlds should belong to all of their players," wants to spearhead an MMO project rooted in FLOSS principles as well as "participative democracy" in both virtual and actual places of game labor.

The next step is clearly for anticorporate players not just to dispute or defect from corporate virtual worlds but to create their own. This step has been taken. Launched in 2004, *agoraXchange* is the working title of an alternative MMO project devised by the political theorist Jacqueline Stevens and the game artist Natalie Bookchin, with prototype funding supported since 2007 by a grant from the University of California (Devis, n.d.). In this virtual world, the rules change. Inheritance has been deemed a mechanism sustaining class privileges over time, an obstacle to a more egalitarian society. Personal wealth left by the deceased will be directed to a transparently run international institution whose mandate is global redistribution to ensure that basic human needs for resources like clean water are met. And no longer will migrants, fleeing from oppression or seeking reunion with family, have reason to fear detainment, deportation, or worse; borders will be opened to the flow of people, not just commodities. Private property will go, too. Land will be held in the trust of the state, leased to individuals and businesses.

Stevens and Bookchin, like many others, view the MMO as a rich laboratory for experimenting with different models of social organization and for studying emergent political behavior. The game's prescribed norms have been a topic of debate among early participants. But *agoraXchange*'s initiation of this discussion is, in our view, a promising multitudinous development toward deploying networked gaming technologies as a platform for planning a new social order. Instead of either embedding the premises of existing institutions or presenting an utterly fantastical scenario, the agora prototype is to be based on "a feasible alternative model for the real world and to witness, through the creative participation of its inhabitants, what that world would look like—what alliances, affinities, and conflicts might arise" (cited in Devis, n.d.).

The idea that virtual worlds might be testing grounds for actual social innovations is one that has recently gained some currency (see Castronova 2007). In 2008 the Institute of the Future, a California nonprofit organization, launched *Superstruct,* the "first massively multiplayer forecast game." Set in the year 2019, it postulates that a Global Extinction Awareness System (GEAS) has forecast human self-destruction by the year 2042 as the result of five simultaneous "super-threats": Quarantine, a result of "declining health and pandemic disease"; Ravenous, the global collapse of the world food system; Power Struggle, "as nations fight for energy supremacy and the world searches for alternative energy solutions"; Outlaw Planet, covering increased surveillance and loss of liberties; and Generation Exile, with a "massive increase in refugees" (Institute for the Future 2009). The aim is for players to collaborate, communicating not only in-game but across e-mail, blogs, and social networks to devise solutions to these problems. We don't necessarily hold any brief for the answers *Superstruct* comes up with—as we've already indicated, the global demographics of gaming promise plenty of scope for bias. But the basic point remains: if the Pentagon and Wall Street can use virtual worlds to plan the Empire, why should communards not use them to think through their escape routes?

AgoraXchange is a virtual world influenced by the wave of writing about "life after capitalism" that accompanied the turn-of-the-millennium counterglobalization movement (Albert 2003). *Superstruct* is clearly informed by the current wave of concern over global warming and ecological disaster. Such experiments actualize the recent suggestion by an eminent computer scientist in the journal *Science* that online games enable large-scale studies of alternative governmental regimes "next to impossible in society at large," including explorations of "how individuals can be induced to cooperate in producing public goods" (Bainbridge 2007). To look at games' potential contribution to collective-goods production, we need, however, to examine further the involvement of games of multitude in struggles over intellectual property.

Software Commons

Online guerrilla warfare throws a massive corporate complex into crisis, brings some of its sectors to the brink of collapse, forces others to rethink their strategies, calls forth drastic countermeasures—but seems to remain undefeatable. Neither a sci-fi game scenario nor a radical fantasy, this is how Todd Hollenshead of id Software characterized the state of the virtual play business to a rapt audience at the Game Developers Conference in 2007 (cited in Radd 2007). He was referring, of course, to piracy. Citing the Electronic Software Association's (ESA 2007b) estimate of $3 billion annual losses by North American publishers to piracy, Hollenshead suggested that illegal copying of games was propelling the computer side of digital play to crisis. Such estimates are suspect, often making the unlikely assumption that all pirated games would otherwise be purchased at market price (Tetzalf 2000). But Hollenshead wasn't being completely hyperbolic about "guerrilla war," at least in regard to the counterinsurgency measures of the game industry: with pirates facing international police crackdowns, multi-million-dollar fines, and multiyear prison terms, and gamers' hardware routinely scanned by digital rights management systems, law enforcement is ramping up in play-space.

Commercial games, like the music and film businesses, are suffering at the hands of rip-and-burn digital culture. This is a return of the repressed: the hacker knowledge that the games industry commodified bites back as new generations of consumers learn to copy and pass on the goods it makes without paying. As we saw with "nomad gamers" chipping consoles (chapter 3), piracy covers a range of practices from large-scale for-profit operations to warez networks inspired by technical challenge and anticorporate politics to small-scale game swapping. We don't simplify or romanticize piracy. Nor are we without sympathy for independent game developers who see revenues disappearing into the black market. The game industry's guerrilla war is, however, a symptom of new forms of networked creativity not easily or productively contained in the commodity form.

This war has generated innumerable conflicts and anomalies. For example, much of the preservation and archiving of game culture is conducted by "abandonware" sites that make available online old games that are no longer sold commercially (Costikyan 2000). All these sites are technically illegal; since U.S. copyright endures for ninety-five years, no game copyright has yet expired. Yet publishers and developers—acquired, merged, and resold—may even be unaware of, or indifferent to, their ownership of game classics and rarities. Persisting despite periodic threats of prosecution, abandonware operators, like pirate librarians of the game world, run in a legal twilight zone. Meanwhile the use of antipiracy technology has raised issues about both privacy invasion and collateral damage. A notorious case was the Starforce Digital Rights Management, whose success in degrading the performance of many players' computers occasioned class-action suits and eventually abandonment by leading game publishers (Loughrey 2006).

Similar uncertainties hang over the creation of new content. A flashpoint is the practice of game modding (see chapter 1) and modders' practice of mixing content from multiple games and other media. The first known intellectual property prosecution of modders occurred when Twentieth Century Fox shut down a *Quake* "Aliens vs. Predator" mod. Fox became notorious for contacting mod teams, demanding they cease production, remove Web sites, surrender files, destroy copies, and reveal the names and addresses of members. A new term—"foxing"—entered gamers' lexicon (Kahless 2001). But other corporations followed suit. Mods for *Quake, Mario,* and *Mortal Kombat* have been foxed to degrees from total shutdown to renaming; a recent high-profile case involves the importation of copyrighted comic-book characters into the superhero game *Freedom Force.* While the pattern of enforcement is highly uneven, the issue hangs as a potential damper over the creativity of both mods and machinima.

In yet other parts of the piracy battlefield, prosecutions have raised far-reaching issues about the scope of corporate control over networked software. Blizzard's early *Warcraft* games were not designed for online play, but players independently created shareware to enable it. Blizzard then constructed its own proprietary multiplayer meeting place, Battlenet. A group of player-programmers promptly reverse-engineered Battlenet software and constructed an alternative network, BnetD. Blizzard sued, claiming BnetD enabled use of pirated games. BnetD's creators said they aimed only to evade notorious Battlenet problems of crashes, slow response, and rampant cheating. They were joined as codefendants by the Electronic Frontier Foundation, which argued that outlawing reverse software engineering would prevent new programs interoperating with older ones, thus allowing companies to eliminate rival products that interface with their own. Courts ruled in favor of Blizzard, in a decision widely seen as pivotal to legal regulation of new media (EFF 2005; Miller 2002; Wen 2002).

While media corporations struggle to contain digital culture within the bounds of profitability, multitudinous counterinitiatives take an opposite direction, trying to legally enlarge the domains of collective intellectual and artistic practice and expand a "knowledge commons" (*Mute* 2005). Two instances are the Free/Libre Open Source Software (FLOSS) movement and the Creative Commons initiative. FLOSS is a movement of libertarian-minded programmers voluntarily collaborating to develop operating systems and software whose source code is available for free. Legal instruments such as the GNU General Public License or other variants of what is colloquially known as copyleft permit users to copy, alter, and redistribute the software provided they allow the same freedoms to subsequent users. Although FLOSS has many internal divisions and factions, it has become a globally important counterforce against corporate lockdown on digital knowledge (Stallman 2005). Creative Commons refers to a growing set of licenses that disaggregate the prerogatives bundled together in conventional copyrights, allowing creators to permit copying with or without attribution, for commercial or noncommercial use, allowing or disallowing derivative works, in a variety of permutations (Lessig 2004). It is an alternative form of copyright, which grants users certain specified permissions regarding what people can do with your created content, rather than insisting, "all rights reserved." Such licenses have now been applied to millions of cultural products of filmmakers, artists, authors, bloggers, and musicians. While the politics of both open-source and Creative Commons licenses are ambivalent, and by no means immune to corporate co-optation, both express a deep restiveness against the corporate controls over intellectual and cultural life and are part of the intellectual property activism that one writer for the *New York Times* declared "the first new social movement of the century" (cited in Sunder 2006, 258).

FLOSS and Creative Commons have had only limited influence on games. The Ryzom free software initiative cited in the previous section is one example of open-source incursion, and online repositories of open-source projects such as SourceForge are littered with hundreds of game proposals, preliminary code strings, and graphics, though most range from modest to abandoned. But the Linux operating system, the most famous creation of the FLOSS community, is very rarely supported by game publishers; indeed, its inhospitability to virtual play is one of the major barriers to its wider adoption. Many of the tactical and serious games discussed earlier in this chapter carry a Creative Commons license. The control of mainstream game production by commercial publishers ensures, however, that licensing remains dominated by standard copyright and the click-through EULA, or end user licensing agreement.

Some of the more innovative game publishers have, however, attempted to assimilate these new developments. In *Second Life*, Linden

Labs allows, in addition to the copyright bestowed on user-generated content, Creative Commons licenses (Mia Wombat 2006). More recently, Linden released the source code for the viewers that enable players to join *Second Life* and then, in April 2007, announced the server software would go open-source. The politics of this move are complex. As Andrew Herman and his coauthors (2006) note, Linden's initial move giving players ownership over virtual property was in part a response to grievances about free labor in virtual worlds, but one that dealt with the issue through the very concepts of individual property ownership on which neoliberal capitalism depends. Throwing some Creative Commons and FLOSS provisions into the mix is part and parcel of Linden's broader corporate strategy, opening access while making money off the selling and taxing of virtual property. In this sense, it is part of a wider corporate drive across the entire Internet sector to reabsorb open source as yet another way of mobilizing the coding intellect of its users (see Hardie 2006). The cutting edge of corporate game strategy thus rests on partially encouraging the very initiatives that, if they were to run "out of control," invite anticapitalist experimentation—precisely what we would expect from the mutually entwined relation of Empire and multitude, where the issue of who is co-opting whom is chronically ambivalent.

Our point, however, is not to predict a major outbreak of copyleft licensing in game culture, though the practice may well become more frequent. It is to suggest that such commons projects are symptomatic of a deep *disparity* between the real conditions of digital production and existing property laws (see Coleman and Dyer-Witheford 2007). Game production, like that of film, music, and all digital arts, exemplifies conditions where creativity rests on derivation from preceding works, boundaries between producers and consumers blur along a continuum, and restrictions on illegal copying and circulation can only be achieved, if at all, by deep invasions of privacy and restrictions of technological capacities. The conditions are, in short, those of highly socialized production, a de facto commons that is incompatible with stringent de jure intellectual property rights. Game culture, we would say, exemplifies practical open-source and Creative Commons practices, *even though it continues to be governed by conventional intellectual property regulations.* It is a practical reality of multitude, ruled by the old law of Empire. This is what makes the "war on piracy" so frustrating to both proprietors and players.

While media capital struggles to either repress or co-opt do-it-yourself digital culture, these attempts at commodification resemble a group of feudal lords trying on the eve of the industrial revolution to figure out how to tithe "a newly invented power loom" (see Boyle 1996, xiv). "Dot.communist" (Barbrook 2001) practices of digital creation and circulation, not just in games but also in other fields, such as P2P, tactical media, grid computing, and microfabrication, are signs of deep tectonic shifts in the forces of production. In this view, the logic of the commons is no anachronistic remnant of fading hacker culture but a premonitory avatar of some yet-to-emerge "commonist" mode of production (see Dyer-Witheford 2002; Strangelove 2005). Such a shift would be marked by protracted crisis, in which heightened policing of intellectual property confronts expanding piracy, a proliferation of freeware and open-source programming, and the migration of much that is inventive not just in games but in digital culture at large to "autonomous zones" and "dark nets" (Bey 2003; Biddle et al. 2002). The full potential of this to reorganize social ways of making, doing, and living could only be realized in the context of a wider transformation of social relations, of the very sort Hardt and Negri suggest as the political project of the multitude.

Conclusion: Strange Contraptions

Hardt and Negri's concept of the multitude reveals the strong presence of the radical French philosopher, psychoanalyst, and activist Félix Guattari. Indeed, in the 1980s Guattari and Negri coauthored a book whose discussion of "integrated world capitalism" anticipates the core thesis of *Empire* (Guattari and Negri 1990, 47–56). What distinguished Guattari and Negri's collaboration was their emphasis on resistance, on "new machines of struggle" (110–21), on the urgent need to "think and live in another way" (131). Very near the end of his life, in 1992, Guattari (1996a) wrote an essay titled "Remaking Social Practices," a short, whirlwind synthesis of some of his long-standing proposals for thinking and acting beyond what we now call Empire. Here, in conclusion, we note the strong affinities between some of the ideas presented in that and related texts and the games of multitude explored in this chapter. Counterplay, dissonant development, tactical games, polity simulators, self-organized worlds, and software commons are six interweaving paths of social activity remaking *ludic* practices.

Guattari envisaged "a new alliance with machines," an alliance that would "join science and technology with human values" (1996a,

267, 264). This requires shattering the subjectivity of what he called the "tele-spectator," the individual reduced to a consumer "passive in front of the screen" (263). "Technological evolutions, combined with social experimentation," would, he imagined, lead into a "post-media" era characterized by "reappropriation . . . of the use of the media" (Guattari 1996b) against the values of the market that dominate our media-machines today. With mounting ecological catastrophe and mental disorientation, Guattari described the remaking of social practices as fundamentally about "exploring the future of humanity," even, perhaps, of "utopia" (1996a, 264). Aspects of game culture resonate strongly with this idea of a "post-media era" of liberated, self-producing subjectivities (1996b, 106–11). But Guattari was also well aware that integrated world capitalism itself invites us to *participate,* not vegetate, noting that it "loosen(s) up the measure of work-time" only to "practice a politics of leisure . . . all the more 'open' (to) better colonize it" (206). Virtual gaming is ambivalent: one face points toward the increasing corporate absorption of unpaid "playbor" to extend the life and profitability of games; the other turns toward intensifying autonomous production, with periodic but increasingly frequent flashes of conflict and outbreaks of anticorporate game activism.

Yet we agree with Guattari when he advises fellow activists to "try to find a way out of the dilemma of having to choose between unyielding refusal or cynical acceptance of the situation" (1996a, 95). Our gamble on games of multitude started from the apparently negligible moment of gamers selecting anti-imperial options in play. This instance of autonomy—a voice that "defines its own coordinates" (Guattari 1996a, 96)—disrupts the manufacture of consensus, of imperial common sense. Such possibility, as we noted, usually arises from, and depends on, the algorithmic choices coded in game programming by commercial developers. The emergence within a few game studios of critical political perspectives is both a reminder that game designers, while subject to bottom-line constraints and genre conventions, do sometimes enjoy a degree of creative autonomy in their immaterial labor, and also a mark of *dissensus,* an act of disengagement from the cultural consensus of integrated world capitalism (Guattari 2000, 50).

But gaming alternatives that open onto truly "new universes of reference" (Guattari 2000, 50) come mainly from outside the play factory. With the post-2000 emergence of tactical games, the virtualities of digital play have for the first time been connected to actual insurgencies of social movements, in perma-temp offices, outside detention centers, within antiwar demonstrations. While tactical games have become part of the multitude's arsenal of mediated resistance, the polity simulators of serious games, though rife with contradictions, also offer prospects for alternative forms of counterplanning and participatory governmentality. Games not only cultivate the imagination of alternative social possibilities; they also present practical tools that may be useful for its actualization. Tactical games, polity simulators, and also the self-organized worlds of MMOs all emerge as part of a wider autoludic culture in which the ability to code, change, and copy digital culture is diffusing.

Such distributed creativity reflects an emergent subjectivity equipped with impressive capacities for designing virtual worlds independently as player intelligence, creative desire, DIY design tools, and platforms for networked collaboration thread more tightly together. This is a critical part of the capacities of multitude. It shows that cognitive capitalism is paradoxically both reliant on, and the host of, a *noncapitalist virtuality,* that of "autonomous production" (Hardt and Negri 2000, 276; Thoburn 2001). This is exactly what we catch a glimpse of in the *Uru* migration and the Free Ryzom Campaign: a geographically diffuse network of intelligent agents declaring their capacity to creatively reproduce a virtual world—without the intermediary of a capitalist corporation. In a longer horizon, the project of going beyond world capitalism requires a revival of utopian imagination. Projects like *agoraXchange* can be understood as a *counteractualization* of an essential virtuality of gameplay: "an escape from particular demands and an exploration of possibilities" (Schott and Yeatman 2005, 93). They support a future-oriented optic that, Guattari stressed, is crucial if the market's emphasis on short-term returns is to be supplanted by a different conception of time capable of preserving humanity.

But the play of multitude still remains locked inside games of Empire. The mechanism of this lockdown is an intellectual property regime that deals all the trump cards for legal control of digital innovation into corporate hands. The inadequacy of this regime to the realities of digital culture is demonstrated by the futile war on piracy, with its colossal waste of resources and inhibition of technological capacity and human creativity. This means that the full potential of self-organized culture can only be realized in a system that relaxes commodification in favor of more shared and open uses of digital resources. "Commons" is a concept that sums up many of the aspirations of the movements of the multitude for collective and democratic, rather than private and plutocratic, ownership in a variety of vital spheres: an ecological commons (of water, atmosphere, fisheries, and forests); a social commons (of public provisions for welfare, health, education, and so on); and, as we have suggested here, a networked commons (of access to the means of communication).

To speak of games of multitude is thus to assert that the possibilities of virtual play exceed its imperial manifestations, and that the desires of many gamers surpass marketers' caricatures of them. Indeed, unlike the virtual-actual traffic that is characteristic of games of Empire, here we saw virtual games nourished by and nourishing the multitude. By proposing "games of multitude," we start asking of digital play what Guattari asked of collective humanity: "How can it find a compass by which to reorient itself?" (1996a, 262). His response, by "remaking social practices," was grounded in a reading of transformations already under way. Games of multitude are, in Guattari's conceptual terms, a "molecular revolution" involving "the effort to not miss anything that could help rebuild a new kind of struggle, a new kind of society" (1996b, 90). Not missing anything includes virtual games. "Strange contraptions, you will tell me, these machines of virtuality, these blocks of mutant percepts and affects, half-object, half-subject," Guattari mused, perhaps (who knows?) contemplating a video game console—yet potentially, he insisted, such "strange contraptions" were "crucial instrument[s]" to "generate other ways of perceiving the world, a new face on things, and even a different turn of events" (1995, 92, 97).

8. Exodus:
The Metaverse and the Mines

The Metaverse

A video available online shows the celebrated game developer Will Wright in conversation with the ambient-music pioneer Brian Eno (ForaTV 2006). They are discussing Wright's then forthcoming game *Spore,* for which Eno composed the score. It is an epic evolutionary game in which the player creates and steers an entire species, growing it from a single-celled organism into a social animal, capable of building world-scale civilizations and eventually of interstellar exploration. As Wright explains to Eno, *Spore* uses "procedural generation" protocols that make it possible to create content in the course of gameplay, "on the fly," rather than having everything completed in development. This promises vast scope and open-endedness for the *Spore* universe. Player-made creatures, buildings, and inventions will be uploaded automatically to a network and then redistributed to populate other players' games. Many of the civilizations a player encounters will thus actually have been designed by other gamers. These interactions will not actually change the fate of the original, which continues to reside on the initial designer's computer or console. Rather, players engage with a copy of the initial creation, with artificial-intelligence technologies emulating the maker's style of play. Each player, however, receives reports of others' interactions—hostile or friendly, cooperative or destructive—with their worlds and of the outcomes in each parallel, replicate existence. The game thus constitutes an "asynchronous metaverse" exploring innumerable potential species pathways.

As he explains these features, Wright demonstrates the gameplay, gradually building a multilimbed, vaguely amphibian race from amoeboid slime to hypertechnological culture. He guides their spaceships to an earthlike planet, whose more primitive inhabitants are at first intimidated into worshiping the invading power by a display of celestial fireworks. But then a tactless abduction sours the relationship. As the colonized fight back, to surprisingly good effect, Wright ruefully remarks that he seems to have "started an interplanetary war." At this point, Eno chips in: "Americans are doing that all the time," he observes. "That's about right . . . No comment there," says an apparently flustered Wright, his hands full now with blasting apart the recently discovered civilization from the heavens. "Time to cut and run," he remarks, as the planet sinks into ruins. "Yes," replies Eno, "the intelligence was wrong." Surveying the devastation, Wright ruminatively suggests that he had better "erase what I've done" and launches into some major terraforming activities. Oceans rise and flood the scorched landscapes: "That's the global warming fast-forward version." The screen shot zooms out, leaving behind the site of apocalypse, scanning the full scope of the game universe, with many planets and solar systems scattered through curling nebulae and vast galactic clouds, a scene of undeniable beauty, full of glittering imaginary worlds created by associated player-producers.

An amusing piece of game promotion, talking up a forthcoming release online to generate viral buzz, Wright and Eno's conversation also raises issues relevant to the intersection of games and Empire. *Spore*'s theme—the making and remaking of whole civilizations and evolutionary lines—suggests the magnitude of the social, economic, and technological transformations under way within global capitalism today, changes fundamentally altering the condition of our species. Wright's and Eno's wry allusions to contemporary events, such as the war in Iraq and the global climate crisis, as they watch their game planet reduced to a smoking wasteland, are symptomatic of a widespread anxiety that these transformations might be on a destructive course. Yet alongside this apprehension, the final moments of the video also convey an appreciative optimism about the new capacities of collective cultural creation, including those of the networked assemblies, of which *Spore* is itself one example.

At the moment of release in 2008, *Spore* was, however, to provide another telling political parable for the age of Empire (BBC 2008a, 2008c). Waging its ongoing corporate war against piracy, Electronic Arts, the game's developer and publisher, embedded in it a digital rights management system that allowed purchasers to install the game only three times, and only a single player using one screen name to use it. This negated both a contemporary technological reality of multiple-machine use, frequent deinstallations and reinstallations, and an entire culture of swapping and sharing. Gamers were furious. Players protested that the DRM made the game "for rent, not sale"; almost universal single-star ratings of the game on Amazon.com focused on the copy-protection system; hundreds of complaints were posted to *Spore* fan sites and gaming Web sites, including EA's official discussion forum. And, needless to say, the game's copy protection was almost instantly broken and the game widely pirated—downloaded via file-sharing networks more than 171,000 times within a few days of its release, an intensity of illegal welcome that seemed directly attributable to the reaction against the DRM measures (Greenberg and Irwin 2008). Within a month, EA had been forced to relax the DRM restriction, allowing five installations and up to five different screen names. Nothing could speak more powerfully to the condition of cognitive capital than the attempt, uncannily reminiscent of the gene-patenting "terminator seed" exploits of biotechnology companies like Monsanto, to shackle Wright's expansive vision of do-it-yourself species development with aggressive privatized intellectual property defenses—or that these attempts should be so loudly rejected and effectively sabotaged by the gamer multitude. We elaborate on these points using the concepts of *species-being, exodus,* and *general intellect.*

Species-Being, Exodus, General Intellect

"Species-being" designates humanity's collective ability to transform its own nature. When a century and half ago, the young Marx (1844) wrote of species-being, he was thinking of the huge transformations that accompanied the transition from traditional agricultural societies to industrial capitalism—the new centrality of market exchange, the advent of factory labor, urbanization, railways, the telegraph, and many other upheavals that profoundly changed the conditions of life. That humans have a social capacity for radical self-alteration, however, is an idea even more applicable to the era of informational technologies, which probably explains why there has been a recent renewed interest in the concept of species-being (see Dyer-Witheford 2004; Harvey 2000; Spivak 1999). The Human Genome Project and biotechnology, for example, bring the ability to alter our species constitution at the genetic level while at the same time global warming shows that we are terraforming our own biosphere in previously unimaginable ways. This is the reality that games like *Spore* play with in their projected fantasies of controlled evolution and designed planets.

There is, however, clearly no guarantee that this human species-changing capacity will turn out well. For Marx, the crucial issue was the way in which its direction was usurped or "alienated" by the private ownership of resources and capitalism's control of the species' co-operative powers. In an Empire dominated by biotechnology corporations like Monsanto, pharmaceutical firms like Merck, energy giants like BP, and weapons merchants such as Lockheed-Martin, this issue is more alive than ever. Today's techno-scientific apparatus can actualize a wide range of posthuman, ahuman, or subhuman conditions. By entrusting its direction to cognitive capitalism and the world market, Empire is navigating the species onto some rather visible reefs: the biospheric disaster of climate change, a health crisis of global epidemics, of which HIV/AIDS is one, and yawning social inequalities dividing a world well seeded with terrifying weapons. Like Wright and Eno, we may be witnessing (but in our case also inhabiting) a planet spiraling into collapse, chronic or acute. It is such issues that inspire uprisings of the multitude we have described and, in the longer term, impel many to think of exodus.

By exodus we mean not an escape on a spaceship to another planet but a social transformation that *exits* Empire. It suggests a process of overcoming Empire not by seizing power but by subtracting support from its institutions and, at the same time, creating other ones. The dominant order is destroyed "not by a massive blow to the head, but through a mass withdrawal from its base, evacuating its means of support" (Virno 1996a, 198). However, this "politics of withdrawal also simultaneously constitutes a new society, a new republic." It is an "engaged withdrawal or founding leave-taking, which both refuses this social order and constructs an alternative" (Virno and Hardt 1996, 262). Negri and Hardt (2000, 212) describe exodus as a "defection" from Empire: a defection that is not just negative but a project of reconstruction—"a complex ensemble of *positive actions*" (Virno 1996a, 198).

There is no blueprint for exodus. Many would say it is a project that defies schematic planning. But there are a growing number of thoughtful sketches of what such a postcapitalist society might look like. Some of the frequent elements include less-free markets; more decentralized, democratic public planning; less commodification and more commons; less wage labor and more self-management; less precarity and more universal provision of basic life needs (see *Turbulence* 2007). To review and evaluate these outlines of a world beyond Empire is completely outside the scope of this study. But we will mention one aspect that is particularly relevant to gaming culture: "general intellect."

General intellect, another concept that autonomists derive from Marx, is also called "collective intelligence" or "social knowledge." Just as collective labor power was necessary for many historical forms of production, so today collective intellectual power is increasingly employed as a direct force of production (see Virno 1996b). This process is enabled by technologies of communication—such as the Internet—that enable collaboration and knowledge sharing on an unprecedented scale. Empire's gamble is that general intellect can be assimilated into the structure of the world market in a capitalist "knowledge economy." However, this process opens new points of conflict, such as those over piracy and network activism. It is evident that the general intellect of networked communication could be used in ways that go beyond the world market and its for-profit priorities. The production and distribution of free and open-source software, the use of digital networks to facilitate various forms of solidarity economics, and the deployment of simulations to assist in democratic environmental and social planning are all examples. In the previous chapter, we proposed six lines along which games might contribute to such a trajectory. Now we want to step back from these specific lines of development to consider at a more general level why video games are a promising component of this project.

Another World

"Another world is possible" was a popular activist slogan at the beginning of the twenty-first century. It is also, in a different register, a gamer slogan, for all games involve the social production of possible worlds. This is the explicit theme of so-called God games such as *Spore*, which, as Wright acknowledges, draws on and combines elements from a number of other games in this broad genre: his own urban-planning and domestic-life *Sim* games; the *Civilization* games of Sid Meir; Peter Molyneux's *Populous* saga of tribes and gods; and a variety of science fiction "4x" (eXplore, eXpand, eXploit, eXterminate) games.

But in a sense *every* game, even apparently very simple ones, is a world. To play is to figure out a universe. To win demands experimentally learning a system, a programmed ecology, or code metabolism whose simple algorithms generate more or less complex events, be they the waves of alien attack in *Space Invaders,* the quest for the emeralds in *Sonic the Hedgehog,* or a metal solo in *Guitar Hero.* Many game designers and theorists have pointed out this "totality-grasping" aspect of playing games. Some have suggested that its logic might be transferable to larger spheres. Twenty years ago, Bill Nichols, in his study of "the work of culture in an age of cybernetic reproduction," suggested that video games had an emancipatory aspect that arose from the gamer experience of "seeing ourselves as part of a larger whole," engaged in an activity where one's individual activity was "regulated at higher levels to conform to predefined constraints" (1987, 112–13). In Nichols's view, this was an engagement with "the set of systemic principles governing order itself." This insight into the constructed, rule-governed nature of systems had, he argued, a liberatory potential to give an intuitive glimpse of "the relativism of social order."

A decade later, Ted Friedman (1995, 1999), drawing on the work of game designers such as Will Wright and Chris Crawford, elaborated this theme of play as systems cognition. Digital games, Friedman wrote, require players to reorganize their perceptions to perceive "complex interrelationships," whether of spatial geometry in *Tetris* or urban planning in *SimCity.* In the latter case, "the result, once the game is over and you step outside, is a new template with which to interpret, understand and cognitively map the city around you." Friedman takes the term "cognitive mapping" from the Marxian theorist Fredric Jameson (1991), who argues that under globalized capital—what we have been calling Empire—a prerequisite for oppositional movements is "an aesthetics of cognitive mapping, a pedagogical political culture which seeks to endow the individual subject with some new heightened sense of its place in the global system." Friedman explicitly builds on Jameson's concept to suggest that "playing a simulation means to become engrossed in a systemic logic that connects a myriad array of causes and effects. The simulation acts as a kind of map-in-time, visually and viscerally (as the player internalizes the game's logic) demonstrating the repercussions and interrelatedness of many different social decisions" (1995, 86). He goes on to make the politically radical implications explicit by observing that while the hopes of the Soviet revolutionary avant-garde filmmaker Sergei

Eisenstein to make a film of Marx's *Capital* were doomed to be frustrated by the narrative conventions of Hollywood, "A computer game based on *Das Kapital,* on the other hand, is easy to imagine" (86). More recent game theorists amplify this point. Alexander Galloway builds on Friedman's work when he observes that "the gamer is not simply playing this or that historical simulation" but instead is "learning, internalizing and becoming intimate with a massive, multipart global algorithm. To play the game means to play the code of the game. To win means to know the system" (2006a, 90–91). He suggests that this makes the "problem of political control . . . coterminous with the entire game. . . . Video games achieve a unique type of political transparency" (92). Ian Bogost's (2006a) suggestion that digital play is driven by a "simulation fever"—the gap between a game's source-systems logic and the gamer's subjective understanding of that logic—points to a similar dynamic.

The concept of games—not just God games but all games—as possible worlds is thus a long-standing one. But the idea is acquiring new dimensions. Since Nichols and Friedman wrote, gaming increasingly involves not just playing with worlds but producing them. Such production—the art of the game designer—has, of course, always been the skill of the cadres of immaterial labor working in games studios. But the inclusion of ever-more-sophisticated editing tools in games, the rise of mod and machinima culture, and a powerful drive toward user-generated content mean that, to a much greater degree than even ten years ago, gamers are involved not just in cognitively mapping pregiven game worlds but in making, or at least tweaking, their systems logic.

This activity is, moreover, profoundly collective. If in game studios the "lone wolf developer" has been supplemented by the hundred-member development team, in game culture as a whole, games are now altered, generated, and made from basic tools in intensely collaborative and networked milieus. The apogee of this activity is, of course, MMOs such as *World of Warcraft,* where populations of millions of players are the cocreators of complex worlds. But there are other examples in different modalities. *Spore*'s asynchronous metaverse is one. Another, which at once offers a whimsical contrast to cosmic futurism while still clearly illustrating a world-making logic, is Sony's *LittleBigPlanet,* a game that plays on the theme of little people in a big world, with teams of weird humanoid-animal hybrids negotiating their way through a complex fantasy environment, using editing tools to place, edit, morph, rotate, and interact with springs, ropes, levers, and motors to hoist or hurl themselves over obstacles, cooperatively sharing their patches across servers worldwide.[1] This turn to user-generated content stands in a contradictory relation to corporate control of game properties: it arises in part from a drive to cut costs, to exploit a diffuse playbor force; it generates an array of conflicts between playbor and publishers; but it also amounts to a devolution of control, to a socialization of the means of production.

Thus game culture revolves around the social production of possible worlds. If games are a means for the collective construction and exploration of possible worlds, it is easy to see why a gaming culture might have an affinity with social change. *Gamers against Empire!* would thus be a happy slogan to end on, and one less completely implausible than it might seem.

The Mines

As we have suggested in these pages, video game culture in many ways presents a quite contrary picture. To say that digital games are deeply embedded in global capitalism is an understatement; while the same can be said of each and every commodity, from cars to sneakers, including every bit of paraphernalia beloved by academics, from laptop to espresso machine, there is something in the sheer gratuitousness of video games, the fact that they are so absolutely and excessively just for fun, that makes them peculiarly paradigmatic of consumer capitalism. Like all such commodities, games come at a price. And to remind us of what this price is, we might consider two episodes from the history of that console's predecessor, the most successful gaming machine of all time, the PS2.

At Christmas 2000, shoppers excited about Sony's much-publicized new console were frustrated by a shortage of machines (Vick 2001). The cause was a blockage to the supply of coltan (columbite-tantalite), a mineral vital for the electrical capacitors used in cell phones, mobile radios, computers, and game consoles, and in short supply because of the dot-com boom (Montague 2002, 105). Eighty percent of the world's coltan deposits are in the Democratic Republic of the Congo (DRC), in a catastrophe zone of globalization wracked by poverty, HIV/AIDS, and chronic warfare.

In the 1990s, Uganda, Rwanda, and their proxy rebel forces invaded the eastern DRC to seize control of areas rich in natural assets. Gold, diamond, copper, cobalt, and timber were an important draw, but "more than any other mineral resource," coltan "attracted the invading forces and lured them into establishing full-fledged commercial operations," appointing local rebel leaders and field commanders to facilitate operations, and hiring middlemen to form relationships with major Western corporations such as Bechtel (Montague 2002, 104; see also Vick 2001). Coltan extraction is dirty, hard, pick-and-shovel work, though well paid, in Congo terms: while the average worker made $10 a month, a coltan miner made anywhere from $10 to $50 a week (Delewala 2001). Child labor was common: one-third of the region's children gave up school to dig (*Seeing Is Believing* 2002). The mining camps of migrant miners, notorious centers of the area's rampaging HIV epidemic, were overseen and protected from rivals by militias, often composed of juvenile soldiers toting AK-47s and rocket launchers, who were in turn paid from coltan revenues.

Sony denied using Congolese coltan, but Wairagala Wakabi (2004) says that cargoes were flown out to Europe under guard by Russian and Ukrainian mercenaries and then found their way by roundabout routes into the production chains of companies such as Nokia, Sony, Compaq, Dell, and Eriksson. Certainly pressure on supplies created by PS2 production contributed, even if indirectly, to a coltan boom at the height of which Rwanda was estimated by a UN Security Council report to be making $320 million a year from occupied mine sites, 80 percent of its military budget (Nolen 2005). Since then precarious Central African peace deals have been negotiated, coltan prices have dropped, and mounting public concern in the West, particularly about the extermination of gorillas and elephants in mining areas, has made some importers circumspect about their sources. And though in 2004 renewed Rwandan invasions highlighted the fact that coltan continues to be a contested resource in a volatile and tragic area, and much coltan production has moved to Australia and Egypt, the sources of rare minerals in the latest generation of game consoles remain opaque.

The PS2's coltan attained a certain notoriety in game culture. But another scandal, involving a different stage of the console life cycle— not production but disposal—is only gradually attracting attention. As the PS3, Xbox 360, and Wii take over retail shelves, millions of older consoles, mainly PS2s, remain scattered around the planet. They will remain in use for a while, perhaps passed on by a gamer to a younger sibling; long after they become utterly uncool in North America, Europe, and Japan, PS2s will continue to be used in countries like Brazil, where gaming has long depended on the cast-off machinery of more-affluent areas. But eventually the PS2s, along with millions of other game-playing consoles, computers, handhelds, and mobile devices, become garbage, part of the extraordinarily toxic e-waste that is regularly shipped to mountainous dumps around the world, especially in Africa, India, and China. These sites not only contaminate the groundwater, soil, and air but are also, in the low-wage zones of Empire, another site of desperate labor conditions, where communities eke out an existence sorting reusable components from these electronic graveyards amid a cauldron of poisons.

Under pressure from environmental and labor campaigns, electronics corporations are gradually revising the final stages of their product cycle to check ecological and human horrors, but only slowly and after prolonged resistance. Greenpeace (2007a, 2007b) issued a report evaluating the progress of consumer electronics corporations in removing hazardous substances from production and introducing take-back and recycling for obsolete devices. It not only gave Sony a mediocre grade (ninth out of thirteen companies) but actually *reduced* its ranking, giving it "penalty points" for showing "corporate double standards" in supporting "producer responsibility" recycling initiatives in Europe but resisting them in the United States. Meanwhile Sony representatives proposed an innovative plan to deposit e-waste not in scrap heaps but in abandoned open-pit mines, to be reprocessed using traditional mining techniques. While this might seem a progressive idea, one of its objectives appeared to be to evade the mounting concerns about e-waste toxicity by placing electronic junk under the traditionally abysmal standards applied to mining wastes; while it is "less costly than traditional electronics recycling," critics say that it could add to "the mining industry's devastating impact on the environment" (Mayfield 2002). And, of course, much of the uptake on this idea seems to come from impoverished regions in countries such as India (Kukday 2007). Thus, in a bizarre return of the repressed, the environmentally destructive and labor-exploiting mines that lie somewhere in the PS2's coltan origins seem set to reappear at the final, e-waste end of its journey.[2] While game virtualities open up all kinds of posthuman possibilities in the metaverse of *Spore,* the species-being options actualized for the laborers of Africa's coltan pits and India's e-waste sites are of a very different sort.

The Money: *The Stock Market Game*

Circulating between the metaverse and the mines is, of course, the money. At the end of the writing of this book, Empire was dealt a blow—and perhaps a boost—in the form of a financial crisis of a magnitude that is eliciting comparisons to the Great Depression. The fiscal meltdown is obviously a blow to global capitalism, because some of its largest corporate entities vaporized, and serious, potentially fatal doubt has been cast on casino-style commerce. Yet, less obviously, it may ultimately prove a boost, because massive devaluation of assets clears the decks for the renewal of accumulation, as national leaders of many of the world's largest economies speak of the need for a properly global (read: imperial) regulatory architecture for the financial system in the hope of lending it an extended lease on life.

Opinion was divided as to how the financial crisis might affect the planetary play factory. On the one hand, there is the optimistic forecast, based on the sector's performance during past economic slumps, that the video game industry is "recession-proof" (Frazier, cited in Kalning 2008). One of the cited reasons for its insulation is that hard economic times have a cocooning effect, with more and more people spending another night in, rather than a costly one out. Gaming, in this context, may be an enjoyable "diversion" from the stress of the precarious state of one's personal finances (Frazier, cited in Kalning 2008). We are easily tempted to recall one of the points made at the start of this book—that empires have long abided by a cultural theory of bread and circuses.

On the other hand, there is the gloomy likelihood that the financial crisis will, sooner rather than later, exact a cost on the games industry (Kalning 2008). Some observed that the credit crunch would make it harder for independent developers to access the all-important advance monies that fund prototyping and production—the risky ventures that often generate the most-experimental games. At the bigger studios, an environment of uncertainty, some commentators predicted, would lead to an even stronger "focus on known profit-generators (i.e., sequels) and less on innovative . . . projects" (Erickson 2008). Others noted that, after a long stretch of employment expansion, the major publishers, like EA, and midsized developers, like Avalanche, were laying off workers by the hundreds (Erickson 2008). Whether the financial crisis was the catalyst of the firings or just a timely explanation for long-planned corporate restructuring was a matter of some dispute (Gaither and Pham 2008). Still others noted that game consoles are costly consumer machines, and as working people are forced to tighten their belts, the console market may expand more slowly, undermining growth across the industry.

At this juncture it is worth remembering that virtual play rose not only out of the era of information war and immaterial work but also out of the casino economy. In his *Empire of Indifference,* Randy Martin (2007) links the informatic risk management strategies of war and finance capital. Video games are part of this conjugation. Their golden age was the time not only of Reagan's first-strike nuclear options but also of deregulated banking, junk bonds, debt escalation, and stock market populism. Making a financial play is a perennial theme of early video and computer games: *Wall Street Kid, Inside Trader, Wall Street Raider, Speculator: The Futures Market Game,* and *Black Monday* all gamed actual investment practices that were themselves becoming virtualized as global money circulated in networks second in sophistication only to the Pentagon's. On one side, these games blend seamlessly with software tools abetting the "financialization of daily life" (Martin 2002): as Atari created its hits, it also made "Bond Analysis" and "Stock Charting" (see Kaltman 2008). On the other flank, these trading games form a continuum with the commercial empire-building tycoon play genre; with the world of *The Sims,* where consumption proceeds divorced from work in the perfect virtual parable for the invested classes of long-boom America; and with the fully monetized economies of MMOs built around the fictive capital of digital platinum, gold, and Linden dollars. It is, we suggest, no coincidence that in the early twenty-first century, "virtual trading" means both online stock market speculation and the buying and selling of digital game goods.

Meanwhile finance capital, ramping through the dot-com spree, the Internet bubble, and the great housing splurge, was, like the military, hot on games. In 1997 a junior trader training in the gamelike simulator of a German finance house posted 130,000 bond futures online, believing the sale was just an exercise. But the play was for real. He had "pressed the wrong button," creating a financial *Ender's Game* scenario; his firm took a loss of some $16 million. The stockbroker Ameritrade created *Darwin: Survival of the Fittest,* a game distributed free to teach customers online trading just in time for the 2001 crash. On the brink of their great fall, the quants on Wall Street were using video game graphics processing units to speed options analytics and other math-intensive applications necessary for derivatives and mortgage-backed securities (Schmerken 2008). They also prepared the future subjects of financialization. In 2008, at the moment of the crash, the annual cycle of *The Stock Market Game* was beginning in North American schools (Levitz 2008). The game, sponsored by Wall Street's largest trade group, the Securities Industry and Financial Markets Association, provides a "curriculum" for a "scholastic contest" in which players get "a hypothetical $100,000 to invest in stocks bonds or mutual funds" and access to a computer system that executes the simulated trades, ranking teams for "bull and bear trophies" (Levitz 2008). As the Dow Jones hit the worst week in its history, some 700,000 players from grades four through twelve tried to pick winners, time the market, and sell short. Two of the game's national sponsors, Merrill Lynch and Wachovia, were annihilated in the financial firestorm. They had bet virtual play would "prime the next generation of customers." Some students learned a different lesson; a thirteen-year-old confessed, "Before all this, I asked my mom to get me stocks for Christmas" but, after experiencing the carnage of *The Stock Market Game*, "told her not to do it" and "asked for a parakeet instead" (Levitz 2008). Millions who didn't go for the bird lost to a ludocapitalism that apparently can't find "Resume Game."

Empire is only too ready to react to such pedagogical moments by advocating self-help solutions for capital's catastrophic excesses. At the same time that *The Stock Market Game* was getting into full swing, the *New York Times* reported that the Treasury Department, "which is spending billions of dollars in taxpayer money to clean up an economic mess brought on in part by all sorts of easy credit," had started an advertising campaign inviting consumers to check into the "Bad Credit Hotel," an online game that "teaches the basics of maintaining good credit" (Dash 2008). The best outcome of the crisis is that such patronizing exhortations to disciplined restraint from the masters of a system that has shown none at all speed a multitude's turn away from the great global game of finance capital to different options—virtual and actual.

Games of Empire

Since the production and consumption of digital games are themselves part of a world market whose profitability depends on dividing and controlling—when necessary by force—various unequal strata, from e-waste miners to gold farmers to "EA spouses" to game-publisher shareholders, it is hardly surprising that so many of the industry's virtualities reproduce and reassert the actualities of Empire. As we have argued throughout this book, most, though not all, of the other worlds that games explore are, in their military, accumulative, and racial logics, extensions, echoes, and intensifications of global capital.

But Empire remains a contested system dependent on social energies that it has to hold under control, but which incessantly depart from its discipline. Some of these insurgencies are regressive fundamentalisms; others are movements of radical democracy. Game culture, though dominated by global corporate-military structures, is crisscrossed by dissenting influences, partly arising from the long genealogy of player-hacking at the core of its high-technology matrix, partly impinging on it from biopolitical movements of counterglobalization, war resistance, and ecological activism. All games of Empire are, it bears repeating, also games of multitude, shot through, in the midst of banal ideological conventionality, with social experimentation and technopolitical potential.

To grasp this paradox, one might say that while games tend to a reactionary imperial *content,* as militarized, marketized, entertainment commodities, they also tend to a radical, multitudinous *form,* as collaborative, constructive, experimental digital productions. This schematization is approximate and simplified—but it points to the deep ambivalence of video game culture.

Such ambiguity opens to different interpretations. In many ways, gaming culture demonstrates the success of Empire in enveloping the new technologies and cultural capacities of immaterial labor and subsuming them as reproducers of an order whose only watchword is "business as usual." Addressing the way in which informational, post-Fordist business has adopted so many apparently iconoclastic and utopian ideas and assimilated them as management techniques and revenue sources, Paolo Virno has written of "the communism of capitalism" (2004, 110). Game capital, rushing to take on team production, modding, machinima artists, MMO populations, digital distributions, and peer-to-peer networks, is a good exemplar of this process in Empire.

Yet this is a door that swings two ways. For in this process of cooptation, Empire cultivates capacities that might exceed its grasp. In this perspective, the imperial content of so many games may turn out to be simply a shell from which the far more radical potentials of the game form eventually break out. Rather than simply swallowing the utopian potential of digital play's possible worlds, commercial game culture might also simultaneously be incubating a culture of system-simulating, self-organized, cooperatively producing hacker-players capable of looking to a future beyond the edge of the global market.

To raise such system-transforming prospects in the context of artifacts as apparently trivial as video games seems grossly disproportionate. But as Ned Rossiter has reminded us, issues of Empire, multitude, and exodus are decided not in the "fantasies of the radical intellectual" but in the quotidian, mundane, often "terribly dull" practices of millions (2007, 214–15). These daily practices involve, for many across the planet, life-and-death survival struggles such as those of coltan miners and e-waste pickers, and, for most, the daily grind of work—but also all the passionate pastimes and imaginative invention by which people re-create themselves amid and in spite of this terror and this dullness. Games on computers, consoles, and mobiles are now among those re-creations played, pirated, and produced across the planet by billions, especially by youthful multitudes, from Shanghai to Toronto to Cairo. These myriad virtual-actual interactions, multiplying second, third, fourth, and nth lives, are part of a much wider recomposition of general intellect proceeding across global digital networks. And this together with changes in biotechnologies and the biosphere is part of what is evidently a massive twenty-first-century alteration in species-being rivaling in scale the changes generated by industrial capitalism, a metamorphosis that, if survivable, points perhaps to an unprecedented intensification of Empire, but also possibly to exodus from it. Virtual games are one molecular component of this undecidable collective mutation, which is revolutionizing life from the mines to the metaverse. In that sense, they are games with worlds to win.

Notes

Introduction

1. The exact population count is disputed: Linden Labs defines a "resident" as "a uniquely named avatar with the right to log into *Second Life,* trade Linden Dollars and visit the Community pages," and records the total number of residents created since the game's launch in 2003 as over eleven million. Many of these are, however, abandoned by players who make only brief incursions. At the time of writing, 459,614 residents had logged in in the last seven days, 914,202 in the last thirty, and 1,497,749 in the last sixty (Second Life 2007). The number of actual human beings behind these virtual identities is unknown, since one person may have several avatars.

2. The origins of Empire games are lost in the mists of very recent digital history. The first game called *Empire* seems to have originated in interpreted BASIC programming code on an HP2000 minicomputer at Evergreen State College in the United States sometime in the 1970s, under the name *Civilization.* When the host computer was retired, the source code was lost, but the authors, Peter Langston and Ben Norten, each independently wrote new versions both named *Empire.* Another claimant is the *Empire* written for PLATO network—a very early attempt at a virtual university instruction system—in 1972, sometimes reckoned as the first networked multiplayer action game. Other early games in the lineage include *Classic Empire,* written around 1977 in the FORTRAN PDP-10 computer at Caltech; *Empire!,* a space combat and trading video game published in 1986 for the ZX Spectrum and Commodore 64; and *World Empire,* a Risk-style computer grand-strategy game published in 1991.

3. Created by Eastwood Real Time Strategy Group, the game is downloadable from http://www.kuda.org/eastwood. For the evident influence of Hardt and Negri on a member of this group, see Lukic 2005.

4. Stallabrass concluded his book by noting that while in advanced capitalism "a truly Gargantuan culture of distraction" holds sway, this culture remained vulnerable to social and natural forces about which most of its participants were oblivious: "The majority of the world's population will not stand our forgetfulness and our condescension forever" (1996, 231). Remembering that Bill Gates's launch party for the Microsoft Xbox, planned for September 2001, was postponed by the destruction of the Twin Towers, it is hard not to find these lines prophetic.

1. Immaterial Labor

1. Gouskos (2008) describes many famous Easter eggs, including more hidden rooms in the Zelda game *The Link to the Past;* the bizarre Secret Cow Level in *Diablo II;* a demonic green ninja in *Mortal Kombat;* and the bonus game *Snail,* which could be activated on the Sega Master System. Arcade companies in the 1980s found these hidden rooms a good means to get kids to keep dropping quarters in the slots, and other adventure games were designed almost entirely around Easter eggs. The Nintendo video game *Super Mario Bros.* included innumerable Easter eggs. Nintendo would start fee-based phone counselor lines and a profitable in-house magazine, *Nintendo Power,* both of which revolved to a significant extent on how to find treasures, secret rooms, and new levels of a game. Some Easter eggs, however, continue the subversive tradition initiated by Robinett. In 1996 the programmer Jacques Servin set out to demonstrate how hegemonically heterosexual videogaming culture was by transforming scantily clad female characters in the hot-tub scenes of Maxis *Sim Copter* into men. "These non-player characters were notoriously friendly, kissing all the other characters they encountered" (Gouskos 2008). Although Servin intended them to only appear occasionally, especially on Friday the thirteenth or on his own birthday, the "gay" NPCs began to proliferate uncontrollably and were discovered by Will Wright, creator of *The Sims.* Servin was terminated for adding unauthorized content and went on to become a member of the famous satirist-activist group the Yes Men.

2. The classic example is Tezuka Osamu's *Tetsuwan Atomu* (Mighty Atom) about a robot boy created by a minister of science to replace a son lost in an accident—an obvious parable of Japan's recovery from nuclear disaster. Because of Osamu's absorption of Disney influences, his work, translated as *Astro-Boy* in TV shows and comics, for some time defined Western perception.

3. Programmers like Brenda Laurel worked for Atari and Activision; others, such as Roberta Williams, ran their own companies; female gamers peopled early MUD communities; women played *Tetris* and *Myst;* many male players remember one girl unbeatable at, say, *Doom* or *Starfox.*

4. After rising swiftly from the mid-1960s, the proportion of bachelor's and master's degrees in computing science that U.S. universities awarded women declined in 1984 and continued to do so for a decade (Cohoon and Aspray 2006, x). Many observers saw video games as both symptom and cause of this reversal.

2. Cognitive Capitalism

1. This and other unreferenced quotations in this chapter are taken from interviews we conducted with video game managers and developers. Due to confidentiality agreements, the identities of the interviewees are not disclosed.

2. In 2004 EA donated eight million dollars to the University of Southern California to launch the Electronic Arts Interactive Entertainment Program, a master's program with courses on programming, scripting, and designing video games. More generally, EA's University Relations program encompasses coordinating research partnerships, inviting guest academic speakers to EA studios, and running an internship program (Delaney 2004b; Pausch 2004).

3. EA Spouse has come out in favor of unionization, observing that while the spate of publicity about work hours has temporarily curbed the imposition of permanent crunch time, "I don't think that will be very long-lived. In my opinion, the only thing that will get publishers to budge is unionization, which I believe to be the best solution" (cited in Hyman 2005).

3. Machinic Subjects

1. The PS2 had an optional hard drive and an add-on for Internet connection, although the promised PS2 Network gaming system was never properly realized.

2. For the later Xbox 360, Microsoft not only wanted new chips but also, to reduce costs, insisted on retaining the intellectual property rights for these devices. An intricate and cutthroat dance of negotiations resulted in IBM and ATI replacing Intel and Nvidia, while Silicon Integrated Systems made the communication and input/output chips, and the memory chips were provided by Samsung and Infineon.

3. Other theorists have also suggested that media spectatorship has become a form of labor. See Smythe 1983 and, more recently, Beller 2006.

4. The ten best-selling Xbox games as of 2005 included two *Star Wars* games, *Battlefront* and *Knights of the Old Republic;* two car-racing games, *Need for Speed: Underground* and *Gotham City Racer;* a *Grand Theft Auto* collection; and the antiterrorist *Splinter Cell.* The exception was *Fable,* a sleeper RPG hit involving an unusual complexity of moral choices.

4. Banal War

1. It must be said, however, that Islam has no monopoly on religious "endgame" simulators. *Left Behind: Eternal Forces,* for instance, is a 2006 title in a "mainstreaming" genre of "Christian gaming" (Halter 2006c, 46). Inspired by the apocalyptic scenarios of the Book of Revelations, the game depicts life on earth when signs of the Rapture have become apparent, the main signal being the restructuring of a UN-like body into something called Global Community. Led by the Antichrist, the Global Community must be battled, and not without violence, by the Tribulation Forces. The main setting of *Left Behind* is, tellingly, New York City.

5. Biopower Play

1. The journey to Guangzhou was taken in 2004; background is from Marks 2004, who clearly took much the same journey at much the same time.

2. David Harvey's (2005a) account of the new imperialism further extends the concept of primitive accumulation to include the seizure of assets by war—for example, the opening of Iraqi oil to foreign private ownership after the U.S. invasion.

3. Paul Rabinow and Nikolas Rose write of "nascent advances in molecular and genomic technologies" as forming a "novel formation of biopower" (2003, 29, 35). They pointedly distance their observations from Hardt and Negri's Marxian interpretation of biopower but find all too good a fit between Empire and the research investments, intellectual property, and marketing campaign of big pharma, the biotech business, and other elements of an emergent capitalist life-science complex.

4. Lazzarato (2002) argues that this interpretation is in fact true to Foucault's injunction that, with respect to the operations of power, "resistance comes first."

5. The distinction is more easily made in Italian, where *potere* conveys "power from above" and *potenza* "power from below." See Virno and Hardt 1996, 263.

6. Such statistics are categorized extensively by players (e.g., www .wowwiki.com, www.thottbot.com), which seem to be almost as thorough as Blizzard's data while offering a large amount of additional information.

7. While in many MMOs it is impossible to complete the game alone, it is possible to solo *World of Warcraft,* though this constrains one from exploring many of its most exciting experiences. This makes *World of Warcraft* a less-social game than predecessors such as *EverQuest.* Nevertheless about 60 percent of *World of Warcraft* players belong to a guild (Williams et al. 2006, 345).

8. According to the *China Daily* newspaper, the Shanghai Regional Court was told that Qiu Chengwei, forty-one, stabbed fellow gamer Zhu Caoyuan repeatedly in the chest after he was led to believe that Zhu had sold his dragon saber following games of *Legend of Mir 3*. The defense claimed that Qiu won the sword last February and lent it to Zhu, who then sold it for 7,200 yuan. "Zhu promised to hand over the cash but an angry Qui lost patience and attacked Zhu at his home, stabbing him in the left chest with great force and killing him," stated the prosecution (Li and Xiaoyang 2005).

9. In a highly complex mix of gamer autonomy and replication of official government positions, Chinese players of the MMO *Far Westward Journey* (with 1.3 million concurrent subscribers) (Varney 2006) mounted what is perhaps the largest political demonstration ever held in a virtual world when some eighty thousand logged on to a single server to protest what was perceived as pro-Japanese content (Jenkins 2006).

10. There also is one documentary film in process at the time of writing: *Chinese Gold Farmers Preview* (Jin 2006).

11. The widely circulated preview of Jin's film contains interviews where gold-farm employees speak quite positively about their jobs; but given the public nature of these testimonials and the precarity of the workers' situation, it is hard to know how to evaluate such statements.

6. Imperial City

1. As George Gerbner (1996) has established, one of the achievements of U.S. mass media under neoliberalism has been to create a false and fearful impression about the ubiquity of crime, providing a rationale for escalating law and order expenditures. There has in actuality not been any universal increase in crime in the United States; on the contrary, before 2005 violent crime rates had *declined* for fifteen years. Nonetheless specific urban zones *have* seen real crime crises, which have become a deep source of cultural fascination in films, music, and, of course, games such as *GTA*.

2. This and other unattributed quotations in this chapter are from dialogue in *Grand Theft Auto*.

3. Barrett's comments on neoliberalism are actually made in relation to *GTA: San Andreas* but apply just as well to *Vice City*.

4. Greg Singh remarks that despite the much-celebrated "freedom" of *San Andreas,* in fact, "the game promotes a task-based strategy required to accumulate material goods in order to progress" such that a "systemic valuation model is placed upon the ludic elements themselves." "The game's overall narrative is arguably used to compel the player through the main missions, the main tasked based element, while the subsidiary

missions and games, which rarely provide the same level of functionality . . . are there to provide a sense of freedom" (2006, 6).

7. Games of Multitude

1. The theme reappears in other genres. The *Final Fantasy* series' exquisitely wrought RPG world of quasi-chivalric character types seems the extreme of "spectacular" gaming. But the famous seventh game (1997) in the series revolves around a conflict between a group of disaffected youths and a multinational conglomerate, Shinra (which, translated from the Japanese, means "New Rome"), a weapons developer whose attempt to drain a universal source of "mako" energy (a clear allegory for biopower) enables it both to attain the status of world government and to cause massive ecological destruction until it is defeated by the activists.

2. Even apparently conventional games betray some dark skepticism toward the Bush era. Consider *Just Cause,* released in 2006, in which we begin by guiding the parachuting Rico Rodriguez—a U.S.-appointed CIA operative—in his freefall to the lush shores of San Esperito on a mission to assassinate President Salvador Mendoza, an oppressive ruler who has become a thorn in the United States' side. Central to game victory is partnering with armed antigovernment revolutionary forces in the mountains and pitting the country's oppositional factions against one another. When finally you approach the presidential palace, there is not much time to contemplate the morality of your mission, and in any case, the mayhem you've fomented is too intense to stop: kill, overthrow, and "Lead a nation to freedom!" (Eidos 2006, 4). Standard imperialist fare? There is just enough irony in *Just Cause* to make it plausible to counterplay as a critical parody of the U.S. role in Latin American politics, interpreting the backstory of the game not just as a jab at the contemporary rhetoric of the war on terror but as a sardonic medley of a controversial history of U.S. intervention, whose modern episodes include the U.S. invasion of Panama in 1989 to oust erstwhile U.S. ally Manuel Noriega—an invasion, we remember, that carried the code name Operation Just Cause—and also a trial run of aerial tactics deployed months later in the first Gulf War (Lindsay-Poland 2003).

3. Two important sites for tracking and discussing tactical games are Watercooler Games, http://www.watercoolergames.org, maintained by Ian Bogost and Gonzalo Frasca, and Selectparks, http://www.selectparks.net.

4. In 2005 we contributed an early essay about "games of empire" (de Peuter and Dyer-Witheford 2005) to *Flack Attack,* a journal virtually published out of the Port, a community-driven space inside *Second Life.* Other articles in a first edition on the theme of autonomy discussed the situation of "prosumers" (self-producing consumers) in *Second Life* and their need for unionizing, the position of sex communities in virtual

worlds, the desire for voluntary submission and slavery, the balkanization of Wikipedia, and the establishing of commons in the gray zones of intellectual property law. The overall orientation of the journal was to explore the possibilities "to act critically or subversively within the framework of somebody else's code and business strategy" in virtual worlds, with the organizers explicitly recognizing that a situation where "the user group voluntarily produce their own consumption . . . relates to the neo-marxist notion of the 'social factory' in which all of life is enclosed within a logic of labor" (Goldin and Senneby 2007). *Flack Attack* appears to have been short-lived, but the issues it raised are central to our considerations here.

8. Exodus

1. *LittleBigPlanet* encountered an obstacle in getting its game to the world market, however. In an actual version of its virtual theme, and a striking illustration of the globalized hybridity of Empire culture, the giant Sony received a lone letter that changed this game's history. Just after *LittleBigPlanet* was released in Europe, days away from its North American launch, the publisher received a complaint that a song that played in the background of the game (performed by an African musician and Muslim, Toumani Diabaté) contained lyrics quoting the Koran, a pairing of the text with the music that was referred to in the letter as "deeply disturbing" to Muslims (cited in Chloe 2008). Sony wasted no time recalling the game where it was already available and delaying its release in North America, repressing an unknown quantity of discs featuring an instrumental version of the licensed song.

2. In a more recent report, specifically aimed at game companies, Greenpeace has called on gamers to persuade Sony, Microsoft, and Nintendo to make their consoles greener. According to the environmental campaign group, console makers have so far "failed to reduce the toxic burden of their products" (Greenpeace 2007c). It accuses Microsoft, Nintendo, and Sony of lagging behind mobile phone and PC manufacturers. In this report, Sony showed up better on recycling policy than Microsoft and Nintendo—having apparently made some rapid progress since the earlier critique—but worse on the high power use of the PS3 compared to that of the Wii and Xbox. Greenpeace accompanied the report with a Web site featuring a short video showing the iconic figures of Nintendo's Mario, Microsoft's Master Chief, and Sony's Kratos discussing the polluting practices of their corporate creators: "One console may not sound like a threat, but try sixty million" (Greenpeace 2007c).

References

Aarseth, Espen. 2001. "Computer Game Studies, Year One." *Game Studies* 1 (1). http://www.gamestudies.org.

Abelson, Max. 2008. "Grand Theft Auto Mogul Prefers 'Vacuous' Neighborhoods." *New York Observer,* 2 May. http://www.observer.com.

Acohido, Byron. 2003. "Hackers Use Xbox for More than Games." *USA Today,* 15 May. http://www.usatoday.com.

Adair, Bill. 2005. "Did the Army Get Out-Gamed?" *St. Petersburg Times,* 20 February. http://sptimes.com.

Albert, Michael. 2003. *Parecon: Life after Capitalism.* London: Verso.

Alexander, Leigh. 2007. "EA Gets Social Networking Dev Super Computer." *Gamasutra,* 8 October. http://gamasutra.com.

———. 2008a. "EA Layoff Plans Reach 1,000." *Gamasutra,* December 19. http://gamasutra.com.

———. 2008b. "EA to Open $20 Million Korean Studio." *Gamasutra,* 14 January. http://gamasutra.com.

———. 2009. "EA's Riccitiello: 'Nintendo Isn't Trying to Dominate the Platform.'" *Gamasutra,* June 9. http://gamasutra.com.

Allen, Thomas B. 1987. *War Games: The Secret World of the Creators, Players, and Policy Makers Rehearsing World War III Today.* New York: McGraw-Hill.

Allerfeldt, Kristofer. 2003. "Race and Restriction: Anti-Asian Immigration Pressures in the Pacific North-west of America during the Progressive Era, 1885–1924." *History* 88 (1): 53–73.

Alliance NumériQC. 2003. *Analyse de positionnement de l'industrie du jeu interactif au Québec.* Montréal: SECOR.

Allison, Anne. 2006. *Millennial Monsters: Japanese Toys and the Global Imagination.* Berkeley: University of California Press.

Alloway, Nola, and Pam Gilbert. 1998. "Video Game Culture: Playing with Masculinity, Violence, and Pleasure." In *Wired Up: Young People and the Electronic Media,* ed. Sue Howard, 95–114. London: Routledge.

Althusser, Louis. 1971. *Lenin and Philosophy and Other Essays.* Trans. Ben Brewster. New York: Monthly Review Press.

Andersen, Nate. 2007. "Video Gaming to Be Twice as Big as Music by 2011." *Ars Technica,* 30 August. http://arstechnica.com.

Anderson, Craig A. 2004. "An Update on the Effect of Playing Violent Video Games." *Journal of Adolescence* 27 (February): 113–22.

Anderson, Craig A., and Brad J. Bushman. 2002. "Human Aggression." *Annual Review of Psychology* 53:27–51.

Androvich, Mark. 2008a. "D.I.C.E. 2008: Says Riccitiello." *Gamesindustry.biz,* 2 August. http://www.gamesindustry.biz.

———. 2008b. "GTA IV: Most Expensive Game Ever Developed?" *Gamesindustry.biz,* 1 May. http://www.gamesindustry.biz.

———. 2008c. "Industry Revenue $57 Billion in 2009, Says DFC." *Gamesindustry.biz,* 30 June. http://www.gamesindustry.biz.

Arrighi, Giovanni. 2003. "Lineages of Empire." In *Debating Empire,* ed. Gopal Balakrishnan, 29–43. New York: Verso.

Asakura, Reiji. 2000. *The Revolutionaries at Sony: The Making of the Sony PlayStation and the Visionaries Who Conquered the World of Video Games.* New York: McGraw-Hill.

Associated Press. 1998. "Trader in Training Pushes Wrong Button." *London Free Press,* 20 November.

Atkinson, Rowland, and Paul Willis. 2007. "Charting the Ludodrome: The Mediation of Urban and Simulated Space and the Rise of the *Flâneur Electronique.*" *Information, Communication, and Society* 10 (6): 818–45.

Au, Wagner James. 2002a. "Weapons of Mass Distraction." *Salon,* 4 October. http://www.salon.com.

———. 2002b. "It's Fun to Kill Guys Wearing Acid-Wash and Members Only Jackets." *Salon,* 11 November. http://www.salon.com.

———. 2007a. "Surveying Second Life." New World Notes blog, 30 April. http://nwn.blogs.com.

———. 2007b. "Offshoring Second Life." New World Notes blog, 18 June. http://nwn.blogs.com.

———. 2007c. "Avatar-Based Workers Unite?" New World Notes blog, 17 September. http://nwn.blogs.com.

———. 2007d. "Fighting the Front." New World Notes blog, 15 January. http://nwn.blogs.com.

Auletta, Ken. 2002. *World War 3.0: Microsoft vs. the U.S. Government, and the Battle to Rule the Digital Age.* New York: Broadway.

Bainbridge, William Sims. 2007. "The Scientific Research Potential of Virtual Worlds." *Science* 317 (July): 472–76.

Balakrishnan, Gopal, ed. 2003. *Debating Empire*. New York: Verso.

Barber, Benjamin. 1995. *Jihad versus McWorld: How Globalism and Tribalism Are Reshaping the World*. New York: Ballantine Books.

Barboza, David. 2005. "Boring Game? Hire a Player." *International Herald Tribune,* 9 December. http://www.iht.com.

Barbrook, Richard. 2001. "Cyber-Communism: How the Americans Are Superseding Capitalism in Cyberspace." Hypermedia Research Centre Web site. http://www.hrc.wmin.ac.uk.

Barbrook, Richard, and Andy Cameron. 1996. "The Californian Ideology." *Science as Culture* 6 (1): 44–72.

Barker, Michael. 2007. "A Force More Powerful: Promoting 'Democracy' through Civil Disobedience." *State of Nature* (Winter). http://www.stateofnature.org.

Barrett, Paul. 2006. "White Thumbs, Black Bodies: Race, Violence, and Neoliberal Fantasies in Grand Theft Auto: San Andreas." *Review of Education/Pedagogy/Cultural Studies* 28 (1): 95–119.

Bascuñán, Rodrigo, and Christian Pearce. 2007. *Enter the Babylon System: Unpacking Gun Culture from Samuel Colt to 50 Cent*. Toronto: Random House.

Bateman, Chris, and Richard Boom. 2006. "Twenty-first Century Game Design: Designing for the Market." *Gamasutra,* 10 November. http://www.gamasutra.com.

BBC. 2003a. "Games at Work May Be Good for You." *BBC News,* 7 November. http://news.bbc.co.uk.

———. 2003b. "Sony in 'Shock and Awe' Blunder." *BBC News,* 16 April. http://news.bbc.co.uk.

———. 2005. "Cost of Games Set to Soar." *BBC News,* 17 November. http://news.bbc.co.uk.

———. 2006a. "Venezuelan Anger at Computer Game." *BBC News,* 26 May. http://news.bbc.co.uk.

———. 2006b. "Gamers Aspire to Take Over World." *BBC News,* 1 December. http://news.bbc.co.uk.

———. 2007a. "*Halo 3* Sales Top £84m in 24 Hours." *BBC News,* 27 September. http://news.bbc.co.uk.

———. 2007b. "The Entertainment Industry in Figures." *BBC News,* 27 September. http://news.bbc.co.uk.

———. 2007c. "Thousands Riot in China Protest." *BBC News,* 12 March. http://news.bbc.co.uk.

———. 2008a. "Copyright Row Dogs Spore Release." *BBC News,* 10 September. http://news.bbc.co.uk.

———. 2008b. "Poor Earning Virtual Gaming Gold." *BBC News,* 22 August. http://news.bbc.co.uk.

———. 2008c. "Spore Copyright Control Relaxed." *BBC News,* 22 September. http://news.bbc.co.uk.

Beck, John C., and Wade Mitchell. 2004. *Got Game: How the Gamer Generation Is Reshaping Business Forever.* Boston: Harvard Business School Publishing.

Beller, Jonathan. 2006. *The Cinematic Mode of Production: Attention Economy and the Society of the Spectacle.* Hanover, N.H.: Dartmouth College Press.

Berardi, Franco (Bifo). 2007. "From Intellectuals to Cognitarians." Trans. Enda Brophy. In *Utopian Pedagogy: Radical Experiments against Neoliberal Globalization,* ed. Mark Coté, Richard J. F. Day, and Greig de Peuter, 133–44. Toronto: University of Toronto Press.

Bergen, Peter L. 2006. *The Osama bin Laden I Knew: An Oral History of Al Qaeda's Leader.* New York: Free Press.

Best, Steve, and Douglas Kellner. 2004. "Debord, Cybersituations, and the Interactive Spectacle." Illuminations Web site. http://www.uta.edu/huma/illuminations.

Bettig, Ronald V. 1997. "The Enclosure of Cyberspace." *Critical Studies in Mass Communication* 14 (2): 138–57.

Beverley, John, and David Houston. 1996. "Notes on Miami." *boundary 2* 23 (2): 19–46.

Bey, Hakim. 2003. *T.A.Z.: The Temporary Autonomous Zone, Ontological Anarchy, Poetic Terrorism.* New York: Autonomedia.

Biddle, Peter, Paul England, Marcus Peinado, and Bryan Willman. 2002. "The Darknet and the Future of Content Distribution." UCLA Department of Economics, Levine's Working Paper Archive. http://www.dklevine.com/archive/darknet.pdf.

Blackmore, Tim. 2005. *War X: Human Extensions in Battlespace.* Toronto: University of Toronto Press.

Bloomberg, Michael R. 2006. "Enforceable, Sustainable, Compassionate." *Wall Street Journal,* 24 May. http://www.opinionjournal.com.

Bogenn, Tim. 2002. *Grand Theft Auto: Vice City: Official Strategy Guide.* New York: Brady Games.

Bogost, Ian. 2006a. *Unit Operations: An Approach to Videogame Criticism.* Cambridge, Mass.: MIT Press.

———. 2006b. "Playing Politics: Videogames for Politics, Activism, and Advocacy." Special issue, *First Monday* 7. http://www.firstmonday.org.

———. 2007. *Persuasive Games: The Expressive Power of Videogames.* Cambridge, Mass.: MIT Press.

Bogost, Ian, and Dan Klainbaum. 2006. "Experiencing Place in Los Santos and Vice City." In *The Meaning and Culture of Grand Theft*

Auto: Critical Essays, ed. Nate Garrelts, 162–76. Jefferson, N.C.: McFarland.

Bollier, David. 2002. *Silent Theft: The Private Plunder of Our Common Wealth.* New York: Routledge.

Boron, Atilio. 2005. *Empire and Imperialism: A Critical Reading of Michael Hardt and Antonio Negri.* London: Zed Books.

Bowditch, Gillian. 2008. "*Grand Theft Auto* Producer Is Godfather of Gaming." *Times Online,* 27 April. http://www.timesonline.co.uk.

Boyer, Crispin. 2008a. "Sweet Land of Liberty." 1UP.com Web site. http://www.1up.com.

———. 2008b. "Motormouth: A GTA Q & A: A Rare Sit-Down with Rockstar Games Founder Sam Houser." 1UP.com Web site. http://www.1up.com.

Boyle, James. 1996. *Shamans, Software, and Spleens: Law and the Construction of the Information Society.* Cambridge, Mass.: Harvard University Press.

Brand, Stewart. 1972. "Spacewar: Fanatic Life and Symbolic Death among the Computer Bums." *Rolling Stone,* 7 December. http://www.wheels.org/spacewar/stone/rolling_stone.html.

Brandon, Boyer. 2007. "Blizzard, Vivendi File Suit against WoW Bot Creator." *Gamasutra,* 22 February. http://www.gamasutra.com.

Breeze, Mary-Anne. 1998. "Attack of the CyberFeminists." *Switch 9.* http://switch.sjsu.edu.

Brenner, Neil, Jamie Peck, and Nik Theodore. 2005. "Neoliberal Urbanism: Cities and the Rule of the Market." Jamie Peck, faculty page, Department of Geography, University of Wisconsin-Madison. http://www.geography.wisc.edu/faculty/peck/Brenner-Peck-Theodore_Neoliberal_urbanism.pdf.

Brophy, Enda. 2006. "System Error: Labour Precarity and Organizing at Microsoft." *Canadian Journal of Communication* 31 (3): 619–38.

Brown, Janelle. 1998. "A Bug Too Far." *Salon,* 19 August. http://www.salon.com.

———. 2000. "Volunteer Revolt." *Salon,* 21 September. http://www.salon.com.

Brown, Russell. 2003. "He Shoots, He Scores." *New Zealand Listener* 190, no. 3302 (23–29 August). http://www.listener.co.nz.

Buchanan, Elizabeth. 2000. "Strangers in the 'Myst' of Videogaming: Ethics and Representation." *Computer Professionals for Social Responsibility Newsletter* 18 (1). http://cpsr.org.

Bulik, Beth Snyder. 2007. "In-game Ads Win Cachet through a Deal with EA." *Advertising Age* 78 (30).

Buncombe, Andrew. 2006. "Bono Drawn into Dispute over Computer Game." *Independent,* 6 July. http://news.independent.co.uk.

Burns, Simon. 2006. "World of Warcraft Profits Tumble in China." *PC Authority,* 22 November. http://www.pcauthority.com.au.

Burrill, Derek. 2008. *Die Tryin': Videogames, Masculinity, Culture.* New York: Peter Lang.

Burston, Jonathan. 2003. "War and the Entertainment Industries: New Research Priorities in an Era of Cyber-Patriotism." In *War and the Media: Reporting Conflict 24/7,* ed. Daya Kishan Thussu and Des Freedman, 163–75. London: Sage.

Caillois, Roger. 1958. *Man, Play, and Games.* Trans. Meyer Barash. Urbana: University of Illinois Press, 2001.

Caoili, Eric. 2008. "World of Warcraft Reaches 11.5 Million Subscribers Worldwide." *Gamasutra,* 23 December. http://www.gamasutra.com.

Carless, Simon. 2006a. "Inside China's Game Outsourcing Biz." *Gamasutra,* 27 July. http://www.gamasutra.com.

———. 2006b. "IGE: Inside the MMO Trading Machine." *Gamasutra,* 25 August. http://www.gamasutra.com.

Carr, Darrah. 2001. "Manhattan Rent Hikes Put the Squeeze on Downtown Dance." *Dance Magazine,* June. http://www.findarticles.com.

Carr, Nicholas. 2006. "Avatars Consume as Much Electricity as Brazilians." Rough Type blog, 5 December. http://www.roughtype.com.

Cassell, Justine, and Henry Jenkins, eds. 1998. *From Barbie to Mortal Kombat: Gender and Computer Games.* Cambridge, Mass.: MIT Press.

Castells, Manuel. 2000. *End of Millennium.* Oxford: Blackwell.

Castronova, Edward. 2001. "Virtual Worlds: A First-Hand Account of Market and Society on the Cyberian Frontier." In *The Gruter Institute Working Papers on Law, Economics, and Evolutionary Biology,* vol. 2. http://www.bepress.com/giwp.

———. 2005a. *Synthetic Worlds: The Business and Culture of Online Games.* Chicago: University of Chicago.

———. 2005b. "The Horde Is Evil." Terra Nova blog, 24 December. http://terranova.blogs.com.

———. 2007. *Exodus to the Virtual World: How Online Fun Is Changing Reality.* New York: Palgrave Macmillan.

"Catching the Gold Farmers." 2007. Google Video, 5 January. http://video.google.ca.

Cawood, Stephen. 2005. *Halo 2: Tips and Tools for Finishing the Fight.* New York: O'Reilly Media.

———. 2006. *The Black Art of Halo Mods.* New York: Sams.

Chairmansteve. 2005. "Game Sales Charts/Computer and Video Game Market Sales." Posted to PCV forum, 1 June. http://forum.pcvsconsole.com.

Chan, Dean. 2005. "Playing with Race: The Ethics of Racialized Representations in E-Games." *International Review of Information Ethics* 4 (December): 25–30.

———. 2006. "Negotiating Intra-Asian Games Networks: On Cultural Proximity, East Asian Games Design, and Chinese Farmers." *Fibre-culture Journal* 8. http://journal.fibreculture.org.

"Chinese Gold Farmers Must Die." 2006. YouTube, 19 November. http://www.youtube.com.

Chomsky, Noam. 2003. *Hegemony or Survival: America's Quest for Global Dominance.* New York: Metropolitan Books.

Christensen, Natasha Chen. 2006. "Geeks at Play: Doing Masculinity in an Online Gaming Site." *Reconstruction* 6, no. 1 (Winter). http://reconstruction.eserver.org.

Chung, Emily. 2005. "Dream Jobs in Hell." *Toronto Star,* 15 August.

Clarren, Rebecca. 2006. "Virtually Dead in Iraq." *Salon,* 16 September. http://www.salon.com.

Cleaver, Harry. 1977. *Reading Capital Politically.* Brighton, UK: Harvester.

Cody, Edward. 2006. "In Face of Rural Unrest, China Rolls Out Reforms." *Washington Post,* 28 January. http://www.washingtonpost.com.

Cohen, Scott. 1984. *Zapped! The Rise and Fall of Atari.* New York: McGraw-Hill.

Cohoon, J. McGrath, and William Aspray, eds. 2006. *Women and Information Technology: Research on Underrepresentation.* Cambridge, Mass.: MIT Press.

Colás, Alejandro. 2007. *Empire.* Cambridge, UK: Polity.

Cole, David. 2006. "Is It Possible to Surpass World of Warcraft?" *Gamasutra,* 29 August. http://www.gamasutra.com.

Coleman, Sarah, and Nick Dyer-Witheford. 2007. "Playing on the Digital Commons: Collectivities, Capital, and Contestation in Videogame Culture." *Media, Culture, and Society* 29 (6): 934–53.

Connelly, Joey. 2003. "Adventure: An Interview with Warren Robinett." Posted to the Jaded Gamer Web site, 13 May. http://www.thejadedgamer.net.

Conroy, Britt. 2005. "Full Spectrum Welfare: How Taxpayers Paid for One of the Nation's Most Profitable Video Games." Taxpayers for Common Sense Web site. http://www.taxpayer.net.

Cooper, Joel, and Diane Mackie. 2006. "Video Games and Aggression in Children." *Journal of Applied Social Psychology* 16 (8): 726–44.

Costikyan, Greg. 2000. "New Front in the Copyright Wars: Out-of-Print Computer Games." *New York Times,* 18 May.

Coté, Mark, Richard J. F. Day, and Greig de Peuter, eds. 2007. *Utopian Pedagogy: Radical Experiments against Neoliberal Globalization.* Toronto: University of Toronto Press.

Cover, Rob. 2004. "New Media Theory: Electronic Games, Democracy, and Reconfiguring the Author-Audience Relationship." *Social Semiotics* 14 (2): 173–91.

Cowan, Danny. 2009. "Critical Reception: Rockstar's *Grand Theft Auto: Chinatown Wars*." *Gamasutra,* 18 March. http://www.gamasutra .com.

Crandall, Jordan. 2004. "Armed Vision." *Multitudes* 15. http://multitudes .samizdat.net.

Dalla Costa, Mariarosa, and Selma James. 1972. *The Power of Women and the Subversion of the Community.* Bristol, UK: Falling Wall Press.

Dash, Eric. 2008. "Consumers Feel the Next Crisis: It's Credit Cards." *New York Times,* 29 October. http://www.nytimes.com.

Davis, Juliet. 2005. "Considerations of the Corporeal: Moving from the Sensorial to the Social Body in Virtual Aesthetic Experience." *Intelligent Agent* 5 (1–2): 1–5. http://www.intelligentagent.com.

Davis, Mike. 1992. *City of Quartz: Excavating the Future in Los Angeles.* New York: Vintage.

———. 1995. "Beyond *Blade Runner:* Urban Control, Ecology of Fear." *Mediamatic.* http://www.mediamatic.net.

———. 1998. *The Ecology of Fear: Los Angeles and the Imagination of Disaster.* New York: Henry Holt.

———. 2002. *Dead Cities and Other Tales.* New York: New Press.

———. 2004. "The Pentagon as Global Slumlord." *Z Magazine,* 19 April. http://www.zmag.org.

Dawson, Ashley. 2007. "Combat in Hell: Cities as the Achilles' Heel of U.S. Imperial Hegemony." *Social Text* 25 (2 91): 169–80.

Debord, Guy. 1967. *Society of the Spectacle.* Detroit, Mich.: Black and Red.

Defense Advanced Research Projects Agency (DARPA). 2007. "BAA 07-56 Deep Green Broad Agency Announcement (BAA)." http://www .defenseindustrydaily.com.

Delaney, Kevin J. 2004a. "Is It Real . . . or Is It Madden? A Videogame Makes It Hard to Tell the Difference." *Wall Street Journal,* 20 September.

———. 2004b. "Electronic Arts Goes to School on Videogames." *Wall Street Journal,* 22 March.

Deleuze, Gilles. 1988. *Spinoza: Practical Philosophy.* San Francisco: City Lights Books.

———. 1992. "Postscript on the Control Societies." *October* 59:3–8.

———. 1995. *Negotiations, 1972–1990.* New York: Columbia University Press.

Deleuze, Gilles, and Félix Guattari. 1983. *Anti-Oedipus.* Vol. 1 of *Capitalism and Schizophrenia.* Trans. Robert Hurley et al. Minneapolis: University of Minnesota Press.

———. 1987. *A Thousand Plateaus*. Vol. 2 of *Capitalism and Schizophrenia*. Trans. Brian Massumi. Minneapolis: University of Minnesota.

———. 1994. *What Is Philosophy?* New York: Columbia University Press.

Deleuze, Gilles, and Claire Parnet. 2002. *Dialogues II*. London: Continuum.

Delewala, Imtiyaz. 2001. "What Is Coltan? The Link between Your Cell Phone and the Congo." *ABC News,* 7 September. http://www.abcnews.com.

Delwiche, Aaron. 2005. Post to Terra Nova blog, 14 November. http://terranova.blogs.com.

DeMaria, Rusel, and Johnny L. Wilson. 2002. *High Score: The Illustrated History of Electronic Games*. Berkeley: McGraw-Hill.

Department of Defense Game Developers' Community (DODGDC). 2005. Department of Defense Game Developers' Community Web site. http://www.dodgamecommunity.com.

de Peuter, Greig, and Nick Dyer-Witheford. 2005. "Games of Empire: A Transversal Media Inquiry." *Flack Attack* 1. http://www.flackattack.org.

Der Derian, James. 2001. *Virtuous War: Mapping the Military-Industrial-Media Entertainment Network*. Boulder, Colo.: Westview Press.

Deuber-Mankowsky, Astrid. 2005. *Lara Croft: Cyber-Heroine*. Minneapolis: University of Minnesota Press.

Devis, Juan. n.d. "Independent Games." KCET Online Web site. http://www.kcet.org.

DFC Intelligence. 2006. "Is It Possible to Surpass World of Warcraft?" San Diego, Calif.: DFC Intelligence Web site, 29 August. http://www.dfcint.com.

Dibbell, Julian. 2006. *Play Money: Or How I Quit My Day Job and Struck It Rich in Virtual Loot Farming*. New York: Perseus Books.

Dobson, Jason. 2006. "Estimate: China to Export $250 Million in Game Accessories." *Gamasutra,* 29 March. http://www.gamasutra.com.

———. 2007. "EA Invests $105 Million in Korean Dev Neowiz." *Gamasutra,* 20 March. http://www.gamasutra.com.

Doctorow, Cory. 2006. "Chinese Censors Get Played." *Globe and Mail,* 25 February. http://www.theglobeandmail.com.

Dominick, Joseph R. 1984. "Videogames, Television Violence, and Aggression in Teenagers." *Journal of Communication* 34 (2): 136–47.

Doree, Adam. 2007. "Welcome to Grand Theft Auto IV." Kikizo Web site, 25 May. http://games.kikizo.com.

Dowling, Amanda, Rodrigo Nunes, and Ben Trott, eds. 2007. *Ephemera* 7 (1). http://www.ephemeraweb.org.

Ducheneaut, Nicolas, Nick Yee, Eric Nickell, and Robert J. Moore.

2006. "Building an MMO with Mass Appeal: A Look at Gameplay in World of Warcraft." *Games and Culture* 1 (4): 281–317.

Dugan, Patrick. 2006. "Hot off the Grill: La Molleindustria's Paolo Pedercini on the McDonald's Video Game." *Gamasutra,* 27 February. http://www.gamasutra.com.

Duncomb, Stephen. 2007. *Dream: Re-imagining Progressive Politics in an Age of Fantasy.* New York: New Press.

Dunn, Kevin C. 2004. "Africa's Ambiguous Relation to Empire and Empire." In *Empire's New Clothes: Reading Hardt and Negri,* ed. Paul A. Passavant and Jodi Dean, 143–62. London: Routledge.

Dyer-Witheford, Nick. 1999. *Cyber-Marx: Cycles and Circuits of Struggle in High-Technology Capitalism.* Urbana: University of Illinois Press.

———. 2001. "Empire, Immaterial Labor, the New Combinations, and the Global Worker." *Rethinking Marxism* 13 (3–4): 70–80.

———. 2002. "E-Capital and the Many-Headed Hydra." In *Critical Perspectives on the Internet,* ed. Greg Elmer, 129–64. Lanham, Md.: Rowman and Littlefield.

———. 2004. "1844/2004/2044: The Return of Species-Being." *Historical Materialism* 12 (4): 1–23.

Dyer-Witheford, Nick, and Zena Sharman. 2005. "The Political Economy of Canada's Video and Computer Game Industry." *Canadian Journal of Communication* 30 (2): 187–210.

EA Academy. 2005. http://www.ea.com.

Eakin, Emily. 2001. "What Is the Next Big Idea? The Buzz Is Growing." *New York Times,* 7 July. http://www.nytimes.com.

EA Spouse. 2004. "EA: The Human Story." EA Spouse blog, 10 November. http://ea-spouse.livejournal.com.

Economist. 2007a. "World of Dealcraft." *Economist,* 6 December. http://www.economist.com.

———. 2007b. "Video-Games Industry: More than a Game." *Economist,* 4 December. http://www.economist.com.

———. 2007c. "Electronic Arts: Looking Forward to the Next Level." *Economist,* 8 February. http://www.economist.com.

———. 2009a. "Internet Use: China Is Number One." *Economist,* 26 January. http://www.economist.com.

———. 2009b. "Intangible Value: Online Gaming in China." *Economist,* 2 April. http://www5.economist.com.

———. 2009c. "Nintendo: Playing a New Game." *Economist,* 16 April. http://www.economist.com.

Edge Magazine. 2003. "The Modern Age." *Edge Magazine* 126:58–67.

———. 2005. "A World Apart." *Edge Magazine* 152:75–81.

———. 2007a. "BlackSite." *Edge Magazine* 178:34–35.

————. 2007b. "A First-Person Philosophy: The Mainstream Shooters with Allegorical Messages." *Edge Magazine* 178:31.

————. 2007c. "Who Dares Wins." *Edge Magazine* 177:63–71.

————. 2007d. "The Console Piracy Squeeze." *Edge Magazine,* 4 July. http://www.edge-online.com.

Edwards, Paul. 1997. *The Closed World: Computers and the Politics of Discourse in Cold War America.* Cambridge, Mass.: MIT Press.

EFF (Electronic Frontier Foundation). 2005. "Federal Court Slams Door on Add-On Innovation." Electronic Frontier Foundation Web site. News release, 1 September. http://www.eff.org.

Eperjesi, John R. 2004. "*Crouching Tiger, Hidden Dragon:* Kung Fu Diplomacy and the Dream of Cultural China." *Asian Studies Review* 28 (1): 25–39.

Erickson, Kris. 2008. "Economic Crisis Hits Game Studios." *PS3 Informer,* 4 November. http://www.ps3informer.com.

ESA (Entertainment Software Association). 2007a. "Top Ten Facts." Electronic Software Association Web site. http://www.theesa.com.

————. 2007b. "Anti-Piracy Frequently Asked Questions." Electronic Software Association Web site. http://www.theesa.com.

————. 2008a. "2008 Sales, Demographics, and Usage Data: Essential Facts about the Computer and Videogame Industry." http://www .theesa.com.

————. 2008b. "Game Player Data." Electronic Software Association Web site. http://www.theesa.com.

Everett, Anna. 2005. "Serious Play: Playing with Race in Contemporary Gaming Culture." In *Handbook of Computer Game Studies,* ed. Joest Raessens and Jeffrey Goldstein, 311–26. Cambridge, Mass.: MIT Press.

Everett, Anna, and S. Craig Watkins. 2008. "The Power of Play: The Portrayals and Performance of Race in Video Games." In *The Ecology of Games: Connecting Youth, Games, and Learning,* ed. Katie Salen, 141–66. Cambridge, Mass.: MIT Press.

"Eyewitness: Farmer's Market." 2005. *PC Gamer Magazine,* 17 July.

Federici, Silvia. 2006. "The Restructuring of Social Reproduction in the United States in the 1970s." *Commoner* 11. http://www.commoner .org.uk.

Feldman, Curt. 2004a. "China Backs Local Game Developers." *GameSpot,* 21 October. http://www.gamespot.com.

————. 2004b. "Employees Readying Class-Action Lawsuit against EA." *GameSpot,* 11 November. http://www.gamespot.com.

————. 2005. "EA Settles Labor-Dispute Lawsuit." *GameSpot,* 5 October. http://www.gamespot.com.

Fernandez, Maria, and Faith Wilding. 2002. "Situating Cyberfeminisms."

In *Domain Errors! Cyberfeminist Practices,* ed. Maria Fernandez and Faith Wilding, 17–28. New York: Autonomedia.

Festinger, Jon. 2005. *Video Game Law.* Markham, Ontario: LexisNexis Butterworths.

Flanagan, Mary. 2002. "Hyperbodies, Hyperknowledge: Women in Games, Women in Cyberpunk, and Strategies of Resistance." In *Reload: Rethinking Women + Cyberculture,* ed. Mary Flanagan and Austin Booth, 424–54. Cambridge, Mass.: MIT Press.

Florian, Ellen. 2004. "Six Lessons from the Fast Lane." *Fortune Magazine,* 6 September. http://www.cnnmoney.com.

ForaTV. 2006. "Will Wright and Brian Eno: Spore Metaverse." Google Video. Presentation at the Long Now Foundation, San Francisco, 26 June. http://video.google.ca.

Fortunati, Leopoldina. 1995. *The Arcane of Reproduction: Housework, Prostitution, Labor, and Capital.* New York: Autonomedia.

———. 2007. "Immaterial Labor and Its Machinization." *Ephemera* 7 (1): 139–57.

Foucault, Michel. 1990. *The History of Sexuality: An Introduction.* Trans. Robert Hurley. New York: Vintage.

———. 2002. "Governmentality." In *Power: Essential Works of Michel Foucault, 1954–1984,* ed. James D. Faubion, 201–22. London: Penguin.

———. 2003. *Society Must Be Defended: Lectures at the College de France, 1975–76.* New York: Picador.

Frasca, Gonzalo. 2004. "Videogames of the Oppressed: Critical Thinking, Education, Tolerance, and Other Trivial Issues." In *First-Person: New Media as Story, Performance, and Game,* ed. Noah Wardrip-Fruin and Pat Harrigan, 85–94. Cambridge, Mass.: MIT Press.

Frauenheim, Ed. 2004. "Electronic Arts Promises Workplace Change." *ZDNET News,* 3 December. http://www.zdnet.com.

Free Software Foundation. 2006. "Freeing a MMORPG—Updated." Free Software Foundation Web site. News release, 21 December. http://www.fsf.org.

Friedman, Ted. 1995. "Making Sense of Software: Computer Games and Interactive Textuality." In *CyberSociety: Computer-Mediated Communication and Community,* ed. Steven G. Jones, 73–89. Redwood, Calif.: Sage.

———. 1999. "Civilization and Its Discontents: Simulation, Subjectivity, and Space." In *On a Silver Platter: CD-ROMs and the Promises of a New Technology,* ed. Greg M. Smith, 135–50. New York: New York University Press.

Fritz, Ben. 2008. "Dan Houser's Very Extended Interview about Everything 'Grand Theft Auto IV' and Rockstar." Cut Scene blog, 19 April. http://weblogs.variety.com/thecutscene.

Full Spectrum Warrior Instruction Manual (FSWIM). 2004. Los Angeles: Pandemic Studios.

Funk, McKenzie. 2007. "I Was a Chinese Internet Addict." *Harper's Magazine* (March): 65–72.

Gaither, Chris, and Alex Pham. 2008. "Game Giant Electronic Arts Posts Losses, Plans Job Cuts." *Los Angeles Times,* 30 October. http://latimesblogs.latimes.com.

Gallaugher, John, and Greg Stoller. 2004. "Software Outsourcing in Vietnam: A Case Study of a Locally Operating Pioneer." *Electronic Journal of Information Systems in Developing Countries* 17 (1): 1–18.

Galloway, Alexander R. 2006a. *Gaming: Essays on Algorithmic Culture.* Minneapolis: University of Minnesota Press.

———. 2006b. "*Warcraft* and Utopia." *CTheory,* 16 February. http://www.ctheory.net.

———. n.d. "A Report on Cyberfeminism: Sadie Plant Relative to VNS Matrix." *Switch* 9. http://switch.sjsu.edu.

Game Informer. 2007. http://www.ruthlesstoonimation.com/gta4.htm.

Game Politics. 2007. "Ebay Bans Virtual Item Auctions." Game Politics Web site, 30 January. http://gamepolitics.com.

Garcia, David, and Geert Lovink. 1997. "The ABC of Tactical Media." E-mail to nettime mailing list, 16 May. http://www.nettime.org.

Gaudiosi, John. 2007. "Electronic Arts Shifts NASCAR 09 to New North Carolina Studio." *GameDaily,* 24 October. http://www.gamedaily.com.

Gerbner, George. 1996. "The Hidden Side of Television Violence." In *Invisible Crises: What Conglomerate Control of Media Means for America and the World,* ed. George Gerbner, Hamid Mowlana, and Herbert Schiller, 27–34. Boulder, Colo.: Westview Press.

Ghattas, Kim. 2002. "Syria Launches Arab War Game." *BBC News,* 31 May. http://news.bbc.co.uk.

Gibson, Elie. 2005. "Microsoft Announces Xbox 360 Manufacturers." *GameIndustry.biz,* 17 August. http://www.gamesindustry.biz.

Gilroy, Paul. 2000. *Against Race: Imagining Political Culture beyond the Color Line.* Cambridge, Mass.: Belknap Press.

Giroux, Henry A. 2006. *Beyond the Spectacle of Terrorism: Global Uncertainty and the Challenge of the New Media.* Boulder, Colo.: Paradigm.

Giumetti, Gary W., and Patrick M. Markey. 2007. "Violent Video Games and Anger as Predictors of Aggression." *Journal of Research in Personality* 41 (6): 1234–43.

Glenny, Misha. 2008. *McMafia: Crime without Frontiers.* London: Random House.

Goldin, Simon, and Senneby, Jakob. 2007. "Enclosure and Enthusiasm: Or Looking for Autonomy in the 'Social Factory.'" goldin+senneby Web site, 31 January. http://www.goldinsenneby.com.

Goldman, Michael. 1998. "Introduction: The Political Resurgence of the Commons." In *Privatizing Nature: Political Struggles for the Global Commons*, ed. Michael Goldman, 1–19. London: Pluto.

Gordon, Larry. 2007. "Virtual War, Real Healing." *Los Angeles Times*, 9 February. http://www.latimes.com.

Gorenfeld, John. 2003. "Get Behind the MULE." *Salon*, 18 March. http://www.salon.com.

Graft, Kris. 2007. "Pearl: Be Wary of Outsourcing Expenses." *Next Generation*, 22 January. http://www.next-gen.biz.

Graham, Stephen. 2007. "War and the City." *New Left Review* 44 (March–April): 121–32.

Greenberg, Andy, and Mary Jane Irwin. 2008. "Spore's Piracy Problem." *Forbes*, 12 September. http://www.forbes.com.

Greenpeace. 2007a. "Guide to Greener Electronics." Version 8. Greenpeace International Web site. http://www.greenpeace.org.

———. 2007b. "Nintendo, Microsoft, and Philips Flunk Toxic Test." Greenpeace International Web site, 27 November. http://www.greenpeace.org.

———. 2007c. "Clash of the Consoles." Greenpeace International Web site. http://www.greenpeace.org.

Griffiths, Mark. 1999. "Violent Video Games and Aggression: A Review of the Literature." *Aggression and Violent Behaviour* 4:203–12.

Griggers, Camilla. 1997. *Becoming Woman*. Minneapolis: University of Minnesota Press.

Grossman, David. 1996. *On Killing: The Psychological Costs of Learning to Kill in War and Society*. New York: Back Bay Books.

Grossman, Dave, and Gloria DeGaetano. 1999. *Stop Teaching Our Kids to Kill: A Call to Action against TV, Movie, and Video Game Violence*. New York: Crown.

Gouskos, Carrie, with Jeff Gerstmann. 2008. "The Greatest Easter Eggs in Gaming." *GameSpot*. http://www.gamespot.com.

The GTA Place. 2008. "Assets." GTA Place Web site. http://www.thegtaplace.com.

Guattari, Félix. 1995. *Chaosmosis: An Ethico-aesthetic Paradigm*. Trans. Paul Bains and Julian Pefanis. Bloomington: Indiana University Press.

———. 1996a. *The Guattari Reader*. Ed. Gary Genosko. Oxford: Blackwell.

———. 1996b. *Soft Subversions*. New York: Semiotext(e).

———. 2000. *The Three Ecologies*. Trans. Ian Pindar and Paul Sutton. London: Athlone.

Guattari, Félix, and Antonio Negri. 1990. *Communists like Us: New Spaces of Liberty, New Lines of Alliance*. Trans. Michael Ryan. New York: Semiotext(e).

Gunter, Barrie. 2004. "Psychological Effects of Video Games." In *Handbook of Computer Game Studies,* ed. Joest Raessens and Jeffrey Goldstein, 145–61. Cambridge, Mass.: MIT Press.

Gwap. 2008. "About Gwap." Gwap Web site. http://www.gwap.com/gwap/about.

Haines, Lizzie. 2004a. *Why Are There So Few Women in Games?* Manchester, UK: Media Training North West. International Game Developers Association Web site. http://www.igda.org.

———. 2004b. *Women and Girls in the Game Industry.* Manchester, UK: Media Training North West. International Game Developers Association Web site. http://www.igda.org.

Halbfinger, David M., and Steven A. Holmes. 2003. "A Nation at War: The Troops; Military Mirrors a Working-Class America." *New York Times,* 30 March. http://www.nytimes.com.

Hall, Kenji. 2006. "The Big Ideas behind Nintendo's Wii." *Business Week,* 16 November. http://www.businessweek.com.

Halter, Ed. 2006a. *From Sun Tzu to Xbox: War and Video Games.* New York: Thunder's Mouth Press.

———. 2006b. "Islamogaming: Looking for Video Games in the Muslim World." *Fox News,* 11 September. http://www.foxnews.com.

———. 2006c. "Play to Pray: A History of Christian Video Games." *Games for Windows* (December): 44–46.

Haraway, Donna. 1985. "Manifesto for Cyborgs: Science, Technology, and Socialist Feminism in the 1980s." *Socialist Review* 80:65–108.

Hardie, Martin. 2006. "Change of the Century: Free Software and the Positive Possibility." *Mute Magazine.* http://www.metamute.org.

Hardt, Michael, and Antonio Negri. 2000. *Empire.* Cambridge, Mass.: Harvard University Press.

———. 2004. *Multitude: War and Democracy in the Age of Empire.* New York: Penguin.

Hart-Landsberg, Martin, and Paul Burkett. 2006. "China and the Dynamics of Transnational Capital Accumulation: Causes and Consequences of Global Restructuring." *Historical Materialism* 14 (3): 3–43.

Harvey, David. 1989. *The Condition of Postmodernity: An Enquiry into the Origins of Cultural Change.* Oxford: Blackwell.

———. 2000. *Spaces of Hope.* Berkeley: University of California Press.

———. 2001. *Spaces of Capital: Towards a Critical Geography.* London: Routledge.

———. 2004. "A Geographer's Perspective on the New American Imperialism." Interview with Harry Kreisler. *Conversations with History.* Institute of International Studies, University of California, Berkeley, 2 March. http://globetrotter.berkeley.edu.

———. 2005a. *The New Imperialism.* Oxford: Polity.

———. 2005b. "Last Days of the U.S. Empire?" *Socialist Worker Online,* 30 July. http://www.socialistworker.co.uk.

———. 2007. *A Brief History of Neoliberalism.* Oxford: Oxford University Press.

Hasselback, Drew. 2000. "Brain Drain Puts Jobs on Hold." *National Post* (Toronto), 10 April.

Heeks, Richard. 2008. "Current Analysis and Future Research Agenda on 'Gold Farming': Real-World Production in Developing Countries for the Virtual Economies of Online Games." Development Informatics Working Paper Series No. 32. http://www.sed.manchester.ac.uk/idpm/research/publications/wp/di/documents/di_wp32.pdf.

Hefflinger, Mark. 2007. "Sony: Virtual Game Item Marketplace Does $1.87 Million in First Year." *Digital Media Wire,* 7 February. http://www.dmwmedia.com.

Herald News Service. 2008. "Electronic Arts to Expand Online in Asia." *Calgary Herald,* 6 June. http://www.canada.com/calgaryherald.

Herbst, Claudia. 2005. "Shock and Awe: Virtual Females and the Sexing of War." *Feminist Media Studies* 5 (3): 311–24.

Herman, Andrew, Rosemary J. Coombe, and Lewis Kaye. 2006. "Your *Second Life*? Goodwill and the Performativity of Intellectual Property in Online Digital Gaming." *Cultural Studies* 20, nos. 2–3 (March–May): 184–210.

Herman, Leonard. 1997. *Phoenix: The Fall and Rise of Videogames.* Union, N.J.: Rolenta Press.

Hermida, Alfred. 2004. "Xbox Live Aims for a Million Gamers." *BBC News,* 8 January. http://news.bbc.co.uk.

Herz, J. C. 1997. *Joystick Nation: How Videogames Ate Our Quarters, Won Our Hearts, and Rewired Our Minds.* Boston: Little, Brown.

Hesseldahl, Arik. 2005. "Microsoft's Red-Ink Game." *Business Week,* 22 November. http://businessweek.com.

Higgin, Tanner. 2006. "Play-Fighting: Understanding Violence in Grand Theft Auto III." In *The Meaning and Culture of Grand Theft Auto: Critical Essays,* ed. Nate Garrelts, 70–87. Jefferson, N.C.: McFarland.

Hill, Dan. 2004. "Los Angeles: Grand Theft Reality." City of Sound blog, 20 December. http://www.cityofsound.com.

Hill, Logan. 2002. "Why Rockstar Games Rule: The Badboys of Rockstar Games." *Wired* 10 (7): 119–21.

Himanen, Pekka. 2001. *The Hacker Ethic and the Spirit of the Information Age.* New York: Random House.

Hobsbawm, Eric. 1998. *Uncommon People: Resistance, Rebellion, and Jazz.* London: Abacus.

Hochschild, Arlie R. 1983. *The Managed Heart: The Commercialization of Human Feeling.* Berkeley: University of California Press.

Hochschild, Arlie R., with Anne Machung 1990. *The Second Shift*. New York: Avon.

Hof, Robert D. 2007. "The End of Work as You Know It." *Business Week*, 20 August. http://www.businessweek.com.

Hogan, Jenny, and Barry Fox. 2005. "Sony Patent Takes First Step towards Real-Life Matrix." *New Scientist*, 7 April. http://www.newscientist .com.

Holmes, Brian. 2007. "Disconnecting the Dots of the Research Triangle: Corporatisation, Flexibilisation, and Militarisation in the Creative Industries." In *MyCreativity Reader: A Critique of Creative Industries*, ed. Geert Lovink and Ned Rossiter, 177–89. Amsterdam: Institute of Network Cultures.

Holmstrom, Nancy, and Richard Smith. 2000. "The Necessity of Gangster Capitalism: Primitive Accumulation in Russia and China." *Monthly Review* 51 (9). http://www.monthlyreview.org.

hooks, bell. 1995. "Cool Tool." *ArtForum* 38, no. 7 (March): 63–66, 110.

Hoover's Company Records. 2008. "Electronic Arts." Hoover's Company Records database, 10 June.

Howard, Pat. 1988. *Breaking the Iron Rice Bowl: Prospects for Socialism in China's Countryside*. New York: M. E. Sharpe.

Howie, Hank. 2005. "Making Great Games in 40 Hours per Week." *Gamasutra*, 31 January. http://www.gamasutra.com.

Huifeng, He. 2005. "Chinese 'Farmers' Strike Cyber Gold." *South China Morning Post*, 25 October. http://english.cri.cn.

Huizinga, Johan. 1921 [1996]. *The Autumn of the Middle Ages*. Chicago: University of Chicago Press.

———. 1944 [1950]. *Homo Ludens: A Study of the Play-Element in Culture*. Boston: Beacon Press.

Humphreys, Sal. 2004. "Commodifying Culture: It's Not Just about the Virtual Sword." In *Proceedings of the Other Players Conference*, ed. J. Heide Smith and M. Sicart. Copenhagen: IT University of Copenhagen.

———. 2005. "Productive Players: Online Computer Games' Challenge to Conventional Media Forms." *Journal of Communication and Critical/Cultural Studies* 2, no. 1 (March): 37–51.

Hyman, Paul. 2005. "Unionize Now?" *Gamasutra*, 22 March. http:// www.gamasutra.com.

———. 2008. "Quality of Life: Does Anyone Still Give a Damn?" *Gamasutra*, 13 May. http://www.gamasutra.com.

IGDA (International Game Developers Association). 2004a. *Quality of Life in the Game Industry: Challenges and Best Practices*. International Game Developers Association Web site. http://www.igda.org.

———. 2004b. "Quality of Life Issues Are Holding Back the Game

Industry: Open Letter from IGDA Board of Directors." International Game Developers Association Web site. 16 November. http://www.igda.org.

———. 2005. *Game Developer Demographics: An Exploration of Workforce Diversity.* International Game Developers Association Web site. http://www.igda.org.

Institute for Creative Technologies (ICT). 2004. University of Southern California, Institute for Creative Technologies Web site. http://www.ict.usc.edu.

———. n.d. "Post-traumatic Stress Disorder Assessment and Treatment." University of Southern California, Institute for Creative Technologies Web site. http://www.ict.usc.edu.

Institute of the Future. 2009. "Superstruct." http://www.superstructgame.org.

Irwin, Mary Jane. 2009. "Riccitiello's Three Rules for Recession." *Edge,* 19 February. http://www.edge-online.com.

Jade, Charles. 2005. "Blizzards Bans a Gold Rush." *Ars Technica,* 15 March. http://www.arstechnica.com.

Jakobsson, Mikael, and T. L. Taylor. 2003. "The Sopranos Meet Ever-Quest: Social Networking in Massively Multiplayer Online Games." In *Proceedings of the 5th International Digital Arts and Culture Conference.* Melbourne: School of Applied Communication, RMIT, Melbourne, 19–23 May. http://hypertext.rmit.edu.au/dac.

James, C. L. R. 1966. *Beyond a Boundary.* London: Hutchinson.

Jameson, Fredric. 1981. *The Political Unconscious: Narrative as a Socially Symbolic Act.* Ithaca, N.Y.: Cornell University Press.

———. 1988. "Cognitive Mapping." In *Marxism and the Interpretation of Culture,* ed. Cary Nelson and Lawrence Grossberg, 347–57. Chicago: University of Illinois Press.

———. 1992. *Postmodernism, or The Cultural Logic of Late Capitalism.* New York: Verso.

Jana, Reena. 2006. "On-the-Job Video Gaming." *Business Week,* 27 March. http://www.businessweek.com.

Jenkins, David. 2005. "China Promotes 'Patriotic' Online Games." *Gamasutra,* 24 August. http://www.gamasutra.com.

———. 2007. "Report Predicts $1.3 Billion Games Market in China." *Gamasutra,* 27 January. http://www.gamasutra.com.

———. 2008a. "EA Acquires Napster Founder's Gaming Social Network." *Gamasutra,* 4 June. http://www.gamasutra.com.

———. 2008b. "EA's Riccitiello: Balance of Power Shifting from Games to Films." *Gamasutra,* 14 April. http://www.gamasutra.com.

———. 2008c. "EA Expands Massive in-Game Advertising Deal." *Gamasutra,* 18 March. http://www.gamasutra.com.

Jenkins, Henry. 1992. *Textual Poachers: Television Fans and Participatory Culture.* New York: Routledge.

———. 1999. "Professor Jenkins Goes to Washington." *Harper's Magazine,* July, 19–23.

———. 2003. "From Barbie to Mortal Kombat: Further Reflections." In *New Media: Theories and Practices of Digitextuality,* ed. Anna Everett and John T. Caldwell, 243–54. New York: Routledge.

———. 2005. "Games: The New Lively Art." In *Handbook of Computer Game Studies,* ed. Joest Raessens and Jeffrey Goldstein, 175–92. Cambridge, Mass.: MIT.

———. 2006a. *Fans, Bloggers, and Gamers: Exploring Participatory Culture.* New York: New York University.

———. 2006b. "National Politics within Virtual Game Worlds: The Case of China." Confessions of an Aca-fan blog, 2 August. http://www.henryjenkins.org.

Jenkins, Henry, with Mary Fuller. 1995. "Nintendo and New World Travel Writing: A Dialogue." In *Cybersociety: Computer-Mediated Communication and Community,* ed. Steven G. Jones, 57–72. Thousand Oaks, Calif.: Sage.

Jhally, Sut. 1989. "Cultural Studies and the Sports/Media Complex." In *Media, Sport, and Society,* ed. Lawrence Werner, 70–93. Newbury Park, Calif.: Sage.

Jin, Ge. 2006. "Chinese Gold Farmers in the Game World." *Consumers, Commodities, and Consumption: A Newsletter of the Consumer Studies Research Network* 7 (2). https://netfiles.uiuc.edu/dtcook/www/CCCnewsletter/7-2.

Johne, Marjo. 2006. "Prize for Playing the Game: A Career." *Globe and Mail* (Toronto), 26 April.

Johns, Jennifer. 2006. "Video Games Production Networks: Value Capture, Power Relations, and Embeddedness." *Journal of Economic Geography* 6:151–80.

Johnson, Steven. 2005. *Everything Bad Is Good for You: How Today's Popular Culture Is Actually Making Us Smarter.* New York: Riverhead.

Joint Chiefs of Staff. 2000. *Joint Vision 2020.* Washington: U.S. Government Printing Office. http://www.dtic.mil/jointvision/jvpub2.htm.

Kahless. 2001. "The Foxing of Mods." 3DactionPlanet Web site, 28 April. http://www.3dactionplanet.com.

Kahney, Leander. 2003. "Games Invade Hollywood's Turf." *Wired,* 9 July. http://wired.com.

Kalning, Kristin. 2008. "Is the Video Game Industry Recession-Proof?" MSNBC, 7 March. http://www.msnbc.com.

Kaltman, Eric. 2008. "Financial Woes." Eric Kaltman's blog. http://www.stanford.edu/group/htgg/cgi-bin/drupal.

Kent, Steven. 2001. *The Ultimate History of Video Games.* Roseville, Calif.: Prima Publishing.

Kerr, Aphra. 2006. *The Business and Culture of Digital Games: Gamework/Gameplay.* London: Sage.

Kiat, Ong Boon. 2008. "Electronic Arts Eyes Asian Growth." *Business Times,* 10 March.

Kim, Kyung Hyun. 2004. *The Remasculinization of Korean Cinema.* Durham, N.C.: Duke University Press.

Kinder, Marsha. 1991. *Playing with Power in Movies, Television, and Videogames: From Muppet Babies to Teenage Mutant Turtles.* Berkeley: University of California Press.

Kinsella, Sharon. 1998. "Amateur Manga Subculture and the *Otaku* Panic." Sharon Kinsella's Web site. http://www.kinsellaresearch.com. Originally published in *Journal of Japanese Studies* 24:289–316.

———. 2000. *Adult Manga: Culture and Power in Contemporary Japanese Society.* Honolulu: University of Hawaii Press.

———. 2005. "The Nationalization of Manga." Japan Society Lecture, School of Oriental and African Studies, London, 11 October. Japan Society of the UK Web site. http://www.japansociety.org.uk/lectures.

Klein, Naomi. 2000. *No Logo: Taking Aim at the Brand Bullies.* Toronto: Knopf.

———. 2007. *The Shock Doctrine: The Rise of Disaster Capitalism.* Toronto: Knopf.

Kline, Stephen, Nick Dyer-Witheford, and Greig de Peuter. 2003. *Digital Play: The Interaction of Culture, Technology, and Marketing.* Montreal and Kingston: McGill-Queen's University Press.

Kohler, Chris. 2004. *Power Up: How Japanese Video Games Gave the World an Extra Life.* New York: Brady Games.

———. 2009. "EA CEO: Recession Is a 'Blessing' for Game Biz." Wired Gamelife blog, 19 February. http://www.wired.com/gamelife.

Koo, Shang. 2006. "The Chinese MMO Cola Wars." *Gamasutra,* 27 November. http://www.gamasutra.com.

———. 2007a. "Game Safety." *Gamasutra,* 22 January. http://www.gamasutra.com.

———. 2007b. "The9." *Gamasutra,* 12 February. http://www.gamasutra.com.

———. 2007c. "Perfect Worlds, Golden Flowers." *Gamasutra,* 8 January. http://www.gamasutra.com.

Korris, James. 2004. "Full Spectrum Warrior: How the Institute for Creative Technologies Built a Cognitive Training Tool for Xbox." University of Southern California, Institute for Creative Technologies Web site. http://www.ict.usc.edu.

Kraemer, Kenneth, and Jason Dedrick. 2001. "Creating a Computer

Industry Giant: China's Industrial Policies and Outcomes in the 1990s."
Center for Research on Information Technology and Organizations,
University of California, Irvine. http://www.crito.uci.edu/git.

Krotoski, Aleks. 2004. *Chicks and Joysticks: An Exploration of Women
and Gaming.* Entertainment and Leisure Software Publishers Association Web site. http://www.elspa.com.

Kücklich, Julian. 2005. "Precarious Playbour: Modders and the Digital
Games Industry." *Fibreculture Journal 5.* http://journal.fibreculture.org.

Kukday, Kavita. 2007. "Making Profit from Mining of E-Waste." *Times
of India,* 8 June. http://timesofindia.indiatimes.com.

Kuma Games. 2006. "Kuma Reality Games Sparks Virtual Dialogue
with Iran over Nuclear Arms Dispute." Kuma Games Web site. News
release, 9 June. http://www.kumawar.com.

Kuma War. 2007. Kuma Games Web site. http://www.kumawar.com.

Kushner, David. 2003. *Masters of Doom: How Two Guys Created an
Empire and Transformed Pop Culture.* New York: Random House.

———. 2004. "Hot Geeks." *Rolling Stone,* 19 August, 100.

———. 2007a. "Road to Ruin: How Grand Theft Auto Hit the Skids."
Wired, 29 March. http://www.wired.com.

———. 2007b. "The Ups and Downs of Take-Two Interactive's Stock
Price." *Wired,* 29 March. http://www.wired.com.

Laclau, Ernesto. 2004. "Can Immanence Explain Social Struggles?"
In *Empire's New Clothes: Reading Hardt and Negri,* ed. Paul A.
Passavant and Jodi Dean, 21–30. London: Routledge.

Laff, Michael. 2007. "Serious Gaming: The Trainer's New Best Friend."
T+D (January): 52–57.

Lake, Chloe. 2008. "Little Big Planet Delayed by Koran Quotes." *News
.com.au,* 20 October. http://www.news.com/au/technology.

Lappe, Anthony, and Dan Goldman. 2007. *Shooting War.* New York:
Warner Books.

Lastowka, Greg. 2005. "You Will Rule the Planes of Power!" Terra Nova
blog, 25 June. http://www.terranova.blogs.com.

———. 2006. "Cultural Borrowing in WoW." Terra Nova blog, 16 May.
http://terranova.blogs.com.

Laurel, Brenda. 2001. *Utopian Entrepreneur.* Cambridge, Mass.: MIT
Press.

Lazarus, Eve. 1999. "New Game." *Marketing* 104, no. 20 (24 May): 9–10.

Lazzarato, Maurizio. 1996. "Immaterial Labour." Trans. Paul Colilli and
Ed Emory. In *Radical Thought in Italy Today,* ed. Paolo Virno and
Michael Hardt, 133–47. Minneapolis: University of Minnesota Press.

———. 2002. "From Biopower to Biopolitics." Trans. Ivan A. Ramirez.
Pli 13:100–111.

———. 2004. "From Capital-Labour to Capital-Life." Trans. Valerie

Fournier, Akseli Virtanen, and Jussi Vähämäki. *Ephemera* 4 (3): 187–208. http://www.ephemeraweb.org.

Lee, James. 2005. "Wage Slaves." 1UP.com Web site. http://www.1up.com.

Lenoir, Timothy. 2000. "All but War Is Simulation: The Military-Entertainment Complex." *Configurations* 8 (3): 289–335.

Lens, Sidney. 2003. *The Forging of the American Empire: From the Revolution to Vietnam: A History of American Imperialism.* London: Pluto Books.

Leonard, David J. 2003. "'Live in Your World, Play in Ours': Race, Video Games, and Consuming the Other." *Studies in Media and Information Literacy Education* 3 (4): 1–9.

———. 2004. "High Tech Blackface: Race, Sports Video Games, and Becoming the Other." *Intelligent Agent* 4 (2). http://www.intelligentagent.com.

———. 2005. "To the White Extreme: Conquering Athletic Space; White Manhood and Racing Reality." In *Digital Gameplay: Essays on the Nexus of Game and Gamer,* ed. Nate Garrelts, 110–30. New York: McFarland.

———. 2006. "Virtual Gangstas, Coming to a Suburban Home Near You: Demonization, Commodification, and Policing Blackness." In *The Meaning and Culture of Grand Theft Auto: Critical Essays,* ed. Nate Garrelts, 49–69. Jefferson, N.C.: McFarland.

Lessig, Lawrence. 2004. *Free Culture: How Big Media Uses Technology and Law to Lock Down Cultures and Control Creativity.* New York: Penguin.

Levitz, Jennifer. 2008. "Playing the Market, These Kids Are Losing a Lot of Play Money." *Wall Street Journal,* 29 October. http://www.online.wsj.com.

Lévy, Pierre. 1998. *Becoming Virtual: Reality in the Digital Age.* New York: Plenum.

Li, Cao, and Jiao Xiaoyang. 2005. "Gamer Slays Rival after Online Dispute." *China Daily,* 30 March. http://www.chinadaily.com.

Lindenschmidt, James W. 2004. "From Virtual Commons to Virtual Enclosures: Revolution and Counter-revolution in the Information Age." *Commoner* 9. http://www.commoner.org.uk.

Lindsay-Poland, John. 2003. *Emperors in the Jungle: The Hidden History of the U.S. in Panama.* Durham, N.C.: Duke University Press.

Linebaugh, Peter, and Marcus Rediker. 2000. *The Many-Headed Hydra: Sailors, Slaves, Commoners, and the Hidden History of the Revolutionary Atlantic.* New York: Verso.

Littlemore, Richard. 1998. "The Totally Awesome Mr. Wong." *B.C. Business Magazine* 26, no. 6 (June): 36–42.

Logan, Tracey. 2004. "Gaming Helps Traders Score Big-Time." *BBC News,* 10 October. http://news.bbc.co.uk.

Loughrey, Paul. 2006. "UbiSoft No Longer Using Starforce Protection." *Gamesindustry.biz,* 18 April. http://www.gamesindustry.biz.

Lovink, Geert, and Florian Schneider. 2003. "A Virtual World Is Possible: From Tactical Media to Digital Multitudes." Makeworlds Web site. http://www.makeworlds.org.

Lowenstein, Doug. 2005. "Electronic Entertainment Expo 2005: State of the Industry Address." Entertainment Software Association Web site. http://www.theesa.com.

Lowood, Henry. 2005. "Real-Time Performance: Machinima and Game Studies." *International Digital Media and Arts Association Journal* 1, no. 3 (Spring): 10–18.

Lucarelli, Stefano, and Andrea Fumagalli. 2008. "Basic Income and Productivity in Cognitive Capitalism." *Review of Social Economy* 66, no. 1 (March): 71–92.

Lukic, Kristian. 2005. "The Enclosure of Societal Changes." In *Alternative Economies, Alternative Societies,* ed. Oliver Ressler and Aneta Szylak, 13–16. Gdansk, Poland: Wyspa Institute of Art.

Luthje, Boy. 2004. "Global Production Networks and Industrial Upgrading in China: The Case of Electronic Contract Manufacturing." *East-West Center Working Papers* 74. East-West Center Web site. http://www.eastwestcenter.org.

Macedonia, Michael R. 2002. "A View from the Military." *Defense Horizons* 11 (April): 6–8.

Mahajan, Rahul. 2003. *Full Spectrum Dominance: U.S. Power in Iraq and Beyond.* New York: Seven Stories.

Malaby, Thomas. 2006. "Parlaying Value: Capital in and beyond Virtual Worlds." *Games and Culture* 1 (2): 141–62.

Manjoo, Farhad. 2008. "Grand Theft Auto IV Is a Dark Urban Masterpiece." Machinist blog, 9 May. http://machinist.salon.com.

Manufactured Landscapes. 2007. DVD. Directed by Jennifer Baichwal. Toronto and Ottawa: Foundry Films, Mercury Films, and National Film Board of Canada.

Maragos, Nich. 2005a. "Study Shows Gaming Gender Equality in Asia." *Gamasutra,* 18 July. http://www.gamasutra.com.

———. 2005b. "Korean MMOs See Shrinking Chinese Market Share." *Gamasutra,* 6 October. http://www.gamasutra.com.

———. 2006. "Chinese Government Quantifies Online Gaming Surge." *Gamasutra,* 12 January. http://www.gamasutra.com.

Marielo. 2006. "Year 2005: History of Lightning's Blade." *World of Warcraft* forum, 1 January. http://www.worldofwarcraft.com.

Markoff, John. 2005. *What the Dormouse Said: How the Sixties*

Counterculture Shaped the Personal Computer Industry. New York: Viking.

Marks, Robert. 2004. "Robert Marks on the Pearl River Delta." *Environmental History* 9 (2): 296–99.

Marriott, Michael. 1999. "Blood, Gore, Sex, and Now Race: Are Game Makers Creating Convincing New Characters or 'High-Tech Blackface'?" *New York Times,* 21 October.

Martin, Randy. 2002. *The Financialization of Daily Life.* Philadelphia: Temple University Press.

———. 2007. *An Empire of Indifference: American War and the Financial Logic of Risk Management.* Durham, N.C.: Duke University Press.

Marx, Karl. 1844. *The Economic and Philosophical Manuscripts.* New York: International, 1962.

———. 1858. *Grundrisse.* London: Penguin, 1973.

———. 1867. *Capital: A Critique of Political Economy, Volume 1.* New York: Vintage, 1976.

Marx, Karl, and Friedrich Engels. 1848. *The Communist Manifesto.* New York: Penguin, 1985.

Massumi, Brian. 1998. "Requiem for Our Prospective Dead (Toward a Participatory Critique of Capitalist Power)." In *Deleuze and Guattari: New Mappings in Politics, Philosophy, and Culture,* ed. Eleanor Kaufman and Kevin Jon Heller, 40–64. Minneapolis: University of Minnesota Press.

———. 2002a. "Translator's Foreword: Pleasures of Philosophy." In *A Thousand Plateaus: Capitalism and Schizophrenia,* by Gilles Deleuze and Félix Guattari, trans. Brian Massumi, ix–xv. Minneapolis: University of Minnesota Press.

———. 2002b. *Parables for the Virtual: Movement, Affect, Sensation.* Durham, N.C.: Duke University Press.

———. 2006. "Fear (The Spectrum Said)." *Multitudes* 23 (January). http://multitudes.samizdat.net.

Matthews, Glenna. 2003. *Silicon Valley, Women, and the California Dream: Gender, Class, and Opportunity in the Twentieth Century.* Stanford, Calif.: Stanford University Press.

Mayfield, Kendra. 2002. "New E-Waste Solution a Mine Idea." *Wired,* 7 June. http://www.wired.com.

McLoud, Scott. 2006. *Making Comics: Storytelling Secrets of Comics, Manga, and Graphic Novels.* New York: Harper.

Menzies, Heather. 1996. *Whose Brave New World: The Information Highway and the New Economy.* Toronto: Between the Lines.

———. 2005. *No Time: Stress and the Crisis of Modern Life.* Toronto: Douglas and McIntyre.

Mia Wombat. 2006. "Mia Wombat: Age of the Conducer." Creative Commons Wiki, 20 April. http://wiki.creativecommons.org.

Michael, David, and Sande Chen. 2006. *Serious Games: Games That Educate, Train, and Inform.* Boston: Course Technology.

Midnight Notes. 1992. *Midnight Oil: Work, Energy, War, 1973–1992.* New York: Autonomedia.

Miller, Ernest. 2002. "Analysis of Blizzard vs. BnetD." *LawMeme,* 26 February. http://research.yale.edu/lawmeme.

Mo, Honge. 2006. "'Gold Farmers' in Virtual World Make Fortune in Reality." *China View,* 21 September. http://news3.xinhuanet.com.

Molleindustria. n.d. Molleindustria Web site. http://www.molleindustria .org.

Montague, Dena. 2002. "Stolen Goods: Coltan and Conflict in the Democratic Republic of Congo." *SAIS Review* 22, no. 1 (Winter–Spring): 103–18.

Moore, David. 2001. "Africa: The Black Hole at the Middle of Empire?" *Rethinking Marxism* 13, nos. 3–4 (September): 100–118.

Morgenstern, Steve. 2007. "The Wright Stuff." Interview with Will Wright. *Popular Science,* 2 August. http://www.popsci.com.

Morini, Christina. 2007. "The Feminization of Labour in Cognitive Capitalism." *Feminist Review* 87:40–59.

Mortensen, Torill Elvira. 2006. "WoW Is the New MUD: Social Gaming from Text to Video." *Games and Culture* 1 (4): 397–413.

Mosco, Vincent. 1996. *The Political Economy of Communication: Rethinking and Renewal.* London: Sage.

———. 1999. "New York.Com: A Political Economy of the 'Informational' City." *Journal of Media Economics* 12 (2): 103–16.

———. 2003. "Whose Ground Zero? Contesting Public Space in Lower Manhattan." Université du Québec à Montréal, GPB Advanced Seminars in Communication Web site. http://www.er.uqam.ca/nobel/ gricis/gpb.

moviebob. 2007. "Super Mario: Working Class Hero." YouTube, 22 May. http://www.youtube.com.

Mumford, Lewis. 1970. *The Myth of the Machine: The Pentagon of Power.* New York: Harcourt Brace.

Muoio, Anna. 2001. "Man with a (Talent) Plan." *Fast Company* 42. http://pf.fastcompany.com.

Murray, Soraya. 2005. "High Art/Low Life: The Art of Playing Grand Theft Auto." *PAG* 27, no. 1 (May): 91–98.

Musgrove, Mike. 2005. "Game Turns Players into Indie Movie Makers." *Washington Post,* 1 December.

Mute Magazine. 2005. "Underneath the Knowledge Commons." *Mute Magazine* 2 (1). London: Mute Publishing.

narcogen. 2005. "Is XBL a Breeding Ground for Sexism." Comment posted to Rampancy forum, 22 June. http://rampancy.net.

Neesan, J. M. 1993. *Commoners: Common Right, Enclosures, and Social Change in England, 1700–1820.* Cambridge, UK: Cambridge University Press.

Negri, Antonio. 1991. *Marx beyond Marx: Lessons on the Grundrisse.* Trans. Harry Cleaver, Michael Ryan, and Maurizio Viano. New York: Autonomedia.

————. 1999. *Insurgencies: Constituent Power and the Modern State.* Trans. Maurizia Boscagli. Minneapolis: University of Minnesota Press.

————. 2002. "The Multitude and the Metropolis." Trans. Arianna Bove. Generation Online Web site. http://www.generation-online.org.

————. 2005. "First Meeting." Multitude and Metropolis blog, 28 November. http://parisgabriel.blogspot.com.

Negri, Antonio, Constantin Petcou, Doina Petrescu, and Anne Querrien. 2007. "What Makes a Biopolitical Space? A Discussion with Toni Negri." *Eurozine,* 17 September. http://www.eurozine.com.

Neubauer, Deane. 2004. "Mixed Blessings of the Megacities." *YaleGlobal,* 24 September. http://yaleglobal.yale.edu.

Newman, James. 2004. *Videogames.* London: Routledge.

News Services. 2007. "EA to Buy Developers from Bono's Firm." *Washington Post,* 12 October. http://www.washingtonpost.com.

Ni, Ching-Ching. 2005. "Game Aims to Make Vintage Communism a Hit with Children." *Concordia Monitor Online,* 5 November. http://www.concordmonitor.com.

Nichols, Bill. 1987. "The Work of Culture in the Age of Cybernetic Systems." *Screen* 29 (1): 22–46.

Nieborg, David B. 2006. "Mods, Nay! Tournaments, Yay! The Appropriation of Contemporary Game Culture by the U.S. Military." *Fibreculture Journal* 8. http://journal.fibreculture.org.

Nijman, Jan. 1997. "Globalization to a Latin Beat: The Miami Growth Machine." *Annals of the American Academy of Political and Social Science* 551 (1): 164–77.

Nitewalkz. 2007. "An Interview with Paolo Pedercini of Molleindustria." Culture Jamming Web site. http://www.culture-jamming.de.

Nolen, Stephanie. 2005. "Is the 'Genocide Credit' Used Up?" *Globe and Mail,* 22 January.

Notes from Nowhere. 2003. *We Are Everywhere: The Irresistible Rise of Global Anticapitalism.* New York: Verso.

Nutt, Christian. 2007. "EA CEO Riccitiello Talks Game Pricing, Creativity." *Gamasutra,* 31 October. http://www.gamasutra.com.

Ochalla, Bryan. 2007. "Who Says Video Games Have to Be Fun? The Rise of Serious Games." *Gamasutra,* 29 June. http://www.gamasutra.com.

O'Dea, Allan. 2009. "How Do Massive Multi-player Online Games (MMOs) Make Money?" *Simple Life Forms,* 12 March. http://www .simplelifeforms.com.

Oliver, Julian. 2004a. "First Person(s): 'Under Siege' and the New Virtual War." SelectParks Web site, 4 September. http://selectparks.net.

———. 2004b. "Interview with Radwan Kasmiya of AFKARMedia." SelectParks Web site, 7 September. http://selectparks.net.

Opensorcery. 2004. "OUT: Operation Urban Terrain." Opensorcery Web site. http://www.opensorcery.net.

Overby, Stephanie. 2003. "Staff Alert." *CIO,* 11 June. http://www.cio .com.au.

Ow, Jeffrey, A. 2000. "The Revenge of the Yellowfaced Cyborg: The Rape of Digital Geishas and the Colonization of Cyber-coolies in 3D Realms' Shadow Warrior." In *Race in Cyberspace,* ed. Beth Kolko, Lisa Nakamura, and Gilbert Rodman, 51–68. New York: Routledge.

Paradise, J. 2005. "Confessions of a Girl Gamer." DailyGame Web site, 22 June. http://www.dailygame.net.

Passavant, Paul A., and Jodi Dean, eds. 2004. *Empire's New Clothes: Reading Hardt and Negri.* London: Routledge.

Pasquinelli, Matteo. 2005. "Radical Machines against the Techno-Empire: From Utopia to Network." Trans. Arianna Bove. *Eurozine,* 19 July. http://www.eurozine.com.

———. 2006. "Immaterial Civil War: Prototypes of Conflict within Cognitive Capitalism." Rekombinant Web site. http://www.rekombinant .org/ImmCivilWar.pdf.

Paul. 2005. "Secrets of Massively Multiplayer Farming." Posted to Game Guides Online. http://www.gameguidesonline.com.

Pausch, Randy. 2004. *An Academic's Field Guide to Electronic Arts: Observations Based on a Residency in the Spring Semester of 2004.* Electronic Arts Web site. http://www.info.ea.com/company/summit/ ea_fieldguide.pdf.

Pearce, Celia. 2006. "Productive Play: Game Culture from the Bottom Up." *Games and Culture* 1 (1): 17–24.

Peck, Michael. 2007. "Constructive Progress: U.S. Army Embraces Games—Sort Of." *Training and Simulation Journal,* 24 December. http://www.tsjonline.com.

Perelman, Michael. 1992. *The Invention of Capitalism: Classical Political Economy and the Secret History of Primitive Accumulation.* Durham, N.C.: Duke University Press.

Pfanner, Eric. 2007. "Internet Pushes the Concept of 'Free' Content." *International Herald Tribune,* 17 January. http://www.iht.com.

Phillips, David. 2009. "New Game in Electronic Arts' Lineup: 'Financial Crisis.'" *BTNet Media,* 8 June. http://industry.bnet.com.

Pieterse, Jan Nederveen. 2004. *Globalization or Empire?* London: Routledge.

Pilieci, Vito. 2008. "Free Gaming Coming Soon." *Leader Post* (Regina), 8 March.

Pinckard, Jane. 2001. "Marketing the X." *Mindjack,* 12 November. http://www.mindjack.com/feature/xad.html.

PlayOn. 2007. "WoW Data Archives." PlayOn blog, 2 March. http://blogs.parc.com/playon.

Poblocki, Kacper. 2002. "Becoming-State: The Bio-cultural Imperialism of Sid Meier's Civilization." *Focaal: European Journal of Anthropology* 39:163–77.

Pomerantz, Dorothy. 2003. "Top of Their Game." *Forbes,* 1 June. http://www.forbes.com.

Poole, Steven. 2000. *Trigger Happy: The Inner Life of Video Games.* London: Fourth Estate.

Portes, Alejandro, and Alex Stepick. 1996. *City on the Edge: The Transformation of Miami.* Berkeley: University of California Press.

Provenzo, Eugene. 1991. *Video Kids: Making Sense of Nintendo.* Cambridge, Mass.: Harvard University Press.

Rabinow, Paul, and Nikolas Rose. 2003. "Thoughts on the Concept of Biopower Today." Molecular Sciences Institute Web site. http://www.molsci.org/files/Rose_Rabinow_Biopower_Today.pdf.

Radd, David. 2007. "Piracy Is Big Business." *Business Week,* 13 March. http://www.businessweek.com.

Raessens, Joest, and Jeffrey Goldstein, eds. 2005. *Handbook of Computer Game Studies.* Cambridge, Mass.: MIT Press.

Ratliff, Evan. 2004. "Sports Rule!" *Wired* 11 (1). http://www.wired.com.

Read, Jason. 2003. *The Micro-politics of Capital: Marx and the Prehistory of the Present.* Albany, N.Y.: State University of New York Press.

Redmond, Dennis. 2006. "Grand Theft Auto: Running and Gunning for the U.S. Empire." In *The Meaning and Culture of Grand Theft Auto: Critical Essays,* ed. Nate Garrelts, 104–14. Jefferson, N.C.: McFarland.

Retort. 2005. *Afflicted Powers: Capital and Spectacle in a New Age of War.* New York: Verso.

Reuters. 2007. "Vivendi Full Year 2006 Revenues Reach EUR 20 Billion." Reuters news agency, 31 January. http://today.reuters.com.

———. 2008. "China Claims Sweet Spot in Tech Food Chain." *China Daily,* 26 May. http://www.chinadaily.com.

———. 2009. "Update 4: World of Warcraft to Help Vivendi Weather Crisis." *Reuters,* 2 March. http://www.reuters.com.

Richards, Birgit, and Jutta Zaremba. 2004. "Gaming with Grrls: Looking for Sheroes in Computer Games." In *Handbook of Computer Game*

Studies, ed. Joest Raessens and Jeffrey Goldstein, 183–200. Cambridge, Mass.: MIT Press.

Richtel, Matt. 2006. "Game Maker Discloses a Subpoena." *New York Times,* 27 June. http://www.nytimes.com.

———. 2008a. "Bid for Game Maker Seen as Effort to Buy Innovation." *New York Times,* 26 February. http://ww.nytimes.com.

———. 2008b. "Electronic Arts Lowers Forecast and Cuts Its Work Force." *New York Times,* 30 October. http://www.nytimes.com.

Rider, Shawn. 2006. "A Bridge Too Far." GamesFirst! Web site, 26 May. http://www.gamesfirst.com.

Roberts, Dexter. 2006. "How Rising Wages Are Changing the Game in China." *Business Week,* 27 March. http://www.businessweek.com.

Robertson, Margaret. 2008. "How Games Will Change the World." *BBC News,* 28 May. http://news.bbc.co.uk.

Robinson, John, and James Tansey. 2006. "Co-production, Emergent Properties, and Strong Interactive Social Research: The Georgia Basin Futures Project." *Science and Public Policy* 33, no. 2 (March): 151–60.

Ross, Andrew. 2004. "Dot-com Urbanism." In *Mediaspace: Place, Scale, and Culture in a Media Age,* ed. Nick Couldry and Anna McCarthy, 145–62. London: Routledge.

———. 2006. *Fast Boat to China: High-Tech Outsourcing and the Consequences of Free Trade; Lessons from Shanghai.* New York: Vintage.

Ross Sorkin, Andrew, and Seth Schiesel. 2008. "Game Maker Bids $2 Billion to Take Over Competitor." *International Herald Tribune,* 26 February.

Rossiter, Ned. 2007. *Organized Networks: Media Theory, Creative Labour, New Institutions.* Rotterdam: NAi Publishers.

RTP (Research Triangle Park). 2008. "Business Climate." Research Triangle Park Web site. http://www.rtp.org.

Rubens, Paul. 2007. "Three Hacker Teams Unlock the PSP." *BBC News,* 26 February. http://news.bbc.co.uk.

Ruberg, Bonnie. 2005. "I'm the Pink One: Women on Xbox Live." Gamegal Web site, 15 August. http://www.gamegal.com.

Rustin, Michael. 2003. "Empire: A Postmodern Theory of Revolution." In *Debating Empire,* ed. Gopal Balakrishnan, 1–18. New York: Verso.

Ryan, Nick. 2009. "Gold Trading Exposed: The Sellers." *Eurogamer,* 25 March. http://www.eurogamer.net.

Sassen, Saskia. 2001. *The Global City: New York, London, Tokyo.* Princeton, N.J.: Princeton University Press.

Schiesel, Seth. 2003. "Some Xbox Fans Microsoft Didn't Aim For." *New York Times,* 10 July. http://www.nytimes.com.

———. 2005. "Conqueror in a War of Virtual Worlds." *New York Times,* 6 September. http://www.nytimes.com.

———. 2007. "A Global Vision from the New Man at EA Sports." *New York Times,* 5 September. http://www.nytimes.com.

———. 2008a. "A Company Looks to Its Creative Side to Regain What It Has Lost." *New York Times,* 19 February. http://www.nytimes.com.

———. 2008b. "Grand Theft Auto Takes on New York." *New York Times,* 28 April. http://www.nytimes.com.

Schiller, Dan. 2007. *How to Think about Information.* Urbana: University of Illinois Press.

———. 2008. "An Update on China in the Political Economy of Information and Communications." *Chinese Journal of Communication* 1 (1): 109–16.

Schleiner, Anne-Marie. 2002. "Velvet-Strike: War Times and Reality Games." Opensorcery Web site. http://www.opensorcery.net.

———. 2004. "Female-Bobs Arrive at Dusk." In *CyberFeminism: Next Protocols,* ed. Claudia Reiche and Verena Kuni, 119–32. New York: Autonomedia.

Schmerken, Ivy. 2008. "Trading Desks Turn to Video Game Technology to Speed Analytics." *Wall Street and Technology.* http://www.wallstreetandtech.com.

Schor, Juliet. 1993. *The Overworked American: The Unexpected Decline of Leisure.* Boston: Basic Books.

Schott, Gareth, and Bevin Yeatman. 2005. "Subverting Game-Play: JFK Reloaded as Performative Space." *Australasian Journal of American Studies* 24, no. 2 (December): 82–94.

Scola, Nancy. 2006. "Avatar Politics: Social Applications of Second Life." Nancy Scola, personal Web site. http://www.nancyscola.com.

Second Life. 2007. "Economic Statistics." Second Life Web site. http://secondlife.com.

Seeing Is Believing: Handicams, Human Rights, and the News. 2002. DVD. Directed by Katerina Cizek and Peter Wintonick. Montreal: Necessary Illusions Productions.

Seth, Sanjay. 2003. "Back to the Future." In *Debating Empire,* ed. Gopal Balakrishnan, 43–51. New York: Verso.

Sheff, David. 1999. *Game Over: How Nintendo Zapped an American Industry, Captured Your Dollars, and Enslaved Your Children.* New York: Random House.

Sheffield, Brandon. 2006. "EA LA's Neil Young on Emotion, IP, and Overtime." *Gamasutra,* 22 May. http://www.gamasutra.com.

Sherry, John L. 2001. "The Effects of Violent Games on Aggression: A≈Meta-Analysis." *Human Communication Research* 27, no. 3 (July): 409–31.

Shields, Rob. 2003. *The Virtual.* London: Routledge.

Shinkle, Eugénie. 2005. "Corporealis Ergo Sum: Affective Response in

Digital Games." In *Digital Gameplay: Essays on the Nexus of Game and Gamer,* ed. Nate Garrelts, 21–33. New York: McFarland.

Silberman, Steve. 2004. "The War Room." *Wired* 12 (9). http://www.wired.com.

Simon, Bart. 2006. "Beyond Cyberspatial Flaneurie: On the Analytic Potential of Living with Digital Games." *Games and Culture* 1 (1): 62–67.

Sinclair, Brendan. 2006. "Activision Faces Labor Suit." *GameSpot,* 20 July. http://www.gamespot.com.

Singer, P. W. 2009. *Wired for War: The Robotics Revolution and Conflict in the Twenty-first Century.* New York: Penguin Press.

Singh, Greg. 2006. "*San Andreas:* Agency, Movement, and Containment; or, How the West Is (Frequently) Won." *Aesthetics of Play: Online Proceedings.* Bergen, Norway, 14–15 October 2005. http://www.aestheticsofplay.org.

Siwek, Stephen E. 2007. *Video Games in the 21st Century: Economic Contributions of the U.S. Entertainment Software Industry.* Entertainment Software Association Web site. http://www.esa.com.

Smith, Charlie. 2006. "The Videogame Explosion." *Georgia Straight,* 5 November. http://www.straight.com.

Smith, David. 2004. "EA Faces Class-Action Overtime Suit." 1UP.com, 11 January. http://www.1up.com.

Smith, Neil. 2002. "New Globalism, New Urbanism: Gentrification as Global Urban Strategy." In *Spaces of Neoliberalism: Urban Restructuring in North America and Western Europe,* ed. Neil Brenner and Nik Theodore, 80–104. Oxford: Blackwell.

Smythe, Dallas. 1983. *Dependency Road: Communications, Capitalism, Consciousness, and Canada.* New York: Ablex.

Soja, Edward W. 2000. *Postmetropolis: Critical Studies of Cities and Regions.* Oxford: Blackwell.

Spivak, Gayatri Chakravorty. 1999. *A Critique of Postcolonial Reason: Toward a History of the Vanishing Present.* Cambridge, Mass.: Harvard University Press.

Stallabrass, Julian. 1993. "Just Gaming." *New Left Review* 198:83–106.

———. 1996. *Gargantua: Manufactured Mass Culture.* New York: Verso.

Stallman, Richard. 2005. "GNU's Not Unix! Free Software, Free Society: Why 'Open Source' Misses the Point of Free Software." Free Software Foundation Web site. http://www.gnu.org.

Steinkuehler, Constance. 2006. "The Mangle of Play." *Games and Culture* 1 (3): 199–213.

Stephenson, William. 1999. "The Microserfs Are Revolting: Sid Meier's Civilization II." *Bad Subjects* 45. http://bad.eserver.org.

Stern, Eddo. 2002. "A Touch of Medieval: Narrative, Magic, and

Computer Technology in Massively Multiplayer Computer Role-Playing Games." *Proceedings of Computer Games and Digital Cultures Conference,* ed. Frans Mäyrä, 257–76. Tampere, Finland: Tampere University Press.

Stockwell, Stephen, and Adam Muir. 2003. "The Military-Entertainment Complex: A New Facet of Information Warfare." *Fibreculture Journal* 1. http://journal.fibreculture.org.

Strangelove, Michael. 2005. *The Empire of Mind: Digital Piracy and the Anti-capitalist Movement.* Toronto: University of Toronto Press.

Sunder, Madhavi. 2006. "IP3." *Stanford Law Review* 59:257–332.

Svensson, Christian. 2005. "Team Structure." *Next Generation,* 21 June. http://www.next-gen.biz.

Takahashi, Dean. 2000. "Electronic Arts Game Plan Is Looking like a Winner." *Wall Street Journal,* 4 May.

———. 2002. *Opening the Xbox: Inside Microsoft's Plan to Unleash an Entertainment Revolution.* New York: Prima.

———. 2004. "Video-Game Workers Sue for Overtime Pay." *San Jose Mercury News,* 12 April. http://www.mercurynews.com.

———. 2005. "Profile: India's Game Developers Target Outsourcing." *San Jose Mercury News,* 5 July. http://blogs.mercurynews.com.

———. 2006. *The Xbox 360 Uncloaked: The Real Story behind Microsoft's Next-Generation Video Game Console.* New York: Lulu Press.

———. 2009. "Take-Two's Strauss Zelnick Talks about Games beyond Grand Theft Auto." *GamesBeat,* 17 June. http://www.games.venturebeat.com.

Taylor, Chris. 1999. "Best Companies to Work for in BC." *BC Business Magazine* 27 (11): 31–51.

Taylor, T. L. 2006a. *Play between Worlds: Exploring Online Game Culture.* Cambridge, Mass.: MIT Press.

———. 2006b. "Does WoW Change Everything? How a PvP Server, Multinational Player Base, and Surveillance Mod Scene Caused Me Pause." *Games and Culture* 1 (6): 318–37.

———. 2003. "'Whose Fame Is This Anyway?': Negotiating Corporate Ownership in a Virtual World." Paper presented at the annual meeting of the International Communication Association, San Diego, Calif., May 27.

Terranova, Tiziana. 2000. "Free Labor: Producing Culture for the Digital Economy." *Social Text* 18 (2 63): 33–58.

Tetzlaf, David. 2000. "Yo-ho-ho and a Server of Warez: Internet Software Piracy and the New Global Information Economy." In *The World Wide Web and Contemporary Cultural Theory,* ed. Andrew Herman and Thomas Swiss, 77–99. New York: Routledge.

Thoburn, Nicholas. 2001. "Autonomous Production? On Negri's 'New Synthesis.'" *Theory, Culture, and Society* 18 (5): 75–96.

Thompson, Clive. 2007. "Playing the Master Race." *Wired*, 12 March. http://www.wired.com.

Thompson, Jack. 2005. "Open Letter to the Members of the Entertainment Software Association." Voodoo Extreme Web site, 14 July. http://www.ve3d/ign.com.

Thompson, Jason. 2008. *Manga: The Complete Guide.* New York: Random House.

Thompson, Tony. 2005. "They Play Games for 10 Hours—and Earn £2.80 in a 'Virtual Sweatshop.'" *Guardian*, 13 March. http://www.theguardian.co.uk.

Thorsen, Tor. 2005a. "Elevation, BioWare, Pandemic Joining Forces." *GameSpot*, 3 November. http://www.gamespot.com.

———. 2005b. "Spot On: The Road to the 360." *GameSpot*, 12 May. http://www.gamespot.com.

———. 2006. "Vivendi Rolling in World of Warcraft Gold." *GameSpot*, 27 July. http://www.gamespot.com.

———. 2007. "Report: Online Game Revs Tripling by 2012." *GameSpot*, 30 May. http://www.gamespot.com.

———. 2008. "Game Stocks Bloodied in Market Meltdown." *GameSpot*, 9 October. http://www.gamespot.com.

———. 2009. "28 Million Xbox 360s Sold, 17 Million on Xbox Live." *GameSpot*, 6 January. http://www.gamespot.com.

Todd, B. 2003. "Million Dollar Mods." *Computer Games* (September): 24–25.

Torill, Elvira Mortensen. 2006. "WoW Is the New MUD: Social Gaming from Text to Video." *Games and Culture* 1 (6): 397–413.

Totilo, Stephen. 2006. "Controversial 'Bad Day L.A.'" MTV News, 30 August. http://www.mtv.com.

———. 2007. "'BlackSite' Pushes Buttons." MTV News, 13 February. http://www.mtv.com.

Trotsky, Leon. 1962. *The Permanent Revolution and Results and Projects.* New York: Pioneer.

Turbulence Collective. 2007. *Turbulence* 1. "What Would It Mean to Win?" http://www.turbulence.org.uk.

Turkle, Sherry. 1997. "Seeing through Computers: Education in a Culture of Simulation." *American Prospect* 31 (March–April): 76–82.

Turner, Fred. 2006. *From Counterculture to Cyberculture: Stewart Brand, the Whole Earth Network, and the Rise of Digital Utopianism.* Chicago: University of Chicago Press.

Varney, Allen. 2006. "Red Blindness." *Escapist* 49 (13 June). http://www.escapistmagazine.com.

———. 2007. "Blowing Up Galaxies." *Escapist* 101 (12 June). http:// www.escapistmagazine.com.

Venezuelan Solidarity Network. 2006. "U2's Bono Backs Insidious Propaganda: Videogame with Venezuela Invasion Theme." *Venezuela Solidarity Network Web site.* Press release, 7 July. http://www .vensolidarity.org.

Vercellone, Carlo. 2005. "The Hypothesis of Cognitive Capitalism." Paper presented at "Towards a Cosmopolitan Marxism," Historical Materialism Annual Conference, 4–6 November, Birkbeck College and School of Oriental and African Studies.

———. 2007a. "Cognitive Capitalism and Models for the Regulation of the Wage Relation: Some Lessons from the Anti-CPE Movement." E-mail to the edu-factory mailing list, 18 April.

———. 2007b. "From Formal Subsumption to General Intellect: Elements for a Marxist Reading of the Thesis of Cognitive Capitalism." *Historical Materialism* 15:13–36.

Verklin, David, and Bernice Kanner. 2007. *Watch This, Listen Up, Click Here: Inside the 300 Billion Dollar Business behind the Media You Constantly Consume.* New York: Wiley.

Vick, Karl. 2001. "Vital Ore Funds Congo's War." *Washington Post,* 19 March. http://www.washingtonpost.com.

"Video Game CEO Convicted of Stock Fraud." 2007. *North Country Gazette,* 15 February. http://www.northcountrygazette.org.

Virno, Paolo. 1996a. "Virtuosity and Revolution: The Political Theory of Exodus." Trans. Ed Emory. In *Radical Thought in Italy: A Potential Politics,* ed. Paolo Virno and Michael Hardt, 189–210. Minneapolis: University of Minnesota Press.

———. 1996b. "Notes on the 'General Intellect.'" Trans. Cesare Casarino. In *Marxism beyond Marxism,* ed. Saree Makdisi, Cesare Casarino, and Rebecca E. Karl, 265–22. New York: Routledge.

———. 2004. *A Grammar of the Multitude.* Trans. Isabella Bertoletti, James Cascaito, and Andrea Casson. New York: Semiotext(e).

———. 2006. *Ambivalencia de la multitud: Entre la innovacion y la negatividad.* Buenos Aires: Tinta Limón.

Virno, Paolo, and Michael Hardt, eds. 1996. *Radical Thought in Italy: A Potential Politics.* Minneapolis: University of Minnesota Press.

Virtual Citizenship Association. 2007. "Virtual Worlds, Real Citizens." *Virtual Citizenship Association Web site.* http://www.virtualcitizenship .org.

Vitka, William, and Chad Chamberlain. 2005. "Game Speak: Jack Thompson." *CBS News,* 25 February. http://www.cbsnews.com.

Vivendi. 2002. "Environment Strengthens Presence in China with Two New Contracts." Press release, 16 December. http://www.secinfo.com.

VNS Matrix. 1991. "VNS Matrix Cyberfeminist Manifesto for the 21st Century." OBN Web site. http://www.obn.org/reading_room.

Wakabi, Wairagala. 2004. "The Arms Smugglers." *New Internationalist* 367 (May). http://www.newint.org.

Warcraft Realms. 2007. "WoW Census." Warcraft Realms Web site. http://www.warcraftrealms.com/census.

Ward, Mark. 2005a. "Deadly Plague Hits Warcraft World." *BBC News,* 22 September. http://news.bbc.co.uk.

———. 2005b. "Warcraft Maker in Spying Row." *BBC News,* 31 October. http://news.bbc.co.uk.

———. 2006. "Gay Rights Win in Warcraft World." *BBC News,* 13 February. http://news.bbc.co.uk.

Wardrip-Fruin, Noah, and Pat Harrigan, eds. 2004. *First Person: New Media as Story, Performance, and Game.* Cambridge, Mass.: MIT Press.

Wark, McKenzie. 2004. *A Hacker Manifesto.* Cambridge, Mass.: Harvard University Press.

———. 2007. *Gamer Theory.* Cambridge, Mass.: Harvard University Press.

Waters, Darren. 2008. "Brain Control Headset for Gamers." *BBC News,* 20 February. http://news.bbc.co.uk.

Webber, Michael, and Ying Zhu. 2005. "Primitive Accumulation, Transition, and Unemployment in China." *SAGES Working Papers in Development,* March. School of International Development, University of Melbourne. http://www.sages.unimelb.edu.au.

Wen, Howard. 2002. "Battle.net Goes to War." *Salon,* 18 April. http://www.salon.com.

Whyte, Murray. 2007. "(Virtual) Reality Bites." *Toronto Star,* 11 March. http://www.thestar.com.

Williams, Dimitri. 2002. "Structure and Competition in the U.S. Home Video Game Industry." *International Journal on Media Management* 4 (1): 41–54.

Williams, Dimitri, Nicolas Ducheneaut, Li Xiong, Nick Yee, and Erik Nickell. 2006. "From Tree House to Barracks: The Social Life of Guilds in World of Warcraft." *Games and Culture* 1 (6): 338–61.

Williams, Raymond. 1976. *Keywords: A Vocabulary of Culture and Society.* London: Fontana Press.

Wilson, James. 2005. "Indie Rocks! Mapping Independent Video Game Design." *Media International Australia* 115 (May): 109–22.

Wilson, Trevor. 2007. "Game Developer's Top Twenty Publishers." *Gamasutra,* 8 January. http://www.gamasutra.com.

Wingfield, Nick. 2007. "EA Chief Cites Need for More Innovative Games." *Wall Street Journal,* 9 July. http://online.wsj.com.

————. 2008. "Electronic Arts Sees Its Revenue Growing by Half."
Wall Street Journal, 13 February. http://www.online.wsj.com.

Wingfield, Nick, and Robert A. Guth. 2004. "Workers at EA Claim They
Are Owed Overtime." *Wall Street Journal,* 19 November. http://www
.online.wsj.com.

Wolf, Mark J. P. 2001. *The Medium of the Video Game.* Austin: University of Texas Press.

Wood, Ellen Meiksins. 2003. "A Manifesto for Global Capital?" In
Debating Empire, ed. Gopal Balakrishnan, 61–82. New York: Verso.

Woodcock, Bruce. 2005. MOGCHART Web site. http://mmogchart.com.

————. 2008. "Total MMOG Active Subscribers." *MMOG.Chart.Com.*
An Analysis of MMOG Subscription Growth. Version 23. 9 April.
http://www.mmogchart.com/Chart4.html.

Wright, Evan. 2005. *Generation Kill: Devil Dogs, Iceman, Captain
America, and the New Face of American War.* New York: Penguin.

Wright, Lawrence. 2006. *The Looming Tower: Al-Qaeda and the Road
to 9/11.* New York: Knopf.

Wright, Steve. 2002. *Storming Heaven: Class Composition and Struggle
in Italian Autonomist Marxism.* London: Pluto.

Xinhua News Agency. 2003. "China Encourages Mass Urban Migration."
People's Daily Online, 28 November. http://english.people.com.

————. 2006. "China Has 26.34m Subscribers Paying for the Online
Games Legend." *China View,* 11 January. http://news.xinhuanet.com/
english.

Yardley, Jim. 2004. "Farmers Being Moved Aside by China's Real Estate
Boom." *New York Times,* 8 December. http://www.nytimes.com.

Ye, Juliet. 2009. "World of Warcraft on Hiatus in China." *China Journal,*
8 June. http://blogs.wsj.com/chinajournal.

Yee, Nick. 2005. "Guild Involvement." PlayOn blog, 13 June. http://
blogs.parc.com/playon.

————. 2006a. "The Labor of Fun: How Video Games Blur the Boundaries of Work and Play." *Games and Culture* 1:68–71.

————. 2006b. "Yi-Shan-Guan." Daedalus Project Web site, 4 January.
http://www.nickyee.com.

————. 2007. "WoW Basic Demographics." Daedalus Project Web site,
23 March. http://www.nickyee.com.

Yoshimi, Shunya. 2000. "Consuming 'America': From Symbol to System."
In *Consumption in Asia: Lifestyles and Identities,* ed. Chua Beng-Huat,
202–24. New York: Routledge.

Young, Jeffrey R. 2007. "The Mud-Wrestling Media Maven from MIT."
Chronicle of Higher Education, 14 September. http://www.chronicle
.com.

Zacharias, Yvonne. 2008. "Inside the EA Magic Factory." *Vancouver Sun*, 15 March. http://www.canada.com/vancouversun.

Zhao, Yuezhi. 2008. *Communication in China: Political Economy, Power, and Conflict*. Lanham, Md.: Rowman and Littlefield.

Zizek, Slavoj. 1999. "The Spectre of Ideology." In *Mapping Ideology*, ed. Slavoj Zizek. New York: Verso.

Zizek, Slavoj, and Glyn Daly. 2004. *Conversations with Zizek*. Cambridge, UK: Polity.

Index

abandonware, 85, 207
accumulation, 148, 177; biopower
and, 124–25, 132, 142; capital,
37, 149, 162–63, 190; cities as
territory of, 154; flexible, 192;
game industry methods of,
xxix; primitive, 117–18, 125,
126, 127, 133, 145, 234n2;
rebellion against, 149–50; renewal of, 25, 225. *See also* gold
farming
Activision Inc., xv, 13, 40, 61
activism/activists, xxi; anticorporate, 212; feminist,
18–23; intellectual property,
209; Japanese, 15–16; ludic,
185–86; media, 198; of the
multitude, xxi, 187–91, 213;
1960s and 1970s, 5, 6, 9, 11,
12, 15–16, 194; online, 203–4;
radical, xv, xxx, 179, 180;
social, xxvii–xxviii. *See also*
tactical games
Adventure, 11, 25
advertising: in-game, xvi, 48; television, 77–78
Afghanistan: fighting in, 103–4,
115

Afkar Media Ltd., 119
Africa: e-waste in, 224; game
manufacturing in, xviii
age, xvii, 89
Age of Empires, xix, 75
agoraXchange, 205, 206, 213
AION, 149
Akira (film), 17
Allison, Anne, 17–18
All New Gen, 18
Alpha Centauri, 192, 193
America's Army, xii–xv, xxviii,
101, 186
Ameritrade, 28, 226
anatomo-politics, 124, 128
Anti-Japan War Online, 136
Apple Inc., 12
arcade games, 11–12, 15, 232n1
Armored Core: Last Raven, 194
ARPANET, 8
artificial intelligence, 15
Asheron's Call, 78, 126
Ashida, Ken'ichiro, 89
Asia: console ownership in, 52;
game manufacturing in, xviii,
50; gaming culture, xvii; im-
material labor in, 14–18; MMO
play in, 127, 132, 135

Bush, George W.: presidency of,
99, 114, 161, 169, 196, 236n2
Bushnell, Nolan, 11–12, 13, 18
businesses. *See* corporations

California: labor law in, 60, 64
Canon Inc., 29
capital, xx, xxi, 6, 11, 18, 226;
accumulation of, 37, 117,
149, 162–63, 190; criminal,
170–78; excesses of, 94, 227;
game-related, 26, 32–33, 149,
190–91, 196, 228; global, 22,
71, 156, 159, 161–62, 177,
187–89, 220–21
capitalism: advanced, 181, 232n4;
American, 164; biopolitics
and, 127; biopower's role in,
124–25, 145; Chinese, 133–34,
145; communist, 188, 228;
criminal, 158; expansion of,
xxix, 150, 160; gaming and,
xvii–xviii, xxviii, 12, 17–18,
32–33; industrial, 19; machines
of, 74–77, 84, 87; militarized,
xiv–xv, xxiii; neoliberalism
and, xxviii, 125, 159–60, 210;
opposition to, xxi, 32, 120;
subjectivities of, 4, 192; urban,
154, 176. *See also* cognitive
capitalism; global capitalism;
ludocapitalism
capital-labor relations, 4–5, 36,
61, 65, 162. *See also* labor
Casino Empire, xix
casino-style commerce, 225, 226
Castle Smurfenstein, 24
Castle Wolfenstein, 24
Castronova, Edward, 131, 138, 151
casual gamers, 52, 68, 80, 89, 91,
94
cell phones: playing games on,
xvi, 68

Chan, Alex, 186–87
Chan, Dean, 135, 144
Changyou.com Limited, 149–50
cheating codes/tools, 113, 141
Chengwei, Qiu, 235n8
China, 123–24; biopower in,
133–34, 145; capitalism in,
133–34, 145; EA's business
in, 50; electronics industry in,
xviii, 77, 134, 145, 149; e-waste
in, 224; gaming culture, xvii,
134–37, 149; gold farming
in, 137–51; MMO playing
in, 133, 134–37, 150, 235n9;
U.S. relations with, xxiii–xxiv,
147–48
Chinatown Wars, 176–77
Chinese Gold Farmers Preview
(film), 235n10, n11
Chinese Hero Registry, The, 136
Christensen, Natasha, 83
cinema. *See* machinima; *and individual films*
Circus Empire, xix
Cisco Systems, Inc., 29
cities: capitalism and, 154; class
warfare in, 173; corruption in,
178–82; digital mapping of,
157, 171; inequalities in, 172;
as key sites of Empire, 153–54,
157–58, 170; neoliberalism
and, 157, 158–64, 169; racialization of, 154, 157, 164–70,
186–87; simulations of, 154,
155–57, 182; violence in, 179,
235n1; wars fought in, 104,
107, 114, 180, 186. *See also*
Grand Theft Auto (GTA) game
series
civilization-building games, 192,
193, 202–6, 215–17, 219, 221
Civilization IV: Age of Empire,
xxi, 198

farming; Linden dollars; platinum, digital; RMT
Cyan Holdings PLC, 24
Cyberlore Studios. *See* Minerva Software
cyborgs. *See* technology: cyborg
cynicism, 169, 178–82

Dance, Dance Revolution, 88
Darfur Is Dying, 201
Dark Age of Camelot, 44, 126, 138
dark nets, 211
Darwin: Survival of the Fittest, 28, 226
Davis, Mike, 104, 154, 182; studies of Los Angeles, 168–69
Deep Green supercomputer, 121–22
Defense Advanced Research Project, 121
Delappe, Joseph, xiv
Deleuze, Gilles, xxi; on capitalism, 74, 87; on Empire, xxx, 90, 94; on machines, 70–71, 77–78, 92; on nomadism, 84; on process of becoming, 18–19; on society of control, 117; on war games, 118
Delta Force, 119
democracy, 100, 169, 188, 204, 205
Democratic Republic of the Congo (DRC), 222–23
Department of Defense Game Development Community, 101–2
Der Derian, James, xv, 101, 102
deterritorialization, 10, 74, 94
Deus Ex series of games, 194
development: concentration of ownership in, 61, 63–66; costs, 40–41, 64; cycles in, 42–43, 56–57; democratization of, 91; design phase, 221; independent, 42, 43; licensing-based, 44–46; military-civilian collaboration in, 104–5, 117–18; organization of, 39, 40–44; third-party, 13; as virtual factory, 48; wash-rinse-repeat strategy, 46, 51. *See also* dissonant development; do-it-yourself (DIY) game making; homebrew game development; publishers/publishing; studios; user-generated content
Diablo II, 232n1
Dibbell, Julian, 126
Digital Equipment Corporation, 8
digital games. *See* virtual games/gaming
digital rights management (DRM) systems, 86, 207–8, 216–17
Disney Company, 45
dissent, digital, xiv–xv, xxviii
dissonant development, 118, 191, 194–97, 211, 212
Distinctive Software, Inc., 49
distribution, 39; EA's control over, 66
do-it-yourself (DIY) game making, 9, 27, 121, 217; culture of, xxv, 6, 197, 203, 210–11. *See also* homebrew game development; modding/mods; playbor force; self-organized worlds; user-generated content
Donkey Kong, 3
Donnelly, Michael, 141–42
Doom, xxiv–xxv, 24–25, 28, 83, 194, 232n3
dot-com boom and bust, 13–14, 125, 172–73, 174, 176, 222–23, 226
Dragon Quest, 16
Dr. J. and Larry Bird Go One on One, 46

Employment Contract Quality of Life Certification, 35

enclosure: concept of, 125–26

end-user license agreements. *See* EULAs

End War, 122

Engels, Friedrich, 187

Eno, Brian, 215–16, 218

Entertainment Software Association (ESA): statistics from, xvi–xvii, 22, 207

E-Recruiter (employment software), 53–54, 65

Escape from Woomera, 185, 187, 197

Escobar, Pablo, 161

ESP Game, 30–31

ET (game), 13

Eternal Darkness, 81

ethnicity, 167, 171; depictions in virtual games, xxvii, 108. *See also* race

EULAs (end-user license agreements), 131, 209; breaches of, 139–40

Europa Universalis III, 193

Europe: EA workforce in, 68; game manufacturing in, xviii, 49, 50, 76, 77; gaming market in, xvii; postindustrial employment shift, 3–4

Everett, Anna, 167

EverQuest, 25, 26, 78, 126, 127–28, 138

EverQuest II (EQ2), 136, 140

e-waste, 224; in China, 145–46

existence: survival and, 170, 171

exodus: concept of, 218–19

EyeToys, 88

Fable, 233n4

Fair Labor Standards Act, 60

farmbots, 139, 141–42, 143

farming. *See* gold farming

Far Westward Journey, 235n9

feminism, 18–23. *See also* women

FIFA Online, 50, 52, 67

50 Cent: Bulletproof, 165

Final Fantasy game series, 17, 132, 236n1

FlatWorld, 102

Flextronics International Ltd., 76

FLOSS (Free/Libre Open Source Software) movement, 208–9, 210. *See also* software: open-source

Food Force, 201

Force More Powerful, A, 201

Fordism, 3, 4, 6, 10, 58, 112, 228

Fortunati, Leopoldina, 19

Foucault, Michel, xx, xxi, 234n4; on biopower, 124–25, 128, 129, 131, 150

4x game series, 192, 219

foxing, 208

Frasca, Gonzalo, 197

Free Culture Game, The, 199

Freedom Force, 208

Free/Libre Open Source Software (FLOSS) movement. *See* FLOSS

Free Ryzom Campaign, 204–5, 209, 213

Free Software Movement, 205, 210

freeware, xix, 9, 52, 198–99, 200, 211. *See also* abandonware

French Democracy, The, 186–87, 197

Friedan, Betty, 18

Friedman, Ted, 220, 221

Full Spectrum Command, 104

full-spectrum dominance, 103–5, 111, 115, 116–18

Full Spectrum Leader, 104

Full Spectrum Warrior (FSW), 98–99, 181; banalization of war in, 116–18; cheating code, 113;

Tech Model Railroad Club (TMRC), 8
technology: antipiracy, 207–8; capital and, 18; culture of, xvi, 118; cyborg, 15, 82, 93, 94, 192; digital, xix; disruptive, 89; global capitalism and, 120–21; information, xx, xxiii, 4, 6, 10; jobs in, 19–20, 22; subversive uses of, 84; of video games, 187, 197. *See also* biotechnologies
Tennis for Two, 8, 11
Terranova, Tiziana, 23, 148
Tetris, 23–24, 28, 220, 232n3
Tetsuwan Atomu (Mighty Atom), 232n2
The9 Limited, 136–37, 149
theocracy, 120, 122
therapies, virtual, 97–98
Third World Farmer, 201
Thompson, Jack, 116, 155
THQ Inc., 104; development of *FSW,* 114, 115
Three Gorges Dam (China), 133, 145
ThreeSF, Inc., 44
Tiger Woods PGA Tour 08, 46
Tomb Raider, 21
Toriyama, Akira, 16
Total War, xix
TPO Gaming, 121
trading, virtual, xxviii, 129, 130, 138, 226–27
Training and Doctrine Command (TRADOC), Project Office for Gaming, 121
training games: business-related, xii, xxviii, 28–33, 138, 200, 226–27; military, xv, 7–8, 28, 98–99, 100, 101–2, 104–5, 116–17, 119–22, 202. *See also* simulations
Trillion Dollar Bailout, 198

Trojan Horses: game consoles as, 75, 78, 88
Truth about Game Development, The, 198
TuboFlex, 197, 198
Twentieth Century Fox Film Corporation, 208
tycoon games, 198–99

UbiSoft Entertainment SA, 63
Uganda, 222–23
Ultima, 24, 25, 26, 44
Ultima Online, 25–26, 126, 138
Under Ash, 119
Under Siege, 119
unemployment: protests against, 186, 187
unionization, 63, 67, 161, 233n3
United States: China relations, xxiii–xxiv, 147–48; games' industry in, xvii, xviii, 53; hegemony of, xxii, xxiii, 17–18; Japanese relations, 15; politics in, 179, 180, 181–82
Unreal, 26
urban areas. *See* cities
Uru, 203, 213
user-generated content, xxvi, 23, 215–17, 221–22; control over, xi–xii, 210; sale of, 79; Sony's attempt at, 90–91. *See also* do-it-yourself (DIY) game making; homebrew game development; modding/mods

Vancouver, Canada: EA's studio in, 41, 42, 47, 56, 59; game set in, 200
Velvet Strike interventions, 186
Venezuela: game set in, 115–16
Venus Matrix (feminist group). *See* VNS Matrix
Vercellone, Carlo, 36–37, 40, 50

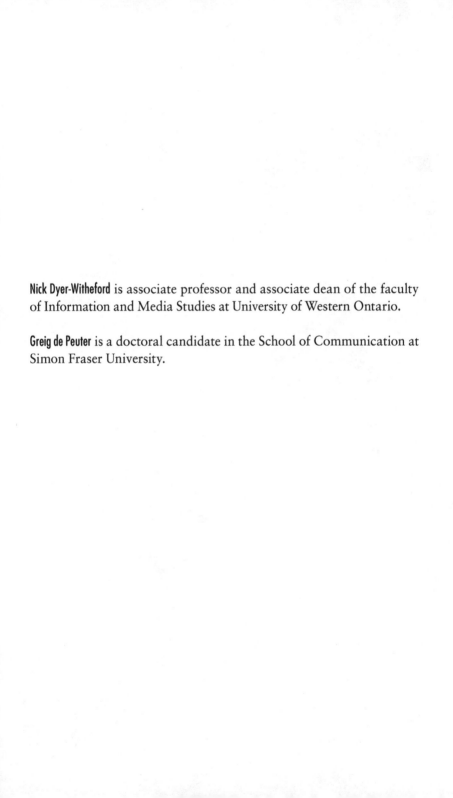

Nick Dyer-Witheford is associate professor and associate dean of the faculty of Information and Media Studies at University of Western Ontario.

Greig de Peuter is a doctoral candidate in the School of Communication at Simon Fraser University.

CPSIA information can be obtained
at www.ICGtesting.com
Printed in the USA
LVHW031930110223
739150LV00002B/47